Fourth Edition

Understanding ARGUMENTS

AN INTRODUCTION TO INFORMAL LOGIC

ROBERT J. FOGELIN
Dartmouth College

WALTER SINNOTT-ARMSTRONG
Dartmouth College

HARCOURT BRACE JOVANOVICH, PUBLISHERS
San Diego   New York   Chicago   Austin   Washington, D.C.
London   Sydney   Tokyo   Toronto

ISBN: 0-15-592672-1

Library of Congress Catalog Card Number: 90-82128

Printed in the United States of America

To Eric, John, Lars, and Miranda
and the colleges of their choice

An argument isn't just contradiction.

Can be.

No it can't. An argument is a connected series of statements intended to establish a proposition.

No it isn't.

Yes it is.

Argument Clinic,
From MONTY PYTHON'S PREVIOUS RECORD

Preface

This book is about arguments. It considers arguments not in the narrow sense of quarrels or squabbles but in the broader, logician's sense of giving reasons in behalf of some claim. Viewing arguments in this way, we see that they are a common feature of daily life, for we are often involved in giving reasons or evaluating reasons given by others. These activities are not only common but important. Deciding what to believe, how to act, how to judge others, and the like all involve assessing reasons and, hence, evaluating arguments.

Traditionally, logic has been considered the most general science dealing with arguments. The task of logic is to discover the fundamental principles for distinguishing good arguments from bad ones.

For certain purposes, arguments are best studied as abstract patterns of reasoning. Logic is not concerned with particular arguments—for example, your attempt to prove that the bank, not you, has made a mistake. The study of those general principles that make certain patterns of argument reasonable (or valid) and other patterns of argument unreasonable (or invalid) is called *formal logic*. Two chapters of this work are dedicated to formal logic.

A different, but complementary, way of viewing an argument is to treat it as a *particular use of language*: arguing is one of the things that we do with words. This approach places stress upon arguing as a linguistic activity. Instead of studying arguments as abstract patterns, it takes them as they occur in their actual employment. It raises questions of the following kind: What is the place of argument within language as a whole? What words or phrases are characteristic of arguments, and how do these words function? What task or tasks are arguments supposed to perform? When an approach to arguments has this emphasis, the study is called *informal logic*. As its subtitle indicates, *Understanding Arguments* is primarily a textbook in informal logic.

The main innovation of this Fourth Edition is the appearance of Walter Sinnott-Armstrong as coauthor, and, with this, a citation to his daughter Miranda on the dedication page.

The text has been revised in a number of substantial ways. At the suggestion of many reviewers, we have restored the discussion of speech act theory to Chapter 1. This was dropped from the Third Edition because a number of those who taught the material said that their students found it too difficult. We are confident that the new discussion will prove more accessible.

The chapter on deep analysis has been expanded. We also moved it, because we have found it most effective to teach deep analysis just after close analysis in Chapter 3.

Chapter 7 now includes a discussion of general conditionals which are found often in everyday language but do not fit into the propositional calculus.

In Chapter 8, instead of developing the modern and classical approaches to existential import in tandem, as was done in previous editions, we have adopted a straightforward modern approach through most of the chapter, reserving remarks on the classical approach to supplementary discussions that can easily be omitted.

Chapter 9, which is on inductive reasoning, has been thoroughly rewritten and contains an important innovation. Instead of using Mill's methods for finding and testing inductive generalizations, we carry out the entire discussion in terms of sufficient conditions and necessary conditions. We think this approach is intuitively clearer than the standard approach, and it is certainly easier to apply. We illustrate this approach by applying it to the first outbreak of Legionnaire's disease.

Chapter 10, "Taking Chances," has been expanded and the terminology brought more in line with current usage.

In Part II, introductory essays have been added to the chapters concerning legal reasoning, moral reasoning, and scientific reasoning.

Finally, we have added new exercises to almost every chapter, and many new discussion questions to provide the basis for class discussion or written assignments.

This new edition has been influenced by our teaching this material with various colleagues, including visitors, at Dartmouth College. This has produced some very lively discussions that have lead to changes, both large and small, throughout the book. In this regard, we wish to thank Mark Bedau, Susan Brison, Timothy Duggan, Deni Elliott, and James Moor of Dartmouth College; David Luban and Douglas MacLean of the University of Maryland; and Susan Russinoff, Carl Wolf, Russell Abrams, and Julia Driver. We are indebted as well to the following reviewers: Sharon Bishop, California State University, Los Angeles; Josiah B. Gould, State University of New York at Albany; James Cargile, University of Virginia; Joseph Campbell, University of Arizona; and James Edward Magruder, Stephen F. Austin State University. At Harcourt Brace Jovanovich we have also received splendid help in the preparation of this fourth edition from Bill McLane, acquisitions editor; Karen Allanson, associate editor; Julia Ross, manuscript editor; Nancy Simerly and James Hughes, designers; David Hough, production manager; and Eleanor Garner, permissions editor.

Robert J. Fogelin
Walter Sinnott-Armstrong

Contents

Part Two   Areas of Argumentation

THE ANALYSIS OF ARGUMENT

1

The Web of Language

As an introduction to our study of informal logic, this chapter will survey the general nature of language. In doing so, it will stress three main ideas. First, language is *conventional*. Words acquire meaning within a rich system of linguistic conventions or rules. An understanding of language demands an understanding of these conventions and rules. We will examine three levels or three kinds of conventions that govern our use of language. Second, the chapter stresses that the uses of language are *diverse*. We sometimes use language to communicate information, but we also use it to ask questions, issue orders, write poetry, keep score, formulate arguments, and perform an almost endless number of other tasks. Third, meaning is often conveyed *indirectly*. To understand the significance of many utterances, we must go beyond what is literally said to examine what is conversationally implied.

LANGUAGE AND ARGUMENT

Logic is the general science of argument: its goal is to lay down principles for distinguishing good arguments from bad arguments. The word "argument" may suggest quarrels or squabbles, but here it is used in the broader, logician's sense of giving reasons for or against some claim. Viewing arguments in this way, we see that they are a common feature of daily life, for we are often involved in giving reasons for things we believe or in evaluating reasons given by others for things they want us to believe. Trying to decide which way to vote in an election, where to go to college, whether to support or oppose capital punishment—all involve weighing and evaluating reasons.

Arguing is also an activity, in particular, a *linguistic* activity. Arguing is one of the many things that we can do with words. In fact, unlike fighting, it is something that we can *only* do with words. Thus, to understand how arguments work, it is important to understand how language works. Unfortunately, our understanding of human languages is far from complete, and linguistics remains a young science where disagreement abounds. Still, certain facts about language are beyond dispute, and recognizing them will provide a background for understanding how arguments work.

LANGUAGE AND CONVENTION

As everyone who has bothered to think about it knows, language is conventional. There seems to be no reason why we, as English speakers, use the word "dog" to refer to dogs rather than to cats, trees, or anything at all. Any word might have been used to stand for anything. Beyond this, there seems to be no reason why we put words together in the way that we do. In English, we put adjectives before the nouns they modify. We thus speak of a *green salad*. In French, adjectives usually follow the noun, and so instead of saying *verte salade* the French say *salade verte*. The conventions of our own language are so much with us that it strikes us as odd when we discover that other languages have different conventions. A French diplomat once praised his own language because, as he said, it followed the natural order of thought. This strikes English speakers as silly, but in seeing what is silly about it, we see that the word order in our own language is conventional as well. This, in turn, may help us guard against treating certain nonstandard dialects of English as inferior because they differ from standard English. Usually such differences do not show a lack of rules, merely the existence of different rules.

Although it is important to realize that our language is conventional, it is also important not to misunderstand this fact. From the idea that language is conventional, it is easy to conclude that language is *arbitrary*. If language is arbitrary, then it might seem that it really doesn't matter which words we use or how we put them together. It takes only a little thought to see that this is not true. If we wish to communicate with others, we must follow the system of conventions that others use. Communication can take place only from *within* a shared system of conventions. Conventions do not destroy meaning by making it arbitrary; conventions bring meaning into existence.

A misunderstanding of the conventions of language can lead to pointless disputes. Sometimes, in the middle of a discussion, someone will declare that "the whole thing is just a matter of definition" or "what you say is true by your definition, false by mine." Now, there are times when definitions are important and the truth of what's said turns upon them, but usually this is not true. Suppose someone has fallen off a cliff and is heading towards certain death on the rocks below. Of course, it is a matter of definition (of convention) that we use the word "death" to describe the result of the sudden sharp stop at the end of the fall. We might have used some other word—perhaps "birth"—instead. But it certainly will not help the person who is falling to change the meaning of the word "death" in the middle of his plunge. It will not do him any good to yell out, "By 'death' I mean 'birth'." It will not help even if *everyone* agrees to use these words in this new way. If we all decided to adopt this new convention, we would then say, "He is falling from the cliff to his certain birth" instead of "He is falling from the cliff to his certain death." But speaking in this way will not change the facts. It will not save him from injury. It will not make those who care about him feel better.

The upshot of this simple example is that the truth of what we say is rarely just a matter of definition. Whether what we have said is true or not will depend, for the most part, on how things stand in the world. For example, if a German wishes to say that snow is black, then he or she will use the words "Schnee ist schwartz." Other Germans will *understand* his words, but unless snow is different in Germany than everyplace else, they will also think that what is being said is false. In general, then, though the *meaning* of what we say is dependent upon convention, the *truth* of what we say is not.

In the last sentence we used the qualifying phrase: "in general". To say that a claim holds *in general* is to acknowledge that there may be exceptions. Such a qualification is needed in this case because sometimes the truth of what we say *is* simply a matter of definition. Take a simple example. The claim that a triangle has three sides is true by definition, because a triangle is defined as a closed, plane figure having three sides. Again, if someone says that sin is wrong, he or she has said something that is true by definition, for a sin is defined as, among other things, something that is wrong.

Consider a more complicated case. Suppose a defender of communism argues that the only true democracies exist in communist states. This person admits that in such states there are no general elections where a large portion of the population is allowed to choose between competing parties, but goes on to say that a genuine democracy exists when the party in power reflects the interests of the masses. Voting, this person might continue, is simply a capitalist trick for bamboozling the people. Here we might challenge the definition of a democracy that this person is using and then be met by the following reply: Why should everyone in the world be bound by the capitalist definition of a democracy? The correct response to this is to say that in a democracy the people *choose* the policies that govern them, or at least the representatives who formulate these policies. When this choice is absent, democracy does not exist. Anyone in favor of another form of government should say what it is and defend it on its own terms.

Sometimes, then, it is important to ask people to define their terms. We should do this whenever we think that someone is distorting the meaning of words to win an argumentative point. But it makes no sense to ask that every word be defined. This would prove an endless task and we would never get around to saying anything in particular.

In sum, people are able to communicate with each other because they share certain linguistic conventions. These conventions could have been very different, and in this sense they are arbitrary. But it does not follow from this that the truth of what we say is also merely arbitrary. In general, the truth of what we say is settled not by an appeal to definition but by a look at the facts. Sometimes, however, the conventions of our language are misused or even abused. Here it does make sense to ask for a definition. It would, however, be absurd to ask that every word be defined.

LEVELS OF LANGUAGE

Linguistic Acts

In the previous section we saw that a language is a system of shared conventions that allows us to communicate with one another. If we pause to look at language, we see that it contains many different kinds of conventions. We have seen that words have meanings conventionally attached to them. The word "dog" is used conventionally to talk about dogs. Proper names are also conventionally assigned, for Harry Jones could have been named Wilbur Jones. Other conventions concern the way in which words can be put together to form sentences. These are often called *grammatical* rules. Using the three words "John," "hit," and "Harry," we can formulate sentences with very different meanings. For example, "John hit Harry" and "Harry hit John." We recognize that these sentences have different meanings because we understand the grammar of our language. This grammatical understanding also allows us to see that the sentence "Hit John Harry" does not mean anything at all—even though the individual words possess meaning. (Notice that "Hit John, Harry!" does mean something: it is a way of telling Harry to hit John.) Grammatical rules are very important, for they play a part in giving a meaning to a sentence as a whole. Admittedly, some of our grammatical rules play only a small role in this important task because they are largely stylistic. If someone says "Everyone take their seats," that person has uttered an ungrammatical sentence since the subject and verb do not agree. The violation of deeper and more fundamental grammatical rules can produce sentences that are unintelligible.

There are, then, at least two kinds of conventions that give meaning to what we say. The ones that assign meaning to individual words are commonly called *semantic* conventions. The conventions that lay down rules for combining words into meaningful wholes are called grammatical or *syntactical* conventions. When these conventions are satisfied, we will say that we have performed a *linguistic act*: we have said something meaningful in a language. Later on we will look more closely at semantic and syntactical conventions, for at times they are a source of fallacies and other confusions. But before we examine the defects of our language, we should first appreciate that language is a powerful and subtle tool. We will next examine the wide variety of jobs that language can perform when used correctly.

Speech Acts

When asked about the function of language, it is natural to reply that we use language to communicate our ideas. But this is only *one* of its uses. This becomes obvious as soon as we set aside our prejudices and take a look at the way our language actually works. Adding up a column of figures is a linguistic activity, but it does not communicate any ideas to others. When I add the figures, I am not even trying to communicate anything to myself: I am trying to figure something out.

Writing a poem is a more interesting example. Sometimes poems convey factual information, and at other times they express philosophical truths. Poems also express emotions. Yet often the most important fact about a poem is that it is an artistic creation in the same way that a painting or a sculpture is an artistic creation. A poem is a linguistic artifact. We get a bad theory of poetry, and may even lessen our appreciation of poetry, if we think of a poem as a mere device for conveying the poet's thoughts and emotions to others. Consider one example:

Upon Julia's Clothes
Robert Herrick

Whenas in silks my Julia goes,
Then, then, methinks, how sweetly flows
The liquefaction of her clothes.

Next when I cast mine eyes, and see
That brave vibration each way free,
O, how that glittering taketh me!

Using a modern idiom, Herrick might have said "Julia's terrific figure turns me on." This second way of speaking leaves little doubt about what Herrick thinks and how he feels about Julia. The poem, by comparison, may fail to some extent in communication, but the chief difference lies elsewhere. Herrick's emotions are, after all, fairly common. His mode of expressing them, however, produces one of the most perfect poems in the English language. A poem is not simply a news broadcast with fancy frills.

Poetry provides an example of language used for purposes other than communication, but beyond that it is a complicated linguistic phenomenon that defies easy analysis. A look at our everyday conversations produces a host of other examples of language being used for different purposes. Grammarians, for example, have divided sentences into various moods:

(1) Indicative
(2) Interrogative
(3) Imperative
(4) Expressive

For example:

(1) He is in England now that spring is here.
(2) Is he in England now that spring is here?
(3) Go to England now that spring is here!
(4) Oh to be in England, now that spring is here!!

The first sentence states a fact; we can use it to communicate information about a person's location. If we use it in this way, what we say will be either true or false. Notice that none of the other sentences can be called either true or false.

Performatives

The different types of sentences recognized by traditional grammarians indicate that we use language to do more than convey information. But this traditional classification of sentences gives only a small idea of the wide variety of things that we can accomplish using language. Sometimes, for example, in using language, we actually *do* things in the strong sense of bringing about a change, sometimes a fundamental change, between individuals. In one familiar setting, if one person says "I do," and another person says "I do," and finally a third person says "I now pronounce you husband and wife," the relationship between the first two people changes in a fundamental way: they are thereby married. With luck, they begin a life of wedded bliss, but they also alter their legal relationship. For example, they may now file joint income tax returns and may not legally marry other people without first getting a divorce.

Sentences of this kind, those that can be used *to bring something about* rather than merely *stating something,* were labeled *performatives* by the philosopher J. L. Austin.[1] He called them performatives in order to bring out the contrast between performing an action and simply describing one. For example, if an umpire shouts, "You're out!" then the batter is out. The umpire is not merely describing the situation, but declaring the batter out. By way of contrast, if someone says "I am the best tennis player in Tennessee," that person is not *thereby* the best tennis player in Tennessee. Becoming the best tennis player in Tennessee is something that you do with a tennis racket, not simply with words.

To avoid complications, we shall concentrate on what Austin called *explicit* performatives. A sentence expresses an explicit performative if it is in the first-person singular indicative present and yields a true statement when it is plugged into the following pattern:

In saying "I ———," I thereby ———.

We will call this the *thereby test.* With some qualifications to be noted later, it provides a convenient way of identifying explicit performatives. Thus, "I congratulate you" expresses an explicit performative, because it is true that in saying "I congratulate you," I thereby congratulate you. Here a quoted expression occurs on the left side of the word "thereby", but not on the right side. This reflects the fact that the *saying,* which is referred to on the left side of the pattern, amounts to the *doing* referred to on the right side of the word "thereby." Applied to the following pairs of sentences, this test shows that the sentences on the left formulate explicit performative (EP) expressions whereas the sentences on the right formulate nonperformative (N) expressions:

I order you to leave. (EP)	I want you to leave. (N)
I apologize. (EP)	I feel sad. (N)

---

[1] *See* for example, J. L. Austin, "Performative Utterances," *Philosophical Papers,* ed. J. O. Urmson and G. J. Warnock, 2nd ed. (Oxford: Clarendon Press, 1970) pp. 233–52.

Notice that with the last pair, in saying "I apologize," I thereby apologize, but *saying* "I am sad" no more makes me sad than saying "I am six feet tall" makes me six feet tall. Apologizing, like congratulating, is something that you can accomplish using words; feeling sad is something that goes on inside you. Finally, questions, imperatives, and exclamations are not explicit performatives, since they cannot be sensibly plugged into the pattern at all. (Try the question "Is there a washroom on this floor?")

▼ EXERCISE I

Using the thereby test, as described above, indicate which of the following sentences express explicit performatives (EP) and which do not express explicit performatives (N):

(1) I resign from this rotten club.
(2) Pierre is the capital of South Dakota.
(3) I order you to leave.
(4) I own the World Trade Towers.
(5) I claim this land for Queen Victoria. (Said by an explorer.)
(6) I'm out of gas.
(7) Get lost!
(8) I bring you official greetings from the Socialist Party of Finland.
(9) Ask not what your country can do for you, but what you can do for your country.
(10) I ask you, are you better off now than you were four years ago?

▼ EXERCISE II

Follow the same instructions for the following dialogue:

(1) Lefty: I assure you that George caught only one fish.
(2) Righty: I already conceded that George caught only one fish.
(3) Righty: My only claim is that George can fish with style.
(4) Lefty: I wonder why you think that.
(5) Lefty: I also deny that he can fish with style.
(6) Righty: My sources told me so.
(7) Righty: Then I saw how he wields a fishing rod.
(8) Righty: And you told me so yourself.
(9) Lefty: I lied.
(10) Lefty: In fact, I am lying right now.

Kinds of Speech Acts. Studying explicit performatives not only helps break the spell of the idea that indicative sentences only serve the purpose of conveying information, it also introduces us to a level of language distinct from that which involves *linguistic acts*. We will call these acts *speech acts*, and the rules that govern them *speech act rules*.

It is difficult to give a precise definition of a speech act, but we can begin explaining this notion by contrasting it with a linguistic act. A linguistic act, as we said, is the act of saying something meaningful in a language. It is important to see that the very same linguistic act can play different roles as it occurs in different contexts. To understand this, consider the use of the word "yes" in each of these contexts:

(1) A: Is there any pizza left?
    B: Yes.

(2) A: Do you promise to pay me back by Friday?
    B: Yes.

(3) A: Do you swear to tell the truth?
    B: Yes.

(4) A: Do you refuse to leave?
    B: Yes.

Here the same linguistic act, uttering the word "yes", is used to make four different moves in a language exchange: to state something, to make a promise, to take an oath, and to refuse to do something. We will call such acts as stating, promising, swearing, and refusing *speech acts*. *A speech act is the conventional move that a remark makes in a language exchange.* It is what we do *in* saying something.[2]

Explicit performatives are important because they provide a systematic way of identifying different kinds of speech acts. The basic idea is this: different speech acts are named by the different verbs that occur in explicit performatives. We can thus use the thereby test to search for different kinds of speech acts. For example:

If I say "I promise," I thereby promise.
  So *promising* is a kind of speech act.
If I say "I resign," I thereby resign.
  So *resigning* is a kind of speech act.
If I say "I apologize," I thereby apologize.
  So *apologizing* is a kind of speech act.
If I say "I question his honesty," I thereby question his honesty.
  So *questioning* is a kind of speech act.

---

[2] Austin calls this an illocutionary act. J. L. Austin, *How to Do Things with Words*, ed., J. O. Urmson and Marina Sbisa, 2nd ed. (Cambridge: Harvard University Press, 1962) pp. 98 ff.

If I say "I conclude that he is guilty," I thereby conclude that he is guilty.

So *concluding* is a kind of speech act.

We will call the main verbs that appear in such explicit performatives *performative verbs*.

Thus far, we have concentrated on the fact that we do a great deal more with language than make statements, assert facts, or describe things. That is, we do more with language than put forward claims that are either true or false. But, of course, we also use language to do these things; so stating, asserting, and describing are themselves kinds of speech acts. This can be shown by using the thereby test:

If I say "I state that I am a U. S. citizen," I thereby state that I am a U. S. citizen.

If I say "I assert that the defendant was in Detroit at the time of the crime," I thereby assert that the defendant was in Detroit at the time.

If I say "I describe him as being dark haired and just over six feet tall," I thereby describe him as being dark haired and just over six feet tall.

We now have a more accurate conception of the way in which language functions than the common one that the function of language is to convey ideas. Making claims that are either true or false is one important kind of speech act, but we perform a great many other kinds of speech acts that are also important. In this brief survey we have identified the following kinds of speech acts:

promising	congratulating	ordering
apologizing	resigning	swearing
pronouncing	refusing	stating
asserting	describing	questioning
concluding		

▼ EXERCISE III

Using a college dictionary, add to the above list by finding ten verbs that can be used to construct sentences (in the first-person singular indicative present) that pass the thereby test.

Discussion Question. The importance of deciding what kind of speech act has been performed is illustrated by the classic case from the law of contracts: *Hawkins v. McGee.*[3] McGee performed an operation on Hawkins's hand that proved unsuccessful, and Hawkins sued for damages. He did not sue on the basis of malpractice but on the basis of breach of contract. His attorney argued that the doctor initiated a contractual relationship by trying to persuade Hawkins to have the oper-

---

[3] Supreme Court of New Hampshire, 1929, 84 N.H. 114, A. 641.

ation by saying such things as "I will guarantee to make the hand a 100 percent perfect hand." He made statements of this kind a number of times and finally Hawkins agreed to undergo the operation. The attorney for the surgeon replied that these words, even if uttered, would not constitute an offer of a contract, but merely expressed a *strong belief.*

It is important to remember that contracts do not have to be written and signed to be binding. A proper verbal offer and acceptance is usually sufficient to constitute a contract.[4] The case then turned on two questions: (i) Did McGee utter the words attributed to him? In other words, did McGee perform the *linguistic act* attributed to him? The jury decided that he did. (ii) The second, more interesting, question was whether these words, when uttered in this particular context, amounted to an offer of contract, as Hawkins maintained, or merely an expression of strong belief, as McGee argued. In other words, the fundamental question in this case was what kind of *speech act* McGee performed when trying to convince Hawkins to have the operation.

Explain how you would settle this case. (The court actually ruled in favor of Hawkins, but you are free to disagree.)

Speech-Act Rules. The distinctive feature of a performative utterance is that, in a sense we have tried to make clear, the saying constitutes a doing of something. In saying "I resign," I am not simply describing my resigning, I am actually resigning. Here, however, an objection might arise. Suppose a soldier, tired of military life, walks up to the drill sergeant and says "I resign." Has the soldier actually resigned? Well, he has tried to resign, but it may be that one is not permitted to resign from the army. Or suppose someone who is a supporter of marriage goes about the streets pronouncing random couples husband and wife. First of all, unless this person is a member of the clergy, a justice of the peace, a ship's captain, or the like, that person will have no right to make such pronouncements. Furthermore, even if this person is, say, a crazed member of the clergy, the pronouncement may still not come off. The parties addressed have to say "I do"; they must have a proper license; and so on. These examples show that a speech act will *not come off* or be *void* unless certain rules or conventions are satisfied. These rules or conventions which must be satisfied for a speech act to come off and not be void, we will call *speech-act rules.* We will look briefly at some of the main types of speech-act rules.

(1) Must the person have a special position to perform the speech act?

---

[4] In general, verbal contracts are binding if it can be shown that the verbal agreement did take place. More technically, a signed document is not a contract but evidence of one. A verbal agreement, though sometimes harder to prove, can also be evidence of a contract.

Sometimes a speech act will come off only if it is performed by someone with an *official position*. We have already seen that for someone to make two people husband and wife by pronouncing them husband and wife, that person must have a certain *official* position. In the same way, although a shortstop can perform the linguistic act of *shouting* "You're out," she cannot perform the speech act of *calling* someone out. Only an umpire can do that. A janitor cannot pronounce a body dead on arrival, even if the body is plainly dead when it arrives at the hospital. That's the job of a doctor or a coroner.

(2) Are there any special words or formulas associated with the speech act?

Sometimes a speech act will come off only if certain *words or formulas* are used. In baseball the umpire must say "strike two," or something very close to this, to call a second strike. In a pick-up game it might be all right to say instead "Hey, that's two bad ones on you, baby!" but that way of calling strikes is not permitted in serious play. Certain legal documents are not valid if they are not properly signed, endorsed, notarized, and so on. In tournament bridge, the only way to bid five clubs is to say, in a flat tone of voice, "Five clubs." This prevents players from conveying extra information by saying such things as "Well, if I really have to, why not five clubs?" or "Five clubs, and you better believe it."

(3) What facts are presupposed in the use of the speech act?

Most speech acts also involve assumptions or presuppositions that certain *facts* obtain. A father cannot bequeath an antique car to his son if he doesn't own one. You cannot resign from the American Civil Liberties Union or the Veterans of Foreign Wars if you are not a member. Apologies are in order only if you have done something wrong.

(4) Is any response or uptake needed to complete the speech act?

Sometimes a speech act will come off only if there is an *uptake* by another person. A person can *offer* a bet by saying "I bet you ten dollars that the Angels win today," but this person will have *made* a bet only if the other person says "Done" or "You're on," shakes hands, or in some other way accepts the bet. A marriage ceremony is completely flawed if one of the parties doesn't say "I do," but instead says "Well, maybe I should think about this for a while."

(5) What feelings and beliefs is the person performing the speech act expected to have?

Thus far, we have considered conventions that must be satisfied for the speech act to come off (for it not to be void). Speech acts can, however, be flawed in another way: they can be *insincere*. If we apologize for something, we are expected to feel sorry for what we have done. Of course, the person who says "I apologize" has apologized even if he or she does not feel sorry, but the apology will not be sincere. If we congratulate someone, we are usually supposed to be pleased with that person's success. If we state something, we are expected to believe what we say. In all three of these cases—in apologizing, congratulating, and stating—we do succeed in performing a speech act, but are subject to criticism because our feelings or beliefs were not appropriate for the kind of speech act we performed.

▼ EXERCISE IV

Give a speech-act analysis of the speech acts named by each of the following performative verbs. That is, for each of these speech acts, answer the five questions given above.

(1) to thank
(2) to deny
(3) to promise
(4) to fire (from employment)
(5) to vote
(6) to give up (in a fight)

Now do the same for five of the ten verbs that you found as answers to Exercise III.

Conversational Acts[5]

In examining first linguistic acts—saying something meaningful in a language—and then speech acts—making a move in a language game—we have largely ignored one of the central features of language: it is primarily an activity that takes place among people. It is usually a social activity. We use language to inform people of things, to get them to do things, to amuse them, to calm them down, and so on. We can capture this aspect of language by introducing the notion of a *conversational exchange*, that is, a situation where one person, the speaker, uses language to bring about some effect in another person, the listener. We will call this act of causing an effect in another a *conversational act*.

Suppose, for example, A says to B, "Radon is seeping into your basement." In this case, A has performed a linguistic act, that is, has uttered a meaningful sentence in the English language. At the same

---

[5] With some variation, this discussion of conversational rules and conversational implication is based on Paul Grice's important essay "Logic and Conversation." It has been reprinted in his *Studies in the Way of Words* (Cambridge: Harvard University Press, 1989). The passages quoted occur between pages 22 and 40 of this work in the same order that they appear here.

time, A has performed a speech act, that is, has made a statement. Beyond this, A has also performed a conversational act, that is, she has *informed B* or *made B aware* that radon is seeping into his basement.

Although we have a rich vocabulary of verbs indicating speech acts, the number of verbs indicating conversational acts is really quite small. The following contrasts may help to bring out the difference between speech acts and conversational acts:

(1) We often *urge* people to do things in order to *persuade* them to do these things.

Here urging is the speech act, persuading is the conversational act.

(2) We often *tell* people something in order to *get them to believe* something.

Here telling is the speech act, getting them to believe something is the conversational act.

(3) We sometimes *warn* people in order to *alert them* or *put them on guard.*

Here warning is the speech act, alerting them or putting them on guard is the conversational act.

The contrast between a speech act and a conversational act is clear in the first example. If I say, "I urge you to go," I thereby urge you to go. This shows urging is a kind of speech act. It makes no sense to say, "I persuade you to go," so persuading is not a speech act. The contrast is no less obvious in the second two cases. Telling and warning are both kinds of speech acts; getting people to believe something and putting them on guard are not.

▼ EXERCISE V

Indicate whether each of the following verbs primarily names a linguistic act, a speech act, a conversational act, or none of these kinds of act. Assume a standard context. Explain your answers.

(1) to inform
(2) to deny
(3) to hum
(4) to mispronounce
(5) to alert
(6) to fire (from employment)
(7) to praise
(8) to convince
(9) to exhale
(10) to whisper

(11) to pledge
(12) to frighten
(13) to advise
(14) to blame
(15) to enlighten
(16) to conclude
(17) to challenge
(18) to amuse
(19) to abbreviate
(20) to condemn

Conversational Rules

Just as there are rules that govern linguistic acts and rules that govern speech acts, there are also rules that govern conversational acts. This is not surprising because conversational exchanges can be complicated interpersonal activities in need of rules to make them effective. These underlying rules are implicitly understood by users of the language, but the philosopher Paul Grice was the first person to examine them in careful detail.

Grice begins with a very general principle, one that he calls the Cooperative Principle (CP):

> Make your conversational contribution such as is required, at the stage at which it occurs, by the accepted purpose or direction of the talk exchange in which you are engaged.

This, of course, is *very* general. It considers a standard case where conversation is a cooperative venture—that is, where the parties have some common goal they are trying to achieve in talking to each other. (A witness being cross-examined is not in such a situation.) The principle states that the parties should use language in a way that contributes toward achieving their common goal. It tells them to cooperate.

This general principle gets more content when we examine other principles that fall under it. With specific reference to contexts in which information is being exchanged, Grice discusses four such principles. The first is the rule of *Quantity* or what we might also call the rule of *Strength*. It tells us to give the right amount of information. More specifically:

(1) Make your contribution as informative as is required (for the current purposes of the exchange); and possibly
(2) Do not make your contribution more informative than is required.

Here is an application of this rule: A person comes rushing up to you and asks, "Where is a fire extinguisher?" You know a fire extinguisher is five floors away in the basement, and you also know that a fire extinguisher is just down the hall. Suppose you say that a fire extinguisher is in the basement. Here you have said something that is true, but you have violated the rule of Quantity. You have failed to reveal an important piece of information that, under the rule of Quantity, you should have produced. A violation of the second version of the rule would look like this: As smoke billows down the hall, you start with the basement, and say where a fire extinguisher is located on each floor.

There is another cluster of rules that Grice calls rules of *Quality*. In general:

Try to make your contribution one that is true.

More specifically:

(1) Do not say what you believe to be false.

(2) Do not say that for which you lack adequate evidence.

In a cooperative activity, you are not supposed to tell lies. Beyond this, you are expected not to talk off the top of your head either. When we make a statement, we can be challenged in the following ways:

Do you really believe that?
Why do you believe that?

That a person has the right to ask such questions shows that statement-making is governed by this rule of *Quality*. In a court of law, we are expected to tell the whole truth and nothing but the truth. The demand for *nothing but the truth* reflects the rule of Quality; the demand for the *whole truth* roughly reflects the rule of Quantity.

The next rule is called the rule of *Relevance*. Simply stated, it says: Be relevant! Though easy to state, the rule is not easy to explain, because relevance itself is a difficult notion. It is, however, easy to illustrate. If someone asks me where he can find a doctor, I might reply that there is a hospital in the next block. Though not a direct answer to his question, it does not violate the rule of relevance since it provides him with a piece of useful information. If, however, in response I tell the person that I like his haircut, then I have violated the rule of relevance. Clear-cut violations of this principle usually involve *changing the subject*. Interruptions are typically violations of the rule of Relevance.

Another rule concerns the *Manner* of our conversation. We are expected to be clear. Under this general rule come various special rules:

(1) Avoid obscurity of expression.

(2) Avoid ambiguity.

(3) Be brief.

(4) Be orderly.

As an example of the fourth part of this rule, in describing a series of events, it is usually important to state them in the order that they occurred.

There are probably many other rules that govern our conversations. *Be polite!* might be one of them. *Be charitable!* is another. That is, we should put the best interpretation on what others say and our replies should reflect this. We should avoid quibbling and being picky. For the most part, however, we will not worry about them.

If we look at basic conversational rules, we notice that these rules sometimes clash, or at least push us in different directions. The rule of Quantity encourages us to give as much information as possible, but this is constrained by the rule of Quality, which restricts our claims to things we believe to be true and can back up with good reasons. The demands of the rule of Quantity can also conflict with the demand for brevity. Again, to be brief, we must sometimes simplify and even falsify, and this can come into conflict with the Quality rule which demands that we say only what we believe to be true. An ongoing conversation is a constant series of adjustments to this background system of rules.

Conversational Implication

We have seen that conversational exchanges are governed by a system of rules that help those involved in the exchange in achieving their goals. Of course, when people make statements, they do not always follow these rules. People withhold information, they lie, they talk off the tops of their heads, they wander off the subject, they talk vaguely and obscurely. Yet in a normal setting where people are cooperating toward a shared goal, they conform quite closely to these rules. If, on the whole, people do not do this, we could not have the linguistic practices we do. If we thought, for example, that people very often lied (even about the most trivial matters), the business of exchanging information would be badly damaged.

But not only do we follow these conventions, we also (1) implicitly realize that we are following them, and (2) expect others to assume that we are following them. This mutual understanding of the commitments involved in a conversational act leads to the following important result: *people are able to convey a great deal of information without actually saying it.*

A simple example will illustrate this: Again suppose that A, with smoke billowing behind him, comes running up to you and asks:

Where is a fire extinguisher?

And you reply:

There is one in the lobby.

As already noted, this commits you to the claim that this is the closest, or at least the most accessible, fire extinguisher. Of course, you haven't actually *said* that it is the closest fire extinguisher, but you have, we might say, *implied* this. When we do not actually say something, but do imply it in virtue of a conversational rule, the implication is called a *conversational implication*.

Conversational implications have a feature that will be important to us later on: if saying something conversationally implies something that is false, this does not show that what has been said is itself false. Saying that Jay has his bags packed conversationally implies (by the rule of Relevance) that he is about to leave. Yet it might be true that Jay has his bags packed and he is not about to leave. This marks the difference between conversational implication and logical implication. Although saying that Jay has his bags packed may conversationally imply he is leaving, the statement "Jay has his bags packed" does not logically imply this. We will begin our discussion of logical implication in the next chapter.

The Pervasiveness of Conversational Implication.   It is important to realize that conversational implication is a pervasive feature of human discourse. It is not something we employ only occasionally for special effect. In fact, virtually every conversation relies upon these implications, and most conversations would fall apart if those involved in them refused to go beyond literal meaning to take into account the implications of saying these things. In the following conversation B is literal-minded in just this way:

> A: Do you know what time it is?
>
> B: Not without looking at my watch.

B has answered A's question, but it is hard to imagine that A received the information that she was looking for. Presumably she wanted to know what time it was, not merely whether B, at this very moment, knew the time. Finding B rather obtuse, A tries again:

> A: Can you tell me what time it is?
>
> B: Oh yes, all I have to do is look at my watch.

Undaunted, A gives it another try:

> A: Will you tell me what time it is?
>
> B: I suppose I will as soon as you ask me.

Finally:

> A: What time is it?
>
> B: Two o'clock.

Notice that in each of these exchanges B gives a direct and accurate answer to A's question, yet, in all but the last answer, he does not provide what A wants. Here we might say that B is taking A's question too literally, but we might better say that the problem is that B is doing nothing *more* than taking A's remarks literally. In a conversational exchange, we expect others to take our remarks in the light of the obvious purpose we have in making them. We expect them to share our commonsense understanding of why people ask questions. People often want to be told the time, but only rarely, for example, when they are trying to synchronize their activities, do they care whether others know what time it is. In his replies, B is totally oblivious to the point of A's questions and, like a computer in a science-fiction movie, gives nothing more than the literally correct answer to the question explicitly asked.

▼ EXERCISE VI

In a standard context, Alice says, "How can you love Gary? He's a male-chauvinist pig." Which of the following does Alice conversationally imply a commitment to? Explain your answers.

(1) Gary is a male-chauvinist pig.
(2) Alice believes Gary is a male-chauvinist pig.
(3) Alice has reason to believe Gary is a male-chauvinist pig.
(4) If someone is a male-chauvinist pig, that is a reason not to love him.
(5) Gary is not also someone who kills women who loves him.
(6) Gary loves Alice.
(7) Alice believes Gary loves Alice.
(8) Alice has reason to believe Gary loves Alice.

Violating Conversational Rules

We can next look at a set of conversational implications that attracted Grice's attention. Sometimes our speech acts *seem* to violate certain conventions. On the assumption that the conversation is good-willed and cooperative, the listener will then attempt to make sense of this in a way that will explain why the speaker is transparently violating a conversational rule. Here is one of Grice's examples. Suppose that A tells B that he wants to visit a friend, C, and the following conversation takes place:

A: Where does C live?
B: Somewhere in southern France.

If A is interested in visiting C, then B's reply is not adequate and thus seems to violate the rule of Quantity. We can explain this departure on the assumption that B does not know exactly where C lives and would thus violate the rule of Quality if he said anything more specific. In this case, B's reply conversationally implies that he does not know exactly where C lives. B is cooperating as much as he can.

In a more extreme case, a person may even flout one of these conventions—that is, obviously violate it. Here is Grice's example and his explanation of it:

> A is writing a testimonial about a pupil who is a candidate for a philosophy job, and the letter reads as follows: "Dear Sir, Mr. X's command of English is excellent, and his attendance at tutorials has been regular, Yours, etc." (Gloss: A cannot be opting out, since if he wished to be uncooperative, why write at all? He cannot be unable, through ignorance, to say more, since the man is his pupil; moreover, he knows that more information is wanted. He must, therefore, be wishing to impart information he is reluctant to write down. This supposition is only tenable on the assumption that he thinks that Mr. X is no good at philosophy. This, then, is what he is implicating.)

This is a case of damning with faint praise.

We can intentionally violate the rule of Relevance by pointedly changing the subject. Grice again:

> At a genteel tea party A says "Mrs. X is an old bag." There is a moment of appalled silence, then B says "The weather has been quite delightful this summer, hasn't it?"

The conversational implication here needs no explanation. We can also violate the demand for brevity and thereby *not* say something that could be said briefly. Here is one final example from Grice:

> Miss X produced a series of sounds which corresponded closely with the score of "Home Sweet Home."

By not saying simply that Miss X *sang* "Home Sweet Home," the speaker indicates, through a conversational implication, that he is not willing to call what she did singing.

Conversational Implication and Rhetorical Devices. Conversational implication is so much a part of our everyday use of language that we hardly notice that we are employing it. Consider how *rhetorical questions* work. Normally, when we ask a question we are seeking information, but not always. If I ask someone, "Can you hurry up?" I certainly know that he *can* hurry up. The point of the question is to force the person to *admit* that he can hurry up, and that in turn suggests that he should. For this reason a rhetorical question can have the force of an assertion or an order. Again, if I say to someone, "Do you expect me to believe that?" I am indicating that the person should answer this question *no*, and thus my question has the force of the assertion, "I *don't* believe that."

It is important to see that the same question can be rhetorical in one context but not in another. If we hear (or think we hear) someone in the basement, I might ask you, "Do you want me to call the police?" Here I am genuinely interested in your opinion, for calling the police might be unnecessary or even dangerous. On the other hand, if I am trying to get someone to move his car from my driveway, these same words will have the force of a rhetorical question. My question "Do you want me to call the police?" has the expected answer *no* and because of this conversationally implies the threat, "If you don't move your car, I'll call the police"—or maybe, "If you don't want me to call the police, move your car!" Rhetorical questions are used (and often abused) in everyday arguments. They are, as we shall see, often a sign of a weakness in an argument.

With rhetorical questions, we expect our words to be taken in a straightforward way. We are asking a question, even though the question itself is not used in the standard (information-seeking) way. At other times, we do not expect our listeners to take even our words at face value. We tend to exaggerate. When people claim to be hungry enough to eat a bear, that usually indicates that they are very hungry. In most cases, it does not dawn on us to take these speech acts at face value, for to do so would be to attribute to the speaker a wildly false belief about his or her powers of ingestion.

Sometimes, then, we do not intend to have our words taken at face value. But even beyond this, we sometimes expect our listeners to interpret us as claiming just the *opposite* of what we assert. This occurs, for example, with *irony* and *sarcasm*. At a crucial point in a game, the second baseman fires the ball ten feet over the first baseman's head and someone shouts: "Great throw." Literally, it was not a great throw; it was just the opposite of a great throw. How does the listener know enough to interpret it in this way? Sometimes this is indicated by tone of voice. A sarcastic tone of voice usually indicates that the person means the opposite of what he or she is saying. But even without the tone of sarcasm, the remark, "Great throw," is not likely to be taken literally. The person who says this knows, after all, that it was not a great throw. He is thus knowingly saying something false, so his utterance violates Grice's first rule of Quality, "Do not say what you believe to be false." Furthermore, the person is not trying to lie or mislead anyone, since everyone knows that the remark is false. This forces us to the conclusion, which we draw immediately, that the person does not wish to be taken literally. By saying something outrageously inappropriate, the person draws attention to the true state of affairs, that is, just how bad the throw really was.

Sometimes, though not always, the use of *metaphors* involves saying something which taken nonmetaphorically would be literally false. If someone says that her professor is an old goat, we do not suppose that she is saying her teacher is a four-footed, often smelly, animal of the genus *Capra*. We automatically take such a remark as metaphorical because the alternative, taking it literally, would be to attribute to the person a belief so wildly out of whack with reality as to border on insanity. Taken as a metaphor, the remark indicates that the speaker finds some striking and salient similarities between her professor and old goats.

Usually metaphorical remarks, taken nonmetaphorically, are literally false—but not always. For example, "No man is an island" is literally true. We treat this remark as a metaphor because, taken literally, it is so obviously and boringly true that we cannot imagine why anyone would want to say it. Taken literally, it would make no greater contribution to the conversation than any other irrelevant truth—for example, that no man is a socket wrench. As a metaphor it is an apt, if somewhat overworked, way of indicating that no one is isolated and self-contained.

These remarks on conversational implication underscore important features concerning the way our language works. First, in using language, we typically convey a great deal more information than is contained in what we actually say. Sometimes, in fact, the main point we are trying to communicate is not put into words at all. Beyond this, what we literally do say is often not meant to be taken literally. We speak loosely, we exaggerate, we employ irony and sarcasm, and we use metaphors. Sometimes these departures from literal assertion cause confusion, and that's one reason why they usually should be avoided in rigorous argument, but in many cases they do no harm and lend vividness and force to our language.

▼ EXERCISE VII

Indicate which, if any, of Grice's conversational rules are violated by the italicized sentence of each of the following conversations. Assume a standard context. More than one rule might be violated.

(1) "What did you get on the last test?" *"Some grade."*
(2) "Don't you think Bernie is an idiot?" *"Nice day, huh?"*
(3) *"The governor is an idiot."*
(4) *"The Lone Ranger rode into the sunset and jumped on his horse."*
(5) "When is Easter next year?" *"Easter will be on April 15 next year."*
(6) *"Without her help, we'd be up a creek without a paddle."*
(7) "Where is Palo Alto?" *"On or near the surface of the Earth."*
(8) *"It will rain tomorrow."* "How do you know?" "I just guessed."
(9) *"Does the dog need to go out for a W-A-L-K?"* (spelled out)
(10) "Why did the chicken cross the road?" *"To get to the other side."*
(11) Psychiatrist: "You're crazy."
Patient: "I want a second opinion."
Psychiatrist: "Okay. *You're ugly,* too."
(12) "This new car is great." *"Sure, and so was the Edsel."*

Deception

In the examples we have examined thus far, a speaker intentionally violates a conversational rule to achieve some special effect—for example, damning with faint praise. It is important in these cases that the listeners *recognize* that a rule is being intentionally broken, for otherwise they may simply be misled. At other times, however, the speaker intentionally breaks conversational rules to mislead his listeners. The speaker may violate Grice's first rule of quality by uttering something he knows to be false with the intention of producing a false belief in his listeners. That's called lying. Notice that lying depends on the general acceptance of the Cooperative Principle. Because people generally assume that people are telling the truth, successful lying is possible.

Flat-out lying is not the only way (and often not the most effective way) of intentionally misleading people. We can say something literally true that, at the same time, conversationally implies something false. This is sometimes called making a *false suggestion*. If a son tells his parents that *he has had some trouble with the car*, that could be true, but deeply misleading, if, in fact, he had totaled it. It would be misleading because it would violate the rule of strength (or Quantity). In saying only that he had *some* trouble with the car, he conversationally implies that nothing very serious happened. He conversationally implies this because, in the context, he is expected to come clean and reveal *all* that actually happened.

A more complex example of false suggestion arose in a lawsuit that went all the way to the Supreme Court.

▼ *Bronston v. United States*
Supreme Court of the United States, 1973
409 U.S. 352

MR. CHIEF JUSTICE BURGER delivered the opinion of the Court.

Petitioner's perjury conviction was founded on the answers given by him as a witness at that bankruptcy hearing, and in particular on the following colloquy with a lawyer for a creditor of Bronston Productions:

"Q. Do you have any bank accounts in Swiss banks, Mr. Bronston?
"A. No, sir.
"Q. Have you ever?
"A. The company had an account here for about six months, in Zurich.
"Q. Have you any nominees who have bank accounts in Swiss banks?
"A. No, sir.
"Q. Have you ever?
"A. No, sir."

It is undisputed that for a period of nearly five years, between October 1959 and June 1964, petitioner had a personal bank account at the International Credit Bank in Geneva, Switzerland, into which he made deposits and upon which he drew checks totaling more than $180,000. It is likewise undisputed that petitioner's answers were literally truthful. (i) Petitioner did not at the time of questioning have a Swiss bank account. (ii) Bronston Productions, Inc., did have the account in Zurich described by petitioner. (iii) Neither at the time of questioning nor before did petitioner have nominees who had Swiss accounts. The government's prosecution for perjury went forward on the theory that in order to mislead his questioner, petitioner answered the second question with literal truthfulness but unresponsively addressed his answer to the company's assets and not to his own—thereby implying that he had no personal Swiss bank account at the relevant time.

It is hard to read the witness's response to the second question in any other way than as a deliberate attempt to mislead the court, for his response plainly implies that he did not have a personal account in a Swiss bank, when, in fact, he did. But the issue before the court was not whether he intentionally misled the court, but whether in doing so he committed perjury. The relevant statute reads as follows:

> Whoever, having taken an oath before a competent tribunal . . . that he will testify . . . truly, . . . willfully and contrary to such oath states or subscribes any material matter which he does not believe to be true, is guilty of perjury. . . . (18 U.S.C. §1621)

The lower courts ruled that Bronston violated this statute and thus had committed perjury. The Supreme Court reversed this decision, in part for the following reasons:

> It should come as no surprise that a participant in a bankruptcy proceeding may have something to conceal and consciously tried to do so, or that a debtor may be embarrassed at his plight and yield information reluctantly. It is the responsibility of the lawyer to probe; testimonial interrogation, and cross examination in particular, is a probing, prying, pressing form of inquiry. If a witness evades, it is the lawyer's responsibility to recognize the evasion and to bring the witness back to the mark, to flush out the whole truth with the tools of adversary examination.

In other words, in a courtroom, where the relationship is typically adversarial rather than cooperative, not all the standard conversational rules are in force, or fully in force. In particular, it would be unrealistic to assume that the rule of Quantity will be consistently honored in a courtroom clash; therefore it becomes the task of the cross-examiner to force the witness to produce all the relevant facts.

▼ EXERCISE VIII

People often say things in order to conversationally imply something else. Assuming a natural conversational setting, what might a person intend to conversationally imply with the following remarks? Briefly explain why each of these conversational implications holds; that is, explain the relationship between what the speaker *literally* says and what he or she intends to convey.

(1) It's getting a little chilly in here.

(2) The crowd didn't actually throw bottles at him. (Said of a rock singer.)

(3) You can trust him if you want to.

(4) I got here before he did. (Said at a lunch counter.)

(5) He hasn't been sent to jail yet.

(6) Do you expect me to believe that?

(7) There are planes leaving every day for China. (Said to a student radical.)

(8) I had some trouble with the car.

(9) These sweet potatoes are very filling.

(10) That exam blew me away.

(11) The West wasn't won with a registered gun.

(12) A midair collision can ruin your whole day.

▼ EXERCISE IX

Each of the following remarks, if taken quite literally, is either false, or otherwise plainly defective. First, explain why each remark is either false or defective on a literal reading. Second, state what you take to be the conversational implication of each remark. Third, explain the source of this conversational implication by making reference to Grice's conversational rules.

(1) "I ain't got nothing but love, babe, eight days a week." (Beatles lyric)

(2) "An army travels on its stomach." (Napoleon)

(3) "The way to a man's heart is through his stomach." (Traditional saying)

(4) "If you have seen one redwood, you've seen them all." (Attributed to James Watt)

(5) "Ich bin ein Berliner." ("I am a Berliner.") (John F. Kennedy, in a speech before the Berlin Wall)

(6) "Let them eat cake!" (Attributed [apparently falsely] to Marie Antoinette upon hearing that the people were rioting for bread).

(7) "It isn't a car, it's a Volkswagen." (Advertisement)

(8) "If God made us in His image, we have certainly returned the compliment." (Voltaire)

(9) "The only thing we have to fear is fear itself." (Franklin D. Roosevelt)

(10) " 'Beauty is truth, truth beauty,'—that is all
Ye know on earth, and all ye need to know."
    (John Keats, *Ode on a Grecian Urn*)

▼ DISCUSSION QUESTIONS

1. Refer back to the dialogue quoted in *Bronston v. United States*. Because it is difficult to read the witnesses's second response as anything but a willful attempt to deceive, why should this case be treated differently from lying? Alternatively, why not drop the demand that witnesses tell the truth, and make it the responsibility of the lawyers to get at the truth itself, rather than just the whole truth, through *probing, prying, pressing inquiry?*

2. During the 1980 presidential campaign, Jimmy Carter made the following statement in Atlanta, Georgia:

   > You have seen in this campaign the stirring of hate and the rebirth of code words like "states' rights" . . . racism has no place in this country.

   In response, George Bush, the Republican vice-presidential nominee, said that he was "appalled at the ugly, mean little remark Jimmy Carter made last night." Beyond the meaning of the literal statement, what are the obvious conversational implications of Carter's statement? Do they amount, as Bush seems to think, to accusing the two principal Republican candidates of racism?

3. In the 1984 presidential campaign, George Bush, referring to the Marines killed in the 1984 Beirut bombing, remarked:

   > And for somebody to suggest, as our opponents have, that these men have died in shame, they had better not tell the parents of these young Marines.

   The next day, Walter Mondale, the Democratic presidential nominee, responded angrily:

   > Mr. Bush, we love this country as much as you do. And Mr. Bush, we honor the men and women who died for our country and we grieve as much for their families as you do.

   He concluded by saying:

   > Apologize, and do it today!

What are the obvious implications of Bush's original remark? Given this, did Mondale have good reasons to demand an apology?

In the days that followed, Bush refused to apologize, even though he could not produce an instance of either Mondale or Ferraro using the word "shame" with respect to the Marines. He quoted Ferraro as saying that the Marines "died or are missing without a purpose and for a policy that's never been explained." He then went on to say:

> Mr. Mondale and Mrs. Ferraro can argue all they want. But the fact is, accusing young men of dying without a purpose and for no reason is in the lexicon of the American people a shame.

The next day, Bush cited the dictionary in defense of his original statement. He quoted Mondale as saying that with the killing of the Marines "once again we're humiliated in this region." Bush then said:

> Abase in Webster's, as I understand it, is defined as deep shame, and when you look up humiliation, it refers you to abase.

Who do you think got the better of this exchange? Why?

AN OVERVIEW

In this chapter we have developed a rather complex picture of the way in which our language functions. In the process we have distinguished three kinds of acts or three levels of acts that are performed when we employ language. We have also examined the rules associated with each kind or level of act. The following outline summarizes this discussion:

THREE LEVELS OF LANGUAGE

Kinds of Acts	Governing Rules
A LINGUISTIC ACT is an act *of* saying something meaningful in a language. It is the basic act that is needed to make anything part of language.	Semantical rules (such as definitions) and syntactical rules (as in grammar).
A SPEECH ACT is the conventional move that a remark makes in a language game. It is what I do *in* saying something. Different speech acts are named by different verbs in explicit performatives. For example, to advise.	Speech-act rules about special agents, formulas, circumstances, facts, and feelings found by speech-act analyses.

A CONVERSATIONAL ACT is the speaker's act of causing a standard kind of effect in the listener. It is what I do *by* saying something. For example, to persuade.

Conversational rules (Cooperative principle; Maxims of Quantity, Quality, Relevance, and Manner.)

▼ EXERCISE X

Someone is trying to solve the following puzzle: One of thirteen balls is heavier than the others, which are of equal weight. In no more than three weighings on a balance scale, determine which ball is the heavier one. The person is stumped so someone says to her: "Begin by putting four balls in each pan of the scale."

Describe the linguistic act, the speech act, and the conversational act of the person who makes this remark.

2

The Language
of Argument

Using the techniques developed in
Chapter 1, this chapter will examine the use of language to formulate arguments and will provide
methods for analyzing genuine arguments in their richness and
complexity. The first stage in analyzing an argument is the discovery of its basic *structure*. To do
this, we will examine the words,
phrases, and special constructions
that indicate the premises and
conclusions of an argument. The
second stage is the study of techniques used to *strengthen* an argument. These include *guarding*
premises so that they are less subject to criticism, offering *assurances* concerning debatable claims,
and *discounting* possible criticisms in advance. Finally, we will
examine the role of *evaluative*
language in arguments.

THE BASIC STRUCTURE OF ARGUMENTS

In the previous chapter, we saw that language is used for a great many purposes beyond stating things that are either true or false. When we issue an order or make a bet, we are not stating anything. Turning now to arguments, we see that they, like orders and bets, are not statements. Although arguments are typically made up of statements, they are not themselves statements. A single example illustrates this:

> Socrates is older than Plato; Plato is older than Aristotle; therefore, Socrates is older than Aristotle.

Taken as a whole, this sentence does *not* express anything either true or false. It is used for a different purpose, namely, to *derive* a conclusion from some premises.

Although arguments are not statements, they are constructed out of statements. Still, arguments are not *just* lists of statements. Here is a simple list of statements:

> Socrates is mortal.
> All men are mortal.
> Socrates is a man.

This is not an argument, because none of these statements is presented as a reason for any of the others.

It is simple to turn this list into an argument. All we have to do is to add the single word "therefore":

> Socrates is mortal.
> All men are mortal.
> Therefore, Socrates is a man.

Now we have an argument. The word "therefore" converts these sentences into an argument by signaling that the statement following it is a conclusion, and that the statement or statements that come before it are offered as reasons in behalf of this conclusion. This argument is a very bad one, since the conclusion does not follow from the reasons stated in its behalf, but it is an argument nonetheless.

There are many other ways to turn this same list into an argument. Here is one:

> Socrates is mortal,
> since all men are mortal,
> and Socrates is a man.

This produces a new argument, and this time it is a good argument, because the conclusion does follow from the premises offered in its behalf.

Notice that the word "since" operates roughly in an opposite way from "therefore." The word "therefore" is a *conclusion marker*, because it indicates that the statement that follows it is a conclusion. In contrast, the word "since" is a *reason marker*, because it indicates that the statement or statements that follow it are reasons. In our example, the conclusion comes before the word "since," but there is a variation on this. Sometimes the conclusion is tacked onto the end of the argument:

Since all men are mortal and Socrates is a man,
Socrates is mortal.

"Since" flags reasons; the remaining connected statement is then taken to be the conclusion, whether it appears at the beginning or at the end of the sentence.

Many other terms are used to introduce an argumentative structure into language by marking out reasons and conclusions. Here is a partial list:

Reason Markers	Conclusion Markers
since	therefore
because	then
for	thus
	so
	hence
	accordingly

We shall call such terms *warranting connectives*, because, in various ways, they each present one or more statements as the *warrant* or backing for some other statement.

It is important to realize that these words are not always used as warranting connectives, that is, as terms that introduce an argumentative structure. The words "since" and "then" are often used as indicators of time, as in "He's been an American citizen since 1973" and "He ate a hot dog, then a hamburger." The word "for" is often used as a preposition, for example, "John works for IBM." Since some of these terms have a variety of meanings, it is not possible to identify warranting connectives in a mechanical way just by looking at words. It is necessary to examine the meaning of words in the context in which they occur. One test of whether a word is functioning as a warranting connective in a particular sentence is whether you can substitute another warranting connective without changing the meaning of the sentence. In the last example, it makes no sense to say "John works since IBM."

There are a variety of other ways to introduce argumentative structure into our language. We can also indicate conclusions and reasons by using certain explicit performatives. If someone says, "I conclude that . . .," the words that follow are given the status of a conclusion. More pretentiously, if someone says, "I here base my argument on the claim that . . .," what comes next is a premise. In fact, a wide variety of phrases is available to signal that an argument is being presented. Here is just a small sample:

from which it follows that . . .
from which we may conclude that . . .
from which we see that . . .
which goes to show that . . .
which establishes that . . .

These are conclusion markers, but they can be turned into reason markers very easily:

which follows from the fact that . . . ,
which we may conclude from the fact that . . . ,
and so on.

Examining actual arguments will show that this list can be extended almost indefinitely.

If . . . , Then . . .

If-then sentences contain a common, but special, kind of warranting connective. If-then sentences are called *conditional* sentences. Though they often occur in arguments, they do not themselves usually present arguments. Consider the following indicative conditional:

If the Dodgers get better hitting, then they will win the Western Division.

The sentence that occurs between the "if" and the "then" is called the *antecedent* of the conditional. The sentence that occurs after the "then" is called its *consequent*. In using an indicative conditional, we are not asserting the truth of its antecedent, and we are usually not asserting the truth of its consequent either. Thus, the person who makes the above remark is not claiming that the Dodgers will win the Western Division. All she is saying is that *if* they get better hitting, they will win. Furthermore, she is not saying that they will get better hitting. The word "if" cancels this suggestion. Because the speaker is not committing herself to either of these claims, she is not presenting an argument; she is not trying to give reasons for the truth of some claim. This makes her claim very different than if she had said, "Since the Dodgers will get better hitting, the Dodgers will win the Western Division."

Yet there is obviously some close connection between conditional statements and arguments. One way of telling someone not to argue is to say that we do not want to hear any ifs, ands, or buts. For indicative conditionals, at least,[1] the following explanation seems reasonable. Although indicative conditionals do not present arguments, they provide a *pattern* that can be converted into an argument whenever the antecedent is taken to be true.[2] Thus, we often hear people argue in the following way:

---

[1] Special problems arise with other conditionals—for example, subjective conditionals. They will not be discussed in this work.

[2] We also get an argument when the consequent is shown to be *false*. This will be discussed in Chapter 7.

If international terrorism continues to grow, there will be a worldwide crisis. But international terrorism will certainly continue to grow, so a world crisis is on the way.

The first sentence is an indicative conditional, and it makes no positive claims about terrorism or a coming world crisis. The next sentence indicates that the antecedent of this conditional is true and proceeds immediately to the conclusion that the consequent must be true as well. This use of indicative conditionals for formulating arguments is typical, and for this reason we shall call the if-then connective a *warranting connective.*

ARGUMENTS IN STANDARD FORM

Since arguments come in all shapes and forms, it will help to have a standard way of presenting arguments. For centuries, logicians have used a format of the following kind:

> All men are mortal.
> Socrates is a man.
> ───────────────
> ∴ Socrates is mortal.

The reasons (or premises) are listed above the line, the conclusion is listed below the line, and the symbol "∴" is read "therefore." Arguments presented this way are said to be in *standard form.*

The notion of a standard form is useful because it helps us see that the same argument can be expressed in different ways. For example, the following two sentences formulate the argument we just now stated in standard form above:

> Socrates is mortal, since all men are mortal, and Socrates is a man.
> All men are mortal, so Socrates is mortal, since he is a man.

More importantly, by putting arguments into standard form, we perform the most obvious, and in some ways most important, step in the analysis of an argument: the identification of premises and conclusions.

▼ EXERCISE I

(a) Identify which of the following sentences expresses an argument.
(b) For each that does,
   (i) circle the warranting connective (or connectives), and
   (ii) restate the argument in standard form.

(1) Since Chicago is north of Boston, and Boston is north of Charleston, Chicago is north of Charleston.

(2) Toward evening, clouds formed and the sky grew darker; then the storm broke.

(3) Texas has a greater area than Topeka, and Topeka has a greater area than the Bronx Zoo, so Texas has a greater area than the Bronx Zoo.

(4) Both houses of Congress may pass a bill, but the president may still veto it.

(5) Other airlines will carry more passengers because United Airlines is on strike.

(6) Since Jesse James left town, taking his gang with him, things have been a lot quieter.

(7) Witches float, because witches are made of wood, and wood floats.

VALIDITY, TRUTH, AND SOUNDNESS

Not all arguments are good arguments, so, having identified an argument, the next task is to *evaluate* it. Evaluating arguments is a complex business, and, in fact, this entire book is aimed primarily at developing procedures for doing so. There are, however, certain fundamental terms used in evaluating arguments that should be introduced from the start. They are validity, truth, and soundness. Here they will be introduced informally; later (in Chapters 7 and 8) they will be examined with more rigor.

Validity

Validity is a technical notion, but it closely matches the common-sense idea of a conclusion *following from* its premises. To say that a conclusion follows from its premises means that the conclusion must be true if the premises are true. We will take this to be our definition of validity: *an argument is valid if and only if it is not possible for all of the premises to be true and the conclusion false.* Looking at it from the other side, we can also say that an argument is valid when, if the conclusion is false, at least one premise must also be false. If you think about it, you will see that these definitions are equivalent.

The following argument passes this test for validity:

> All Senators are paid.
> Sam Nunn is a Senator.
> ─────────────
> ∴ Sam Nunn is paid.

The conclusion of this argument is true, but, if it were false, one of the premises would also have to be false. If Nunn were not paid, either Nunn would not be a Senator or not all Senators would be paid. So this argument is valid. Contrast this with a different argument:

All Senators are paid.
Sam Nunn is paid.

∴ Sam Nunn is a Senator.

The conclusion is true again, but we get a very different picture when we ask what would happen if the conclusion were false. If Nunn were not a Senator, both premises still might be true; it would still be possible that all Senators are paid and Nunn is paid (for some other job). Thus, this argument is not valid.

Given our definition of validity, it should be clear why validity is valuable: there can be no valid arguments that lead us from true premises to a false conclusion. This should square with your commonsense ideas about reasoning: if you reason well, you should not be led from truth into error. This makes validity one criterion for a good *deductive* argument, since deductive arguments are put forward as meeting this standard. Other arguments—inductive arguments—are not intended to meet this rigorous standard. The criteria for evaluating inductive arguments will be examined in Chapter 9. For now we will concentrate solely on deductive arguments.

Truth

Although a deductive argument must be valid to be a good argument, validity is not enough. One reason is that an argument can be valid even when all of the statements that it contains are false:

All clowns are from Tennessee.
Sam Nunn is a clown.

∴ Sam Nunn is from Tennessee.

This is a bad argument, because both of its premises are false. Nonetheless, this argument does satisfy our definition of validity: if all of the premises were true, then the conclusion could not be false. This makes it obvious that validity is not the same as truth. It also makes it obvious that another requirement of a good argument is that *all of its premises must be true*.

Soundness

We thus make at least two demands of a deductive argument that we will accept as proving its conclusion:

(1) The argument must be valid.
(2) The premises must be true.

When an argument meets both these standards, it is said to be *sound.* If it fails to meet either one, it is *unsound.* Thus, an argument is unsound if it is invalid, and it is also unsound if at least one of its premises is false.

	Premises True	At Least One False Premise
Valid	Sound	Unsound
Invalid	Unsound	Unsound

Soundness has one great benefit: a sound argument must have a true conclusion. We know this because its premises are true, and it is valid, so it is not possible that its premises are true and its conclusion is false. This is why people who seek truth want sound arguments.

▼ EXERCISE II

Indicate whether each of the following series of statements is an argument and, if so, whether it is valid and whether it is sound. Explain your answers where necessary.

(1) Bill Cook went bald, and most men go bald.
(2) Bill Cook went bald, because most men go bald.
(3) Most professors agree that they are paid too little, so they are.
(4) Republicans agree that SDI will work, and it will.
(5) If this school were at the South Pole, I'd be at the South Pole. But I'm not at the South Pole. Therefore, this school is not at the South Pole.
(6) There can't be a largest six-digit number, because six-digit numbers are numbers, and there is no largest number.
(7) Lee can't run a company right, since he can't do anything right.
(8) David Letterman is over 5 feet tall, so he is over 2 feet tall.
(9) Since Bush is president, he must have won the election.

▼ EXERCISE III

Assume that the truth-value assignments given to the right of each statement are correct.

(1) All seniors are arrogant. (T)
(2) All arrogant people are immodest. (T)
(3) All arrogant people are seniors. (F)
(4) All seniors are immodest. (T)

Using these somewhat arbitrarily assigned truth values, label each of the following arguments as (a) either valid or invalid and (b) either sound or unsound.

(a) All seniors are arrogant.
All arrogant people are immodest.

∴ All seniors are immodest.

(b) All seniors are immodest.
   All arrogant people are immodest.
   ∴ All seniors are arrogant.

(c) All arrogant people are seniors.
   All seniors are immodest.
   ∴ All arrogant people are immodest.

(d) All arrogant people are immodest.
   All seniors are immodest.
   ∴ All seniors are immodest.

▼ EXERCISE IV

Using this new set of statements and assigned truth values,

(1) All talented people are insightful. (T)
(2) All talented people are ugly. (F)
(3) All seniors are ugly. (F)
(4) All seniors are talented. (F)
(5) All ugly people are insightful. (T)
(6) All seniors are insightful. (F)
(7) All ugly people are seniors. (F)

construct arguments with two premises and a conclusion such that:

(a) The argument is valid, but all the premises are false, and the conclusion is false as well.
(b) The argument is valid, both premises are false, and the conclusion is true.
(c) The argument is valid, one premise is true, one premise false, and the conclusion is true.
(d) The argument is valid, one premise is true, one false, and the conclusion is false.

▼ EXERCISE V

Indicate whether each of the following sentences is true. For those that are true, explain why they are true. For those that are false, show why they are false by giving an example.

(1) Every argument with a false conclusion is invalid.
(2) Every argument with a false premise is invalid.
(3) Every argument with a false premise and a false conclusion is invalid.
(4) Every argument with a false premise and a true conclusion is invalid.

(5) Every argument with true premises and a false conclusion is invalid.

(6) Every argument with a true conclusion is sound.

(7) Every argument with a false conclusion is unsound.

A PROBLEM AND SOME SOLUTIONS

Although soundness guarantees a true conclusion, we usually expect even more from an argument than soundness. In the first place, an argument can be sound, but trivially uninteresting:

> Nigeria is in Africa.
>
> ∴ Nigeria is in Africa.

Here the premise is true. The argument is also valid, because the premise cannot be true without the conclusion (which repeats it) being true as well. Yet the argument is completely worthless as a proof that Nigeria is in Africa. The reason is that this argument is *circular*. We will examine circular arguments in detail later on in Chapter 5, but it is obvious why such arguments are useless. If A is trying to prove something to B that B has doubts about, then citing the very matter in question will not do any good. In general, for A to prove something to B, A must marshall facts that B accepts and then show that they justify the claim at issue. In circular arguments, the doubt about the conclusion immediately turns into a doubt about the premise as well.

Now A seems to run into a problem. A cannot cite a proposition as a reason for *itself*, for that would be circular reasoning. If, however, A cites some *other* propositions as premises leading to A's conclusion, the question naturally arises as to why B should accept these premises. Doesn't A have to present arguments for A's premises as well? Yet if A does that, A will just introduce further premises that are also in need of proof, and so on indefinitely. It now looks as if every argument, to be successful, will have to be infinitely long!

The answer to this ancient problem depends on the fact that the activity of arguing or presenting reasons relies on a shared set of beliefs and a certain amount of trust. When I present reasons, I try to cite these shared beliefs—things that will not *in fact* be challenged. Beyond this, I expect people to believe me when I cite information that only I possess. But there are limits to this, for people do believe things that are false and sometimes lie about what they know to be true. This presents a practical problem: how can I present my reasons in a way that does not produce just another demand for an argument—a demand for more reasons? Here we use three main strategies:

(1) *Assuring:* indicating that there are back-up reasons even though we are not giving them right now.

(2) *Guarding:* weakening our claims so that they are less subject to attack.

(3) *Discounting:* anticipating criticisms and dismissing them.

In these ways we build a defensive perimeter around our premises. Each of these defenses is useful, but each can also be abused.

Assuring

When will we want to give assurances about some statement we have made? If we state something that we know everyone believes, assurances are not necessary. For that matter, if everyone believes something, we may not even state it at all; we let others fill in this step in the argument. We offer assurances when we think that someone might challenge what we say.

There are many ways to give assurances. Sometimes we cite authorities:

Doctors agree . . .
Recent studies have shown . . .
An unimpeachable source close to the White House says . . .
It has been established that . . .

Here we do not actually cite reasons. We merely indicate that they can be produced on demand. When the authority is trusted, this is often sufficient, but authorities often can and should be questioned. This topic will be discussed more fully in Chapter 5. Another way to give assurances is to comment on the strength of our own belief:

I'm certain that . . .
I'm sure that . . .
I can assure you that . . .
Over the years, I have become more and more convinced that . . .

Again we do not cite reasons, but we conversationally imply that there is some reason why we feel so sure. A third kind of assurance abuses the audience:

Everyone with any sense agrees that . . .
Of course, no one will deny that . . .
It is just common sense that . . .
There is no question that . . .
Nobody but a fool would deny that . . .

These assurances not only do not give any reason, they also suggest that there is something wrong with you if you ask for a reason. We can call this *the trick of abusive assurances.*

Although many assurances are legitimate, we as critics should always view assurances with some suspicion. Following the conversational rule of Quality, we should expect people to give assurances only when they have good reasons to do so. Yet, in point of fact, assuring remarks often mark the weakest parts of the argument, not the strongest parts. If someone says "I hardly need argue that. . . ," it is often useful to ask why he has gone to the trouble of saying it. In particular, when we distrust an argument—as we sometimes do—this is precisely the place to look for weakness. If assurances are used, they are used for some reason. Sometimes the reason is a good one. Sometimes, however, it is a bad one. In honest argumentation, they save time and simplify discussion. In a dishonest argument, they are used to paper over cracks.

Guarding

Guarding represents a different strategy for protecting premises from attack. We reduce our claim to something less strong. Thus, instead of saying "all," we say "many." Instead of saying something straight out, we use a qualifying phrase like "it is likely that . . . ," "it is very possible that . . . ," and so on. Law school professors like the phrase "it is arguable that. . . ." This is wonderfully noncommittal, for it really doesn't indicate how strong the argument is, yet it does get the statement into the argument.

Broadly speaking, there are three ways of guarding what we say:

(1) Weakening the *extent* of what has been said: retreating from "all" to "most" to "a few" to "some," and so on.

(2) Using *probability* phrases like "it is virtually certain that . . . ," "it is likely that . . . ," and so on.

(3) Describing our *cognitive* state: moving from "I know that . . ." to "I believe that . . ." to "I tend to believe that . . ."

These guarding phrases are often legitimate and useful. If you want to argue that a friend needs fire insurance for her house, you don't need to claim that her house *will* burn down. All you need to claim is that there is a real *chance* that her house will burn down. Your argument is better if you start with this weaker premise, because it is easier to defend, and it is enough to support your conclusion.

If we weaken a claim sufficiently, we can make it completely immune to criticism. What can be said against a remark of the following kind: "There is some small chance that perhaps a few politicians are honest on at least some occasions"? You would have to have a *very* low opinion of politicians to deny this statement. On the other hand, if we weaken our premises too much, we pay a price. The premise no longer gives strong support to the conclusion. When the guard goes too far, it has degenerated into a *hedge*.

The goal is to find a *middle way:* We should weaken our premises sufficiently to avoid criticism, but not weaken them so much that they no longer provide strong enough evidence for the conclusion. Balancing these factors is one of the most important strategies in making and criticizing arguments.

Just as it was useful to zero in on assuring terms, it is useful to keep track of guarding terms. Guarding terms are easily corrupted. One common trick is to *insinuate* into a conversation things that cannot be stated explicitly. Consider the effect of the following remark: "Perhaps the secretary of state has not been candid with the Congress." This doesn't actually say that the secretary has been less than candid with the Congress, but it suggests it. Furthermore, it suggests it in a way that is hard to combat.

A more subtle device for corrupting guarding terms is to introduce a statement in a guarded form and then go on to speak as if it were not guarded at all. After a while, the word "perhaps" disappears.

> Perhaps the secretary of state has not been candid with the Congress. Of course, he has a right to his own views, but this is a democracy where officials are accountable to Congress. So even the secretary of state cannot escape justice.

This corruption of guarding can be called *the trick of the disappearing hedge.*

Discounting

The general pattern of discounting is to cite a possible criticism in order to reject it or counter it. Notice how different the following statements sound:

> The ring is beautiful, but expensive.
> The ring is expensive, but beautiful.

Both statements assert the very same facts—that the ring is beautiful and that the ring is expensive. Both statements also suggest that there is some opposition between these facts. Yet these statements operate in different ways. We might use the first as a reason for *not* buying the ring; we can use the second as a reason *for* buying it. The first sentence acknowledges that the ring is beautiful, but overrides this by pointing out that it is expensive. In reverse fashion, the second statement acknowledges that the ring is expensive, but overrides this by pointing out that it is beautiful. Such assertions of the form "A but B" thus have four components:

(1) The assertion of A.
(2) The assertion of B.
(3) The suggestion of some opposition between A and B.
(4) The indication that the truth of B is more important than the truth of A.

The word "but" thus discounts the statement that comes before it in favor of the statement that follows it.

"Although" is also a discounting connective, but it operates in reverse fashion from the word "but." We can see this using the same example:

Although the ring is expensive, it is beautiful.
Although the ring is beautiful, it is expensive.

Here the statement following the word "although" is discounted in favor of the connected statement. A partial list of terms that function as discounting connectives includes the following conjunctions:

although	but
though	however
even if	nonetheless
still	nevertheless
	yet

The clearest cases of discounting occur when we are dealing with facts that point in different directions. We discount the fact that goes against the position we wish to take. Discounting is, however, often more subtle than this. We sometimes use discounting to block certain conversational implications of what we have said. This comes out in examples of the following kind:

Jones is an aggressive player, but he is not dirty.
The situation is difficult, but not hopeless.
The Democrats have the upper hand in Congress, but only for the time being.
A truce has been declared, but who knows for how long?

Take the first example. There is no opposition between the fact that Jones is aggressive and the fact that he is not dirty. Both would be reasons to pick Jones for our team. However, the assertion that Jones is aggressive might suggest that he is dirty. The but-clause cancels this suggestion without, of course, denying that Jones is aggressive.

The nuances of discounting terms can be very subtle, and a correct analysis is not always easy. All the same, the role of discounting terms is often very important. It can be very effective in an argument to beat your opponents to the punch by anticipating and discounting criticisms before your opponents can raise them. The proper use of discounting can also help to avoid side issues and tangents.

But discounting terms can be abused. People often spend time discounting weak objections to their views to avoid other objections which they know are harder to counter. Another common trick is *discounting straw men*. Consider the following remark: "A new building would be great, but we can't build it for free." This doesn't actually say that the speaker's opponents think we can build a new building for free, but it does conversationally imply that they think this, since otherwise it would be irrelevant to discount that objection. The speaker is thus trying to make the opponents look bad by putting words into their mouths— words that they would never say themselves. To prevent tricks like this, we need to ask whether a discounted criticism is one that really would be raised, and whether there are stronger criticisms that should be raised.

▼ EXERCISE VI

For each of the numbered words or expressions in the following sentences indicate whether it is a warranting connective, an assuring term, a guarding term, a discounting term, or none of these. For each warranting connective, specify what the conclusion and the reasons are, and for each discounting term, specify what criticism is being discounted and what the response to this criticism is.

(1) *Although* [1] no mechanism has been discovered, *most* [2] *researchers in the field agree* [3] that smoking *greatly increases the chances* [4] of heart disease.

(2) *Since* [5] *historically* [6] public debt leads to inflation, *there can be no doubt* [7] that, *despite* [8] recent trends, inflation will return.

(3) *Take it from me,* [9] there hasn't been a decent centerfielder *since* [10] Joe Dimaggio.

(4) *Whatever anyone tells you,* [11] there is *little* [12] to the rumor that Queen Elizabeth will step down *for* [13] her son Prince Charles.

(5) The early deaths of Janis Joplin and Jimi Hendrix *show* [14] how *really* [15] dangerous drugs are.

(6) I *think* [16] he is out back somewhere.

(7) I *think,* [17] *therefore* [18] I am.

(8) I *think,* [19] therefore I *think* [20] I am.

▼ EXERCISE VII

(a) Construct three new and interesting examples of statements containing assuring terms.

(b) Do the same for guarding terms.

(c) Do the same for discounting terms, and indicate which statement is being discounted in favor of the other.

EVALUATIVE LANGUAGE

Although some words in our language are relatively neutral, others carry strong positive or negative connotations. They are used not just to describe but to *evaluate*. The clearest cases of evaluative language occur when we say that something is *good* or *bad*, that some course of action is *right* or *wrong*, or that it *should* or *should not* (or *ought* or *ought not* to) be done. Other evaluative terms are restricted to more specific areas. A fertilizer would not normally be called *beautiful* or *ugly*, but it can be a *bargain* or a *ripoff*. Soldiers and firemen are evaluated positively when they are called *brave*, but couches cannot be *brave*. Couches are good in other ways: they can be *comfortable*.

Positive and negative connotations can be subtle. Consider a word like "clever". Descriptively, it indicates quick mental ability and carries a positive connotation. In contrast, "cunning," which has much the same descriptive content, often carries a negative connotation. It thus makes a difference which one of these words we choose. It also makes a difference where we apply them. You can praise a light opera by calling it clever, but it would surely be taken as a criticism if you called a grand opera clever. This, needless to say, turns upon the rule of Quantity. Grand operas are supposed to be more than clever. When something is supposed to be profound and serious, it is insulting just to call it clever. Prayers, for example, should not be clever.

Sometimes innocuous words can shift connotations. The word "too" is the perfect example of this. This word introduces a negative connotation, sometimes turning a positive quality into a negative one. Compare the following sentences:

John is smart.	John is too smart.
John is honest.	John is too honest.
John is ambitious.	John is too ambitious.
John is nice.	John is too nice.
John is friendly.	John is too friendly.

The word "too" indicates an excess, and thereby contains a criticism. If you look at the items in the second column, you will see that the criticism is sometimes rather brutal—for example, calling someone "too friendly."

To understand evaluations, we can ask what they are used to do on the three levels of language discussed in Chapter 1. On the *linguistic* level, to call something good is to utter a meaningful sentence. The meaning of the term "good" is very controversial, but one theory is that to call something good is simply to say that it meets the relevant standards. This is pretty empty until the standards are specified, but that is because the word "good" is applied to so many different subjects, and the context determines which standards are relevant. When we say that Hondas are good cars, we are probably applying standards that involve reliability, efficiency, comfort, and so on. More specific evaluative terms like "brave" invoke particular standards: a brave person must not show too much fear in the face of danger. In addition to invoking standards, when we call something "good," we are also often performing *speech acts* of praising the thing and expressing our approval. When we call something "bad," we are often criticizing or condemning. In particular contexts, we might also call something "good" or "bad" as part of a speech act of giving advice or justifying a decision. On the *conversational* level, we are usually trying to evoke similar appraisals in our audience and often to persuade someone to act in a certain way.

Because of these many uses, evaluative statements stand in contrast to utterances that *merely express* personal feelings. If I say that I just love SpaghettiOs, then I am expressing a personal taste, one that I realize others may not share. On the other hand, if I call something *good* or *bad*, then I am going beyond my personal feelings—I am making a claim to objectivity. Since I am invoking a standard, I need to be able to specify the standard and show that it applies. Thus, in general, if a person makes an evaluative claim (a value judgment), we have a right to ask for the reasons that back this evaluative claim.

Slanting

It is important to see that there is nothing intrinsically wrong with using evaluative and expressive language. Sometimes forceful language is justified. At times, however, people use evaluative language without offering any justification for the evaluations they make. At other times they use highly charged language as a substitute for argument. When either of these latter things takes place, we are dealing with *slanting*. Slanting involves the improper use of evaluative language to place something in a good or bad light without adequate justification.

Ethnic and racial slurs are obvious examples of slanted language. To say that someone is a Jew is to comment on his or her ethnic origin. To call someone a "kike" conveys the same information, but combines it with an expression of contempt. Actually, in this area, connotations are so prevalent that we have to look to scientific language to find more or less neutral language. For example, "white" is a positive term, whereas "whitey" (and "honkey") are negative. "Caucasian" is more or less scientific and neutral. Here we must use the guarding expression "more or less" because all the language in this area is highly charged. For many, "black" is a positive term, and "nigger" is a term of contempt, but "Negro" is not really neutral in the way, for example, that "Mongolian" is. These tensions in the language reflect deeper tensions in our society.

We should also notice that the connotations of a word vary with context. They depend on who is saying what to whom. An irresponsible conservative will accuse his liberal opponents of being communists, thereby associating them with an organization generally held in contempt in this country. On the other hand, it wouldn't have made sense to *accuse* Lenin of having been a communist. That's not something that Lenin would want to deny—he was proud of it. In the reverse fashion, radicals sometimes call their more conservative opponents fascists. Again, it would not have made sense to *accuse* Hitler or Mussolini of being fascists. From their point of view, being a fascist was something good, not bad. Thus, even where the descriptive meaning of a word remains more or less fixed, the positive and negative connotations can vary with context. Calling someone a liberal can count as praise, as an attack from the right, or as an attack from the left, depending on the speaker and the audience.

Persuasive Definitions

A particularly subtle form of slanting involves the use of a definition to gain an argumentative advantage. Charles L. Stevenson calls such definitions *persuasive definitions*.[3] Here is an example:

> Russian Communism is really state capitalism.

Who would say this? Certainly not a capitalist, who thinks capitalism is a good thing and communism is bad. Nor would old-line Russian Communists say this, because they think that capitalism is bad and have no desire to associate their system with it. On the other hand, this is just the kind of statement that a Chinese Communist might use against the Russians. To a Chinese Communist, capitalism is a bad thing, so calling Russian Communism "state capitalism" applies all the standard attacks against capitalism to the Russians. The pattern looks like this:

| Something to be criticized | Definitional link | Something considered bad |

Here is another example that uses the same pattern:

> Admissions quotas in favor of minorities are nothing more than reverse discrimination.

Since discrimination is usually thought to be something bad, a person will have a hard time making a case for minority quotas if he is trapped into accepting "reverse discrimination" as a defining description of a system of minority quotas. On the other side, defenders of admissions quotas tend to call them "affirmative action." This is just another persuasive definition in the other direction: it associates something to be

---

[3] Charles L. Stevenson, "Persuasive Definitions," *Mind* XLVII (July 1938).

praised with something good. Sometimes these definitions are crude and heavy handed, for example:

Abortion is fetal murder.

Since murder is, by definition, a wrongful act of killing, this definition assumes the very point at issue. At other times the argumentative move can be quite subtle, for example:

Abortion is the killing of an unborn person.

At first sight, this definition may seem neutral. It does not contain any obviously charged word like "murder." All the same, it is one of the central issues in the debate over abortion whether a human fetus is already a person. (*See* Chapter 12.) This is a matter to be established by argument, not by definition. In general we have a right to be suspicious of anyone who tries to gain an argumentative advantage through an appeal to definitions. Confronted with a definition in the midst of an argument, we should always ask whether the definition clarifies the issues or merely slants them.

▼ EXERCISE VIII

For each of the following sentences, construct two others—one that reverses the evaluative force and one that is more or less neutral. The symbol 0 stands for neutral, + for positive evaluative force, and − for negative evaluative force.

Example: − Professor Conrad is rude.
  + Professor Conrad is uncompromisingly honest in his criticisms.
  0 Professor Conrad often upsets people with his criticisms.

(1) − Martin is a lazy lout.
(2) + Brenda is vivacious.
(3) + John is a natural leader.
(4) + Selby is a methodical worker.
(5) − Marsha is a snob.
(6) + Clara is imaginative.
(7) − Bartlett is a buffoon.
(8) − Wayne is a goody-goody.
(9) − Sidney talks incessantly.
(10) − Dudley is a weenie.
(11) ? Floyd is a hot dog. (Decide whether this is + or −.)
(12) + Martha is liberated.
(13) + Ralph is sensitive.
(14) ? Betty is a fierce competitor. (Decide whether this is + or −.)
(15) − Psychology is a trendy department.
(16) − This is a Mickey Mouse exercise.

▼ EXERCISE IX

For each of the following persuasive definitions, indicate who would use it and why:

(1) Stinginess is charity at home.

(2) Communism is true democracy.

(3) Communism is fascism without property.

(4) "The better part of valor is discretion." (Said by Falstaff in Shakespeare's *Henry IV*, Part One, 5.4. 119–20.)

(5) The Sixties really began in 1965, after the civil rights movement was over.

ARGUMENTATIVE PERFORMATIVES

We have looked at many acts that are performed in arguments. Speakers can draw conclusions, give reasons, assure, guard, discount, and evaluate. Since these are speech acts, it should come as no surprise that many of these acts can also be done by explicit performatives which pass the thereby test:

> If I say, "I conclude that such and such," I thereby conclude that such and such.
> If I say, "I base my argument on the claim that such and such," I thereby base my argument on that claim.
> If I say, "I assure you that he will meet you," I thereby assure you that he will meet you.[4]
> If I say, "I limit my claim to only some students," then I thereby limit my claim to only some students.
> If I say, "I reply that such and such," I reply that such and such.
> If I say, "I evaluate his performance very highly," I thereby evaluate his performance very highly.

Once we see that these performatives can make moves in arguments, it is easy to think of many more:

> If I say, "I claim he is lying," I thereby claim he is lying.
> If I say, "I deny the charge," I thereby deny the charge.
> If I say, "I concede the point," I thereby concede the point.
> If I say, "I stipulate that such and such," I thereby stipulate that such and such.

When a performative is used to make a move in an argument, we will call it an *argumentative performative*. As with other performatives, it makes no sense to deny these sentences. If a lawyer finishes his speech to the jury by saying, "I conclude that the evidence merits acquittal," it would

---

[4] This is a tricky case, because you might not feel assured, but even then I could still say to him, "I assured him that you would meet him, but I don't think he believed me."

be ridiculous for someone to say, "No you don't!" We may disagree that the evidence merits acquittal, but we cannot disagree that the lawyer has drawn this conclusion.

Of course, we can also make these argumentative moves in other ways. Instead of saying, "I deny that," we can say, "That's not so," "No way," or "Oh, yeah?" Since there are so many ways to make each move, why do we have argumentative performatives at all? Part of the answer is that argumentative performatives make our argumentative moves explicit. If I want to make it perfectly clear *that* I am disagreeing and also exactly what *part* of my opponent's argument I am disagreeing with, I can do this by saying "I deny that. . . ." We usually reserve argumentative performatives for the *important* parts of opposing arguments.

Performatives also allow *subtle* moves to be made in the course of an argument. Sometimes an arguer will say, "I grant the point for the sake of argument" (thereby granting the point for the sake of argument). This is a powerful move if it can be carried off, for nothing is better than refuting an opponent on his own grounds. This device also contains an escape hatch, for if our efforts go badly, we can still challenge the statement previously granted just for the sake of argument. Somewhat differently, we can say, "I reserve comment" (thereby reserving comment). Here we neither reject nor accept a claim (even for the sake of argument). We let it pass until we see what is made of it. This is a useful tactical device. By reserving comment we can avoid being drawn into irrelevant discussions that will cloud the issue. At other times we do not know what we want to say in response to a particular point or we are not quite sure what the person is going to make of it. Reserving comment is a way of not sticking our necks out prematurely. Argumentative performatives are, then, powerful and subtle tools for making many different kinds of moves in an argument.

▼ DISCUSSION QUESTION

It is sometimes not clear whether certain terms are evaluative or have any negative connotations. One controversial area is the language used in talking about women. To take just one example, Robin Lakoff discusses the term "lady":[5]

> . . . if, in a particular sentence, both *woman* and *lady* might be used, the use of the latter tends to trivialize the subject matter under discussion, often subtly ridiculing the woman involved. Thus, for example, a mention in the San Francisco *Chronicle* of January 31, 1972, of Madalyn Murray O'Hair as the "lady atheist" reduces her position to that of a

---

[5] From *Language and Woman's Place* (New York: Harper and Row, 1975). Lakoff follows a common practice of putting a '*' before any expression that is linguistically anomalous.

scatterbrained eccentric, or at any rate, one who need not be taken seriously. Even *woman atheist* is scarcely defensible: first, because her sex is irrelevant to the philosophical position, and second, because her name makes it clear in any event. But *lady* makes matters still worse. Similarly a reference to a *woman sculptor* is only mildly annoying (since there is no term **male sculptor,* the discrepancy suggests that such activity is normal for a man but not for a woman), but still it could be used with reference to a serious artist. *Lady sculptor,* on the other hand, strikes me as a slur against the artist, deliberate or not, implying that the woman's art is frivolous, something she does to fend off the boredom of suburban housewifery, or at any rate, nothing of moment in the art world. Serious artists have shows, not *dilettantes.* So we hear of *one-woman shows,* but never *one-lady shows.*

Another realm of usage in which *lady* contrasts with *woman* is in titles of organizations. It seems that organizations of women who have a serious purpose (not merely that of spending time with one another) cannot use the word *lady* in their titles, but less serious ones may. Compare the *Ladies' Auxiliary* of a men's group, or the *Thursday Evening Ladies Browning and Garden Society,* with **Ladies' Lib* or **Ladies Strike for Peace. . . .*

Besides or possibly because of being explicitly devoid of sexual connotation, *lady* carries with it overtones recalling the age of chivalry: the exalted stature of the person so referred to, her existence above the common sphere. This makes the term seem polite at first, but we must also remember that these implications are perilous: they suggest that a "lady" is helpless, and cannot do things for herself. In this respect the use of a word like *lady* is parallel to the act of opening doors for women—or ladies. At first blush it is flattering: the object of the flattery feels honored, cherished and so forth; but by the same token, she is also considered helpless and not in control of her own destiny. Women who protest that they *like* receiving these little courtesies, and object to being liberated from them, should reflect a bit on their deeper meaning and see how much they like *that.*

Do you agree with Lakoff's claims about the connotations of the term 'lady'? Why or why not? In your opinion, which other terms used to refer to women reflect a sexist bias in our society? Lakoff also discusses "mistress," "girl," "widow," "spinster," and, of course, "Mrs." (as opposed to "Ms."). You should also consider terms like "broad" and "chick."

Finally, you might want to collect a series of articles concerning women and see whether they reveal a sexist bias. One way to bring this matter into sharper focus is to compare the language used about a woman with the language used about a man in a similar context—for example, in a description of the individual's appointment to some high position. Pay attention not only to what is mentioned but also to what is left out, such as when a woman's spouse is mentioned but a man's spouse is not.

3

The Art of
Close Analysis

This chapter will be largely dedicated to a single purpose: the close and careful analysis of a speech drawn from the *Congressional Record*, using the argumentative devices introduced in Chapter 2. The point of this study is to show in detail how these methods of analysis can be applied to an actual argument of some richness and complexity.

AN EXTENDED EXAMPLE

It is now time to apply all of these notions to a genuine argument. Our example will be a debate that occurred in the House of Representatives on the question of whether there should be an increase in the allowance given to members of the House for clerical help—the so-called "clerk hire allowance." The argument against the increase presented by Representative Kyl (Republican, Iowa) will be examined in detail. We will put it under an analytic microscope.

The choice of this example may seem odd, for the question of clerk hire allowance is not one of the burning issues of our time. This, in fact, is one reason for choosing it. It will be useful to begin with an example where feelings do not run high to learn the habit of objective analysis. Later on we shall examine arguments where almost everyone has strong feelings and try to maintain an objective standpoint even there. The example is a good one for two other reasons: (1) it contains most of the argumentative devices we have listed, and (2) relatively speaking, it is quite a strong argument. This last remark may seem ironic after we seemingly tear the argument quite to shreds, but in comparison to other arguments we shall examine, it stands up quite well.

We can begin by reading through the section of the *Congressional Record*[1] without comment:

▼ *Clerk Hire Allowance, House of Representatives*

Mr. FRIEDEL. Mr. Speaker, by direction of the Committee on House Administration, I call up the resolution (H. Res. 219) to increase the basic clerk hire allowance of each Member of the House, and for other purposes, and ask for its immediate consideration.

The Clerk read the resolution as follows:

Resolved, That effective April 1, 1961, there shall be paid out of the contingent fund of the House, until otherwise provided by law, such sums as may be necessary to increase the basic clerk hire allowance of each Member and the Resident Commissioner from Puerto Rico by an additional $3,000 per annum, and each such Member and Resident Commissioner shall be entitled to one clerk in addition to those to which he is otherwise entitled by law.

Mr. FRIEDEL. Mr. Speaker, this resolution allows an additional $3,000 per annum for clerk hire and an additional clerk for each Member of the House and the Resident Commissioner from Puerto Rico. Our subcom-

---

[1] *Congressional Record*, Vol. 107, Part 3 (March 15, 1961), pp. 4059–60.

mittee heard the testimony, and we were convinced of the need for this provision to be made. A few Members are paying out of their own pockets for additional clerk hire. This $3,000 is the minimum amount we felt was necessary to help Members pay the expenses of running their offices. Of course, we know that the mail is not as heavy in some of the districts as it is in others, and, of course, if the Member does not use the money, it remains in the contingent fund.

Mr. KYL. Mr. Speaker, will the gentleman yield?

Mr. FRIEDEL. I yield to the gentleman from Iowa [Mr. KYL] for a statement.

Mr. KYL. Mr. Speaker, I oppose this measure. I oppose it first because it is expensive. I further oppose it because it is untimely.

I do not intend to belabor this first contention. We have been presented a budget of about $82 billion. We have had recommended to us a whole series of additional programs or extensions of programs for priming the pump, for depressed areas, for the needy, for unemployed, for river pollution projects, and recreation projects, aid to education, and many more. All are listed as "must" activities. These extensions are not within the budget. Furthermore, if business conditions are as deplorable as the newspapers indicate, the Government's income will not be as high as anticipated. It is not enough to say we are spending so much now, a little more will not hurt. What we spend, we will either have to recover in taxes, or add to the staggering national debt.

The amount of increase does not appear large. I trust, however, there is no one among us who would suggest that the addition of a clerk would not entail allowances for another desk, another typewriter, more materials, and it is not beyond the realm of possibility that the next step would then be a request for additional office space, and ultimately new buildings. Some will say, "All the Members will not use their maximum, so the cost will not be great." And this is true. If the exceptions are sufficient in number to constitute a valid argument, then there is no broad general need for this measure. Furthermore, some Members will use these additional funds to raise salaries. Competition will force all salaries upward in all offices and then on committee staffs, and so on. We may even find ourselves in a position of paying more money for fewer clerks and in a tighter bind on per person workload.

This measure proposes to increase the allowance from $17,500 base clerical allowance to $20,500 base salary allowance. No member of this House can tell us what this means in gross salary. That computation is almost impossible. Such a completely absurd system has developed through the years on salary computations for clerical hire that we have under discussion a mathematical monstrosity. We are usually told that the gross allowed is approximately $35,000. This is inaccurate. In one office the total might be less than $35,000 and in another, in complete compliance with the law and without any conscious padding, the amount may be in excess of $42,000. This is possible because of a weird set of formulae which determine that three clerks at $5,000 cost less than five clerks at $3,000. Five times three might total the same as three times five everywhere else in the world—but not in figuring clerk hire in the House.

This is an application of an absurdity. It is a violation of bookkeeping principles, accounting principles, business principles and a violation of commonsense. Listen to the formula:

First, 20 percent increase of first $1,200; 10 percent additional from $1,200 to $4,600; 5 percent further additional from $4,600 to $7,000.

Second, after applying the increases provided in paragraph 1, add an additional 14 percent or a flat $250 whichever is the greater, but this increase must not exceed 25 percent.

Third, after applying the increases provided in both paragraphs 1 and 2, add an additional increase of 10 percent in lieu of overtime.

Fourth, after applying the increases provided in paragraphs 1, 2, and 3, add an additional increase of $330.

Fifth, after applying the increases provided in paragraphs 1, 2, 3, and 4, add an additional increase of 5 percent.

Sixth, after applying the increases provided in paragraphs 1, 2, 3, 4, and 5, add an additional increase of 10 percent but not more than $800 nor less than $300 a year.

Seventh, after applying the increases provided in paragraphs 1, 2, 3, 4, 5, and 6, add an additional increase of 7½ percent.

Eighth, after applying the increases provided in paragraphs 1, 2, 3, 4, 5, 6, and 7, add an additional increase of 10 percent.

Ninth, after applying the increases provided in paragraphs 1, 2, 3, 4, 5, 6, 7, and 8, add an additional increase of 7½ percent.

The Disbursing Office has a set of tables to figure house salaries for office staffs and for about 900 other employees. It contains 45 sheets with 40 entries per sheet. In the Senate, at least, they have simplified the process some by figuring their base in multiples of 60, thus eliminating 11 categories. Committee staffers, incidentally, have an $8,880 base in comparison to the House $7,000 base limitation.

Now, Mr. Speaker, I have planned to introduce an amendment or a substitute which would grant additional clerk hire where there is a demonstrable need based on heavier than average population or "election at large" and possible other factors. But after becoming involved in this mathematical maze, I realize the folly of proceeding one step until we have corrected this situation. We can offer all kinds of excuses for avoiding a solution. We cannot offer reasonable arguments that it should not be done or that it cannot be done.

Someone has suggested that the Members of this great body prefer to keep the present program because someone back in the home district might object to the gross figures. I know this is not so. When a Representative is busy on minimum wage, or aid to education, or civil rights, such matters of housekeeping seem too picayune to merit attention. The Member simply checks the table and hires what he can hire under the provisions and then forgets the whole business. But I know the Members also want the people back home to realize that what we do here is open and frank and accurate, and that we set an example in businesslike procedures. The more we can demonstrate responsibility the greater will be the faith in Congress.

May I summarize. It is obvious that some Members need more clerical help because of large population and large land area. I have been working for some time with the best help we can get, on a measure which would take these items into consideration. Those Members who are really in need of assistance should realize that this temporary, hastily conceived proposition we debate today will probably obviate their getting a satisfactory total solution.

First, we should await redistricting of the Nation.

Second, we should consider appropriate allowance for oversize districts considering both population and total geographic area.

Finally, I hope we can develop a sound and sensible formula for computing salaries of office clerks and other statutory employees in the same category.

Before going any further, it will be useful to record your general reactions to this speech. Perhaps you think that on the whole Kyl gives a well-reasoned argument in behalf of his position. Alternatively, you might think that he is making a big fuss over nothing, trying to confuse people with numbers, and just generally being obnoxious. When you are finished examining this argument in detail, you can look back and ask yourself why you formed this original impression and how, if at all, you have changed your mind.

The first step in the close analysis of an argument is to go through the text, labeling the various argumentative devices we have examined. Here some abbreviations will be useful:

warranting connective	W
assuring term	A
guarding term	G
discounting term	D
argumentative performative	AP
evaluative term	E (+ *or* −)
rhetorical device	R

The last label is a catch-all for the various rhetorical devices discussed in Chapter 1, such as rhetorical questions, irony, metaphor, and so on. There is no label for slanting, because the decision whether or not the use of evaluative terms amounts to slanting depends on the justification the writer provides for employing them. Often this decision can only be made after the entire argument is examined.

Even this simple process of labeling brings out features of an argument that could pass by unnoticed. It also directs us to ask sharp critical questions. To see this, we can look at each part of the argument in detail.

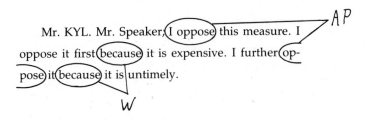

Mr. KYL. Mr. Speaker, I oppose this measure. I oppose it first because it is expensive. I further oppose it because it is untimely.

This is a model of clarity. By the use of a performative utterance in the opening sentence, Kyl makes it clear that he opposes the measure. Then by twice using the warranting connective "because," he gives his two main reasons for opposing it: *it is expensive* and *it is untimely*. We must now see if he makes good each of these claims. This paragraph begins the argument for the claim that the measure is expensive:

> I do not intend to belabor this first contention. — A
>
> We have been presented a budget of about $82 bil-
> lion. We have had recommended to us a whole se-
> ries of additional programs or extensions of programs
> for priming the pump, for depressed areas, for the
> needy, for unemployed, for river pollution projects,
> and recreation projects, aid to education, and many — R
> more. All are listed as *must* activities. These ex-
> tensions are not within the budget. Furthermore, if — W
> business conditions are as deplorable as the news- — G
> papers indicate, the Government's income will not be
> as high as anticipated. It is not enough to say we are — R
> spending so much now, a little more will not hurt.
> What we spend, we will either have to recover in
> taxes, or add to the staggering national debt.

(a) "I do not intend to belabor this first contention. . . ." This is an example of *assuring*. The conversational implication is that the point is so obvious that little has to be said in its support. Yet there is something strange going on here. Having said that he will *not* belabor the claim that the bill is expensive, Kyl actually goes on to say quite a bit on the subject. It is a good idea to look closely when someone says that he or she is not going to do something, for often just the opposite is happening. For example, saying "I am not suggesting that Smith is dishonest" is one way of suggesting that Smith *is* dishonest. If no such suggestion is being made, why raise the issue at all?

(b) Kyl now proceeds in a rather flat way, stating that the proposed budget comes to $82 billion and that it contains many new programs and extensions of former programs. Since these are matters of public record and nobody is likely to deny them, there is no need for guarding or assuring. Kyl also claims, without qualification, that these extensions are not within the budget. This recital of facts does, however, carry an important conversational implication: Since the budget is already out of balance, any further extensions should be viewed with suspicion.

(c) Putting the word "must" in quotation marks, or saying it in a sarcastic tone of voice, is a common device for denying something. The plain suggestion is that some of these measures are *not* must activities at all. We see the same device in a more dramatic fashion when Marc Antony ironically repeats, "Brutus is an honorable man." Anyway, Kyl here suggests that some of the items already in the budget are not necessary. He does this, of course, without defending this suggestion.

(d) "If business conditions are as deplorable as the newspapers indicate, the Government's income will not be as high as anticipated." The sentence as a whole is an *indicative conditional* (with the word "then" dropped out). As such, the sentence does not produce an argument, but instead, provides a pattern for an argument. For the moment, let's drop out the phrase "as the newspapers indicate"; we then get:

> If business conditions are deplorable, then the Government's income
> will not be as high as anticipated.

This seems like a perfectly reasonable conditional claim, and if Kyl could establish that business conditions *are* deplorable, he would have moved his argument along in an important way. Yet, he doesn't say that business conditions are deplorable; instead, he slides in the *guarding* expression "as the newspapers *indicate*." Thus the premises of his argument come to this:

(1) If business conditions are deplorable, then the Government's income will not be as high as anticipated.

(2) Newspapers indicate that business conditions are deplorable.

Given the highly guarded second premise, no strong conclusion follows.[2]

---

[2] This passage also contains a vague *appeal to authority*, since no specific newspaper is cited. We will discuss appeals to authority in Chapter 5.

(e) "It is not enough to say we are spending so much now, a little more will not hurt." The opening phrase is, of course, used to deny what follows it. Kyl is plainly rejecting the argument that we are spending so much now, a little more will not hurt. Yet his argument has a peculiar twist, for who would come right out and make such an argument? If you stop to think for a minute, it should be clear that nobody would want to put it that way. An opponent, for example, would use quite different phrasing. He might say something like this: "Considering the large benefits that will flow from this measure, it is more than worth the small costs." What Kyl has done is to attribute a bad argument to his opponents and then reject it in an indignant tone. This is a common device, and when it is used, it is often useful to ask whether anyone would actually argue or speak in the way suggested. When the answer to this question is no, as it often is, we have what was called "the trick of discounting straw men" in Chapter 2. In such cases, it is useful to ask what the speaker's opponent would have said instead. This leads to a further question: Has the arguer even addressed himself to the *real* arguments of his opponents?

So far, Kyl has not addressed himself to the first main point of his argument, that the measure is *expensive*. This is not a criticism, because he is really making the preliminary point that the matter of expense is significant. Here he has stated some incontestable facts—for example, that the budget is already out of balance. Beyond this he has indicated, with varying degrees of strength, that the financial situation is grave. It is against this background that the detailed argument concerning the cost of the measure is actually presented in the next paragraph.

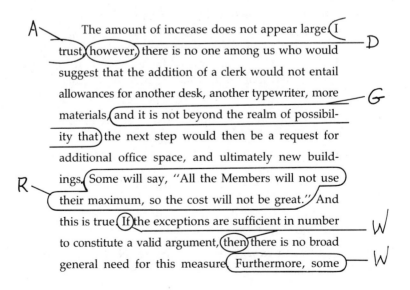

Members will use these additional funds to raise salaries. Competition will force all salaries upward in all offices and then on committee staffs, and so on.

G — We (may even) find ourselves in a position of paying more money for fewer clerks and in a tighter bind on per person workload.

(a) "The amount of increase does not appear large." Words like "appear" and "seem" are sometimes used for guarding, but we must be careful not to apply labels in an unthinking way. The above sentence is the beginning of a *discounting* argument. As soon as you hear this sentence, you can feel that a word like "but" or "however" is about to appear. Sure enough, it does.

(b) "I trust, however, there is no one among us who would suggest that the addition of a clerk would not entail allowances for another desk, another typewriter, more materials. . . ." This is the beginning of Kyl's argument that is intended to rebut the argument that the increase in expenses will not be large. Appearances to the contrary, he is saying, the increase will be large. He then ticks off some additional expenses that are entailed by hiring new clerks. Notice that the whole sentence is covered by the assuring phrase: "I trust . . . that there is no one among us who would suggest. . . ." This implies that anyone who would make such a suggestion is merely stupid. But the trouble with Kyl's argument so far is this: He has pointed out genuine additional expenses, but they are not, after all, very large. It is important for him to get some genuinely large sums of money into his argument. This is the point of his next remark:

(c) "And it is not beyond the realm of possibility, that the next step would then be a request for additional office space, and ultimately new buildings." Here, at last, we have some genuinely large sums of money in the picture, but the difficulty is that the entire claim is totally guarded by the phrase, "it is not beyond the realm of possibility." There are very few things that *are* beyond the realm of possibility. Kyl's problem, then, is this: There are certain additional expenses that he can point to without qualification, but these tend to be small. On the other hand, when he points out genuinely large expenses, he can only do so in a guarded way. So we are still waiting for a proof that the expense will be large. (Parenthetically, it should be pointed out that Kyl's prediction of new buildings actually came true.)

(d) "Some will say, 'All the Members will not use their maximum, so the cost will not be great.' And this is true. If the exceptions are sufficient in number to constitute a valid argument, then there is no broad general need for this measure." This looks like a "tricky" argument, and for this reason alone it demands close attention. The phrase "some will say" is a standard way of beginning a discounting argument. This *is*, in fact, a discounting argument, but its form is rather subtle. Kyl cites what some will say, and then adds, somewhat surprisingly: "And this is true." To understand what is going on here, we must have a good feel for conversational implication. Kyl imagines someone reasoning in the following way:

> All the Members will not use their maximum.
> So the cost will not be great.
> Therefore, since the measure will not be expensive, let's adopt it.

Given the same starting point, Kyl tries to derive just the *opposite* conclusion along the following lines:

> All the Members will not use their maximum.
> If very few use their maximum, then the cost will not be great.
> But if very few use their maximum, then there is no broad general need for this measure.
> Therefore, whether it is expensive or not, we should reject this measure.

In order to get clear about this argument, we can put it into schematic form:

Kyl's argument
If (1) expensive, then   → Reject
If (2) inexpensive, then, because that demonstrates no general
need,   → Reject
The opposite argument
If (1) inexpensive, then   → Accept
If (2) expensive, then, because that demonstrates a general
need,   → Accept

When the arguments are spread out in this fashion, it should be clear that they have equal strength. Both are no good. The question that must be settled is this: Does a genuine need exist that can be met in an economically sound manner? If there is no need for the measure, then it should be rejected however inexpensive. Again, if there is a need then some expense is worth paying. The real problem is to balance the need against expense and then to decide on this basis whether the measure as a whole is worth adopting. Kyl's argument is a *sophistry* because it has no tendency to answer the real question at hand. By a sophistry we shall mean a clever but fallacious argument intended to establish a point through trickery. Incidentally, it is one of the marks of a sophistical argument that, though it may baffle, it almost never convinces. I think that very few readers will have found this argument persuasive even if they could not say exactly what is wrong with it.

The appearance of a sophistical argument (or even a complex and tangled argument) is a sign that the argument is weak. Remember, where a case is strong, people usually argue in a straightforward way.

(e) "Furthermore, some Members will use these additional funds to raise salaries. Competition will force all salaries upward in all offices and then on committee staffs, and so on." The word "furthermore" signals that further *reasons* are forthcoming. Here Kyl returns to the argument that the measure is more expensive than it might at first sight appear. Notice that he speaks here in an unqualified way: no guarding appears. Yet the critic is bound to ask whether Kyl has any right to make these projections. Beyond this, Kyl here projects a *parade of horrors*. He pictures this measure leading by gradual steps to quite disastrous consequences. Here the little phrase "and so on" carries a great burden in the argument. Once more, we must simply ask ourselves whether these projections seem reasonable.

(f) "We may even find ourselves in a position of paying more money for fewer clerks and in a tighter bind on per person workload." Once more, the use of a strong guarding expression takes back most of the force of the argument. Notice that if Kyl could have said straight out that the measure *will* put us in a position of paying more money for fewer clerks and in a tighter bind on per person workload, that would have counted as a very strong objection. You can hardly do better in criticizing a position than showing that it will have just the opposite result from what is intended. In fact, however, Kyl has not established this; he has only said that this is something that we "may even find."

Before we turn to the second half of Kyl's argument, which we shall see in a moment is much stronger, we should point out that our analysis has not been entirely fair. Speaking before the House of Representatives, Kyl is in an *adversary* situation. He is not trying to prove things for all time; rather, he is responding to a position held by others. Part of what he is doing is *raising objections,* and a sensitive evaluation of the argument demands a detailed understanding of the nuances of the debate. But even granting this, it should be remembered that objections themselves must be made for good reasons. The problem so far in Kyl's argument is that the major reasons behind his objections have constantly been guarded in a very strong way.

Turning now to the second part of Kyl's argument—that the measure is untimely—we see that he moves along in a clear and direct way with little guarding.

> This measure proposes to increase the allow-
> ance from $17,500 base clerical allowance to $20,500
> base salary allowance. No member of this House can

tell us what this means in gross salary. That com- — *E –*
putation is (almost) impossible. Such (a completely absurd system) has developed through the years on
salary computations for clerical hire that we have — *E –*
under discussion a (mathematical monstrosity.) We are
usually told that the gross allowed is approximately
$35,000. This is inaccurate. In one office the total
might be less than $35,000 and in another, in com-
plete compliance with the law and without any conscious padding, the amount may be in excess of — *E –*
$42,000. This is possible because of a (weird set of
formulae) which determines that three clerks at $5,000
cost less than five clerks at $3,000. (Five times three
might total the same as three times five everywhere — *R*
else in the world—but not in figuring clerk hire in
the House.)

    This is an application of (an absurdity.) It is a vi- *E –*
olation of bookkeeping principles, accounting principles, business principles and a (violation of
commonsense.) Listen to the formula. . . .

The main point of the argument is clear enough: Kyl is saying that the
present system of clerk salary allowance is utterly confusing, and this
matter should be straightened out before *any* other measures in this
area are adopted. There is, of course, a great deal of negative evaluation in this passage. Notice the words and phrases that Kyl uses:

> completely absurd system
> weird set of formulae
> a violation of common sense
> mathematical monstrosity
> an absurdity

There is also a dash of irony in the remark that five times three might
total the same as three times five everywhere else in the world, but not
in figuring clerk hire in the House. Remember, there is nothing wrong
with using negative evaluative and expressive terms if they are de-
served. We would only describe the use of such terms as *slanting* if

they were used without adequate justification. Looking at the nine-step formula on page 56, you can decide for yourself whether Kyl is on strong grounds in using this negative language.

Now, Mr. Speaker, I have planned to introduce an amendment or a substitute which would grant additional clerk hire where there is a demonstrable need based on heavier than average population or "election at large" and possible other factors.

(a) This passage rejects any suggestion that Kyl is unaware that a genuine problem does exist in some districts. It also indicates that he is willing to do something about it.

(b) The phrase "and possible other factors" is not very important, but it seems to be included to anticipate other reasons for clerk hire that should at least be considered.

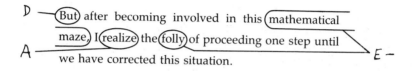

D — But after becoming involved in this (mathematical maze,) I (realize) the (folly) of proceeding one step until
A ———— we have corrected this situation. > E –

(a) Here Kyl clearly states his reason for saying that the measure is untimely. Notice that the reason offered has been well documented and is not hedged in by qualifications.

(b) The phrases "mathematical maze" and "folly" are again negatively evaluative.

We can offer all kinds of (excuses) for avoiding a   E –
solution. (We cannot offer reasonable arguments that) —— A
it should not be done or that it cannot be done.

(a) Notice that the first sentence ridicules the opponents' arguments by calling them *excuses*, a term with negative connotations. The second sentence gives assurances that such a solution can be found.

Someone has suggested that the Members of this great body prefer to keep the present program because someone back in the home district might object to the gross figures. (I know) this is not so. When —A

D — whole business. (But)(I know) the Members also want

the people back home to realize that what we do

E+ — here is (open and frank and accurate,) and that we set

a Representative is busy on minimum wage, or aid
to education, or civil rights, such matters of housekeeping seem too picayune to merit attention. The
Member simply checks the table and hires what he
can hire under the provisions and then forgets the
whole business. (But)(I know) the Members also want —A
the people back home to realize that what we do
here is (open and frank and accurate,) and that we set
an example in businesslike procedures. The more we
can demonstrate responsibility the greater will be the
faith in Congress.

(a) Once more the seas of rhetoric run high. Someone (though not
Kyl himself) has suggested that the Members of the House wish to
conceal information. He disavows the very thought that he would make
such a suggestion by the sentence "I know this is not so." All the
same, he has gotten this suggestion into the argument.

(b) Kyl then suggests another reason why the Members of the House
will not be concerned with this measure: it is too *picayune*. The last two
sentences rebut the suggestion that it is too small to merit close attention. Even on small matters, the more the House is "open and frank
and accurate," the more it will "set an example in businesslike procedures" and thus "demonstrate responsibility" that will increase "the
faith in Congress." This is actually an important part of Kyl's argument, for presumably his main problem is to get the other Members of
the House to take the matter seriously.

May I summarize. (It is obvious that) some Mem- — A

bers need more clerical help (because) of large popu- — W

lation and large land area. /I have been working for) — A

some time with the best help we can get, /on a mea-

sure which would take these items into considera-

tion. Those Members who are really in need of

A — assistance should (realize) that this (temporary, hastily — E−

conceived) proposition we debate today will (probably) — G

obviate their getting a satisfactory total solution.

(a) This is a concise summary. Kyl once more assures the House that he is aware that a genuine problem exists. He also indicates that he is working on it.

(b) The phrase "temporary, hastily conceived proposition we debate today" refers back to his arguments concerning untimeliness.

(c) The claim that "it will probably obviate their getting a satisfactory total solution" refers back to the economic argument. Notice, however, that, as before, the economic claim is guarded by the word "probably."

First, we should await redistricting of the Nation.

Second, we should consider appropriate allowance for oversize districts considering both population and total geographic area.

Finally, I hope we can develop a sound and sensible formula for computing salaries of office clerks and other statutory employees in the same category.

E+

This is straightforward except that a new factor is introduced: we should await redistricting of the nation. This was not mentioned earlier in the argument, and so seems a bit out of place in a summary. Perhaps the point is so obvious that it did not need any argument to support it. On the other hand, it is often useful to keep track of things that are smuggled into the argument at the very end. If redistricting was about to occur in the *near* future, this would give a strong reason for delaying action on the measure. Because the point is potentially so strong, we might wonder why Kyl has made so little of it. Here, perhaps, we are getting too subtle.

▼ EXERCISE I

The following is part of a speech by Ronald Reagan entitled "Peace and National Security" which was delivered on March 23, 1983. In it he argues for a program which he called the Strategic Defense Initiative (SDI) and which his opponents called "Star Wars." Various phrases are numbered for your comment after you have read the whole passage.

REAGAN ON SDI OR STAR WARS

The subject I want to discuss with you, peace and national security, is both *timely and important*. [1] Timely, *because* [2] I've reached a decision which offers a new *hope* [3] for our children in the 21st century—a decision I will tell you about in a few minutes—*and* [4] important because there is a very big decision that you must make for yourselves. . . .[5]

One of [6] the most important *contributions* [7] we can make is, *of course,* [8] to lower the level of all arms, and particularly nuclear arms. We're engaged in several negotiations with the Soviet Union to bring about a mutual reduction of weapons. I will report to you a week from tomorrow my thoughts on that score. *But* [9] *let me just say,* [10] I'm *totally committed* [11] to this course. [12]

If the Soviet Union will join us in our effort to achieve major arms reduction, [13] we will have succeeded in *stabilizing the nuclear balance.* [14] *Nevertheless,* [15] it will still be necessary to rely on the *specter* [16] of retaliation, on *mutual threat.* [17] And that's a *sad* [18] commentary on the human condition. *Wouldn't it be better to save lives than to avenge them?* [19] Are we not *capable* [20] of demonstrating our peaceful intentions by applying all our abilities and our ingenuity to achieving a *truly lasting stability* [21]? I *think* [22] we are. Indeed, we *must.* [23]

After careful consultation with my advisers, including the Joint Chiefs of Staff, [24] I *believe* [25] there is a way. *Let me share* [26] with you a *vision of the future which offers hope.* [27] It is that we embark on a program to counter the awesome Soviet missile threat with measures that are *defensive.* [28] Let us turn to the very strengths in technology that spawned our great industrial base and that have given us *the quality of life that we enjoy today.* [29]

What *if* [30] free people could live *secure* [31] in the knowledge that their security did not rest upon the *threat of instant U.S. retaliation* [32] to deter a Soviet attack, that we could intercept and destroy strategic ballistic missiles before they reached our own soil and that of our allies![33]

I know [34] this is a formidable, technical task, one that *may* [35] not be accomplished before the end of this century. *Yet,* [36] current technology has attained a level of sophistication where it's *reasonable for us to begin* [37] this effort. It will take years, *probably* [38] decades of effort on many fronts. There will be *failures and setbacks,* [39] just as there will be successes and breakthroughs. And as we proceed, we must remain constant in preserving the nuclear deterrent and maintaining a solid capability for flexible response. [40] *But* [41] *isn't it worth every investment necessary to free the world from the threat of nuclear war?* [42] *We know* [43] it is.

For each of the numbered expressions, either answer the question or label the argumentative move, if any, using these abbreviations:

> W = a warranting connective or phrase
> A = an assuring term
> G = a guarding term
> D = a discounting term
> E− = a negative evaluative term
> E+ = a positive evaluative term
> R = a rhetorical device
> AP = an argumentative performative
> N = none of the above

[1]-[4]: Write labels.
[5]: Why does Reagan start out in this way?
[6]-[11]: Write labels.
[12]: What is the overall point of this second paragraph?
[13]: What does this if-clause conversationally imply?
[14]-[22]: Write labels.
[23]: What is Reagan saying that we must do? Who, if anyone, would deny that we must do this?
[24]-[28]: Write labels.
[29]: Why does Reagan praise technology? How does this help his argument?
[30]-[32]: Write labels.
[33]: What is supposed to be the answer to this question? Why does Reagan ask it?
[34]-[38]: Write labels.
[39]: Why does Reagan admit that there will be "failures and setbacks"? Who is his main audience here?
[40]: Why does Reagan mention these other weapons systems? Who is his main audience here?
[41]-[43]: Write labels.

▼ EXERCISE II

Provide a close analysis of each of the following passages by circling and labelling each of the key argumentative terms. Then state what you take to be the central conclusions and premises. What criticisms, if any, do you have of each argument?

Passage 1:

23 This article appeared in the *New York Times* on September 22, 1989.

▼ Barney Frank's Right to Judgment

If Representative Barney Frank knew a male prostitute was selling sex from Mr. Frank's Washington apartment, he cannot remain in the House. If he was unaware of what went on while he was back in Massachusetts, he is guilty only of admitted abysmal judgment and misplaced trust in a man he had hired for household errands.

Who should decide? Mr. Frank has put the issue to the House Ethics Committee, and he rightly rejects the counsel of friends and admirers to resign now. Some Democrats want him to leave to avoid another ethics cloud over their party. Republicans call for his resignation, but probably wouldn't mind his staying around as a punching bag. But to press him to resign now would deprive the House of a chance to debate the issue of personal behavior and public ethics. Worse, it would deny him a just conclusion.

Only last spring the House used the resignation of Speaker Jim Wright as an excuse to avoid deciding when a favor from a legislator's friend becomes an impermissible gift. If Mr. Frank's account is correct, his case raises the issue of what kind of personal behavior disqualifies public officials—drinking, philandering, consorting with prostitutes, or what? These issues need evaluation. The public can't drive people out of office without some agreed standards.

Mr. Frank was indisputably stupid, whether or not he proves more blameworthy. But his defense is plausible on currently available evidence. The prostitute had the capacity to deceive the Congressman; he drove Mr. Frank to and from the airport and knew his schedule. It's pertinent that the Congressman, who later made his homosexuality known to the public, fired the prostitute even though doing so then risked disclosure.

The evidence could show Mr. Frank was highly culpable, or merely misguided, or that he took unacceptable risks to his own reputation and that of the House. But those judgments ought to be made on evidence, not the opinion and speculation that have preoccupied Washington for weeks. Mr. Frank deserves to be judged, after his trial.

Passage 2:

This advertisement (top, p. 71) first appeared in the late 1960s or early 1970s in the *New York Times* and was written by Tiffany's chairman of that period, Walter Hoving.

Passage 3:

This letter to the editor (bottom, p. 71) appeared in the *New York Times,* June 16, 1985. It begins with a reference to an earlier article on fraternities by Fred M. Hechinger, but knowledge of that article is not necessary for understanding Rev. Stemper's argument.

Fraternities, Where Men May Come to Terms with Other Men

To the Editor:

"The Fraternities Show Signs of New Strength," Fred M. Hechinger's analysis of the nature of college fraternities (Science Times, May 21) and the reason for their present growth is superficial. Apart from its condescending tone, it misses the point.

College fraternities are growing today because college curriculums are increasingly technical, preprofessional, competitive, and in most instances remote from the principal challenge of finding meaning in life. Their growth is not unrelated to the rapid rise in teen-age suicide: a pervasive sense that no one—certainly no institution—really cares for the nation's youth.

Local college fraternity chapters provide the only segment of the undergraduate's life he controls. Thus, it is one of the few arenas open to creative expression in self-government, same-sex relationships, and forensic abilities apart from some evaluatory scrutiny by thesis-grading, recommendation-writing members of college faculties and administrations.

Within a fraternity, a student can live without looking over his shoulder—if, in fact, this is still possible in our society. If there is occasional violence associated with initiations and reprehensible treatment of women, the cause is much more deeply rooted in the materialism of our culture, which reduces "life" to "career."

In borrowing from older fraternal and classical traditions, modern college fraternities have provided in the 1980's symbolic structures within which men might come to terms with other men. Far from "a return to a macho kind of adolescence tinged with elitist exclusivity," nurturing, compassion and empathy are commonplace in the college fraternity—sometimes for the first and last time in a man's life with other male friends.

Such vulnerabilities come hard for most young men. A collegiate brotherhood provides the same shelter, in social terms, as a room of one's own provides or a first automobile in adolescence. It is a symbol of self.

A disturbing aspect of the article is the equation of college fraternities with antifeminism. Women have taught men in recent years the meaning of solidarity. A genuine tragedy of our times is that men's liberation movements were a casualty of the post-1960s era.

A man—and a male institution—may affirm a feminist critique of society and still seek to enrich male bonding. One could argue that an objective of feminism is that men should get on with other men in more constructive ways. Fraternities and fraternal orders are the only institutions in our society that have this objective as a primary and lasting goal. For this reason alone, cynical superficiality should give way to honest respect.

(Rev.) WILLIAM H. STEMPER JR.
New York, May 24, 1985

The writer is bishop's vicar for corporate affairs of the Episcopal Diocese of New York.

▼ EXERCISE III

Practice close analysis some more by doing close analyses of

(1) an editorial from your local paper or
(2) one of the articles in part 2 of this book or
(3) the last paper that you wrote in another course.

▼ DISCUSSION QUESTIONS

1. If, as some social critics have maintained, the pervasive nature of television has created generation upon generation of intellectually passive automatons, why study close analysis?

2. Earlier we identified sophistry as a clever but fallacious argument intended to establish a point through trickery. What is the best sophistical argument you have ever encountered? Why is it sophistical?

3. Television commercials are often arguments in miniature. Recount several recent commercials and identify the argumentative devices at work.

4

Deep Analysis

Arguments in everyday life rarely occur in isolation. They usually come in the middle of much that is not essential to the argument itself. Everyday arguments are also rarely complete. Essential premises are often omitted. Such omissions are often tolerable because we are able to convey a great deal of information indirectly by conversational implication. However, to give a critical evaluation of an argument, it is necessary to isolate the argument from extraneous surroundings, to make explicit unstated parts of the argument, and to arrange them in a systematic order. This puts us in a better position to decide on the soundness or unsoundness of the argument in question. This chapter will develop methods for reconstructing arguments so that they may be understood and evaluated in a fair and systematic fashion. These methods will then be illustrated by applying them to a disagreement which depends on fundamental principles.

GETTING DOWN TO BASICS

To understand an argument, it is useful to put it into standard form. As we saw in Chapter 2, this is done by writing down the premises, then a line, then the symbol "∴", and then the conclusion. That is all we write down. But there is often a lot more in the passage that includes the argument. It is not uncommon for the stated argument to stretch over several pages, whereas the basic argument has only a few premises and a single conclusion.

One reason is that people often go off on *tangents*. They start to argue for one claim, but that reminds them of something else, so they talk about that for a while, then they finally return to their original topic. Such tangents can be completely irrelevant or just unnecessary, but they often make it very hard to follow the argument. Some people even go off on tangents on purpose to confuse their opponents and hide gaping holes in their arguments. This might be called the trick of excess verbiage. It violates the rules of Relevance and of Manner. To focus on the argument itself, we need to look carefully at each sentence to determine whether that particular sentence affects the validity of the argument or the truth of its premises.[1] If we decide that a sentence is not necessary for the argument, we should not add it when we list the premises and conclusion in standard form. Of course, we have to be careful not to omit anything that would improve the argument, but including irrelevant material simply makes the task of analyzing the argument more difficult.

Another source of extra material is *repetition*. People often repeat their main points to remind their audience of what was said earlier. Repetition is more subtle when it is used to explain something. A point can often be clarified by restating it in a new way. Repetition can also function as a kind of assurance, as an expression of confidence, or as an indication of how important a point is. Some writers seem to think that if they say something often enough, people will come to believe it. Whether or not this trick works, when two sentences say equivalent things, there is no need to list both when the argument is put into standard form. Listing the same premise twice will not make the argument any better from a logical point of view.

Sometimes *guarding* terms can also be dropped. If I say, "I think Miranda is at home, so we can meet her there," this argument might be represented in standard form as this:

I think Miranda is at home.

∴ We can meet her there.

---

[1] Other factors are important in inductive arguments. We will discuss inductive arguments in Chapter 9.

But this is misleading. My *thoughts* are not what make us able to meet Miranda at home. It is the *fact* that Miranda is at home that provides a reason for the conclusion. Thus, it is clearer to drop the guarding phrase ('I think') when putting the argument into standard form. But you have to be careful. Not all guarding phrases can be dropped. If a friend says that you ought to buckle your seat belt, because accidents can happen, it would distort her argument to drop the guarding term ('can'), since she is not claiming that there definitely will be an accident, or even that there probably will be one. The *chance* of an accident is significant enough to show that you ought to buckle your seat belt, so the guarding term should be kept when the argument is put into standard form.

It is also possible to drop *assuring* terms in some cases. Suppose someone says, "You obviously cannot play golf in Alaska in January, so there's no point in bringing your clubs." There is no need to keep the assuring term ("obviously") in the premise. It might even be misleading, since the issue is whether the premise is true, not whether it is obvious. The argument cannot be refuted by showing that, even though you can't play golf in Alaska in January, this is not obvious, since there might be indoor golf courses. In other cases, assuring terms cannot be dropped without losing the whole argument. For example, if someone argues that "We know that poverty causes crime, because many studies have shown that it does," the assuring phrase ("studies have shown that . . .") cannot be dropped without turning the argument into an empty shell: "We know that poverty causes crime, because it does."

There is no mechanical method for determining when guarding or assuring terms and phrases can be dropped, or whether certain sentences are unnecessary tangents. We have to look closely at what is being said and think hard about what is needed to support the conclusion. It takes great skill, care, and insight to pare an argument down to its essential core without omitting anything that would make it better.

▼ EXERCISE I

Put the following arguments into standard form and omit anything that does not affect the validity of the argument or the truth of its premises.

(1) Philadelphia is rich in history, but it is not now the capital of the United States, so the United States Congress must meet somewhere else.

(2) Not everybody whom you invited is going to come to your party. Some of them will not come. So this room should be big enough.

(3) I know that my wife is at home, since I just called her there.

(4) I'm not sure, but this argument is probably valid. Hence, it is sound if its premises are true.

(5) Some students could not concentrate on the lecture because they did not eat lunch before class.

(6) Yes, Virginia, there is still a Santa Cruz, so the earthquake was not that bad after all.

(7) Dukakis will probably win, since experts agree that more women support him.

(8) It is clear that married people are happier, so marriage must be a good thing.

CLARIFYING CRUCIAL TERMS

After the essential premises and conclusion are isolated, we often need to clarify these claims before we can begin our logical analysis. The goal here is not perfect clarity, for there probably is no such thing. It is, however, often necessary to eliminate ambiguity and reduce vagueness before we can give an argument a fair assessment. In particular, it is often necessary to specify the referents of pronouns, since such references can depend on a context which is changed when the argument is put into standard form. Another common problem is exemplified when someone argues like this:

You should just say no to drugs, because drugs are dangerous.

Is the premise about some drugs, most drugs, all drugs, or drugs of a certain kind? What about alcohol, nicotine, or aspirin? It might seem obvious what was meant: illegal drugs. But we cannot begin to evaluate this argument if we do not know the extent of what is claimed. Of course, we should not try to clarify every term in the argument. Even if this were possible, it would only make the argument extremely long and boring. Instead, our goal is to clarify anything that seems likely to produce confusion later if it is not cleared up now. As our analysis continues, we can always return and clarify more as the need arises, but it is better to get the obvious problems out of the way at the start.

DISSECTING THE ARGUMENT

A single sentence often includes several different clauses which make separate claims. When this happens, it is useful to dissect the sentence into its smallest parts, so that we can investigate each part separately. Simpler steps are easier to follow than complex ones, so we can understand the argument better when it is broken down. Dissection makes us more likely to notice any flaws in the argument. It also makes us able to pinpoint exactly where the argument fails, if it does.

The process of dissecting an argument is a skill that can be learned only by practice. Let's start with a simple example:

Joe won his bet, because all he had to do was eat five pounds of oysters, and he ate nine dozen, which weigh more than five pounds.

The simplest unpacking of this argument yields the following restatement in standard form:

All Joe had to do was eat five pounds of oysters, and he ate nine dozen, which weigh more than five pounds.

∴ Joe won his bet.

If we think about the premise of this argument, we see that it actually contains three claims. The argument will be clearer if we separate these claims into independent premises and add a few words for the sake of clarity. The following, then, is a better representation of this argument:

All Joe had to do (to win his bet) was eat five pounds of oysters.
Joe ate nine dozen (oysters).
Nine dozen oysters weigh more than five pounds.

∴ Joe won his bet.

With the premise split up in this way, it becomes obvious that there are three separate ways in which the argument can fail. One possibility is that Joe had to do more than just eat five pounds of oysters in order to win his bet. Maybe he bet that he could eat five pounds in one minute. Another possibility is that Joe did not really eat nine dozen oysters. Maybe he really ate one dozen oysters cut into nine dozen pieces. A final way that the argument could fail is if nine dozen oysters do not weigh more than five pounds. Maybe the oysters that Joe ate were very small, or maybe nine dozen oysters weigh more than five pounds only when they are still in their shells, but Joe didn't eat the shells. In any case, breaking down complex premises into simpler ones makes it is easier to see exactly where the argument goes wrong, if it does.

Although it is a good idea to break down the premises of an argument where this is possible, we have to be careful not to do this in a way that changes the logical structure of the argument. Suppose someone argues like this:

Socialism is doomed to failure because it does not provide the incentives that are needed for a prosperous economy.

The simplest representation of this argument yields the following standard form:

Socialism does not provide the incentives that are needed for a prosperous economy.

∴ Socialism is doomed to failure.

It is very tempting to break up the first premise into two parts:

> Socialism does not provide incentives.
> Incentives are needed for a prosperous economy.
>
> ∴ Socialism is doomed to failure.

In this form, the argument is open to a fatal objection: socialism *does* provide *some* incentives. Workers often get public recognition when they surpass their quotas in socialist economies. But this does not refute the original argument. The point of the original argument was not that socialism does not provide any incentives at all but only that socialism does not provide enough incentives or the right kind of incentives to create a prosperous economy. This point is lost if we break up the premise in the way suggested. A better attempt is this:

> Socialism does not provide adequate incentives.
> Adequate incentives are needed for a prosperous economy.
>
> ∴ Socialism is doomed to failure.

The problem now is to specify when incentives are "adequate". What kinds of incentives are needed? How much of these incentives? The process of dissection has thus brought out a central issue in this argument, and we cannot evaluate the argument until we go back and clarify the premises further.

ARRANGING SUB-ARGUMENTS

When the premises of an argument are dissected, it often becomes clear that some of these premises are intended as reasons for others. The premises then form a chain of simpler arguments that culminate in the ultimate conclusion, but only after some intermediate steps. Consider this argument:

> There's no way I can finish my paper before the 9 o'clock show, since I have to do the reading first, so I won't even start writing until at least 9 o'clock.

It might seem tempting to put this argument into standard form as:

> I have to do the reading first.
> I won't even start writing until at least 9 o'clock.
>
> ∴ I can't finish my paper before the 9 o'clock show.

This reformulation does include all three parts of the original argument, but it does not indicate the correct role for each part. The two warranting connectives in the original argument indicate that there are really *two* conclusions. The word "since" indicates that what precedes it is a conclusion, and the word "so" indicates that what follows it is also a conclusion. We cannot represent this as a single argument in standard form, since each argument in standard form can have only one conclusion. Thus, the original sentence must have included two arguments. The relation between these arguments should be clear: the conclusion of the first argument functions as a premise or reason in the second argument. To represent this, we let the two arguments form a chain. This is the first argument:

> I have to do the reading first.
> _____
>
> ∴ I won't even start writing until at least 9 o'clock.

This is the second argument:

> I won't even start writing until at least 9 o'clock.
> _____
>
> ∴ I can't finish my paper before the 9 o'clock show.

We can then write these arguments in a chain like this:

> I have to do the reading first.
> _____
>
> ∴ I won't even start writing until at least 9 o'clock.
> _____
>
> ∴ I can't finish my paper before the 9 o'clock show.

Such chains of reasoning are very common. This is a simple example, but some argument chains can get so complex that you might need a flow chart to follow them.

Although it is often illuminating to break an argument into stages, this can be misleading if done incorrectly. For example, the first sentence of Kyl's speech cited in Chapter 3 read as follows: "Mr. Speaker, I oppose this measure. I oppose it first because it is expensive. I further oppose it because it is untimely." Here we have two separate reasons for the same conclusion. They cannot be put into any chain of arguments because the claim that the measure is expensive is not a reason to believe it is untimely, nor is the claim that it is untimely a reason to believe that it is expensive. We have to be careful not to confuse a chain of arguments leading to a conclusion with multiple (or parallel) arguments leading to the same conclusion.

▼ EXERCISE II

Put the following arguments into standard form. Break up the premises and form chains of arguments wherever this can be done without distorting the argument.

(1) I know Pat can't be a father, because she is not a male. So she can't be a grandfather either.

(2) Since many newly emerging nations do not have the capital resources necessary for sustained growth, they will continue to need help from industrial nations to avoid mass starvation.

(3) Either Jack is a fool or Mary is a crook, because she ended up with all of his money.

(4) A strategic arms reductions treaty cannot be safe, because the Soviets are much too paranoid to permit surprise inspections, and there is no way to verify reductions in mobile missiles without surprise inspections, since mobile missiles could be moved as soon as the inspections were announced.

(5) Since he won the lottery, he's rich and lucky, so he'll probably do well in the stock market, too, unless his luck runs out.

SUPPRESSED PREMISES

Shared Facts

Arguments in everyday life are rarely completely explicit. They usually depend on unstated facts understood by those involved in the conversation. Thus, if we are told that Chester Arthur was a president of the United States, we have a right to conclude a great many things about him—for example, that at the time he was president, he was a live human being. Appeals to facts of this kind lie behind the following argument:

> Benjamin Franklin could not have been our second president because he died before the second election was held.

This argument obviously turns on a question of fact: Did Franklin die before the second presidential election was held? (He did.) The argument would not be sound if this explicit premise were not true. But the argument also depends on a more general principle that ties the premise and conclusion together, namely, that the dead are not eligible for the presidency. This new premise is needed to make the argument valid (and also sound). In fact, the argument is not valid unless we also add that the second president served after the second election and that people cannot come back to life after they die.

Traditionally, logicians have called premises that seem too obvious to mention *suppressed* or *unstated* premises. An argument depending upon suppressed premises is called an *enthymeme* and is said to be *enthymematic*. If we look at arguments that occur in daily life, we discover that they are, almost without exception, enthymematic. Therefore, to trace out the pathway between premises and conclusion, it is usually necessary to fill in these suppressed premises that serve as connecting links between the stated premises and the conclusion.

Suppressed premises often concern rules or conventions that might have been otherwise. Our example assumed that the dead cannot be president, but we can imagine a society in which the deceased are elected to public office as an honor (something like posthumous induction into the Baseball Hall of Fame). However, our national government is not like that, and this is something that most Americans know. This makes it odd to come right out and say that the deceased cannot hold public office. In most settings, this would involve a violation of the conversational rule of Strength.

But even if it would be odd to state it, this fact plays a central role in the argument. To assert the conclusion without believing the suppressed premise would involve a violation of the conversational rule of Quality, since the speaker would not have adequate reasons for his conclusion. Furthermore, if this suppressed premise were not true, to give the explicit premise as a reason would violate the conversational rule of Relevance (just as it would be irrelevant to point out that Babe Ruth is dead when someone asks whether he is in the Baseball Hall of Fame). For these reasons, anyone who gives the original argument conversationally implies a commitment to the suppressed premise.

Suppressed premises are not always so obvious. A somewhat more complicated example is this:

> Henry Kissinger cannot become president because he was born in Germany.

Why should being from Germany disqualify someone from being president of the United States? It seems odd that the Founding Fathers should have something against that particular part of the world. The answer is that the argument depends upon a more general suppressed premise:

> Only a native-born American citizen may become president of the United States.

It is this provision of the United States Constitution that lies at the heart of the argument. Knowing this provision is, of course, a more special piece of knowledge than knowing that you have to be alive to be president. For this reason, more people will see the force of the first argument than the second. The second argument assumes an audience with more specialized knowledge.

The argument still has to draw a connection between being born in Germany and being a native-born United States citizen. So it turns out that the argument has two stages:

> Kissinger was born in Germany.
> Germany has never been part of the United States.
> Someone who was born outside the United States cannot be
> a native-born United States citizen.
> _____
> Therefore, Kissinger is not a native-born United States citizen.
> Only a native-born United States citizen may become president of the
>   United States.
> _____
> Therefore, Kissinger cannot become president of the United States.

Now the argument is valid. However, the argument is not sound, because two of the suppressed premises that were added are not true. There are exceptions to them.

The exception to the suppressed premise about who is a native-born citizen is well known to United States citizens who live overseas. People who were born in Germany are still United States citizens if their parents were United States citizens. They also seem to count as native-born citizens, since they were not naturalized. This is not completely settled,[2] but it doesn't matter here, since Henry Kissinger's parents were not United States citizens when he was born. Thus, the first part of the argument can be reformulated as follows:

Kissinger was born in Germany.
Germany has never been part of the United States.
Kissinger's parents were not United States citizens when he was born.
Someone who was born outside the United States and whose parents were not United States citizens when he or she was born cannot be a native-born United States citizen.

Therefore, Kissinger is not a native-born United States citizen.

This much of the argument is now sound.

The exception to the suppressed premise about who can become president is less well known. The Constitution does allow people who are not native-born citizens to become president if they were born before the adoption of the Constitution. Of course, Kissinger was born long after the adoption of the Constitution, so the second part of the argument can be reformulated as follows:

Kissinger is not a native-born United States citizen.
Kissinger was born after the ratification of the Constitution.
Only a native-born United States citizen or a United States citizen who was born before the adoption of the Constitution can become president of the United States.

Therefore, Kissinger cannot become president of the United States.

Now both parts of the argument are sound, and so is the argument as a whole.

An argument with a single premise has grown to include six premises and an intermediate conclusion. Some of the added premises are obvious, but others are less well known, so we cannot assume that the person who gave the original argument had the more complete argument in mind. And many people would be convinced by the original argument even without all of these added complexities. Nonetheless, the many suppressed premises are necessary to make the argument sound, and seeing this brings out the assumptions that must be true

---

[2] Contrast Montana v. Kennedy, 366 U.S. 308, 312 (1961) with Rogers v. Bellei, 401 U.S. 815 (1971).

for the conclusion to follow from the premises. This process of making everything explicit enables us to assess these background assumptions directly.

Linguistic Principles

Often an argument is valid, but it is not clear *why* it is valid. It is not clear how the conclusion follows from the premises. Arguments are like pathways between premises and conclusions, and some of these pathways are more complicated than others. Yet even the simplest arguments reveal hidden complexities when examined closely. For example, there is no question that the following argument is valid:

> Harriet is in New York with her son.
> _____
>
> Therefore, Harriet's son is in New York.

It is not possible for the premise to be true and the conclusion false. If asked why this conclusion follows from the premises, it would be natural to reply that you cannot be someplace with somebody unless that person is there too. This is not something we usually spell out, but, nonetheless, it is the principle that takes us from the premise to the conclusion.

One thing to notice about this principle is that it is quite general, that is, it does not depend on any special features of the people or places involved. If Benjamin is in St. Louis with his daughter, then Benjamin's daughter is in St. Louis. Although the references have changed, the general pattern of the argument has remained the same. Furthermore, the principle that lies behind this inference will seem obvious to anyone who understands the words used to formulate it. For this reason we shall say that principles of this kind are basically *linguistic* in character.

If we look at arguments as they occur in everyday life, we will discover that almost all of them turn on unstated linguistic principles. To cite just one more example, if a wife is taller than her husband, then there is at least one woman who is taller than at least one man. This inference relies on the principle that husbands are men and wives are women. We do not usually state these linguistic principles, for to do so will often violate the rule of Strength, discussed in Chapter 1. (Try to imagine a context in which you would come right out and say, "Husbands, you know, are men." Unless you were speaking to someone just learning the language, this would be a very peculiar remark to make.) But even if in most cases it would be peculiar to come right out and state such linguistic principles, our arguments typically presuppose them. This observation reveals yet another way in which our daily use of language moves within a rich, though largely unnoticed, framework of rules.

Other Kinds of Suppressed Premises

We have examined two kinds of suppressed premises: those that are factual, and others that are linguistic. Many arguments also contain unstated *moral* premises. Consider the following argument as a case in point:

> You shouldn't buy pornography, because it leads to violence towards women.

This argument clearly relies on the principle that you should not buy anything that leads to violence towards women. A different example comes from *religion:*

> You shouldn't take the name of the Lord in vain, because this shows disrespect.

The suppressed premise here is that you shouldn't do anything that shows disrespect (to the Lord). More examples could be given, but the point should be clear: Most arguments depend on unstated assumptions, and these assumptions come in many different kinds.

Uses of Suppressed Premises

Talk about *suppressed* premises sounds a bit like suppressing a rebellion or an ugly thought, and using *hidden* premises may sound somewhat sneaky. But we are not using either of these expressions with such negative connotations. A suppressed or hidden premise is simply an *unstated* premise. Now, it is often legitimate to leave premises unstated. This will be legitimate if (i) those who are given the argument can easily supply these unstated premises for themselves and (ii) the unstated premises are not themselves controversial. If done properly, the suppression of premises can add greatly to the efficiency of language. Indeed, without the judicious suppression of obvious premises, many arguments would become too cumbersome to be effective.

Suppressed premises can also be used improperly. People sometimes suppress questionable assumptions so that their opponents will not notice where their argument goes astray. For example, when election debates turn to the topic of crime, we often hear arguments like this:

> My opponent is opposed to the death penalty, so he must be soft on crime.

The response sometimes sounds like this:

> Since my opponent continues to support the death penalty, he must not have read the most recent studies which show that the death penalty does not deter crime.

The first argument assumes that anyone who is opposed to the death penalty is soft on crime, and the second argument assumes that anyone who read the studies in question would be convinced by them and would turn against the death penalty. Both of these assumptions are questionable, and the questions they raise are central to the debate. If we want to understand these issues and address them directly, we have to bring out these suppressed premises explicitly.

▼ EXERCISE III

The following arguments depend for their validity on suppressed premises of various kinds. For each of the following arguments, list enough suppressed premises to make the argument valid and to show why it is valid. This might require several suppressed premises of various kinds.

Example: Carol has no sisters, because all her siblings are brothers.
Suppressed Premises: A brother is not a sister.
A sister would be a sibling.

(1) Madonna is under 35. Therefore, she cannot run for president of the United States.

(2) Nixon couldn't have been president in 1950, since he was still in the Senate.

(3) 81 is not a prime number, because 81 is divisible by 3.

(4) There's no one named Rupert here; we have only female patients.

(5) Columbus did not discover the New World, because the Vikings explored Newfoundland centuries earlier.

(6) If there were survivors, they would have been found by now. [as a way of arguing that there are no survivors]

(7) Lincoln could not have met Washington, because Washington was dead before Lincoln was born.

(8) Philadelphia cannot play Los Angeles in the World Series, since they are both in the National League.

(9) Mildred must be over 43, since she has a daughter who is 36.

(10) He cannot be a grandfather, because he never had children.

(11) That's not acid rock; you can understand the lyrics.

(12) Harold can't play in the Super Bowl, because he broke his leg.

(13) Minute must be a basketball player, since he's so tall.

(14) Dan is either stupid or very cunning, so he must be stupid.

(15) Susan refuses to work on Saturdays, which shows she is lazy and inflexible.

(16) Jim told me that Bathsheba is a professor, so she can't be a student, since professors must already have degrees.

(17) SDI will never work unless we are very lucky or the Russians are friendly, so we can't rely on it.

(18) SDI will never work, because it will require powerful lasers which we cannot even begin to build at this time.

THE METHOD OF RECONSTRUCTION

We can summarize the discussion so far by listing the steps that need to be taken in reconstructing an argument. The first two steps were discussed in Chapters 2 and 3.

(1) Do a *close analysis* of the passage containing the argument.

(2) List all explicit premises and the conclusion in *standard form*.

(3) *Clarify* the premises and the conclusion where necessary.

(4) *Break up* the premises and the conclusion into smaller parts where this is possible.

(5) *Arrange* the parts of the argument into a chain of sub-arguments where this is possible.

(6) Assess each argument and sub-argument for *validity*.[3]

(7) If any argument or sub-argument is not valid, or if it is not clear why it is valid, add *suppressed premises* that will show how to get from the premises to the conclusion.

(8) Assess the *truth* of the premises.

This method is not intended to be mechanical. Each step requires care and intelligence. As a result, a given argument can be reconstructed in various ways with varying degrees of illumination and insight. The goal of this method is to reveal as much of the structure of an argument as needed and to learn from it as much as you can. Different reconstructions approach more or less closely to this goal.

The whole process is more complex than our discussion thus far has suggested. This is especially clear in the last three steps. They must be carried out together. In deciding whether an argument is acceptable, we try to find a set of true suppressed premises which, if added to the stated premises, yields a sound argument for the conclusion. Two problems typically arise when we make this effort:

(1) We find a set of premises strong enough to support the conclusion, but at least one of these premises is false.

(2) We modify the premises to avoid falsehood, but the conclusion no longer follows from them.

---

[3] With inductive arguments we assess the argument for *strength* instead of validity. Inductive arguments will be examined in Chapter 9.

The reconstruction of an argument typically involves shifting back and forth between the demand for a valid argument and the demand for true premises. Eventually, we either show the argument to be sound or we abandon the effort. In the latter case, we conclude that the argument in question has no sound reconstruction. Now it is possible that *we* were at fault in not finding a reconstruction that showed the argument to be sound. Perhaps we did not show enough ingenuity in searching for a suppressed premise that would do the trick. There is, in fact, no purely formal or mechanical way of dealing with this problem. A person presenting an argument may reasonably leave out steps, provided that they can be easily filled in by those to whom the argument is addressed. So in analyzing an argument, we should be charitable, but our charity has limits. After a reasonable search for those suppressed premises that would show the argument to be sound, we should not blame ourselves if we fail to find them. Rather, the blame shifts to the person who formulated the argument for not doing so clearly.

▼ EXERCISE IV

Practice the method of reconstruction on one or more of the following:

(1)   the passages at the end of Chapter 3
(2)   an editorial from your local paper
(3)   your last term paper or a friend's last term paper
(4)   one of the articles in Part 2

DIGGING DEEPER

After we have reconstructed an argument as well as we can, doubts still might arise about its premises. If we agree with its premises, others might deny them or ask why they are true. If we disagree with some premise, we may be able to understand the source of our disagreement better if we determine why it is believed by other people— including the person who gave the argument. Either way, it is useful to try to construct *supporting* arguments for the premises that might be questioned. These supporting arguments are not parts of the explicit argument or even its reconstruction; they are further arguments back in a chain of arguments.

When we look for further arguments to support the premises in an argument, we might then wonder whether the premises of this new argument can be accepted without supporting arguments as well. We seem faced with the unpleasant task of producing endless chains of argument. When pressed in this way to give reasons for our reasons, and reasons for our reasons for our reasons, and so on, we eventually come upon fundamental principles—principles for which we cannot give any deeper argument. These fundamental principles can concern morality, religion, politics, and our general views concerning the nature of the world. We often argue within a framework of such principles without actually stating them because we assume (sometimes incorrectly!) that others accept them as well. When someone argues that the arms race should be ended because it will lead to the annihilation of the human race, he or she will not feel called upon to say explicitly, "And the annihilation of the human race would be a very bad thing." That, after all, is something that most people take for granted. Though fundamental principles are often obvious and generally accepted, at times it is not clear what principles are being assumed and just how acceptable they really are. Then we need to make our assumptions explicit and to look for deeper arguments, continuing the process as far as we can. There is a limit to how far we can go, but the deeper we go, the better we understand our own views as well as the views of our opponents.

▼ EXERCISE V

The following arguments depend for their validity on suppressed premises. First, state what these underlying premises might be. In some cases, there might be more than one. Second, determine whether these are fundamental in the sense just described. If not, try to give supporting arguments for the premises in each argument until you arrive at principles that are fundamental. Remember, you do not have to accept an argument to detect its underlying principles and to understand the kind of argument that could be used to support it.

Example: General Snork has no right to rule, because he came to power by a military coup.

Suppressed Premise: Someone who came to power by a military coup has no right to rule.

Supporting Argument:

Someone has a right to rule only if he or she has been elected by the people.
Someone who comes to power by a military coup has not been elected by the people.
∴ Someone who came to power by a military coup has no right to rule.

(Further support for the first premise might be provided by some theory of democracy.)

(1)   You cannot say that Kirk is guilty because he has not even been tried yet.

(2) If people can vote and be drafted at 18, then they should be allowed to drink at 18.

(3) We have no right to attack left-wing dictatorships if we support right-wing dictatorships.

(4) If high deficits continue, then inflation will return.

(5) If getting good grades is so easy, why don't more people do it? [as a way of arguing that getting good grades is not so easy]

(6) It is wrong to punish someone just to make an example of him.

(7) Morris does not deserve his wealth, because he merely inherited it.

CAPITAL PUNISHMENT

We can illustrate these methods of deep analysis at work by examining the difficult question of the constitutionality of capital punishment. It has been argued before the Supreme Court that the death penalty should be declared unconstitutional because it violates the provision in the Constitution against "cruel and unusual punishments." The explicitly stated argument has the following form:

> The death penalty violates the constitutional prohibition against cruel and unusual punishments.
>
> Therefore, the death penalty should be ruled unconstitutional.

The argument plainly depends upon two suppressed premises:

> SP1: The death penalty involves cruel and unusual punishment.
>
> SP2: Anything that violates a constitutional prohibition should be declared unconstitutional.

So the argument more fully spelled out looks like this:

(1) SP: The death penalty involves cruel and unusual punishment.
(2) The Constitution prohibits cruel and unusual punishments.

(3) Therefore, the Constitution prohibits the death penalty.
(4) SP: Anything that the Constitution prohibits should be declared unconstitutional.

(5) Therefore, the death penalty should be declared unconstitutional.

This reconstruction seems to be a fair representation of the intent of the original argument.

We can now turn to an assessment of this argument. First, the argument is valid: given the premises, the conclusion does follow. So we can turn our attention to the plausibility of the premises themselves. The second premise is clearly true, for the Constitution does, in fact, prohibit cruel and unusual punishments. The Eighth Amendment reads, "Excessive bail shall not be required, nor excessive fines imposed, nor cruel and unusual punishments inflicted." It is not clear, however, just what this prohibition amounts to. In particular, does the punishment have to be *both* cruel and unusual to be prohibited, or is it sufficient for it to be *either* cruel or unusual? This would make a big difference if cruel punishments were usual, or if some unusual punishments were not cruel. For the moment, let us interpret the language as meaning both cruel and unusual.

Premise (4) seems uncontroversial. Indeed, it may sound like a truism to say that anything that violates a constitutional provision should be declared unconstitutional. As a matter of fact, this notion was once controversial, for nothing in the Constitution gives the courts the right to declare acts of legislators unconstitutional and hence void. The courts have acquired and consolidated this right in the years since 1789, and it is still sometimes challenged by those who think that it gives the courts too much power. But even if the judiciary's power to declare laws unconstitutional is not itself a constitutionally stated power, it is so much an accepted part of our system that no one would challenge it in a courtroom procedure today.

Although premise (4) has a more complicated backing than most people realize, it is obviously the first premise—"The death penalty involves cruel and unusual punishment"—that forms the heart of the argument. What we would expect, then, is a good supporting argument to be put forward in its behalf. Consider the following argument intended to support this claim:

> That killing someone is cruel should go without saying. The important issue is whether such a penalty is unusual. That execution is an unusual penalty is seen from examining court records. Whether a person committing a particular crime will be given the death penalty depends on the kind of legal aid he is given, his willingness to enter into plea bargaining, the personality of the judge, the beliefs and attitudes of the jury, and a great many other considerations. In fact, only in a small percentage of the cases in which it might apply is the death penalty actually handed down.

Let us concentrate on the part of this argument intended to show that the death penalty is an unusual punishment. Of course, in civilized nations the death penalty is reserved for a small range of crimes; but the fact that it is not widespread is hardly the point at issue. The point of the argument is that the death penalty is unusual even for those crimes that are punishable by death. The above passage also enumerates several factors that determine who, among those convicted of crimes punishable by death, actually receives a death sentence. Why are these factors mentioned? The clear suggestion is that it is unfair for sentencing to depend on factors of these kinds. We can then restate the argument more carefully as follows:

The death sentence is given to only a small percentage of those found
guilty of crimes punishable by death.
Among those found guilty of crimes punishable by death, who is given
the death sentence depends on factors that should not affect sentencing.
A punishment is unusual in the relevant sense if it is given to only a
small percentage of cases where it is available and if who gets it depends on factors that should not affect sentencing.

Therefore, the death penalty is an unusual punishment in the relevant
sense.

Now we can spread the entire argument out before us:

(1)   Killing someone is a cruel act.
(2)   The death penalty involves killing someone.

(3)   Therefore, the death penalty is cruel.
(4)   The death sentence is given to only a small percentage of those
       found guilty of crimes punishable by death.
(5)   Among those found guilty of crimes punishable by death, who is
       given the death sentence depends on factors that should not affect
       sentencing.
(6)   A punishment is unusual in the relevant sense if it is given in
       only a small percentage of cases where it is available and if who
       gets it depends on factors that should not affect sentencing.

(7)   Therefore, the death penalty is an unusual punishment in the rel-
       evant sense.
(8)   Therefore, the death penalty is both cruel and unusual in the rele-
       vant sense.
(9)   The Constitution prohibits cruel and unusual punishments.

(10) Therefore, the Constitution prohibits the death penalty.
(11) Anything that the Constitution prohibits should be declared un-
       constitutional.

(12) Therefore, the death penalty should be declared unconstitutional.

These propositions provide at least the skeleton of an argument with
some force. The conclusion does seem to follow from the premises,
and the premises themselves seem plausible. It seems, then, that we
have produced a charitable reconstruction of the argument.

    We can now see how an opponent might respond to it. One par-
ticularly probing objection goes like this:

    It is certainly true that only a small percentage of those who commit
    capital offenses are actually sentenced to death, but this fact does not
    reflect badly on the law but on its administration. If judges and juries
    met their obligations, more people who deserve the death penalty
    would receive it, and the use of it would no longer be unusual. What is
    needed, then, is judicial reform and not the removal of the death pen-
    alty on constitutional grounds.

This response is probing because it insists on a distinction between a law itself and the effects of its application or, more pointedly, its misapplication. Since this distinction was not drawn in the argument above, it is not clear which premise is denied in this response. Probably the best interpretation is that this response denies premise (6) because it is not the death penalty itself that is unusual in the relevant sense when the conditions in premise (6) are met. Instead, it is the present administration of the death penalty that is problematic.

To meet this objection, the original argument could be strengthened in the following way:

> A law should not be judged in isolation from the likely effects of implementing it. Because of the very nature of our system of criminal justice, for the foreseeable future, the death penalty will almost certainly continue to be applied in only a small percentage of cases where it is available, and those who receive it will be determined partly by factors which make sentencing unfair. The death penalty will therefore remain an unusual punishment, so it should be declared unconstitutional.

This argument suggests ways to avoid the above objection by strengthening premises (4)–(6) of the above argument. The new versions of these premises can be spelled out in the following way:

(4*) It is very likely in the foreseeable future that the death sentence will continue to be given to only a small percentage of those found guilty of crimes punishable by death.

(5*) It is very likely in the foreseeable future that, among those found guilty of crimes punishable by death, who is given the death sentence will continue to depend on factors that should not affect sentencing.

(6*) A punishment is unusual in the relevant sense if it is very likely in the foreseeable future that it will be given in only a small percentage of cases where it is available and who gets it will depend on factors that should not affect sentencing.

(7*) Therefore, the death penalty is unusual in the relevant sense.

Of course, an opponent can still respond that these premises are false if he or she can show that there is some way to avoid the problems which are alleged by premises (4*) and (5*). However, this will not be easy to show if the argument is right about "the very nature of our system of criminal justice."

Another kind of question is raised by premise (6*). Should a law be declared unconstitutional whenever there is a good chance that it will be abused in ways that infringe on constitutional rights? Of course, a great many laws have this potential—for example, all laws involving police power. This is why certain police powers have been limited by court ruling. Strict rules governing interrogations and wiretaps are two results. However, only an extremist would suggest that we should abolish all police powers because of the inevitable risk of unconstitutional abuse. Accordingly, those who argue in favor of the death penalty might try to show that the problems in the application of the death penalty are not sufficiently important to be considered constitutionally intolerable.

The supporter of the death penalty can sharpen and extend this criticism in the following way:

> Those who argue against the constitutionality of the death penalty on the grounds that it is a cruel and unusual punishment use the expression "cruel and unusual" in a way wholly different from that intended by the framers of the Eighth Amendment. By "cruel" they had in mind punishments that involved torture. By "unusual" they meant bizarre or ghoulish punishments of the kind that often formed part of public spectacles in barbaric times. Modern methods of execution are neither cruel nor unusual in the constitutionally relevant senses of these words. Therefore, laws demanding the death penalty cannot be declared unconstitutional on the grounds that they either directly or indirectly involve a punishment that is cruel and unusual.

The core of this counter-argument can be expressed as follows:

(1) In appeals to the Constitution, its words must be taken as they were originally intended.

(2) Modern methods of carrying out a death penalty are neither "cruel" nor "unusual" if these words are interpreted as they were originally intended.

(3) Therefore, the death penalty cannot be declared unconstitutional on the ground that it violates the amendment against cruel and unusual punishments.

The second premise of this argument states a matter of historical fact that might not be altogether easy to verify. The chances are, however, that it comes close to the truth. Given this, the opponent of the death penalty must either attack the first premise or find some other grounds for holding that the death penalty should be declared unconstitutional.

The first premise may seem like a truism, for how can a document guide conduct if anyone can reinterpret its words regardless of what was intended? The literal meaning of the document is simply its meaning; everything else is interpretation. Of course, there are times when it is not easy to discover what its meaning is. (In the present case, for example, it is not clear whether the Eighth Amendment prohibits punishments that are either cruel or unusual or only those that are both cruel and unusual.) It seems unlikely, however, that those who drafted the Eighth Amendment used either the word "cruel" or the word "unusual" in the ways they are employed in the anti–capital punishment argument.

Does this last concession end the debate in favor of those who reject the anti–capital punishment argument we have been examining?

The argument certainly seems to be weakened, but there are those who would take a bold course by simply denying the first premise of the argument used to refute them. They would deny, that is, that we are bound to read the Constitution in the way intended by its framers. An argument in favor of this position might look something like this:

> The great bulk of the Constitution was written in an age almost wholly different from our own. To cite just two examples of this: Women were denied fundamental rights of full citizenship, and slavery was a constitutionally accepted feature of national life. The Constitution has remained a live and relevant document just because it has undergone constant reinterpretation. So even if it is true that the expression "cruel and unusual" meant something quite special to those who framed the Eighth Amendment, plainly a humane desire to make punishment more civilized lay behind it. The present reading of this amendment is in the spirit of its original intention and simply makes it applicable to our own times.

The argument has now moved to an entirely new level: one concerning whether the Constitution should be read strictly in accord with the original intentions of those who wrote it or more freely to accommodate modern realities.

We shall not pursue the discussion further into these complex areas. Instead, we should consider how we were led into them. Recall that our original argument did not concern the general question of whether capital punishment is right or wrong. The argument turned on a much more specific point: Does the death penalty violate the prohibition against cruel and unusual punishments in the Eighth Amendment to the United States Constitution? The argument with which we began seemed to be a straightforward proof that it does. Yet, as we explored principles that lay in back of this deceptively simple argument, the issue became broader and more complex. We finally reached a point at which the force of the original argument was seen to depend on what we consider the proper way to interpret the Constitution—strictly or more freely. If we now go on to ask which method of interpretation is best, we will have to look at the role of the courts and, more generally, the purpose of government. Eventually we will come to fundamental principles for which we can give no further argument.

CONCLUSION

In examining the question of the constitutionality of capital punishment, we have had to compress a very complicated discussion into very few pages. All that we have been able to do is to *begin* to show how the issues involved in this complex debate can be sorted out and then addressed intelligently. There is, however, no guarantee that these procedures, however far they are carried out, must eventually settle this or any other fundamental dispute. It is entirely possible that the parties to a dispute may reach a point where they encounter a fundamental or rock-bottom disagreement that they cannot resolve. They disagree, and cannot conceive of any deeper principles that could resolve their disagreement. But even if this happens, they will at least understand the source of their disagreement. They will not be arguing at cross purposes, as so often happens in the discussion of important issues. Finally, even if they continue to disagree, they may come to appreciate that others may view things quite differently from the way they do. Nothing guarantees this, but this in turn may help them deal with their basic disagreements in an intelligent, humane, and civilized way.

▼ EXERCISE VI

The final argument in our examination of whether or not the death penalty violates the Constitution attempts to show that the Constitution must be read in a free or liberal way that makes it relevant to present society. Filling in suppressed premises where necessary, restate this argument as a sequence of explicit steps. After you have given the argument the strongest restatement you can, evaluate it for its soundness.

▼ DISCUSSION QUESTIONS

1. How could the argument of the last section be supported by deeper principles? How would you determine whether the Constitution should be interpreted strictly or freely?

2. How can you tell when you have reached a fundamental principle? Must every argument start with some basic claim for which no further argument can be given or for which you can give no argument?

3. In what ways, if any, does reconstructing an argument help you to understand and evaluate it?

5

Fallacies

In this chapter we shall examine some of the standard ways in which arguments can be defective. Defects in arguments will be considered under three main headings: fallacies of *clarity,* fallacies of *relevance,* and fallacies of *vacuity.* Fallacies of clarity arise when language is not used precisely enough for the argumentative context. Vagueness and ambiguity, two common forms of unclarity, will be defined and discussed in detail. Fallacies of relevance arise when a claim is made which, true or not, has no tendency to establish the point at issue. Such irrelevance comes in endless forms, but only two will be discussed in detail: arguments *ad hominem* and *appeals to authority.* Fallacies of vacuity arise when an argument doesn't get anywhere, either because the conclusion is somehow included already in the premises, or because the conclusion is empty. *Circular arguments* and arguments that *beg the question* fall into this category. So do positions that make themselves immune to criticism by being *self-sealing.*

FALLACIES OF CLARITY

In a good argument, a person states a conclusion clearly and then, with equal clarity, gives reasons for this conclusion. The arguments of everyday life often fall short of this standard. Usually, unclear language is a sign of unclear thought. There are times, however, when people are intentionally unclear—their goal is to confuse others. This is called *obfuscation*.

Before we look at the various ways in which language can be unclear, a word of caution is needed. There is no such thing as absolute clarity. Whether something is clear or not depends on the context in which it occurs. A botanist does not use the commonsense vocabulary in describing and classifying plants. At the same time, it would usually be foolish for a person to use botanical terms in describing the appearance of his backyard. Thus, as Aristotle said, it is the mark of an educated person not to expect more rigor than the subject matter will allow. Because clarity and rigor are context-dependent, it takes judgment and good sense to pitch an argument at the right level.

Vagueness

Perhaps the most common form of unclarity is *vagueness*. It arises in the following way. Many of our concepts admit of *borderline cases*. The standard example is baldness. A person with a full-flowing head of hair is not bald. A person without a hair on his head is bald. In between, however, there is a range of cases where we are not prepared to say definitely whether the person is bald or not. Here we say something less definite, such as that this person is "going" bald. Notice that our inability to apply the concept of baldness in this borderline case is not due to ignorance. It will not help, for example, to count the number of hairs on the person's head. Even if we knew the exact number, we would still not be able to say whether the person was bald or not. The same is true of most adjectives that concern properties admitting of degrees—for example, rich, healthy, tall, wise, and ruthless. We can also encounter borderline cases with common nouns. Consider the common noun "game." Baseball is a game and so is chess, but how about tossing a frisbee? Is that a game? Is Russian roulette a game? Are prizefighting and bullfighting games? As we try to answer these questions, we feel an inclination to say yes and an inclination to say no. This uncertainty shows that these concepts admit of borderline cases.

For the most part this feature of our language—that we use terms without sharply defined limits—causes little difficulty. In fact, this is a useful feature of our language, for suppose we *did* have to count the number of hairs on a person's head before we could say whether that person was bald or not. Yet difficulties can arise when borderline cases themselves are at issue. Suppose that a state passes a law forbidding all actions that tend to corrupt the public morals. The law is backed up by stiff fines and imprisonment. There will be many cases that clearly fall under this law and many cases that clearly do not fall under it. But in a very wide range of cases, it will just not be clear whether they fall under this law or not. Here we shall say that the law is *vague*. Laws are sometimes held unconstitutional for this very reason. In calling the law vague, we are *criticizing* it. We are not simply noticing the existence of borderline cases, for there will usually be borderline cases no matter how careful we are. We shall say, then, that *a concept is vague, if, in a given context, it leaves open too wide a range of borderline cases for the successful and legitimate use of that concept in that context.*

To further illustrate this notion of context dependence, consider the expression "light football player." There are, of course, borderline cases between those football players who are light and those who are not light. But on these grounds alone we would not say that the expression is vague. It is a perfectly serviceable expression, and we can indicate borderline cases by saying, "Jones is a bit light for a football player." Suppose, however, that Ohio State and Cal Tech wish to have a game between their light football players. It is obvious that the previous understanding of what counts as being light is too vague for this new context. At Ohio State, anyone under 210 pounds is considered light. At Cal Tech, anyone over 150 pounds is considered heavy. What is needed then is a ruling—for example, anyone under 175 pounds will be considered a lightweight. This example illustrates a common situation. A concept that is perfectly okay in one area becomes vague when applied to some other (usually more specialized) area. This vagueness is removed by adopting more precise rules. Vagueness is resolved by definition.

▼ EXERCISE I

Each of the following sentences contains words or expressions that are potentially vague. Describe a context where this vagueness might make a difference, and then reduce this vagueness by replacing the italicized expression with one that is more precise. For example:

Harold has a bad reputation.

Context: This is vague when the issue is whether to hire Harold as a bank security guard, since some but not all kinds of bad reputation are relevant. We can reduce the vagueness by saying:
Harold is a known thief.

(1) John has *a nice income.*
(2) Cocaine is *a dangerous drug.*
(3) Marian is *a clever woman.*
(4) Nancy is *a terrific tennis player.*

(5) Mark is *not doing too well.*

(6) Hank's *a big fellow.*

(7) Bush *won comfortably.*

(8) Kevin *worked like a dog.*

Heaps and Slippery Slopes. The existence of borderline cases makes possible various styles of fallacious reasoning that have been identified (and used) since ancient times. One such argument was called the *argument from the heap,* for it was intended to show that it is impossible to produce a heap of sand by adding one grain at a time. As a variation on this, we will show that no one can become rich. The argument goes as follows:

(1) If someone has one cent, he is not rich.

(2) If someone is not rich, then giving him one cent will not make him rich.

∴ (3) No matter how many times you give a person a cent, that person will not pass from not being rich to being rich.

Everyone will agree that there is something wrong with this argument, for if we hand over a billion pennies to someone one at a time, that person will be worth ten million dollars. If he or she started out with nothing, that would certainly count as passing from not being rich to being rich.

Although there is some disagreement among philosophers about the correct way to analyze arguments of this kind, we can see that it turns upon borderline cases in the following way: If we laid down a ruling (maybe for tax purposes) that anyone with a million dollars or more is rich and anyone with less than this is not rich, then the argument would fail. A person with $999,999.99 would pass from not being rich to being rich when given a single penny. But, of course, we do not use the word "rich" with this precision. We know some clear cases of people who are rich and some other clear cases of people who are not rich. In between there is a fuzzy area where we are not prepared to say that people either are or are not rich. In this fuzzy area, a penny one way or the other will make no difference. Once we see the form of the argument from the heap, we see how we might "prove" that nobody is tall, fat, or bald and, finally, that there are no heaps. Wherever we find one thing passing over into its opposite through a gradual series of borderline cases, we can pull the following trick: find some increase that will not be large enough to carry us outside the borderline area, and then use the pattern of argument given above.

But what exactly is wrong with the argument from the heap? As a matter of fact, this is not an easy question to answer and remains a subject of debate. Here is one way of viewing the problem. Consider a case where we would all agree that a person would pass from being fat to being thin by losing at least 100 pounds. Now if this person lost an ounce a day for five years, he or she would have lost at least this much. Of course, there would be no particular day on which this person would pass from being fat to not being fat. Yet losing an ounce a day for five years is *equivalent* to losing more than 100 pounds. So the argument from the heap seems to depend upon the idea that a series of insignificant changes cannot be equivalent to a significant change. Surely this is a strange assumption. Here we might be met with the reply that, for a change to occur, it must occur at some particular time and place. The answer is that this merely shows a misunderstanding of concepts that admit of borderline cases. With concepts like this, changes can occur gradually over long stretches of time.

We can examine this issue more closely by looking at a near cousin to arguments from the heap—so-called slippery slope arguments. *Slippery slope* arguments exploit borderline cases in a different way than arguments from the heap. With slippery slope arguments we inch our way through the borderline area to show that there is *no real difference* between things at opposite ends of a scale. Whereas the argument from the heap was used in an effort to show that nobody is really bald, a slippery slope argument could be trotted out to try to show that there is no real difference between being bald and not being bald.

Slippery slope arguments are no better than arguments from the heap, but, strangely, they are sometimes taken quite seriously. Consider the difference between living and nonliving things:

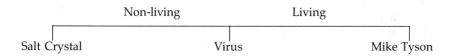

We all agree that a salt crystal is *not* alive. Yet a salt crystal is very similar to other more complex crystals, and these crystals are similar to certain viruses. We might even say that a virus just *is* a highly complex crystalline structure. But a virus is on the borderline between living and nonliving things. A virus does not take nourishment and does not reproduce itself. Instead, a virus invades the reproductive mechanisms of cells, and these cells then produce the virus. As viruses become more complex, the differences between them and higher life forms become less obvious. Through a whole series of such small transitions, we finally reach a creature who is obviously alive: Mike Tyson. So far, we have merely described a series of gradual transitions along a *continuum*. We get a slippery slope argument when we draw the following conclusion from these facts: There is no genuine difference between living and nonliving things since living processes are nothing more than complex nonliving processes. The opposite conclusion might also be drawn, namely, that everything is really alive, and what we call inanimate objects simply have a low level of life.

Slippery slope arguments have been used to deny the difference between sanity and insanity, health and sickness, and amateur and professional athletics. (We can imagine someone saying that a professional athlete is just an athlete who gets paid more than other athletes who are called "amateurs.") All such arguments depend upon the following principles:

(1) We should not draw a distinction between things that are not significantly different.

(2) If A is not significantly different from B and B is not significantly different from C, then A is not significantly different from C.

This first principle is interesting, complicated, and at least *generally* true. We shall examine it more closely in a moment. The second principle is obviously false. As already noted, a series of insignificant differences can add up to a significant difference. As Senator Everett Dirksen once said, "A billion dollars here and a billion dollars there can add up to some real money."

Where Do You Draw the Line?   We can turn now to some arguments concerning borderline cases that can be much more important. In the middle of an argument a person can offer a challenge by asking the question, "Where do you draw the line?" This challenge can arise only when there is a range of intermediate or borderline cases where a line is difficult to draw. But sometimes, even if the line is difficult to draw, this challenge is out of place. If I say that Willie Mays was a superstar, I will not be refuted if I cannot draw a sharp dividing line between athletes who are superstars and those who are not. There are some difficult borderline cases, but Willie Mays isn't one of them. Nor will we be impressed if someone tells us that the difference between Willie Mays and the thousands of players who never made it to the major leagues is "just a *matter of degree.*" What is wrong with this phrase is the emphasis on the word "just", which suggests that differences of degree don't count. Of course, it is a matter of degree, but the difference in degree is so great that it should be marked by a special word.

There are, however, occasions when a challenge to drawing a line is relevant. For example, most schools and universities have grading systems that draw a fundamental distinction between passing grades and failing grades. Of course, a person who barely passes a course does not perform very differently from one who barely fails a course, yet they are treated very differently. Students who barely pass a course get credit for it; those who barely fail it do not. This, in turn, can lead to serious consequences in an academic career and even beyond it. It is entirely reasonable to ask for a justification of a procedure that treats cases that are so similar in such strikingly different ways. We are not just being tender-hearted; we are raising an issue of *fairness* or *justice*. It seems unfair to treat very similar cases in strikingly different ways.

Questions concerning where a line should be drawn often raise problems for law and legislation. For example, the United States Supreme Court, in *California v. Carney*, had to rule on the following issue. Generally, given reasonable cause, the police do not have to obtain a warrant to search a motor vehicle, for the obvious reason that the vehicle might be driven away while the police go to a judge to obtain one. On the other hand, with few exceptions, the police may not search a person's home without a search warrant. In this particular case the vehicle was an "oversized van, fully mobile," parked in a downtown parking lot in San Diego. Looking for marijuana, the San Diego Police searched it without first obtaining a warrant. Because the van was a fully mobile vehicle, it seemed to fall under the first principle, but because it also served as its owner's home, it seemed to fall under the second. The difficulty, as the Court saw, was that there is a grey area between those things that clearly are motor vehicles and not homes (for example, a motorcycle) and those things that clearly are homes and not motor vehicles (for example, an apartment house). Chief Justice Warren Burger wondered about a mobile home in a trailer park hooked up to utility lines with its wheels removed. Justice Sandra Day O'Connor asked whether a tent, because it too is highly mobile, could also be searched without a warrant. As the discussion continued, houseboats (with or without motors or oars), covered wagons, and finally a house being moved from one place to another on a trailer truck came under examination. In the end, our highest court decided that the van in question certainly was a vehicle and could be searched without first obtaining a warrant to do so. As for the other examples it considered, the Court, as it often does, deferred action.[1]

Questions about where to draw the line often have even more important implications than the case just examined. Consider the death penalty. Most societies have reserved the death penalty for those crimes they consider the most serious. But where should we draw the line between crimes punishable by death and crimes not punishable by death? Is the death penalty appropriate for rape? For drug dealing? For drunk drivers who cause deaths in accidents? Wherever we draw the line, it seems to be an unavoidable consequence of the death penalty that similar cases will be treated in radically different ways. A defender of the death penalty can argue that it is not unfair since, once the line is

---

[1] The case was reported by Linda Greenhouse in "Of Tents with Wheels and Houses with Oars," *The New York Times*, May 15, 1985.

drawn, the public will have fair warning about which crimes are subject to the death penalty and which are not. It will then be up to each person to decide to risk his or her life by crossing this line. It remains a matter of debate, however, whether the law can be administered in a way that makes this argument plausible. If the laws themselves are administered in an arbitrary way, arguments of this kind lose their force.

The completeness and finality of death raises a profoundly difficult problem in another area too: the legalization of abortion. Some people think that abortion is never justified and ought to be declared totally illegal. Others think that abortion doesn't need any justification at all and should be completely legalized. Between these extremes, many people believe that abortion is justified in certain circumstances but not in others. There are also those who think that abortion should be allowed for a certain number of months of pregnancy, but not thereafter. People holding these middle positions face the problem of deciding where to draw a line, and for this reason they are subject to criticism from both extreme positions.

This problem admits of no easy solution. Since every line we draw will seem arbitrary to some extent, the only way a person who holds a middle position can face this problem honestly is to argue that it is better to draw some line—even a somewhat arbitrary one—than to draw no line at all. Of course, this does not tell us *where* to draw the line, and that problem will not be easy to solve. Nonetheless, the recognition that some line is needed can often help to locate the real issues, and this is the first step towards a reasonable position.

▼ EXERCISE II

Determine whether each of the following arguments provides any support, or adequate support, for its conclusion.

(1) We shouldn't require eye tests for bus drivers because it's only a matter of degree between perfect eyesight and legal blindness.

(2) Nobody should be committed against his or her will to a mental institution, because there is no real difference between insanity and extreme eccentricity.

(3) "But officer, I shouldn't get a speeding ticket for going 56 miles per hour, since my driving did not all of a sudden get more dangerous when I passed the speed limit of 55."

(4) Pornography shouldn't be illegal, because there is no way to draw a line between pornography and erotic art.

(5) Marijuana should be legal, because it is not really any more dangerous than alcohol or nicotine.

▼ EXERCISE III

For your own amusement, construct your own examples of an argument from the heap and a slippery slope argument.

▼ EXERCISE IV

More seriously, discuss the following cases where drawing a sharp line can produce important moral, social, or political problems. In each case, explain why, if at all, a definite line should be drawn, and then how this line can be drawn, if at all, in a reasonable way.

(1) speed limits
(2) voting age
(3) drinking age
(4) draft age
(5) retirement age
(6) pornography
(7) sanity
(8) time period for legal abortion

Ambiguity

The idea of *vagueness* is based upon a common feature of words in our language. Many of them leave open a range of borderline cases. The notion of ambiguity is also based upon a common feature of our language. Words often have a number of different meanings. For example, *The New Merriam-Webster Pocket Dictionary* has the following entry under the word "cardinal":

Cardinal *adj.* 1: of basic importance: Chief, Main, Primary,
2: of cardinal red color
n. 1: an ecclesiastical official of the Roman Catholic Church ranking next below the Pope, 2: a bright red, 3: any of several American finches of which the male is bright red.

In the plural, "The Cardinals" is the name of an athletic team that inhabits St. Louis; "cardinal" also describes the numbers used in simple counting.

It is not likely that people would get confused about these very different meanings of the word "cardinal," but we might imagine a priest, a bird watcher, and a baseball fan all hearing the remark, "The cardinals are in town." The priest would prepare for a solemn occasion, the bird watcher would get out his binoculars, and the baseball fan would head for the stadium. *If an expression is used in such a way that it is not possible to tell which of a number of possible meanings is intended, we will say that it is used ambiguously.*

Actually, the term "ambiguous" itself seems to be ambiguous. As defined above, an expression is used ambiguously if it is obscure or unclear what meaning is intended. Using this definition, the word "bank" is not used ambiguously in the following sentence:

Joan deposited $500 in the bank and got a receipt.

Some writers, however, call an expression ambiguous simply if it admits of more than one interpretation without adding that it is not possible to tell which of a number of possible meanings is intended. With this definition, the above sentence is ambiguous because it could mean that Joan placed $500 on a river bank, and someone, for whatever reason, gave her a receipt for doing so. On this second definition of ambiguity, virtually every expression is ambiguous, since virtually every expression admits of more than one interpretation. On our first definition, only expressions that are misleading or potentially misleading will be called ambiguous. In what follows we will use the word "ambiguous" according to the first definition.

In everyday life, context usually settles which of a variety of meanings is appropriate. Yet sometimes genuine misunderstandings do arise. An American and a European discussing "football" may have different games in mind. The European is talking about what *we* call "soccer;" the American is talking about what *they* call "American football." It is characteristic of the ambiguous use of a term that when it comes to light we are likely to say something like, "Oh, you mean *that* kind of cardinal!" or "Oh, you were talking about *American* football!" In a context where the use of a word is ambiguous, we do not know *which* of two meanings to attach to a word. In a context where the use of a word is vague, we cannot attach any *clear* meaning to the use of a word.

So far we have talked about the ambiguity of terms or individual words. But sometimes we do not know which interpretation to give to a phrase or a sentence because its grammar or syntax admits of more than one interpretation. Thus, if we talk about *the conquest of the Persians*, we might be referring either to the Persians' conquering someone or to someone's conquering the Persians. Sometimes the grammar of a sentence leaves open a great many possible interpretations. For example, consider the sentence:

Only sons marry only daughters.

One thing that this might mean is that a person who is a male only child will marry a person who is a female only child. Again, it might mean that sons are the only persons who only marry daughters. Other interpretations are possible as well.[2]

The process of rewriting a sentence so that its meaning becomes

---

[2] This example comes from Paul Benacerraf.

clear is called *disambiguating* the sentence. One way of disambiguating a sentence is to rewrite it as a whole, spelling things out in detail. That's how we disambiguated the sentence "Only sons marry only daughters." Another procedure is to continue the sentence in a way that supplies a context that forces one interpretation over others. Consider the sentence: "Mary had a little lamb." Notice how the meaning changes completely under the following continuations:

(1) Mary had a little lamb; it followed her to school.
(2) Mary had a little lamb and then a little broccoli.

Just in passing, it is not altogether obvious how we should describe the ambiguity in the sentence "Mary had a little lamb." The most obvious suggestion is that the word "had" is ambiguous, meaning "owned" on the first reading and "ate" on a second reading. Notice, however, that this also forces alternative readings for the expression "a little lamb." Presumably, it was a small whole live lamb that followed Mary to school, whereas it would have been a small piece of cooked lamb that she ate. So if we try to locate the ambiguity in particular words, we must say that not only the word "had" but also the word "lamb" is being used ambiguously. This is a reasonable approach, but another is available. In everyday speech we often leave things out. Thus, instead of saying "Mary had a little *piece of meat derived from a* lamb *to eat,*" we just say "Mary had a little lamb," dropping out the italicized words on the assumption that they will be understood. In most contexts, such deletions cause no misunderstanding. But sometimes deletions are misunderstood, and this can produce ambiguity.

▼ EXERCISE V

Show that each of the following sentences admits of at least two interpretations either by rewriting the sentence as a whole in two different ways or by expanding the sentence two different ways in order to clarify the context.

    Example: Kenneth let us down.
    Rewriting: Kenneth lowered us.
              Kenneth disappointed us.
    Expanding: Kenneth let us down with a rope.
              Kenneth let us down just when we needed him.

(1) Reggie Jackson was safe at home.
(2) I don't know what state Meredith is in.
(3) Where did you get bitten?
(4) The President sent her congratulations.
(5) Visiting professors can be boring.

(6) There is some explanation for everything.

(7) Wendy ran the marathon.

(8) The meaning of the term "altering" is changing.

▼ EXERCISE VI

Perform the same exercise on the following newspaper headlines. They actually appeared in print and are collected in a marvelous book entitled *Squad Helps Dog Bite Victim.*[3]

(1) Milk Drinkers Turn to Powder

(2) Anti-busing Rider Killed by Senate

(3) Gandhi Stoned in Rally in India

(4) College Graduates Blind Senior Citizen

(5) Jumping Bean Prices Affect the Poor

(6) Tuna Biting off Washington Coast

(7) Time for Football and Meatball Stew

(8) Police Kill Man with Ax

(9) Squad Helps Dog Bite Victim

▼ EXERCISE VII

Ambiguous headlines often carry unfortunate double meanings. Rewrite each of the following sentences to correct this.[4]

> Example: Prostitutes Appeal to Pope
> Revision: Prostitutes Petition Pope

(1) Legalized Outhouses Aired by Legislature

(2) Survivor of Siamese Twins Joins Parents

(3) Judge Permits Club to Continue Sex Bar

(4) Teenage Prostitution Problem Is Mounting

Fallacies of Ambiguity. Ambiguity can cause misunderstanding. More often, it produces hilarious or embarassing side effects, and it is hard to get your arguments taken seriously if your listeners are giggling over an unintended *double entendre*. Ambiguity can also generate bad arguments that are said to involve the *fallacy of equivocation*. An argument is said to commit this fallacy when it uses the same term or larger expression in different senses in different parts of the argument. An example,

---

[3] Columbia Journalism Review Editors, *Squad Helps Dog Bite Victim & Other Flubs from the Nation's Press* (Garden City, N.Y.: Doubleday, 1980).

[4] These examples also come from *Squad Helps Dog Bite Victim.*

attributed to Bertrand Russell, illustrates this fallacy. The following is a perfectly good argument:

> (1) The Apostles were followers of Christ.
>   Paul was an Apostle.
> ∴   Paul was a follower of Christ.

The following argument, though grammatically similar, is obviously a bad argument:

> (2) The Apostles were twelve.
>   Paul was an Apostle.
> ∴   Paul was twelve.

At a superficial level, it is natural to read the conclusion as saying that Paul was *twelve years old*. But if we interpret the first premise in the same way, then the argument, though valid, is unsound—because the first premise, on this reading, is false. The Apostles, at the time they were Apostles, were not twelve years old.

There is, however, a better way of reading the argument that reveals a deeper ambiguity. The first premise obviously means that the Apostles were *twelve in number*. Using this interpretation, let's look at the argument again.

> (3) The Apostles were twelve in number.
>   Paul was an Apostle.
> ∴   Paul was twelve in number.

Having clarified the meaning of the word "twelve", we get an argument with a conclusion that is false, and, indeed, barely makes sense. What went wrong? Both premises are true, so, since the conclusion is false, the argument must be invalid. But why is it invalid? The answer lies in the correct interpretation of the second premise. To say that Paul was an Apostle means that Paul was a *member* of the Apostles. Taken this way, the argument looks like this:

> (4) The Apostles were twelve in number.
>   Paul was a member of the Apostles.
> ∴   Paul was a member of a group with twelve members.

This, of course, is a sound argument. We get a fallacy of equivocation when, as in (2) and (3), expressions in the premises and the conclusion are interpreted in different ways.

Such fallacies of equivocation do not often cause serious confusion in the common affairs of life. It is hard to imagine, for example, anyone that would be convinced that Paul was twelve (either in age or in number) by the argument given above. Nonetheless, ambiguity does cause serious confusion in other cases. It should be clear how to deal with an argument that may trade on ambiguity to produce a fallacy of equivocation: *restate the argument with sufficient clarity so that the premises and conclusion can be given only one reasonable interpretation.*

▼ EXERCISE VIII

Each of the following arguments trades on an ambiguity. For each, locate the ambiguity by showing that one or more of the statements can be interpreted in different ways.

(1) You passed no one on the road; therefore, you walked faster than no one.

(2) Everything must have a cause; therefore, something must be the cause of everything.

(3) Six is an odd number of legs for a horse, and odd numbers cannot be divided by two, so six cannot be divided by two.

(4) I have a right to buy lottery tickets. Therefore, when I buy lottery tickets, I am doing something right.

(5) If I have only one friend, then I cannot say that I have any number of friends. So one is not a number. (*From* Timothy Duggan.)

(6) "The only proof capable of being given that an object is visible is that people actually see it. The only proof that a sound is audible is that people hear it. In like manner, the sole evidence it is possible to produce that anything is desirable is that people actually desire it." (J. S. Mill in his *Utilitarianism.*)

(7) "Many people criticize my paper as a scandalous rumor mill, but we print what we do because it is in the public interest. That is obvious from our circulation and the many letters we receive. This shows how much interest the public takes in our work." (*From* Deni Elliott.)

Definitions

It is sometimes suggested that a great many disputes could be avoided if people simply took the precaution of defining their terms. To some extent this is true, but definitions will not solve all problems, and a mindless insistence upon definitions can turn a serious discussion into a semantic quibble. Furthermore, definitions themselves can be confusing or obfuscating as, for example, when an economist tells us:

I define inflation as too much money chasing too few goods.

Not only is this definition metaphorical and obscure, it also has a theory of the causes of inflation built into it.

Definitions are, of course, important, but to use them correctly we must realize that they come in various forms and can be distinguished by the purposes that they serve. There are at least five kinds of definition to be distinguished.

(1) *Lexical, or dictionary, definitions:* We consult a dictionary when we are ignorant about the meaning of a word in a particular language. Except for an occasional diagram, a dictionary explains the meaning of a word by using other words that, presumably, the reader already understands. If you do not happen to know what the words "jejune," "ketone," or "Kreis" mean, then you can look these words up in an English, a scientific, and a German dictionary respectively. Lexical definitions supply us with factual information about the standard meaning of words in a particular language. They are the most common kind of definition.

(2) *Disambiguating definitions* tell us in which sense a word is being used. (When I said that the banks were collapsing, I meant the river banks, not the financial institutions.) Disambiguating definitions tell us which lexical definition is intended in a particular context.

(3) *Stipulative definitions* are used to assign a meaning to a new (usually technical) term or to assign a new or special meaning to a familiar term. They have the following general form: "By such and such expression we will mean so and so." Thus mathematicians introduced the new term "googol" to stand for the number expressed by 1 followed by one hundred zeroes. Physicists use words like "charm," "color," and "strangeness" to stand for features of subatomic particles. Stipulative definitions do not report what a word means; they give a new word a meaning or an old word a new meaning.

(4) *Precising definitions* are used to resolve vagueness. They are used to draw a sharp (or sharper) boundary around the extension of a term which, in ordinary usage, has a fuzzy or indeterminate boundary. For example, for most purposes it is not important to decide how big a population center must be in order to count as a city rather than as a town. We can deal with the borderline cases by using such phrases as "very small city" or "quite a large town." On most occasions it will not make much difference which phrase we use. Yet it is not hard to imagine a situation in which it might make a difference whether a center of population is a city or not. As a city, it might be eligible for redevelopment funds that are not available to towns. Here a precising definition—a definition that draws a sharp boundary where none formerly existed—is essential.

Precising definitions are a combination of stipulative definitions and lexical definitions. Like stipulative definitions, they involve a decision. They are not completely arbitrary, however, since they usually conform to the generally accepted meaning of a term. It would be reasonable to define a city as any population center with more than 50,000 people. It would be unreasonable to define a city as any population center with more than 17 people. Precising definitions are also not arbitrary for another reason: they often have important effects. If redevelopment funds are to be distributed only to cities, then to define cities as having more than 50,000 people will deny those funds to smaller population centers. Consequently, we need some reason to resolve the vagueness of the term "city" in one way rather than another. We need an argument to show that one precising definition is better than the others.

(5) Finally, *systematic definitions* are introduced to give a systematic order or structure to a subject matter. For example, in mathematics, every term must be either a primitive (undefined) term or a term defined by means of these primitive terms. By a series of such definitions the terms in the theory are placed in systematic relationships with one another. In a similar way, we might try to represent family relationships using only the primitive notions of parent, male, and female. We could then construct definitions of the following kind:

> "A is the brother of B." = "A and B have the same parents and A is male."
> "A is B's grandmother." = "A is a parent of a parent of B and A is female."[5]

Things become more complicated when we try to define such notions as "second cousin once removed," yet by extending these definitions from simple to more complicated cases, our system of family relationships can be given a systematic presentation.

Formulating systematic definitions for family relationships is relatively easy, but similar activities in science and mathematics can demand genius. It often takes deep insight into a subject to see which concepts are genuinely fundamental and which are secondary and derivative. When Sir Issac Newton defined force in terms of mass and acceleration, he was not simply stating how he proposed to use certain words; he was introducing a fundamental conceptual relationship for the understanding of the physical world.

The Role of Definitions.   In the middle of discussions people often ask for definitions or even state, usually with an air of triumph, that everything depends upon the way you define your terms. We saw in the opening chapter that definitions are not always needed, and, in most cases, issues do not turn upon the way in which words are defined. When asked for a definition, it is appropriate to reply: "What sort of definition do you want, and why do you want it?" Of course, the re-

---

[5]   Notice that in these definitions an individual word is not defined in isolation; instead, a whole sentence containing the word is replaced by another whole sentence in which the defined word does not appear. Definitions of this kind are called "contextual definitions" because a context containing the word is the unit of definition. Lexical, disambiguating, stipulative, and precising definitions can also be presented in this contextual form.

quest for a definition is perfectly in order if you are using a word in a way that departs from customary usage, or using it in some special way of your own, or using a word that is too vague for the given context, or using a word in an ambiguous way. In such cases the demand for a definition represents an important move within the argument rather than a distraction from it.

▼ EXERCISE IX

1. Find the lexical definitions for the words "jejune" and "clarion."
2. Give a stipulative definition for the word "klurg." Stipulate a word to stand for the chunks of ice that form under car fenders in winter.
3. Give precising definitions for the words "book," "alcoholic beverage," "dead," and "fast." In each case, supply a context that gives your precising definition a point.
4. Give disambiguating definitions for the words "run," "pen," "game," "painting," and "fast." In each case, supply a context where your definition might avoid a confusion.
5. Using the notions of parent(s), male, and female as basic, give systematic definitions of the following family relationships:
   (a) A and B are sisters.
   (b) A is B's niece.
   (c) A is B's half brother.
   (d) A is B's cousin.
   (e) A is B's second cousin.

FALLACIES OF RELEVANCE

In a good argument we present statements that are true in order to offer support for some conclusion. One way to depart from this ideal is to state things that are certainly true, but have no bearing on the truth of the conclusion. Speaking and arguing in this way violates what Grice calls the rule of Relevance. Now we might wonder why irrelevant remarks can have any influence at all. The answer is that we generally assume that a person's remarks are relevant, for this is one of the conditions for smooth and successful conversation. That it is possible to exploit people by violating this natural assumption is shown in the following passage from *The Catcher in the Rye*.

. . . the new elevator boy was sort of on the stupid side. I told him, in this very casual voice, to take me up the Dicksteins.

He had the elevator doors all shut and all, and was all set to take me up, and then he turned around and said, "They ain't in. They're at a party on the fourteenth floor."

"That's all right," I said. "I'm supposed to wait for them. I'm their nephew."

He gave me this sort of stupid, suspicious look. "You better wait in the lobby, fella," he said.

"I'd like to—I really would," I said. "But I have a bad leg. I have to hold it in a certain position. I think I'd better sit down in the chair outside their door."

He didn't know what the hell I was talking about, so all he said was "oh" and took me up. Not bad, boy. It's funny. All you have to do is say something nobody understands and they'll do practically anything you want them to.[6]

It's clear what is going on here. When someone offers something as a reason, it is conversationally implied that there is some connection between it and the thing being argued for. In most cases the connection is obvious and there is no need to spell it out. In other cases the connection is not obvious, but in the spirit of cooperation others are willing to assume that the connection exists. In the present case, there seems to be no connection between having a bad leg and sitting in one particular chair. Why, then, doesn't the elevator operator challenge this statement? Part of the reason is that it is not easy to challenge what people say; among other things, it is not polite. But politeness doesn't seem to hold the elevator operator back; instead, he does not want to appear stupid. The person who offers a reason conversationally implies a connection, and we do not like to admit that we fail to see this connection. This combination of generosity and fear of looking stupid leads us to accept all sorts of irrelevant statements as reasons.

Fallacies of relevance are surprisingly common in everyday life. The best strategy for dealing with them is simply to cross out all irrelevant claims and then see what is left. Sometimes nothing is left. On the other hand, we should not be heavy-handed in making charges of irrelevance. Sometimes the occurrence of irrelevance is innocent; good arguments often contain irrelevant asides. More importantly, relevance is often secured by way of a conversational implication, so we really have to know what is going on in a given context to decide whether a remark is relevant or not. We can illustrate this last point by examining two kinds of arguments that often involve fallacies of irrelevance: *arguments ad hominem* and *appeals to authority*.

Arguments ad Hominem

Literally, an *argument ad hominem* is an argument directed against the person arguing rather than against the argument itself. On the face of it, this seems to involve irrelevance, for the character of the person

---

[6] J. D. Salinger, *The Catcher in the Rye* (New York: Bantam Books), pp. 157–58.

should have nothing to do with the truth of what she says or the soundness of her argument. But consider a case in point, the following exchange:

A: It is time for the United States to develop more normal relations with Cuba.

B: Yeah, so you can make a bundle importing cigars from those Commies.

B's reply is certainly an ad hominem attack; it is an attack upon the motives of the speaker and not upon what the speaker has said. Yet the remark is not without some relevance—it is not off the wall. In a conversational exchange, we rely on the integrity of the person who is speaking, and when we have reasons to believe that the person's integrity is questionable, we sometimes say so. This is the significance of B's remark. She points to a fact that gives some reason not to trust A's integrity in a discussion of United States relations with Cuba. We will therefore have to draw a distinction between an ad hominem *attack* and an ad hominem *fallacy*. In the context of an argument, we sometimes challenge a person's *right* to perform certain speech acts. We will call this an *ad hominem attack*. On the other hand, an attack of this kind is sometimes illicitly turned into an attack on the *truth* of what a person says or on the *soundness* of what that person argues. We then have an instance of an *ad hominem fallacy*. In an ad hominem fallacy, irrelevant, though perhaps true, statements about the arguer are improperly used to attack the argument itself. This is a fallacy, for, in general, the truth of a statement or the soundness of an argument does not depend upon the character of the person arguing.

To return to the previous example, suppose that A actually produces a very strong argument in favor of the conclusion that the United States should develop more normal relations with Cuba, and B again replies: "Yeah, so you can make a bundle importing cigars from those Commies." It is entirely possible that A will make a great deal of money importing cigars if relations are normalized. This may even be why he has adopted the position he has. If so, B's ad hominem attack on A may be well founded. On the other hand, if this attack on A's character is used as a reason for rejecting the argument itself or its conclusion, then we have an ad hominem fallacy.

One mark of an ad hominem fallacy is that the personal attack may have nothing to do with the matter at hand. A person's physical appearance, ethnic background, sex, bathing habits, or dress may sometimes give us reason to challenge the soundness of that person's argument, but usually they do not. Ad hominem fallacies deal almost exclusively in such matters.

▼ EXERCISE X

Explain the point of each of the following remarks, and specify exactly which argument or position is being criticized. Then decide whether or not each remark involves an ad hominem fallacy.

(1) After an economist predicts an upturn in the economy, someone responds, "If you're so smart, why ain't you rich?"

(2) After Congress passes a military draft, critics respond, "If members of Congress were eligible for the draft, they would not vote for it."

(3) Rejecting atheism, someone remarks, "There are no atheists in foxholes."

(4) Attacking people who defend abortion, Ronald Reagan said, "I've noticed that everybody that is for abortion has already been born."

(5) Attacking male opponents of abortion, someone says, "Men have no right to say anything about abortion."

(6) Joshua is dishonest, so you can't trust a thing he says.

▼ DISCUSSION QUESTIONS

1. In the biblical story of Job, Job is described as a person who "was blameless and upright, one who feared God and turned away from evil." Satan challenges God to allow him to subject Job to the worst calamities to see whether Job's faith will remain unchanged. After the most extreme misfortunes, Job finally cries out and asks why he should be made to suffer so.

   > Then the Lord answered Job out of the whirlwind:
   > Who is this that darkens counsel by words without knowledge?
   > Gird up your loins like a man.
   > I will question you, and you shall declare to me.
   > Where were you when I laid the foundations of the earth?
   > Tell me, if you have understanding.

   Does God's response to Job involve an ad hominem fallacy?

2. In a heated discussion people will sometimes ask an opponent "Why are you being so defensive?" This is obviously a rhetorical question. What is the point of this question? Does it implicitly involve an ad hominem fallacy?

Appeals to Authority

Often in the midst of an argument we cite an authority to back up what we say. As we saw in Chapter 2, this is a standard way of offering assurances. In citing an authority, instead of giving reasons for what we say, we indicate that someone (the authority cited) could give them. Although logicians sometimes speak of the *fallacy* of appealing to authorities, we should notice in the first place that there is often nothing wrong with citing authorities or experts to support what we say. An authority is a person or institution with a privileged position concerning certain information. Through training, a doctor is an expert on certain diseases. A person who works in the Department of Agriculture can be an expert on America's soybean production. Someone who grew up in the swamps might be an expert on trapping muskrats. Since some people stand in a better position to know things than others, there is nothing wrong with citing them as authorities. In fact, an appeal to experts and authorities is essential if we are to make up our minds on subjects outside our own range of competence.

At the same time, appeals to authority can be abused, and there are some obvious questions we should ask whenever such an appeal is made. Most obviously, we should always ask *whether the person cited is, in fact, an authority in the area under discussion.* If an answer to this question is no, then we are dealing with a fallacy of *relevance.* For example, being a movie star does not qualify a person to speak on the merits of a particular brand of toothpaste. Endorsements by athletes of hair creams, deodorants, beer, and automobiles are in the same boat. Of course, we have to be careful in making this charge. It is possible that certain athletes make systematic studies of deodorants before giving one deodorant their endorsement. But it is not likely.

Of course, most people realize that athletes, movie stars, and the like are featured in advertisements primarily to attract attention and not because they are experts concerning the products they are endorsing. It is more surprising how often the wrong authorities are brought in to judge serious matters. To cite one example, Uri Geller had little difficulty in convincing a group of distinguished British scientists that he possessed psychic powers. In particular, he was able to convince them that he could bend spoons by mental powers alone. In contrast, James Randi, a professional magician, had little difficulty in detecting and duplicating the tricks that bamboozled the scientific observers. The remarkable feature of this case was not that a group of scientists could be fooled by a magician, but rather that these scientists assumed that they had the expertise necessary to decide whether a paranormal phenomenon had taken place or not. After all, the most obvious explanation of Geller's feats was that he had somehow cheated. To test this possibility, what was needed, as it turned out, was not a scientist with impeccable scholarly credentials, but a magician who could do the same tricks himself and therefore knew what to look for.[7]

It is, of course, difficult to decide whether someone is an expert in a field when you yourself are not. There are, however, certain clues

---

[7] For an entertaining and instructive account of this case, *see* James Randi's *The Magic of Uri Geller* (New York: Ballantine Books, 1975).

that will help you make this decision. If the supposed authority claims to have knowledge of things that he or she could not possibly possess—for example, about private conversations the person could not have heard, then you have very little reason to trust other things that person has to say. You know that he or she has no qualms about making things up. Furthermore, it is often possible to spot-check certain claims to make sure that they are correct. It may take one expert to tell another, but it often takes little more than good common sense and an unwillingness to be fooled to detect a fraud.

Even in those cases where it is clear that the person cited is an expert in the field, we can still ask *whether the question is of the kind that can now be settled by an appeal to experts.* It is important to raise this question, because authorities often disagree, and since they disagree, some of them must be wrong. In fact, sometimes the very best experts simply get things wrong. For example, in 1932 Albert Einstein, who was surely an expert in the field, declared that "there is not the slightest indication that (nuclear) energy will ever be obtainable. It would mean that the atom would have to be shattered at will." Just a year later, the atom was, in fact, split. Even so, a leading British physicist, Lord Ernest Rutherford, insisted that the splitting of the atom would not lead to the development of nuclear power, saying, "The energy produced by the atom is a very poor kind of thing. Anyone who expects a source of power from the transformation of these atoms is talking moonshine."[8] Given the knowledge available at the time, both Einstein and Rutherford may have been justified in their claims, but their assertions were, after all, more speculations than scientifically justified statements of fact. The lesson to be learned from this is that the very best experts are sometimes fallible, and become more fallible when they go beyond established facts in their discipline to speculate about the future.

Although this may seem obvious, we often forget to ask *whether the authority has been cited correctly.* When a person cites an authority, he or she is making a factual claim that so-and-so holds some particular view. Sometimes the claim is false. Here is an example:

> According to medical authorities, poison ivy is contagious when it is oozing.

If someone told you this, you would probably believe it. In fact, the citation is incorrect. According to medical authorities, poison ivy is never

---

[8] Both quotations are cited in *The Experts Speak,* by Christopher Cerf and Victor Navasky (New York: Pantheon Books, 1984), p. 215. This work contains a marvelous collection of false, and sometimes just plain stupid, things that have been claimed by experts. One notable example is the remark made by the Union general John B. Sedgwick just before being fatally shot in the head by a Confederate marksman: "They couldn't hit an elephant at this dist—" (cited on p. 135).

contagious. Yet many people hold that it is contagious, and they think that they have medical opinion on their side. It is hard to deal with people who cite authorities incorrectly, for we do not carry an almanac or encyclopedia around with us. Yet, again, it is a good idea to spot-check appeals to authority, for, short of lying, people often twist authorities to support their own opinions.

It is also worth asking *whether the authority cited can be trusted to tell the truth*. To put this more bluntly, we should ask whether a particular authority has any good reason to lie or misrepresent facts. Presumably, the officials who know most about Russian food production will be the heads of the various agricultural bureaus. But it would be utterly naïve to take their reports at face value. Failures in agricultural production have been a standing embarrassment of the Russian economy, and, as a consequence, there is pressure at every level to make things look as good as possible. Even if the state officials were inclined to tell the truth, which is a charitable assumption, the information they receive is probably not very accurate.

Experts also lie because it can bring fame and professional advancement. Science, sometimes at the very highest level, has been embarrassed by problems of the falsification and misrepresentation of data. Consider the case of Sir Cyril Burt. Burt's research concerned the inheritance of intelligence. More specifically, he wanted to show that there is a significant correlation between the intelligence quotients (IQs) of parents and their children. The difficulty was to find a way to screen out other influences—for example, that of home environment. To overcome this, Burt undertook a systematic study of identical twins who had been separated at birth and raised in various social settings. His study revealed a very high correlation between the IQs of these twins and that gave strong reason to believe that IQ, to some significant extent, depends on heredity rather than environment. Unfortunately, Burt's data, or at least a significantly large portion of it, were cooked—that is, made up.

It is interesting that Burt's bogus research could go unchallenged for so long. It is also interesting how he was finally unmasked. First of all, his results seemed to many to be too good to be true. He claimed to have found more than 50 identical twins who had been separated at birth and raised in contrasting environments. Given the rarity of such twins, that's a very large number to have found. Secondly, the correlations he claimed to find were extremely high, indeed, much higher than usually found in research in this area. Both of these facts raised suspicions. Stephen Jay Gould describes Burt's final undoing as follows:

Princeton psychologist Leon Kamin first noted that, while Burt had increased his sample of twins from fewer than twenty to more than fifty in a series of publications, the average correlation between pairs for IQ remained unchanged to the third decimal place—a statistical situation so unlikely that it matches our vernacular definition of impossible. Then, in 1976, Oliver Gillie, medical correspondent of the London *Sunday Times*, elevated the charge from inexcusable carelessness to conscious fakery. Gillie discovered among many other things, that Burt's two "collaborators" . . . the women who supposedly collected and processed his data, either never existed at all, or at least could not have been in contact with Burt while he wrote the papers bearing their names.[9]

Outright fraud of this kind, especially by someone so highly placed, is, admittedly, uncommon. Yet it does occur, and provides a good reason for being suspicious of authorities, especially when their results have not been given independent confirmation.

One last question we can ask is *why the appeal to authority is being made at all?* To cite an authority is to give assurances and, as we noticed earlier, we usually give assurances to strengthen the weak points in our arguments. It is surprising how often we can see what is wrong with an argument just by noticing where it is backed by appeals to authority. Beyond this, we should be suspicious of arguments that rely on too many authorities. (We might call this the fallacy of excessive footnotes.) Good arguments tend to stand on their own.

To go back to the beginning, reliance on experts and authorities is unavoidable in our complicated and specialized world. Yet we can still be critical of appeals to authority by asking these questions:

(1) Is the authority cited in fact an authority in the area under discussion?
(2) Is this the kind of question that can now be settled by expert opinion?
(3) Has the authority been cited correctly?
(4) Can the authority cited be trusted to tell the truth?
(5) Why is an appeal to authority being made at all?

▼ EXERCISE XI

Answer the five questions in the text about each of the following appeals to authority, and decide whether each argument is legitimate or fallacious.

(1) Ben and Jerry's ice cream must be the best, because Fat Fred eats it all the time, and he says it's great.
(2) My friend Joe says this movie is hilarious, so it must be worth watching.

---

9 Stephen Jay Gould, *The Mismeasure of Man* (New York: W. W. Norton, 1981), p. 234.

(3) Michael Jordan says that Air Jordan sneakers are springier, so they must be springier.

(4) The surgeon general says that smoking is hazardous to your health, so it is.

(5) The surgeon general says that abortion is immoral, so it is.

(6) True Christians ought to give away all of their money, because the Bible says, "Blessed are the poor."

FALLACIES OF VACUITY

Circular Reasoning and Begging the Question

One purpose of arguments is to establish the truth of a claim to someone who doubts it. In a typical situation, A makes a claim, B raises objections to it, then A tries to find reasons justifying the original statement. Schematically:

A asserts that p is true.
B raises objections $x, y,$ and z against it.
A then offers reasons to overcome these objections.

To start with the simplest case, A cannot meet B's challenge simply by repeating the original assertion. If someone is maintaining that arms races inevitably leads to war, it will not help to offer as a justification for this the very claim that arms races inevitably lead to war. Here the person is using a statement as both a conclusion and a premise for that conclusion. This is called *circular reasoning*. The argument would look like this:

Arms races inevitably lead to war.
∴ Arms races inevitably lead to war.

The argument is, of course, *valid*, since the premise cannot be true without the conclusion being true as well. Furthermore, if the premise is true, then the argument is *sound* as well. All the same, the argument has no force in this conversational setting because any objection that B has to the conclusion is straight off an objection to the premise, since they are identical.

In fact, people do not usually commit the fallacy of circular reasoning in such a transparent way. Often circular reasoning is disguised by restating the conclusion in different words. Furthermore, a statement may first be put forward as a conclusion to be proved, and then only much later used as a premise in its own behalf. In a complex argument this is sometimes very difficult to detect.

Closely related to the fallacy of circular reasoning is the subtle fallacy called *begging the question*. In circular reasoning, the same statement (or an equivalent of it) appears in an argument both as a conclusion and as a premise in its own behalf. In begging the question, a premise is used that *presupposes* or *depends* upon the point at issue. We can think of begging the question as a less transparent form of circular reasoning. The following argument begs the question:

> It's always wrong to murder human beings.
> Capital punishment involves murdering human beings.

∴ Capital punishment is wrong.

Here the first premise is definitionally true, since calling something murder implies that it is a wrongful killing. The second premise is, however, question begging, for in calling capital punishment murder, the point at issue has been assumed, that is, that capital punishment is something wrong.

More subtle than this, opponents of abortion typically refer to the *human fetus* as an *unborn baby* or simply as a *baby*. It may seem a matter of indifference how the fetus is referred to, but this is not true. One of the central points in the debate over abortion is whether the fetus has the status of a person and thus has the rights that a person has. It is generally acknowledged in our society that babies are persons and therefore have the rights of persons. By referring to the fetus as an unborn baby (or simply as a baby), a point that demands argument is taken for granted without argument, and that counts as begging the question. Of course, many opponents of abortion argue for the claim that a human fetus has the moral status of a person and thus do not beg this central question in the debate. But if they give no independent argument, then they do beg the question.

Similarly, if someone argues the pro-choice position simply on the grounds that a woman has a right to control the destiny of her own body, this also begs an important question, because it takes for granted the claim that the fetus is part of a woman's body and not an independent being with rights of its own. Of course, defenders of the pro-choice position need not beg the question in this way, but they often do.

Although the notion of circular reasoning can be defined quite precisely—the conclusion (or its equivalent) is used as a premise in its own behalf—the idea of begging the question is more elusive. Whether a particular claim is question begging will depend upon the context in which it appears. An argument is question begging if it relies, either explicitly or implicitly, on things which, in the argumentative context, are matters of dispute. Thus referring to a human fetus as a baby will be question begging in contexts in which the moral status of the fetus is at issue, but it may not be question begging when this is not an issue.

▼ EXERCISE XII

Explain how each of the following remarks could involve either circular reasoning or begging the question. Your analysis can change depending upon the kind of context you imagine.

(1) Capitalism is the only correct economic system, because without it free enterprise is impossible.

(2) Gun control laws are wrong, because they violate the citizen's right to bear arms.

(3) Intoxicating beverages should be banned, because they can make people drunk.

(4) The Bible is the inerrant word of God, because God speaks only the truth, and because repeatedly in the Bible God tells us that the Bible consists of His words.

(5) We have to accept change, because without change there is no progress.

(6) Premarital sex is wrong, because premarital sex is fornication, and fornication is a sin.

(7) The drinking age should be lowered to eighteen, because eighteen-year-olds are mature enough to drink.

(8) College athletes should be paid to play sports, because they are professionals anyway.

Self-Sealers and Vacuity

It is characteristic of certain positions that no evidence can *possibly* refute them. This may seem like a wonderful feature for a position to have. In fact, however, it *usually* makes the position useless. We can start with a silly example. A Perfect Sage claims to be able to predict the future in detail. The Perfect Sage's predictions take the following form:

Two weeks from today at 4:37 you are going to be doing *exactly* what you will be doing.

Of course, whatever you are doing at that time will be exactly what you are doing, so this prediction cannot possibly be wrong. But, of course, it doesn't tell us anything in particular about the future. *Whatever* happens, the prediction is going to be true, and this is just what is wrong with it. The prediction is *empty* or *vacuous*.

People do not, of course, go around making predictions of the kind just noticed, but they do sometimes hold positions that are empty or vacuous in just the same way. A clairvoyant claims to be able to predict the future, but every time a prediction fails, he says that this just proves that someone set up bad vibrations that interfered with his visions. So if the prediction turns out to be true, he claims that this shows his clairvoyance; if it does turn out to be false, he cites this as evidence of interference. No matter what happens, then, the clairvoyant's claim to be clairvoyant cannot be refuted. His claim to clairvoyance is as empty and vacuous as Perfect Sage's prediction.

Positions that are set up in this way so that nothing can possibly refute them we will call *self-sealers*.[10] A self-sealing position is one that is so constructed that no evidence can possibly be brought against it no matter what happens. This shows its vacuity, and it is precisely for this reason that we reject it.

People do not usually hold self-sealing positions in a blatant way; they tend to back into them. A person who holds that the American economy is controlled by an international Jewish conspiracy will point out people of Jewish extraction (or with Jewish names) who occupy important positions in financial institutions. This at least counts as evidence, though not very strong evidence. There are a great many people in these institutions who are not Jews. To counter this claim, the person now argues that many of these other people are secretly Jews or are tools of the Jewish conspiracy. The Jews have allowed some non-Jews to hold important positions to conceal their conspiracy. What evidence is there for this? Well, really none, but that only helps to prove how clever the Jewish conspiracy is. At this point, the position has become self-sealing, for all evidence cited against the existence of the conspiracy will be converted into evidence *for* its cleverness.

Self-sealing arguments are hard to deal with, for people who use them will often shift their ground. A person will begin by holding a significant position that implies that facts are one way rather than another, but under the pressure of criticism will self-seal the position so that no evidence can possibly count against it. That is, the person will slide back and forth between two positions: one that is not self-sealed, and so is significant, but subject to refutation, and another that is self-sealed, and so is not subject to criticism, but is insignificant. The charge that is leveled against a theory that vacillates in this way is that it is either *vacuous* or *false*. It is vacuous if self-sealing, false if not.

One way of challenging a self-sealing position is to ask what possible fact could prove it wrong. This is a good question to ask, but it can be misunderstood and met with the triumphant reply: "Nothing can prove my position wrong, because it is right." A better way to show the insignificance of a self-sealing theory is to put the challenge in a different form: "If your position has any significance, it should tell us that certain things will occur whereas certain other things will not

---

[10]   We owe this phrase to Ted Honderich, who owes it, directly or indirectly, to Leon Lipson.

occur. If it cannot do this, it really tells us nothing at all; so please make some specific predictions and we will see how they come out."

Ideologies and world views tend to be self-sealing. The Marxist ideology sometimes has this quality. If you fail to see the truth of the Marxist ideology, that just shows that your social consciousness has not been raised. The very fact that you reject the Marxist ideology shows that you are not yet capable of understanding it and that you are in need of reeducation. This is perfect self-sealing. Sometimes psychoanalytic theory gets involved in this same kind of self-sealing. People who vigorously disagree with certain psychoanalytic claims can be accused of repressing these facts. If a boy denies that he wants to murder his father and sleep with his mother, this itself can be taken as evidence of the strength of these desires and of his unwillingness to acknowledge them. If this kind of reasoning gets out of hand, then psychoanalytic theory also becomes self-sealing and empty. Freud was aware of this danger and warned against it.

So far, we have seen two ways in which an argument can be self-sealing: (1) it can invent an *ad hoc* or arbitrary way of dismissing every possible criticism. The clairvoyant can always point to interfering conditions without going to the trouble of saying what they are. The anti-Semite can always cite Jewish cleverness to explain away counterevidence. (2) A theory can counter criticism by attacking its critics. The critic of Marxism is charged with having a decadent bourgeois consciousness which blinds him to the facts of class conflict. The critic's response to psychoanalytic theory is analyzed (and then dismissed) as repression, a reaction formation, or something or other. Here self-sealing is achieved through an ad hominem fallacy.

Yet another form of self-sealing is this: (3) words are used in such a way that a position becomes true *by definition.* For example, a person makes the strong claim that all human actions are selfish. This is an interesting remark, but it seems to be false, for it is easy to think of cases where people have acted in self-sacrificing ways. To counter these obvious objections, the argument takes the following turn: When a person acts in a self-sacrificing way, what that person *wants* to do is help another even at his own expense. This is his desire or motive, and that is what he acts to fulfill. So the action is selfish after all, since the person is acting to achieve what he wants. It should be obvious that this is a self-sealing move, for it will not help to cite any possible behavior—even heroic self-destructive behavior—as counterevidence.

It is not hard to see what has happened in this case. The arguer has chosen to use the word "selfish" in a new and peculiar way: a person is said to act selfishly if he acts to do what he desires to do. This is not what we usually mean by this word. We say that a person acts selfishly if he is too much concerned with his own interests at the expense of the interests of others. On this standard use of the word "selfish" there are any number of counterexamples to the claim that all human actions are selfish. But these counterexamples do not apply when the word "selfish" is used in a new way, where "acting selfishly" comes close to meaning just "acting." The point is that under this new meaning of "selfish" it becomes empty (or almost empty) to say that all human actions are selfish. We are thus back to a familiar situation: Under one interpretation (the ordinary interpretation), the claim that all human actions are selfish is interesting but false. Under another interpretation (an extraordinary interpretation), the claim is true but uninteresting. The position gets all its *apparent* interest and plausibility from a rapid two-step back and forth between these positions.

Self-sealing arguments are not easy to handle, for they change their form under pressure. The best strategy is to begin by charging a person who uses such an argument with saying something trivial, vacuous, or boring. If, to meet this charge, he or she says something quite specific and important, then argument can proceed along normal lines. But it is not always easy to get down to brass tacks in this way. This becomes clear if you examine an argument between a Marxist and an anti-Marxist, or between individuals with different religious views. Their positions are sealed against objections from each other, and the arguments are almost always at cross purposes.   .

▼ DISCUSSION QUESTIONS

(1) During the nineteenth century evidence mounted that apparently showed that the earth has existed for millions, perhaps hundreds of millions, of years. This seemed to contradict the account given in Genesis that holds that the earth was created less than 10,000 years ago. In response to this challenge, Philip Henry Gosse replied roughly as follows: In creating Adam and Eve, God would endow them with a navel, and thus it would seem that they had been born in the normal way and thus also seem that they had existed for a number of years before they were created by God. Beyond this, their hair, fingernails, bones, and so on would all show evidence of growth, again giving evidence of previous existence. The same would be true of the trees that surrounded them in the Garden of Eden which would have rings. Furthermore, the sediment in rivers would suggest that they had flowed for many years in the past. In sum, although the earth was created fairly recently, God would have created it in a way that would make it appear that it had existed for many years, perhaps millions of years, in the past. Thus, the actual creation of the earth less than 10,000

years ago is compatible with scientific evidence that suggests that it is much older than this. Evaluate this line of reasoning.

(2) Is Darwin's theory of evolution self-sealing because it depends on the principle of the survival of the fittest?

_____

6

Other Uses of Arguments

In earlier chapters we have spoken about arguments as if their only function was to prove something or to justify some claim. This chapter will attempt to correct this one-sided view by exploring uses of argument other than justification. Sometimes the primary intention of an argument is not to establish some truth but to *refute* an argument. The patterns of successful refutations mirror the criteria for a sound and significant argument, for the point of a refutory argument is to show that one of these criteria has not been met. Another important use of arguments is to formulate *explanations*. In seeking an explanation, we are not trying to prove that something is true; we are trying to understand *why* it is true. One way of making sense out of a perplexing event is to present an argument that shows how the occurrence of that event in particular circumstances can be derived from general principles. Scientific explanations often take this form. Finally, the chapter considers excuses, treating them as a special kind of explanation, namely as an explanation of conduct intended to put it in a better light. As we shall see, these different uses of argument have distinctive criteria of adequacy, and we will examine them in detail.

REFUTATIONS

To refute an argument is to show that it is no good. Some writers, however, have incorrectly used this term to mean something much weaker. They say such things as that Colonel North refuted the charges brought against him, meaning nothing more by this than that he rejected them, rebutted them, or attacked them. This, however, is not what the word "refute" means. To refute the charges brought against him, Colonel North would have to *prove* that these charges were erroneous. Refuting a charge requires using an argument against it. This takes a lot more work than simply denying it.

Nonetheless, it is important to remember that we can refute an *argument* without proving that its conclusion is false. A refutation of an argument is sufficient if it raises objections that cannot be answered and that show why the argument does not adequately establish its conclusion.

For deductive arguments, refutations take two main forms: (1) we can show that the conclusion does not follow from the premises,[1] and (2) we can argue that some of the premises are dubious or even false.[2] We will discuss these two methods of refutation in turn.

That's Just Like Arguing . . .

We know that an argument is no good if it starts from true premises and leads to a false conclusion. Often, however, we cannot point this out to refute an argument because the truth or falsity of the conclusion is the very thing at issue. Here a typical device is to point out that by arguing in the same way, we *can* get a result that is unsatisfactory. A wonderfully simple example of this style of argument occurred in the English Parliamentary debate on capital punishment. One member of Parliament was defending the death penalty on the grounds that the alternative, life in prison, was much more cruel. He was met with the following reply: On this principle, those found guilty of first-degree murder ought to be given life in prison and the death penalty should be given to those who commit some lesser offense. Notice that the reply is not decisive as it stands. The first speaker could go on to call for the abolition of life imprisonment and then keep the death penalty as the most severe punishment. Alternatively, he could simply *accept*

---

[1] To refute an inductive argument, it is not enough to show that it is not valid. You need to show that the argument is weak by inductive standards. We will discuss inductive arguments and their standards in Chapter 9.

[2] Some arguments cannot be refuted in either of these ways but can still be refuted by showing that they commit another fallacy. For example, some circular arguments are sound, but they are no good because they are circular. Fallacies were discussed in Chapter 5.

the idea that life imprisonment—not the death penalty—is the most severe penalty and apply it to first-degree murder. In point of fact, however, the first speaker was certainly unwilling to accept either of these alternatives. He simply tried a rhetorical trick and got caught.

Refuting an argument by showing that it is *just like another* argument that is obviously no good is a common device in everyday discussions. Here is another example:

A: If I had a higher salary, I could buy more things, so if everyone had higher salaries, everyone could buy more things.

B: That's just like arguing that if one person stands up at a ball game he will get a better view, so if everyone stands up, everyone will get a better view.

At first sight, it may not be obvious whether A's style of reasoning is valid or not. B's response shows that it is invalid by providing an instance where the same style of reasoning takes us from something true to something false. This, then, is the general method for showing that an argument is invalid: give an example of an argument with the same basic form where the inference clearly takes us from something true to

something false. Admittedly, this procedure is not precise, for we have given no explanation of the notion that two arguments have the *same basic form*. (This topic will be discussed more carefully in Chapters 7 and 8.) Yet it remains a fact that people can often see that two arguments have the same basic form and, through seeing this, decide that an argument presented to them is invalid. This ability is the basis of sound logical judgment. It is also the basis of wit. It's at best mildly funny to say that if God had wanted us to fly, he would have given us wings. You have to be fairly clever to reply at once: "If God had wanted us to stay on the ground, he would have given us roots."

▼ EXERCISE I

For each of the following arguments, find another with the same basic form where the premise or premises are true and the conclusion is false.

(1) If tea is dangerous, so is coffee.

   Tea isn't dangerous, so coffee isn't either.
(2) If a country becomes wealthy, then its people become wealthy as well.
(3) You cannot pass a law against dangerous drugs because there is no way of drawing a sharp line between dangerous and nondangerous drugs.
(4) If you have never written a novel, then you are in no position to make judgments about novels.
(5) If a person has nothing to hide, he or she should not object to being investigated.
(6) Women are the natural persons to raise children, because they are the ones who give them birth.
(7) Radicals should not be granted freedom of speech, because they deny this freedom to others.
(8) Since everyone acts from his or her own motives, everyone's actions are selfish.
(9) Why not smoke? The longer you smoke the longer you live.

Counterexamples

The second main way to attack an argument is to challenge the truth of one of its premises. We can argue that there is no good reason to accept a particular premise as true, asking, for example, "How do you know that?" or, more strongly, we can argue that the premise is actually false. In this second case, we refute an argument by refuting one of its premises.

As an example of this second method of refutation, we can examine St. Augustine's attack on astrology. For centuries many people have believed in astrology. They have believed, that is, that their lives are determined to a significant extent by the configuration of the stars at the time of their birth. As evidence for this, astrologers often point out successful predictions that they have made in the past. St. Augustine presented a beautiful refutation of this argument in his *Confessions*. St. Augustine tells us that he was captivated by astrology until his conversion to Christianity. He then abandoned it, he says, for the following reason:

> I turned my attention to the case of twins, who are generally born within a short time of each other. Whatever significance in the natural order the astrologers may attribute to this interval of time, it is too short to be appreciated by human observation and no allowance can be made for it in the charts which an astrologer has to consult in order to cast a true horoscope. His predictions, then, will not be true, because he would have consulted the same charts for both Esau and Jacob and would have made the same predictions for each of them, whereas it is a fact that the same things did not happen to them both. Therefore, either he would have been wrong in his predictions or, if his forecast was correct, he would not have predicted the same future for each. And yet he would have consulted the same chart in each case. This proves

that if he had foretold the truth, it would have been by luck, not by skill.[3]

The central move in St. Augustine's attack upon astrologers' defense of their profession is to challenge a key premise of their argument. In particular, he produces what is called a *counterexample* to the claim that the position of the stars at the time of birth determines the kind of life a person will lead thereafter. By citing the very different lives that twins have led, he offers a counterexample to this claimed connection.

Counterexamples are typically aimed at universal claims. This is true because a *single* contrary instance will show that a universal claim is false. If someone claims that *all* snakes lay eggs, then pointing out that the black snake bears its young alive is sufficient to refute this claim. If the person retreats to the somewhat weaker claim that *most* snakes lay eggs, the guarding term makes it much harder to refute the claim. A single example of a snake that bears its young alive is not enough; to refute this claim, we would have to show that a majority of snakes do not lay eggs. Here, instead of trying to refute his statement, we may ask him to produce his *argument* in behalf of it. We can then attack this argument. Finally, if the person retreats to the very weak claim that at least some snakes lay eggs, then his statement becomes very difficult to refute. Even if it were false (which it is not), to show this we would have to check every fool snake and establish that it does not lay eggs. So, as a rough-and-ready rule, we can say that the stronger a statement is, the more subject it is to refutation; the weaker it is, the less subject it is to refutation.

Citing the fact that black snakes bear their young alive to refute the claim that all snakes lay eggs is called presenting a *counterexample*. The pattern of reasoning is perfectly simple: If someone claims that *everything* of a certain kind has a certain feature, we need find only *one* thing of that kind lacking that feature to refute the claim. Although the pattern of argument is simple in form, it is not always easy to think of counterexamples. Some people are much better at it than others. Socrates was a genius in this respect. He wandered through the streets of ancient Athens questioning various people—often important political figures—challenging them to explain what they meant by various terms such as *justice, knowledge, courage, friendship,* and *piety.* As narrated by Plato, these exchanges all fall into a standard pattern: Socrates asks for a definition of some important notion; after some skirmishing, a definition is offered; Socrates immediately finds a counterexample to this definition; the definition is then changed or replaced by another; once

---

[3] St. Augustine, *Confessions,* R. S. Pine-Coffin, trans. (Harmondsworth, England: Penguin Books, 1961), p. 142.

more Socrates produces a counterexample; and so on. With effortless ease, Socrates seemed able to produce counterexamples to any definition or any principle that others offered. There is no better introduction to the art of giving counterexamples than a specimen of the Socratic method.

Theaetetus was a brilliant young man, gifted in mathematics. In the dialogue that bears his name, Theaetetus and Socrates try (unsuccessfully) to arrive at a correct definition of *knowledge*. They notice an important difference between knowledge and mere belief: It is possible for someone to *believe* something that is false, but it is not possible for someone to *know* something that is false. This leads Theaetetus to suggest a simple definition of knowledge: Knowledge equals true belief. After all, someone cannot have a true belief concerning something that is false. This proposed definition is refuted in the following exchange:

> *Socrates:* [There is] a whole profession to prove that true belief is not knowledge.
> *Theaetetus:* How so? What profession?
> *Socrates:* The profession of those paragons of intellect known as orators and lawyers. There you have men who use their skill to produce conviction, not by instruction, but by making people believe whatever they want them to believe. You can hardly imagine teachers so clever as to be able, in the short time allowed by the clock, to instruct their hearers thoroughly in the true facts of a case of robbery or other violence which those hearers had not witnessed.
> *Theaetetus:* No, I cannot imagine that; but they can convince them.
> *Socrates:* And by convincing you mean making them believe something.
> *Theaetetus:* Of course.
> *Socrates:* And when a jury is rightly convinced of facts which can be known only by an eye-witness, then, judging by hearsay and accepting a true belief, they are judging without knowledge, although, if they find the right verdict, their conviction is correct?
> *Theaetetus:* Certainly.
> *Socrates:* But if true belief and knowledge were the same thing, the best of jurymen could never have a correct belief without knowledge. It now appears that they must be different things.[4]

One thing to notice about this counterexample is that it is *completely decisive* in the sense that no adequate response is available. Theaetetus does not dig in his heels and insist that the ignorant members of the jury do know that the person is innocent provided only that they believe it and it is true. Faced with the counterexample, he retreats at once. Why is this? Why not stay with the definition and reject the counterexample as false? The answer is that for many concepts there is

---

[4] Plato, *Theaetetus*, Francis M. Cornford, trans., in his *Plato's Theory of Knowledge* (New York: Liberal Arts Press, 1957), p. 141.

general agreement about their application to particular cases, even if there is no general agreement about a correct definition. To take an extreme example, everyone agrees that Hitler was a dictator (even Hitler), and no one supposes that Thomas Jefferson was a dictator (even his enemies). So any definition of *a dictator* that would lead us to say that Hitler was not a dictator and Thomas Jefferson was a dictator must be wrong. A less extreme example is the notion of negligence—an idea important in the law. We have some perfectly clear cases of negligence: a person amusing himself by setting off skyrockets in the Sistine Chapel, for example. On the other hand, a person who deliberately drives off a road to avoid striking a child is clearly *not* acting negligently. In between these clear cases there are any number of difficult ones that help give lawyers a living. Because of these borderline cases, no perfectly exact definition of negligence is possible. But any definition of negligence that does not square with the clear cases is just plain wrong, and this can be shown by citing one of these clear cases as a counterexample.

Ethics is an area where arguments often turn upon counterexamples. Although various forms of relativity remain fashionable, in our day-to-day life there is a surprisingly wide range of agreement concerning what actions are right and what actions are wrong. That is, whatever theory we might hold, we usually agree about particular cases. We tend not to notice this agreement because disagreement is interesting and exciting, whereas agreement is not. The task of an ethical theory is to discover those principles which tell us what actions are right and what actions are wrong. One important test of an ethical theory is whether it squares with these clear cases where agreement exists.

Consider the Utilitarian Principle. According to that principle, an action is right if it is the action that will produce the greatest possible total happiness. Admittedly, the idea of happiness is vague and stands in need of explanation. For this discussion, however, we can ignore this complication. At first sight, this principle has much to recommend it. How, we might ask, could it ever be better to act in a way that produces less happiness than would be produced by acting in another way? Furthermore, the world would be a much better place if people uniformly followed this principle. All the same, the Utilitarian Principle is subject to a counterexample that has led most—though not all—philosophers to reject it as the *single* basic principle of ethics. One version of this counterexample goes as follows: It is certainly possible for a society to exist where a small slave population leading a wretched life allows the rest of the population to lead a blissfully happy life. In such a society, any other arrangement would, in fact, lower the total happiness. For example, any attempt to improve the lives of the slaves would be overbalanced by a loss of happiness in the slave-holding class. This may seem like a far-fetched situation, but if it were to occur, the utilitarian would have to approve of this society and argue against any changes in it. To most people this is unacceptable, for it offends our sense of fairness. "Why," we want to ask, "should one segment of society be assigned wretched lives so that others can be happy? How can the society be morally sound when human rights are infringed on in this way?" Considerations of this kind have led *most* philosophers to abandon strict utilitarianism as the single principle of morality. Some philosophers have modified the principle to meet objections; some have supplemented it with other principles; some have simply rejected it in favor of another theory.

Sometimes counterexamples force clarification. Consider the traditional moral precept, "Do unto others as you would have them do unto you." Like utilitarianism, this principle captures an important moral insight, but, if taken quite literally, it is even more subject to counterexamples. Jones, a sado-masochist, enjoys beating other people. When asked whether he would like to be treated in that way, he replies, "Yes." It is obvious that the Golden Rule was not intended to approve of Jones's behavior. The task, then, is to reformulate this rule to avoid this counterexample.

No discussion of counterexamples is complete without a mention of the Morgenbesser Retort. Though the exact story is now shrouded in the mists of time, it has come down to us from the 1950s in the following form. In a lecture, a British philosopher remarked that he knew of many languages where a double negative means an affirmative, but not one language where a double affirmative means a negative. From the back of the room came Morgenbesser's famous retort: "Yeah, Yeah."

▼ **EXERCISE II**

Find a counterexample to each of the following claims:

> Example: *Claim:* "Sugar" is the only word in which an *s* is pronounced *sh.*
> *Counterexample:* Oh *sure.*

(1) What you don't know can't hurt you.

(2) You can never get enough of a good thing.

(3) You shouldn't ask someone to do something that you are not willing to do yourself.

(4) It is always wrong to tell a lie.

(5) You can't be too careful.

(6) It's all right to treat someone in a given way provided that you do not mind being treated that way yourself.

(7) Three points determine a plane.

These two cases are more difficult:

(8) If it is wrong for one person to do something, then it must be wrong for everyone to do it.

(9) Wherever you use the word "nearly," you could use the word "almost" instead, without affecting that truth or the good sense of what you have said.

▼ EXERCISE III

Explain why there cannot be any counterexamples to the following claims.

(1) Killing is usually wrong.
(2) A short person is a person.
(3) Every horse is an animal.
(4) Nothing is both red all over and green all over at the same time.
(5) $2 + 2 = 4$.

EXPLANATIONS

Explanations answer questions about *how* or *why* something happened. We explain how a mongoose got out of his cage by pointing to a hole he dug under the fence. We explain why Smith was acquitted by saying that he got off on a technicality. The purpose of explanations is to make sense out of things. Sometimes simply filling in the details of a story provides an explanation. For example, we can explain how a two-year-old girl foiled a bank robbery by saying that the robber tripped over her while fleeing from the bank. Here we have made sense out of an unusual event by putting it in the context of a plausible *narrative*. It is unusual for a two-year-old girl to foil a bank robbery, but there is nothing unusual about a person tripping over a child when running recklessly at full speed.

Very many of our explanations in everyday life have this narrative form. One standard puzzle specifically calls for this kind of explanation. We are told, for example, of a person who, when alone, always rides an elevator to the eighteenth floor, gets off, and then walks up the remaining five floors to her apartment. We want to know why she behaves in this way. Various lame suggestions are made: she likes to visit people on her way home; she's taking exercise; and so on. None of these explanations makes sense because none accounts for the *invariability* of her behavior. Surely she isn't visiting friends when she comes home at five in the morning, nor is this a reasonable time for taking exercise. Her behavior is completely explained, however, when we are told a single fact: that she is quite short and can reach only up to the button for the eighteenth floor. When she is alone, that is as far as she can take the elevator.

Although the narrative is probably the most common form of explanation in everyday life, we also use *arguments* for giving explanations. We can explain a certain event by deriving it from established principles and accepted facts. This derivation has the form of an argument. Although explanations of this kind do occur in daily life, the clearest examples come from science. A scientist can explain the movements of a complex mechanism by deriving them from the laws of mechanics. A psychologist can explain a person's apparently strange behavior by citing laws governing the unconscious mind. Broadly speaking, the pattern of explanation will employ an argument of the following form:

> General principles or laws.
> A statement of initial conditions.
> ────────────────────────────────
> ∴ A statement of the phenomenon to be explained.

By "initial conditions" we mean those facts in the context which, together with the general principles and laws, allow us to derive the result that the event to be explained will occur.

This sounds very abstract, which it is, but one extended example should clarify these ideas. Suppose we put an ice cube into a glass and then fill the glass to the very brim. It will look something like this:

What will happen when the ice cube melts? Will the water overflow? Will it remain at the same level? Will it actually go down? Here we are asking for a *prediction*, and it will, of course, make sense to ask a person to *justify* whatever prediction he or she makes.

Stumped by this question, we let the ice cube melt to see what happens. In fact, the water level remains unchanged. We are no longer faced with a problem of prediction, for we can now see what happened: When ice cubes melt (or, anyway, when *this* ice cube melted), the water level stays the same (or, at least, it stayed the same in *this* case). After a few experiments we convince ourselves that this result always occurs. We now have a new question: *Why* does this occur? In short, we want an explanation of this phenomenon. The explanation turns upon the law of buoyancy:

An object is buoyed up by a force equal to the weight of the water it displaces.

So if we put an object in water, it will continue to sink until it displaces a volume of water whose weight is equal to its own weight. (An object heavier than water will continue to sink, but it will feel lighter under water.) With all this in mind, go back to the original problem. In the following diagram, the shaded area indicates the volume of water displaced by the ice cube.

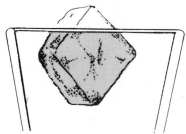

We know from the law of buoyancy that the weight of the ice cube will be equal to the weight of the volume of water it displaces. But an ice cube is itself simply water in a solid state. It is a quantity of water equal to the quantity of water it displaces. More simply, when it melts, it will exactly fill in the volume of water it displaced, so the water level will remain unchanged.

We can now see how this explanation conforms to the argumentative pattern mentioned above:

General principles or laws. Initial conditions. ——————————————— ∴ Phenomenon to be explained.	(Primarily the law of buoyancy.) (An ice cube floating in a glass of water filled to the brim.) (The level of the water remaining unchanged after the ice cube melts.)

There are some things to notice about this explanation. First of all, it is a pretty good explanation. People with only a slight understanding of science can follow it and see why the water level remains unchanged. We should also notice that it is not a *complete* explanation, for certain things are simply taken for granted—for example, that things do not change weight when they pass from a solid to a liquid state. To put the explanation into perfect argumentative form, this assumption and many others would have to be stated explicitly. This is never done in everyday life, and is only rarely done in the most exact sciences.

Here is an example of an explanation that is less technical. Houses in Indonesia sometimes have their electrical outlets in the middle of the wall rather than at floor level. Why? A beginning of an explanation is that flooding is a danger in the Netherlands. Citing this fact does not help much, however, unless one remembers that Indonesia was formerly a Dutch colony. Even remembering this leaves gaps in the explanation. We can understand why the Dutch might put their electrical outlets above floor level in the Netherlands. It is safer in a country where flooding is a danger. Is flooding, then, a similar danger in Indonesia? Apparently not. So why did the Dutch continue this practice in Indonesia? To answer this question we must cite another broad principle: Colonial settlers tend to preserve their home customs, practices, and styles. In this particular case, the Dutch continued to build Dutch-looking houses with the electrical outlets where (for them) they are normally placed—that is, in the middle of the wall rather than at floor level.

Even though this is not a scientific explanation, notice that it shares many features of the scientific explanation examined previously. First we have a curious fact: the location of electrical outlets in some houses in Indonesia. By way of explanation, certain important facts are cited:

Indonesia was a Dutch colony.
Flooding is a danger in the Netherlands.
(And so on.)

These facts are then woven together by certain general principles:

Where flooding is a danger, it is safer to put electrical outlets above floor level.
Colonial settlers tend to preserve their home customs, practices, and styles even when their practical significance is diminished.
(And so on.)

Taken together, these facts and principles make sense of an anomalous fact—that is, they explain it.[5]

Explanations are satisfactory for *practical* purposes if they remove bewilderment or surprise. An explanation is satisfactory if it tells us *how* or *why* something happened in a way that is relevant to the concerns of a particular context. But how far can explanations go? In explaining why the water level remains the same when the ice cube melts, we cited the law of buoyancy. Now why should that law be true? What explains *it*? To explain the law of buoyancy, we would have to derive it from other laws that are more general and, perhaps, more intelligible. In fact, this has been done. Archimedes simultaneously proved and explained the Law of Buoyancy by deriving it from the Laws of the Lever. How about the Laws of the Lever? Can they be proved and

---

[5] This example comes from Alan Ross Anderson.

explained by deriving them from still higher and more comprehensive laws? Perhaps. Yet reasons give out, and sooner or later explanation and justification come to an end. It is the task of science and all rational inquiry to move that boundary further and further back.

▼ EXERCISE IV

Write a brief argument to explain each of the following. Indicate what facts and what general principles are employed in your explanations. (Don't forget those principles that may seem too obvious to mention.)

(1) Why a lighter-than-air balloon rises.
(2) Why there is an infield fly rule in baseball.
(3) Why there is an international date line.
(4) Why there are more psychoanalysts in New York City than in any other city or, for that matter, in most countries in the world.
(5) Why the cost of food tends to be higher in city slums than in wealthy suburbs.

EXCUSES

Sometimes we are charged with acting in an improper or particularly stupid way. There are various ways that we can defend ourselves against such a charge. First, we can deny that we performed the action in question. We might then offer what's called an *alibi* intended to show that we did not perform the action in question. If we admit performing the action, we then have two main options. (1) We can try to *justify* the action, that is, show that it was not improper or stupid but was the right thing to do. (2) We can admit that we performed the action and also admit that it was improper or stupid and then offer an *excuse* intended to show that we were not responsible for what we did.

The following exchanges between A and B illustrate these different kinds of defense.

A: Why did you shove Harold into the gulch?
B: I didn't shove him into the gulch; I was nowhere near him.

Here B's response formulates an *alibi*, because B is denying that he performed the action at all.

A: Why did you shove Harold into the gulch?
B: He was about to be shot by an assassin.

Here B admits that he did shove Harold into the gulch. His response is supposed to explain why B did what he did, and it is also supposed to *justify* B's action by showing that it was the right thing to do. To accomplish this, all B does is cite the single fact that an assassin was about to shoot Harold, but this justification also depends upon some general principles that are so obvious that we simply take them for granted. For example, we assume that saving a person's life is, in general, a good thing; that a person in a gulch is less likely to be struck by a bullet than a person standing in plain view; that the amount of harm that might come from falling into a gulch is much less than the harm that would be caused by being struck by a bullet. Against the background of these principles and others, B's remark explains his otherwise inexplicable conduct by showing that it was *justified*.

Next, notice what happens when we change the example in the following way:

A: Why did you shove Harold into the gulch?
B: I mistakenly thought that he was about to be shot.

B's remark still explains why he acted as he did; we can still understand his behavior. But this remark no longer justifies, or at least fully justifies, his conduct, since he does not claim that what he did was the right thing to do. He thought it was the right thing to do at the time, but now he admits that he was mistaken. Here we would say that B is offering an *excuse* for what he did. Broadly speaking, *an excuse is an explanation of human behavior intended to put it in a better light*. It will often happen that even the best possible light will involve the admission of some wrongdoing. In the third dialogue, B admits to having made a mistake. In some contexts this might be a serious admission, but in the present context B does better admitting that he was, perhaps, stupid, rather than acknowledging that he shoved poor Harold into the gulch as an act of sheer malice.

Even if B admits that he maliciously pushed Harold into the gulch, he may offer a weaker kind of excuse that cites *mitigating circumstances*:

A: Why did you shove Harold into the gulch?
B: He was bugging me all afternoon.

Now, you are not supposed to push people into gulches just because they have been bugging you, so B's response does not justify his conduct. Yet it does provide a *partial* excuse, and thus makes it seem less vicious than if B had pushed Harold into the gulch with no provocation whatsoever.

We evaluate excuses in much the same way that we evaluate other explanations. An excuse will involve statements of fact, and these may be either true or false. We can also challenge the background principles employed in the excuse. We will not be impressed by someone who tells us that he ran seven stoplights so that he would not be late for a kickoff. The desire to make a kickoff does not excuse such obviously dangerous behavior. Finally, as with other explanations, the facts together with the background principles should make sense out of a piece of behavior.

To evaluate an excuse, we can ask the following questions:

(1) Broadly speaking, what are the facts?
(2) With what is the person being charged?
(3) What lesser wrong will the person settle for instead?
(4) How does the excuse answer the more serious charge?

In our third dialogue, (1) B shoved Harold into a gulch. (2) On the face of it, this looks like an attempt to injure Harold. (3) B is willing to admit that he made a mistake of fact. (4) Given this admission, his action was not malicious because it can be seen as a laudable, if flawed, attempt to save Harold from death or serious injury.

▼ EXERCISE V

Determine whether each of the following is being offered as an alibi, a justification, or an excuse. Is each adequate for its intended use?

(1) People with an IQ of 40 should not be given the death penalty, because they are not capable of understanding the consequences of their actions.
(2) I had a very good reason to steal the drug: my wife would have died without it.
(3) Alice shouldn't be kept after school with the rest of the class. She can't be the one who threw the eraser, because she was in the bathroom.
(4) I had to give him the money. He would have killed me if I didn't.
(5) I just couldn't stop myself. When I saw the money lying on the ground, I had to take it. Then I just couldn't bring myself to turn it in. You would have done the same thing.

▼ EXERCISE VI

Imagine that you have written a letter home asking for money. In the closing paragraph, you feel called upon to offer some excuse for not writing for two months. Write such an excuse (not just an apology) in a perfectly natural way, and then analyze it, using the questions given above.

▼ EXERCISE VII

In William Shakespeare's *Much Ado About Nothing*, Benedict, after previously denouncing women and marriage in the strongest terms, is trapped into falling in love with Beatrice. In the following passage he attempts to explain his sudden turnabout. Using the four questions given above, analyze this passage.

I may chance have some odd quirks and remnants of wit broken on me because I have railed so long against marriage. But doth not the appetite alter? A man loves the meat in his youth that he cannot endure in his age. Shall gulps and sentences and these paper bullets of the brain awe a man from the career of his humor? No, the world must be peopled. When I said I would die a bachelor, I did not think I should live till I were married.

▼ EXERCISE VIII

Find an example of a public official offering an excuse for something he or she has done. Analyze its structure using the above four questions.

▼ DISCUSSION QUESTIONS

(1) In general it is wrong to suppose that refuting an argument shows its conclusion to be false. Why?

(2) It is sometimes said that science tells us *how* things happen but does not tell us *why* they happen. In what ways is this contention right, and in what ways is it wrong?

(3) When a claim is made that someone's conduct is *inexcusable*, what precisely is being asserted? How does it differ from calling the conduct simply bad or even very bad?

(4) Taken literally, "Excuse me" is a request. For what?

7

The Formal Analysis of Argument: Part One

This chapter will examine some more technical procedures for analyzing arguments. In particular, it will consider the notion of validity, for this is the central concept of logic. The first part of the chapter will show how the notion of validity first introduced in Chapter 2 can be developed rigorously in one area, the so-called Propositional Calculus. This branch of logic deals with those connectives like "and" and "or" that allow us to build up complex propositions from simpler ones. Throughout most of the chapter, the focus will be theoretical rather than immediately practical. It is intended to provide insight into the concept of validity by examining it in an ideal setting. The chapter will close with a discussion of the relationship between the ideal language of symbolic logic and the language we ordinarily speak.

VALIDITY AND THE FORMAL ANALYSIS OF ARGUMENT

When we carry out an informal analysis of argument, we pay close attention to the key terms used to present the argument and then ask ourselves whether these key terms have been used properly. So far, we have no exact techniques for answering the question: Is such and such a term used correctly? We rely, instead, on logical instincts which, on the whole, are pretty good. In a great many cases, people can tell whether one claim follows from another. But if we ask the average intelligent person *why* the one claim follows from the other, he or she will probably have little to say except, perhaps, that it is just obvious. That is, it is often easy to see *that* one claim follows from another, but to explain *why* turns out to be difficult. The purpose of this chapter is to get some better idea of what we mean when we assert that one claim follows from another.

This quality of "following from" is called validity, as we saw in Chapter 2. The focus of our attention will be largely on the *concept* of validity. We are not, for the time being at least, interested in whether this or that argument is valid—we want to understand validity itself. To this end, the arguments we will examine are so simple that you will not be able to imagine anyone not understanding them at a glance. Who needs logic to deal with arguments of this kind? There is, however, good reason for dealing with simple—trivially simple—arguments at the start. The analytic approach to a complex issue is first to break it down into sub-issues, repeating the process until we reach problems simple enough to be solved. After these simpler problems are solved, we can reverse the process and construct solutions to larger and more complex problems. When done correctly, the *result* of such an analytic process may seem dull and obvious—and it often is. The *discovery* of such a process, in contrast, often demands the insight of genius.

THE PROPOSITIONAL CALCULUS

Conjunction

The first system of arguments that we shall examine concerns propositional (or sentential) connectives. Propositional connectives are terms that allow us to build new propositions from old ones, usually combining two or more propositions into a single proposition. For example, given the propositions "John is tall" and "Harry is short," we can use the term "and" to *conjoin* them, forming a single compound proposition: "John is tall and Harry is short." Now let us look carefully at this simple word "and" and ask how it functions. "And," in fact, is a curious word, for it doesn't seem to stand for anything, at least in the way in which a proper name ("Churchill") and a common noun ("dog") seem to stand for things. Instead of asking what this word stands for, we can ask a different question: What *truth conditions* govern this connective? That is, under what conditions are propositions containing this connective true? To answer this question, we imagine every possible way in which the component propositions can be true or false. Then for each combination we decide what truth value to assign to the entire proposition. This may sound complicated, but an example will make it clear:

John is tall.	Harry is short.	John is tall and Harry is short.
T	T	T
T	F	F
F	T	F
F	F	F

Here the first two columns cover every possibility for the component propositions to be either true or false. The third column states the truth value of the whole proposition for each combination. Pretty obviously, the conjunction of two propositions is true if both of the component propositions are true; otherwise it is false. It should also be obvious that our reflections have not depended on the particular propositions we have selected. We could have been talking about dinosaurs instead of people, and we still would have come to the conclusion that the conjunction of two propositions is true if both propositions are true, but false otherwise. This neglect of the particular content of propositions is what makes our account *formal*. To reflect the generality of our concerns, we can drop the reference to particular sentences altogether and use variables instead. Just as the letters x, y, and z can stand for arbitrary numbers in mathematics, we can let the letters $p, q, r, s, \ldots$ stand for arbitrary propositions in logic. We will also use the symbol "&" for "and."

Consider the expression "p & q." Is it true or false? There is obviously no answer to this question. This is not because we do not know what "p" and "q" stand for, for in fact "p" and "q" do not stand for anything at all. Thus "p & q" is not a statement, but a pattern for a whole series of statements. To reflect this, we shall say that "p & q" is a propositional form. It is a pattern, or form, for a whole series of statements, including "John is tall and Harry is short." To repeat the central idea, we can pass from a proposition to a propositional form by uniformly replacing statements with statement variables.

Proposition	Propositional form
John is tall and Harry is short.	p & q

When we proceed in the opposite direction by uniformly substituting propositions for propositional variables, we get what we shall call a substitution instance of that propositional form.

Propositional form	Substitution instance
p & q	Roses are red and violets are blue.

Thus, "John is tall and Harry is short" and "Roses are red and violets are blue" are both substitution instances of the propositional form "*p* & *q*."

These ideas are perfectly simple, but to be clear about them, it is important to notice that "*p*" is also a statement form with *every* statement, including "Roses are red and violets are blue," as its substitution instances. There is no rule against substituting complex statements for statement variables. Perhaps a bit more surprisingly, our definitions allow "Roses are red and roses are red" to be a substitution instance of "*p* & *q*." We get a substitution instance of a statement form by uniformly replacing the same variable by the same statement throughout. We have not said that different variables must be replaced by different statements throughout. The rule is this:

Different variables may be replaced by the same statement, but different statements may not be replaced by the same variable.

To summarize the discussion thus far:

"Roses are red and violets are blue" is a substitution instance of "*p* & *q*."
"Roses are red and violets are blue" is also a substitution instance of "*p*."
"Roses are red and roses are red" is a substitution instance of "*p* & q."
"Roses are red and roses are red" is a substitution instance of "*p* & *p*."
"Roses are red and violets are blue" is *not* a substitution instance of "*p* & *p*."
"Roses are red" is *not* a substitution instance of "*p* & *p*."

We are in a position to give a perfectly general definition of conjunction, using propositional variables where previously we used specific propositions.

p	q	p & q
T	T	T
T	F	F
F	T	F
F	F	F

There is no limit to the number of propositions we can conjoin to form a new proposition. "Roses are red and violets are blue; sugar is sweet and so are you" is a substitution instance of "(*p* & *q* & *r* & *s*)." We can also use parentheses to group propositions together. This last example could be treated as a substitution instance of "((*p* & *q*) & (*r* & *s*))," that is, as a conjunction containing two conjunctions. Later we will see that parentheses can make an important difference to the meaning of a total proposition.

One cautionary note. The word "and" is not always used to connect two distinct sentences. Sometimes a sentence has to be rewritten to see that it is equivalent to a sentence of this form. For example, "Steffie Graf and Martina Navratilova are tennis players" is simply a short way of saying "Steffie Graf is a tennis player and Martina Navratilova is a tennis player." At other times, the word "and" is not used to produce a conjunction of propositions. For example, "Steffie Graf and Martina Navratilova are playing each other" does not mean that "Steffie Graf is playing each other and Martina Navratilova is playing each other." That doesn't even make sense. The original sentence does not express a conjunction of two propositions; it expresses a single proposition about two people taken as a group. At other times it is unclear whether a sentence expresses a conjunction of propositions or a single proposition about a group. "Steffie and Martina are playing tennis" could be taken either way. When a sentence containing the word "and" expresses the conjunction of two propositions, we will say that it expresses a *propositional conjunction*. When a sentence containing "and" does not express the conjunction of two propositions, we will say that it expresses a *non-propositional conjunction*. In this chapter we are only concerned with sentences that express propositional conjunctions.

▼ EXERCISE I

The proposition "The night is young and you're so beautiful" is a substitution instance of which of the following statement forms?

(1) p

(2) $p \ \& \ q$

(3) $p \ \& \ r$

(4) $p \ \& \ p$

(5) p or q

_____

▼ EXERCISE II

Find three statement forms of which the following statement is a substitution instance:

The night is young and you're so beautiful and my flight leaves in thirty minutes.

_____

Validity for Conjunction

Now we can look at an argument involving conjunction. Here is one that is ridiculously simple:

Harry is short and John is tall.

∴ Harry is short.

This argument is obviously valid. But why is the argument valid? Why does the conclusion follow from the premise? The answer in this case seems obvious, but we will spell it out in detail as a guide for more difficult cases. Suppose we replace these particular statements by statement forms, using a different variable for each distinct statement throughout the argument. This yields what we shall call an *argument form*, for example:

$$p \ \& \ q$$
$$\therefore p$$

This is a pattern for endlessly many arguments, each of which is called a substitution instance of this argument form. Every argument that has this general form will also be valid. It really doesn't matter which propositions we put back into this schema; the resulting argument will be valid—so long as we are careful to substitute the same statement for the same variable throughout.

Let us pursue this matter further. If an argument has true premises and a false conclusion, then we know at once that it is invalid. But in saying that an argument is *valid*, we are not only saying that it does not have true premises and a false conclusion; we are saying that the argument *cannot* have a false conclusion when the premises are true. Sometimes this is true because the argument has a structure or form that rules out the very possibility of true premises and a false conclusion. We can appeal to the notion of an argument form to make sense out of this idea. A somewhat more complicated truth table will make this clear:

		Premise	Conclusion
p	q	$p \ \& \ q$	p
T	T	T	T
T	F	F	T
F	T	F	F
F	F	F	F

The first two columns give all the combinations for the truth values of the statements that we might substitute for p and q. The third column gives the truth value of the premise for each of these combinations. (This column is the same as the definition for "&" given above.) Finally, the fourth column gives the truth value for the conclusion for each combination. (Here, of course, this merely involves repeating the first column. Later on, things will become more complicated and interesting.) If we look at this truth table, we see that no matter how we make substitutions for the variables, we never get a case where the premise is true and the conclusion is false. In the first line, the premise is true and the conclusion is also true. In the remaining three lines the premise is not true, so the possibility of the premise being true and the conclusion false does not arise. Here it is important to remember that a valid argument can have false premises, for one proposition can follow from another that is false. Of course, an argument that is sound cannot have a false premise, since a sound argument is defined as a valid argument with true premises. But our subject here is validity, not soundness.

Let us summarize this discussion. In the case we have examined, validity depends on the form of an argument and not on its particular content. A first principle, then, is this:

An argument is valid if it is a substitution instance of a valid argument form.

So the argument "Harry is short and John is tall, therefore Harry is short" is valid because it is a substitution instance of the valid argument form "p & q $\therefore$ p."

Next we must ask what makes an argument form valid. The answer to this is given in this principle:

An argument form is valid if it has no substitution instances where the premises are true and the conclusion is false.

We have just seen that the argument form "p & q $\therefore$ p" meets this test. The truth-table analysis showed that. Incidentally, we can use the same truth table to show that the following argument is valid:

John is tall.	p
Harry is short.	q
$\therefore$ John is tall and Harry is short.	$\therefore$ p & q

The argument on the left is a substitution instance of the argument form on the right, and a glance at the truth table will show that there can be no cases where all the premises could be true and the conclusion false. This pretty well tells the story of the logical properties of the logical connective we call conjunction.

Notice that we have not said that *every* argument that is valid is so in virtue of its form. There may be arguments where the conclusion follows from the premises but where we cannot show that the argument's validity is a matter of logical form. There are, in fact, some obviously valid arguments that have yet to be shown to be valid in terms of their form. Explaining validity by means of logical form has been an ideal of logical theory, but there are arguments, many of them quite commonplace, where this ideal has yet to be adequately fulfilled.

Many arguments in mathematics fall into this category. At present, however, we shall only consider arguments where the strategy we used for analyzing conjunction continues to work.

Disjunction

Just as we can form a conjunction of two propositions by using the connective "and," we can form a *disjunction* of two propositions by using the connective "or," as in the following compound sentence:

John will win or Harry will win.

Again, it is easy to see that the truth of this whole statement depends on the truth of the component statements. If they are both false, then the statement as a whole is false. If just one of them is true, then the statement as a whole is true. But suppose they are both true, what shall we say then? Sometimes when we say "either-or" we seem to rule out the possibility of both. "You may have chicken or steak" probably means that you cannot have both. Sometimes, however, both are not ruled out—for example, when we say to someone, "If you want to see tall mountains, go to California or Colorado." So one way (in fact, the standard way) to deal with this problem is to say that "or" has two meanings: one *exclusive*, which rules out both, and one *inclusive*, which does not rule out both. We could thus give two truth-table definitions, one for each of these uses of the word "or":

	Exclusive				Inclusive	
p	q	p or q		p	q	p or q
T	T	F		T	T	T
T	F	T		T	F	T
F	T	T		F	T	T
F	F	F		F	F	F

For reasons that will become clear in a moment, we will adopt the inclusive sense of the word "or." Where necessary, we will define the exclusive sense using the inclusive sense as a starting point. Logicians symbolize *disjunctions* using the connective "v." The truth table for this connective has the following form:

p	q	p v q
T	T	T
T	F	T
F	T	T
F	F	F

We shall look at some arguments involving this connective in a moment.

Negation

With conjunction and disjunction, we begin with two propositions and construct a new proposition from them. There is another way in which we can construct a new proposition from another—through *negating* it. Given the proposition "John is clever," we can get a new proposition "John is not clever" simply by inserting the word "not" in the correct place in the sentence. What, exactly, does the word "not" mean? This can be a difficult question to answer, especially if we begin with the assumption that all words stand for things. Does it stand for nothing or, maybe, nothingness? Although some respectable philosophers have sometimes spoken in this way, it is important to see that the word "not" does not stand for anything at all. It has an altogether different function in the language. To see this, think how conjunction and disjunction work. Given two propositions, the word "and" allows us to construct another proposition that is true only when both original propositions are true, and is false otherwise. With disjunction, given two propositions, the word "or" allows us to construct another proposition that is false only when both the original propositions are false, and true otherwise. Our truth-table definitions reflect these facts. Using these definitions as models, how should we define *negation?* A parallel answer is that the negation of a proposition is true just in case the original proposition is false and it is false just in case the original proposition is true. Using the symbol "$\sim$" to stand for negation, this gives us the following truth-table definition:

p	$\sim p$
T	F
F	T

How Truth-Functional Connectives Work

We have now defined conjunction, disjunction, and negation. That, all by itself, is sufficient to complete the branch of modern logic called Propositional Logic. The definitions themselves may seem peculiar. They do not look like the definitions we find in a dictionary. But the form of these definitions is important, for it tells us something interesting about the character of such words as "and," "or," and "not." Two things are worth noting: (1) These expressions are used to construct new propositions from old. (2) The newly constructed proposition is always a *truth function* of the original propositions—that is, the truth value of the new proposition is always determined by the truth value of the original propositions. For this reason they are called *truth-functional connectives.* (Of course, with negation, we start with a *single* proposition.) For example, suppose that "*A*" and "*B*" are two true propositions and "*G*" and "*H*" are two false propositions. We can then determine the truth values of more complex propositions built from them using conjunction, disjunction, and negation. Sometimes the correct assignment is obvious at a glance:

A & B	True
A & G	False
~G	True
A v H	True
~A & G	False

As noted earlier, parentheses can be used to distinguish groupings. Sometimes the placement of parentheses can make an important difference, as in the following two expressions:

$$~A \& G \qquad ~(A \& G)$$

Notice that in one expression the negation symbol applies only to the proposition "A," whereas in the other expression it applies to the entire proposition "(A & G)." The first expression above is false, then, and the second expression is true. Only the second expression translates "Not both A & G." Both of these expressions are different from "~A & ~B," which means "Neither A nor B."

As expressions become more complex, we reach a point where it is no longer obvious how the truth values of the component propositions determine the truth value of the entire proposition. Here a regular procedure is helpful. The easiest method is to fill in the truth values of the basic propositions and then, step by step, make assignments progressively wider, going from the inside out. For example:

$$~((A \lor G) \& ~(~H \& B))$$
$$~((T \lor F) \& ~(~F \& T))$$
$$~((T \lor F) \& ~(T \& T))$$
$$~(T \& ~(T))$$
$$~(T \& F)$$
$$~(F)$$
$$T$$

With very little practice, you can master this technique in dealing with even highly complex examples.

▼ EXERCISE III

Given that "A," "B," and "C" are true propositions and "X," "Y," and "Z" are false propositions, determine the truth values of the following complex propositions:

(1) (A v Z) & B

(2) ~(Z v Z)

(3) ~~(A v B)

(4) (A v X) & (B v Z)

(5) $(A \& X) \vee (B \& Z)$

(6) $\sim(A \vee (Z \vee X))$

(7) $\sim(A \vee \sim(Z \vee X))$

(8) $\sim Z \vee (Z \& A)$

(9) $A \vee ((\sim B \& C) \vee \sim(\sim B \vee \sim(Z \vee B)))$

(10) $A \& ((\sim B \& C) \vee \sim(\sim B \vee \sim(Z \vee B)))$

TESTING FOR VALIDITY

But what is the point of all this? In everyday life we rarely run into an expression as complicated as the one given in our example. Our purpose here is to sharpen our sensitivity to how truth-functional connectives work, and then to express our insights in clear ways. This is important because the validity of many arguments depends on the logical features of these truth-functional connectives. We can now turn directly to this subject.

Earlier we saw that every argument of the form "$p \& q \therefore p$" will be valid. This is obvious in itself, but we saw that this claim could be justified by an appeal to truth tables. A truth-table analysis shows us that an argument of this form can never have an instance where the premise is true and the conclusion is false. We can now apply this same technique to arguments that are more complex. In the beginning we will take arguments that are still easy to follow without the use of technical help. At the end, we will consider some arguments that most people cannot follow without guidance.

Consider the following argument:

> Valarie is either a doctor or a lawyer.
> Valarie is neither a doctor nor a stockbroker.
>
> Therefore, Valarie is a lawyer.

We can use the following abbreviations:

D = Valarie is a doctor.
L = Valarie is a lawyer.
S = Valarie is a stockbroker.

Using these abbreviations, the argument and its counterpart argument form look like this:

$$\begin{array}{cc}
D \vee L & p \vee q \\
\underline{\sim(L \vee S)} & \underline{\sim(q \vee r)} \\
\therefore D & \therefore p
\end{array}$$

The expression on the right gives the argument *form* of the argument presented on the left. To see whether the argument is valid, we ask if the argument form is valid. The procedure is cumbersome, but perfectly mechanical:

| | | | Pr. | Pr. | | Cn. |
| | | | | | | |
p	q	r	$(p \lor q)$	$(q \lor r)$	$\sim(q \lor r)$	p
T	T	T	T	T	F	T
T	T	F	T	T	F	T
T	F	T	T	T	F	T
T	F	F	T	F	T	T	O.K.
F	T	T	T	T	F	F
F	T	F	T	T	F	F
F	F	T	F	T	F	F
F	F	F	F	F	T	F

Notice that there is only one combination of truth values where both premises are true, and in that case the conclusion is true as well. So the original argument is valid since it is an instance of a valid argument form, that is, an argument form with no instances of true premises combined with a false conclusion.

This last truth table may need some explaining. First, why do we get eight rows in this truth table where before we got only four? The answer to this is that we need to test the argument form for *every possible combination of truth values* for the component propositions. With two variables, there are four combinations: (TT), (TF), (FT), and (FF). With three variables, there are eight combinations: (TTT), (TTF), (TFT), (TFF), (FTT), (FTF), (FFT), and (FFF). The general rule is this: If an argument form has n variables, the truth table used in its analysis must have 2^n rows. For four variables there will be sixteen rows; for five variables, thirty-two rows; for six variables, sixty-four rows; and so on. You can be sure that you capture all possible combinations of truth values by using the following pattern in constructing the columns of your truth table:

First column	*Second column*	*Third column* . . .
First half T's, second half F's	First quarter T's, second quarter F's	First eighth T's, second eighth F's

A glance at the earlier examples in this chapter will show that we have been using this pattern. Of course, as soon as an argument becomes at all complex, these truth tables become very large indeed. But there is no need to worry about this, since we will not consider arguments with many variables. Those who do turn to a computer for help.

The style of the truth table above is also significant. The premises (Pr.) are plainly labeled and so is the conclusion (Cn.). A line is drawn under every row where the premises are all true. (In this case, there is only one such row.) If the conclusion on this line is also true, it is marked "O.K." If every line where the premises are all true is O.K., the argument form is valid. Marking all this out may seem rather childish, but it is worth doing. First, it helps guard against mistakes; more importantly, it draws one's attention to the purpose of the procedure being used. Cranking out truth tables without understanding what they are about—or even why they might be helpful—does not enlighten the mind or elevate the spirit.

For the sake of contrast, we can next consider an invalid argument:

> Valarie is either a doctor or a lawyer.
> Valarie is not both a lawyer and a stockbroker.
> ___
> Therefore, Valarie is a doctor.

Using the same abbreviations as earlier, this becomes:

$$D \lor L \qquad\qquad p \lor q$$
$$\underline{\sim(L \,\&\, S)} \qquad \underline{\sim(q \,\&\, r)}$$
$$\therefore D \qquad\qquad\quad \therefore p$$

The truth table analysis for this argument has the following form:

			Pr.	Pr.		Cn.	
p	q	r	$(p \lor q)$	$(q \,\&\, r)$	$\sim(q \,\&\, r)$	p	
T	T	T	T	T	F	T	
T	T	F	T	F	T	T	OK
T	F	T	T	F	T	T	OK
T	F	F	T	F	T	T	OK
F	T	T	T	T	F	F	
F	T	F	T	F	T	F	NO invalid
F	F	T	F	F	T	F	
F	F	F	F	F	T	F	

This time, we find four rows where all the premises are true. In three cases the conclusion is true as well, but in one of these cases (Row 6), the conclusion is false. This row is marked "invalid." Notice that every row where all of the premises are true is marked either as "O.K." or as "invalid." If even one row is marked "invalid," then the argument form as a whole is invalid. The argument form is thus invalid, since it is possible for it to have a substitution instance where all the premises are true and the conclusion is false.

The labeling not only shows that the argument form is invalid, it also shows *why* it is invalid. Each row that is marked "invalid" shows a combination of truth values which make the premises true and the conclusion false. Row six presents the combination where Valarie is not a doctor, is a lawyer, and is not a stockbroker. With these assignments, it will be true that she is either a doctor or a lawyer (Premise 1), also true that she is not both a stockbroker and a doctor (Premise 2), yet false that she is a doctor (the Conclusion).

▼ EXERCISE IV

Using the truth-table technique outlined above, test the following argument forms for validity:

(1) $p \lor q$

$\underline{\quad p \quad}$

∴ $\sim q$

(2) $\underline{\sim(p \lor q)}$

∴ $\sim q$

(3) $\sim(p \& q)$

$\underline{\quad \sim q \quad}$

∴ $\sim p$

(4) p

$\underline{\quad \sim(p \lor q) \quad}$

∴ $\sim q$

(5) p

$\underline{\quad \sim(p \lor q) \quad}$

∴ r

(6) $\underline{(p \& q) \lor (p \& r)}$

∴ $p \& (q \lor r)$

(7) $\underline{(p \lor q) \& (p \lor r)}$

∴ $p \& (q \lor r)$

(8) $\underline{p \& q \quad}$

∴ $(p \lor r) \& q$

SOME FURTHER CONNECTIVES

We have developed the logic of propositions using only three basic notions corresponding (perhaps roughly) to the English words "and," "or," and "not." Now let us go back to the question of the two possible senses of the word "or"—one exclusive and the other inclusive. Sometimes "or" seems to rule out the possibility that both options are open; at other times "or" seems to allow this possibility. This is the difference between exclusive and inclusive disjunction, respectively.

Suppose we use the symbol "$\underline{\lor}$" to stand for exclusive disjunction. (After this discussion, we will not use it again.) We could then define this new connective in the following way:

$$(p \veebar q) = \text{(by definition)} ((p \lor q) \ \& \ \sim(p \ \& \ q))$$

It is not hard to see that the expression on the right side of this definition captures the force of exclusive disjunction. Since we can always define exclusive disjunction when we want it, there is no need to introduce in into our system of basic notions.

▼ EXERCISE V

Construct a truth-table analysis of the expression on the right side of the preceding definition and compare it with the truth-table definition of exclusive disjunction given earlier in this chapter.

Actually, in analyzing arguments we have been defining new logical connectives without much thinking about it. For example, "not both p and q" was symbolized as "$\sim(p \ \& \ q)$." "Neither p nor q" was symbolized as "$\sim(p \lor q)$." Let us look more closely at the example "$\sim(p \lor q)$." Perhaps we should have symbolized it as "$\sim p \ \& \ \sim q$." As a matter of fact, we could have used this symbolization, because the two expressions amount to the same thing. Again, this may be obvious, but we can prove it by using a truth table in yet another way. Compare the truth-table analysis of these two expressions:

p	q	$\sim p$	$\sim q$	$\sim p \ \& \ \sim q$	$(p \lor q)$	$\sim(p \lor q)$
T	T	F	F	F	T	F
T	F	F	T	F	T	F
F	T	T	F	F	T	F
F	F	T	T	T	F	T

Under "$\sim p \ \& \ \sim q$" we find the column (FFFT), and we find the same sequence under "$\sim(p \lor q)$." This shows that, for every possible substitution we make, these two expressions will yield statements of the same truth value. We shall say that these statement forms are *truth-functionally equivalent*.

Given the notion of truth-functional equivalence, the problem of more than one translation can often be solved. If two translations are truth-functionally equivalent, then it does not matter which one we use in testing for validity. Of course, some translations will seem more natural than others. For example, "$p \lor q$" is truth-functionally equivalent to

$$\sim((\sim p \ \& \ \sim p) \ \& \ (\sim q \lor \sim q))$$

The first expression is obviously more natural than the second, even though they are truth-functionally equivalent.

▼ EXERCISE VI

Use truth tables to test which of the following propositional forms are truth-functionally equivalent to each other.

(1) $\sim(p \vee \sim q)$

(2) $\sim(\sim p \vee \sim q)$

(3) $\sim p \mathbin{\&} q$

(4) $p \mathbin{\&} q$

▼ SUMMARY

So far in this chapter we have seen that by using conjunction, disjunction, and negation, it is possible to construct complex statements out of simple statements. A distinctive feature of compound statements constructed in these three ways is that the truth of the compound statement is always a function of the truth of its component propositions. Thus, these three notions allow us to construct truth-functionally compound statements. Some arguments depend for their validity simply upon these truth-functional connectives. When this is so, it is possible to test for validity in a purely mechanical way. This can be done through the use of truth tables. Thus, in this area at least, we are able to give a clear account of validity and to specify exact procedures for testing for validity. Now we shall go on to examine an area where the application of this approach is more problematic. It concerns *conditionals*.

CONDITIONALS

Conditionals often occur in arguments. They have the form, "If _____, then _____." What goes in the first blank of this pattern is called the *antecedent* of the conditional; what goes in the second blank is called its *consequent*. Sometimes conditionals appear in the indicative mood:

If it rains, the crop will be saved.

Sometimes they occur in the subjunctive mood:

If it had rained, the crop would have been saved.

There are also conditional imperatives:

If a fire breaks out, call the fire department first!

There are conditional promises:

If you get into trouble, give me a call and I promise to help you.

Indeed, conditionals get a great deal of use in our language, often in arguments. It is important, therefore, to understand them.

Unfortunately, there is no general agreement among experts concerning the correct way to analyze conditionals. We will simplify matters, and avoid some of these controversies, by considering only indicative conditionals. We will not examine conditional imperatives, conditional promises, or subjunctive conditionals. Furthermore, at the start, we will examine only what we will call *propositional conditionals*. We get a propositional conditional by substituting indicative sentences that express propositions—something either true or false—into the schema: If _____, then _____. Or, to use technical language already introduced, a propositional conditional is a substitution instance of "If p, then q" where "p" and "q" are propositional variables. Of the four conditional sentences listed above, only the first is a propositional conditional.

Even if we restrict our attention to propositional conditionals, this will not avoid all controversy. A number of competing theories exist concerning the correct analysis of propositional conditionals, and no consensus has been reached concerning which is right. It may seem surprising that disagreement should exist concerning such a simple and fundamental notion as the if-then construction, but it does. In what follows we will first describe the most standard treatment of propositional conditionals, and then consider a number of alternatives to it.

Truth Tables for Conditionals

For conjunction, disjunction, and negation, the truth-table methods provided an approach that was at once plausible and effective. A propositional conditional is also compounded out of two simpler propositions, and this suggests that we might be able to offer a truth-table definition for these conditionals as well. What should the truth table look like? When we try to answer this question, we get stuck almost at once, for it is unclear how we should fill in the table in three out of four cases.

p	q	If p, then q.
T	T	?
T	F	F
F	T	?
F	F	?

It seems obvious that a conditional cannot be true if the antecedent is true and the consequent false. We record this by putting an F in the second row. But suppose "p" and "q" are replaced by two arbitrary true propositions, say, "two plus two equals four" and "Chile is in South America." What shall we say about the conditional:

If two plus two equals four, then Chile is in South America.

The first thing to say is that this is a *very* strange statement, because the arithmetical remark in the antecedent doesn't seem to have anything to do with the geographical remark in the consequent. So this conditional is odd—indeed, extremely odd—but is it true or false? At this point a reasonable response is bafflement.

Now consider the following argument, which is intended to solve all these problems by giving good reasons for assigning truth values in each row of the truth table. First, it seems obvious that if "If p, then q" is true, then it is not the case that "p" is true and "q" is false. That in turn means that "$\sim(p \ \& \ \sim q)$" must be true. The following, then, seems to be a valid argument form:

$$\text{If } p, \text{ then } q$$
$$\therefore \ \sim(p \ \& \ \sim q)$$

Second, we can reason in the opposite direction. Suppose that we know that "$\sim(p \ \& \ \sim q)$" is true. For this to be true, "$p \ \& \ \sim q$" must be false. We know that from the truth-table definition of negation. Next let us suppose that "p" is true. Then "$\sim q$" must be false. We know that from the truth-table definition of conjunction. Finally, if "$\sim q$" is false, then "q" itself must be true. This line of reasoning is supposed to show that the following argument form is valid.

$$\sim(p \ \& \ \sim q)$$
$$\therefore \ \text{If } p, \text{ then } q$$

The first step in the argument was intended to show that we can validly derive "$\sim(p \ \& \ \sim q)$" from "If p, then q." The second step was intended to show that the derivation can be run in the other direction. But if each of these expressions is derivable from the other, this suggests that they are equivalent. We use this background argument as a justification of the following definition:

If p, then q = (by definition) Not both p and not q.

We can put this into symbols using a horseshoe to symbolize the conditional connective:

$p \supset q$ = (by definition) $\sim(p \ \& \ \sim q)$

Given this definition, we can now construct the truth table for propositional conditionals. It is simply the truth table for "$\sim(p \ \& \ \sim q)$":

p	q	$\sim(p \ \& \ \sim q)$	$(p \supset q)$	$(\sim p \ \text{v} \ q)$
T	T	T	T	T
T	F	F	F	F
F	T	T	T	T
F	F	T	T	T

Notice that "$\sim(p \ \& \ \sim q)$" is also truth-functionally equivalent to the expression "$(\sim p \ \text{v} \ q)$." We have cited it here because "$(\sim p \ \text{v} \ q)$" has traditionally been used to define "$p \supset q$." For reasons that are now obscure, when a conditional is defined in this truth-functional way, it is called a *material conditional*.

Now let us suppose, for the moment, that the notion of a material conditional corresponds exactly with our idea of a propositional conditional. What would follow from this? The answer is that we could treat conditionals in the same way in which we have treated conjunction, disjunction, and negation. A propositional conditional would be just one more kind of truth-functionally compound statement capable of definition by truth tables. Furthermore, arguments that depend on this notion (together with conjunction, disjunction, and negation) could be settled by appeal to truth-table techniques. Let us pause for a moment to examine this.

One of the most common patterns of reasoning is called *modus ponens*. It looks like this:

$$\text{If } p, \text{ then } q. \qquad\qquad p \supset q$$
$$\underline{\qquad p \qquad} \qquad\qquad \underline{\quad p \quad}$$
$$\therefore q \qquad\qquad\qquad \therefore q$$

The truth-table definition of material implication shows at once that this pattern of argument is valid.

Pr.		Pr.	Cn.	
p	q	$p \supset q$	q	
T	T	T	T	
T	F	F	F	O.K.
F	T	T	T	
F	F	T	F	

▼ **EXERCISE VII**

Show that the argument form called *modus tollens* is valid. It looks like this:

$$p \supset q$$
$$\underline{\sim q}$$
$$\therefore \sim p$$

These same techniques allow us to show that one of the traditional fallacies is, indeed, a fallacy. It is called the fallacy of *denying the antecedent*, and it looks like this:

$$p \supset q$$
$$\underline{\sim p}$$
$$\therefore \sim q$$

The truth-table analysis showing the invalidity of this argument has the following form:

		Pr.	Pr.	Cn.
p	q	$p \supset q$	$\sim p$	$\sim q$
T	T	T	F	F
T	F	F	F	T
F	T	T	T	F	NO valid invalid
F	F	T	T	T	OK

▼ EXERCISE VIII

A second standard fallacy is called *affirming the consequent*. It looks like this:

$$p \supset q$$
$$q$$
$$\therefore p$$

Using truth-table techniques, show that this argument form is invalid.

We can examine one last argument that has been historically significant. It is called the *hypothetical syllogism* and has the following form:

$$p \supset q$$
$$q \supset r$$
$$\therefore p \supset r$$

Since we are dealing with an argument form containing three variables, we must perform the boring task of constructing a truth table with eight rows:

			Pr.	Pr.	Cn.
p	q	r	$p \supset q$	$q \supset r$	$p \supset r$
T	T	T	T	T	T	OK
T	T	F	T	F	F
T	F	T	F	T	T
T	F	F	F	T	F
F	T	T	T	T	T	OK
F	T	F	T	F	T
F	F	T	T	T	T	OK
F	F	F	T	T	T	OK

This is fit work for a computer, not for a human being, but it is important to see that it actually works.

Why is it important to see that these techniques work? Most people, after all, could see that hypothetical syllogisms are correct without going through all this tedious business. We seem only to be piling boredom on top of triviality. This protest deserves an answer. Suppose we ask someone *why* he or she thinks that the conclusion follows from the premises in a hypothetical syllogism. The person might answer that anyone can see that—something, by the way, that is false. Beyond this, he or she might say that it all depends upon the meanings of the words, or that it is all a matter of definition. But if we go on to ask *which words* and *what definitions,* most people will fall silent. What we have done is to discover that the validity of some arguments depends on the meanings of such words as "and," "or," "not," and "if-then." We have then gone on to give explicit definitions of these terms—definitions, by the way, that help us to see how these terms function in an argument. Finally, by getting all these *simple* things right, we have produced what is called a *decision procedure* for determining the validity of every argument involving only conjunctions, disjunctions, negations, and propositional conditionals. Our truth-table techniques give us a mechanical procedure for settling questions of validity in this area. In fact, truth-table techniques have practical applications, for example, in computer programming. But the important point here is that through understanding how these techniques work, we can gain a deeper insight into the notion of validity.

▼ EXERCISE IX

Using the truth-table techniques employed above, test the following argument forms for validity. (For your own entertainment, guess about the validity of the argument form before working it out.)

(1) $p \supset q$

$\therefore q \supset p$

(2) $p \supset q$

$\therefore \sim q \supset \sim p$

(3) $(p \lor q) \supset r$

$\therefore p \supset r$

(4) $(p \,\&\, q) \supset r$

$\therefore p \supset r$

(5) $p \supset q$

$q \supset r$

$\therefore p \supset (q \,\&\, r)$

(6)　$(p \lor q) \And (p \lor r)$
　　$\sim r$
　　―――――――――
　　$\therefore \sim q \supset p$

(7)　$(p \supset q) \And (p \supset \sim r)$
　　$r \And \sim q$
　　―――――――――
　　$\therefore \sim p$

(8)　$p \supset q$
　　$q \supset r$
　　―――――――――
　　$\therefore \sim r \supset \sim p$

(9)　$p \supset (q \supset r)$
　　―――――――――
　　$\therefore (p \And q) \supset r$

(10)　$p \supset (q \supset r)$
　　$p \supset q$
　　―――――――――
　　$\therefore r$

Logical Language and Everyday Language

Early in this chapter we started out by talking about such common words as "and" and "or," and then slipped over to talking about *conjunction* and *disjunction*. The transition was a bit sneaky, but intentional. To understand what is going on here, we can ask how closely these logical notions that we have defined match their everyday counterparts. We will start with conjunction, and then come back to the more difficult question of conditionals.

At first sight, the match between conjunction as we have defined it and the everyday use of the word "and" may seem pretty bad. To begin with, in everyday discourse, we do not go about conjoining random bits of information. We do not say, for example, that two plus two equals four and Chile is in South America. We already know why we do not say such things, for unless the context is quite extraordinary, this is bound to violate the rule of Relevance. But if we are interested in validity, the rule of Relevance—together with all other pragmatic rules—is simply beside the point. When dealing with validity, we are only interested in one question: if the premises of an argument are true, must the conclusion be true as well? Pragmatic rules, as we saw in Chapter 1, do not affect truth.

The truth-functional notion of conjunction is also insensitive to another important feature of our everyday discourse: by reducing all conjunctions to their bare truth-functional content, it often misses the argumentative point of a conjunction. We have already seen that the following remarks have a very different force in the context of an argument:

The ring is beautiful, but expensive.
The ring is expensive, but beautiful.

These two remarks point in opposite directions in the context of an actual argument, but from a purely truth-functional point of view we treat them as equivalent. We translate the first sentence as "*B & E*" and the second as "*E & B*". Their truth-functional equivalence is too obvious to need proof. Similar oddities arise for all discounting terms, such as "although," "whereas," "however," and so on.

It might seem that if formal analysis cannot distinguish an "and" from a "but," then it can hardly be of any use at all. This is not true. A formal analysis of an argument will tell us just one thing: whether the argument is valid or not. If we expect the analysis to tell us more than this, we will be disappointed. It is important to remember two things: (1) we expect deductive arguments to be valid; (2) usually we expect much more than this from an argument. To elaborate upon the second point, we usually expect an argument to be sound as well as valid—we expect the premises to be true. Beyond this, we expect the argument to be informative, intelligible, convincing, and so forth. Validity, then, is an important aspect of an argument and formal analysis helps us to evaluate it. But validity is not the only aspect of an argument that concerns us; in many contexts it is not even our chief concern.

We can now look at our analysis of conditionals, for here we find some striking departures between the logician's analysis and everyday use. The following argument forms are both valid:

$$(1)\ \frac{p}{\therefore q \supset p} \qquad (2)\ \frac{\sim p}{\therefore p \supset q}$$

▼ EXERCISE X

Check the validity of the above argument forms using truth tables.

Yet, though valid, both argument forms seem odd—so odd that they have actually been called *paradoxical*. The first argument form seems to say this: If a proposition is true, then it is *implied by* any proposition whatsoever. Here is an example of an argument that satisfies this argument form and is therefore valid:

    Lincoln was president.
So: If the moon is made of cheese, Lincoln was president.

This is a very peculiar argument to call valid. First, we want to know what moon has to do with Lincoln's having been president. Beyond this, how can his having been president depend upon a blatant falsehood? We can give these questions even more force by noticing that even the following argument is valid:

    Lincoln was president.
So: If Lincoln was not president, then Lincoln was president.

Both arguments are instances of the valid argument form: $p \therefore q \supset p$.

The other argument form is also paradoxical. It seems to say a false proposition implies any proposition whatsoever. The following is an instance of this argument form:

Lincoln was president.
So: If Lincoln was not president, then the moon is made of cheese.

Here it is hard to see what the falsehood that Lincoln was not president has to do with the composition of the moon.

At this point, nonphilosophers become impatient, whereas philosophers become worried. We started out with principles that seemed to be both obvious and simple. Now, quite suddenly, we are being overwhelmed with a whole series of peculiar results. What in the world has happened, and what should be done about it? Philosophers remain divided in the answers they give to these questions. The responses fall into two main categories: (1) Simply give up the idea that conditionals can be defined truth-functionally and search for a different and better analysis of conditionals that avoids the difficulties involved in truth-functional analysis. (2) Take the difficult line and argue that there is nothing wrong with calling the above argument forms valid.

The first approach is highly technical and cannot be pursued in detail in this book. The general idea is this: Instead of identifying "If p then q" with "Not both p and not q," identify it with "Not *possibly* both p and not q." This provides a stronger notion of a conditional and avoids some—though not all—of the problems concerning conditionals. This theory is given a systematic development by offering a logical analysis of the notion of possibility. This branch of logic is called *modal* logic, and has shown remarkable development in recent years.

The second line has been taken by Paul Grice, whose theories played a prominent part in Chapter 1. He acknowledges—as anyone must—that the two argument forms above are decidedly odd. He denies, however, that this oddness has anything to do with *validity*. Validity concerns one thing and one thing only: a relationship between premises and conclusion. An argument is valid if the premises cannot be true without the conclusion being true as well. The above argument forms are valid by this definition of validity.

Of course, arguments can be defective in all sorts of other ways. Look at the first argument form. Since "q" can be replaced by any proposition (true or false), the rule of Relevance will often be violated. It is worth pointing out violations of the rule of Relevance, but, according to Grice, this has nothing to do with validity. Now if we look at the second argument form we see that it can also lead to arguments that contain a violation of the rule of Relevance. Beyond this, arguments having these forms can also involve violations of the rule of Quantity. A conditional will be true just in case the consequent is true.

Given this, it doesn't matter to the truth of the whole conditional whether the antecedent is true or false. Again, a conditional is true just in case the antecedent is false—and it doesn't matter, given this, whether the consequent is true or false. Yet it can be very misleading to *use* a conditional on the basis of these logical features. For example, it would be very misleading for a museum guard to say, "If you give me five dollars, then I will let you into the exhibition," when, in fact, he will admit you in any case. For Grice, this is misleading since it violates the rule of Quantity. Yet, strictly speaking, it is not false. Strictly speaking, it is true.

The Grice line is attractive, for, among other things, it allows us to accept the truth-functional account of conditionals with all its simplicity. Yet sometimes it is difficult to swallow. Consider the following remark:

If God exists, then there is evil in the world.

If Grice's analysis is correct, even the most pious will have to admit that this conditional is true, provided only that he is willing to admit that there is evil in the world. Yet this conditional plainly suggests that God's existence has something to do with the evil in the world, and the pious will wish to deny this suggestion. Grice would agree: the conditional plainly suggests that there is some connection between God's existence and the evil in the world—presumably, that is the point of connecting them in a conditional. All the same, this is something that is conversationally implied, not asserted, and once more we come to the conclusion that this conditional could be misleading—and therefore is in need of criticism and correction—but is still, strictly speaking, true.

Philosophers and logicians have had various responses to Grice's position. No consensus has emerged on this issue. The authors of this book find it on the whole convincing and therefore have adopted it. This will have two advantages: (1) This appeal to pragmatics fits in well with our previous discussions, and (2) it provides a way of keeping the logic simple and within the range of a beginning student. Other philosophers and logicians continue to work toward a definition superior to the truth-table definition for indicative conditionals.

Other Conditionals in Ordinary Language

So far we have considered only one form in which propositional conditionals appear in everyday language: the conditional "If *p*, then *q*." But propositional conditionals come in a variety of forms and some of them demand careful treatment.

We can first consider the contrast between constructions using "if" and those using "only if":

(1) I'll clean the barn if Hazel will help me.
(2) I'll clean the barn only if Hazel will help me.

Adopting the following abbreviations:

B = I'll clean the barn.
H = Hazel will help me.

the first sentence is translated as follows:

$H \supset B$

Notice that in the prose version of (1), the antecedent and consequent appear in reverse order. "q if p" means the same thing as "If p, then q."

How shall we translate the second sentence? Here we should move slowly and first notice what seems incontestable: If Hazel does not help me, then I will not clean the barn. This is translated in the following way:

$\sim H \supset \sim B$

And that is equivalent to:

$B \supset H$

If this equivalence is not obvious, it can be quickly established using a truth table.

A more difficult question arises when we ask whether an implication runs the other way. When I say that I will clean the barn only if Hazel will help me, am I committing myself to cleaning the barn if she does help me? There is a strong temptation to answer the question yes and then give a fuller translation of (2) in the following way:

$(B \supset H) \& (H \supset B)$

Logicians call such two-way implications *biconditionals,* and we shall discuss them in a moment. But adding this second conjunct is almost surely a mistake, for we can think of parallel cases where we would not be tempted to include it. A government regulation might read as follows:

> A student may receive a New York State Scholarship only if the student attends a New York State school.

From this it does not follow that anyone who attends a New York State school may receive a New York State Scholarship. There may be other requirements as well, for example, being a New York State resident.

Why were we tempted to use a biconditional in translating sentences containing the connective "only if"? Why, that is, are we tempted to think that the statement "I'll clean the barn only if Hazel will help me" implies "If Hazel helps me, then I will clean the barn"? The answer turns upon the notion of conversational implication first met in Chapter 1. If I am *not* going to clean the barn whether Hazel helps me or not, then it will be misleading—a violation of the rule of Quantity—to say that I will clean the barn only if Hazel helps me. For this reason, in many contexts, the *use* of a sentence of the form "p only if q" will conversationally imply a commitment to "p if and only if q."

We can next look at sentences of the form "*p* if and only if *q*"—so-called biconditionals. If I say that I will clean the barn if and only if Hazel will help me, then I am saying that I will clean it if she helps and I will not clean it if she does not. Translated, this becomes:

(*H* ⊃ *B*) & (~*H* ⊃ ~*B*)

This is equivalent to:

(*H* ⊃ *B*) & (*B* ⊃ *H*)

We thus have an implication going both ways—the characteristic form of a biconditional. In fact, constructions containing the expression "if and only if" do not often appear in everyday speech. They appear almost exclusively in technical or legal writing. In ordinary conversation, we capture the force of a biconditional by saying something like this:

I will clean the barn, but only if Hazel helps me.

The decision whether to translate a remark of everyday conversation into a conditional or a biconditional is often subtle and difficult. We have already noticed that the use of sentences of the form "*p* only if *q*" will often conversationally imply a commitment to the biconditional "*p* if and only if *q*." In the same way, the *use* of the conditional "*p* if *q*" will also carry this same implication. If I plan to clean the barn whether Hazel helps me or not, it will certainly be misleading—again, a violation of the rule of Quantity—to say that I will clean the barn *if* Hazel helps me.

We can close this discussion by considering one further, rather difficult, case. What is the force of saying "*p* unless *q*"? Is this a biconditional, or just a conditional? If it is just a conditional, which way does the implication go? There is a strong temptation to treat this as a biconditional, but the following example shows this to be wrong:

Bush will lose the election unless he carries the Northeast.

This sentence clearly indicates that Bush will not win the election if he does not carry the Northeast. Using abbreviations:

N = Bush will carry the Northeast.
L = Bush will lose the election.
~*N* ⊃ *L*

The original statement does not imply—even conversationally—that he will win the election if he does carry the Northeast. Thus,

"*p* unless *q*" = "~*q* ⊃ *p*"

We can also note that "~*p* unless *q*" means the same thing as "*p* only if *q*," and they both translate:

p ⊃ *q*

So far, then we have the following results:

	Translates	Often Conversationally Implies
q if *p*	$p \supset q$	$(p \supset q) \ \& \ (q \supset p)$
q only if *p*	$q \supset p$	$(p \supset q) \ \& \ (q \supset p)$
p unless *q*	$\sim q \supset p$	$(p \supset \sim q) \ \& \ (\sim q \supset p)$

▼ EXERCISE XI

Translate each of the following sentences into symbolic notation, using the suggested symbols as abbreviations.

(1) The Reds will win only if the Dodgers collapse. *(R, D)*
(2) The Steelers will win if their defense holds up. *(S, D)*
(3) If it rains or snows, the game will be called off. *(R, S, O)*
(4) Unless there is a panic, stock prices will continue to rise. *(P, R)*
(5) If the house comes up for sale and if I have money in hand, I will bid on it. *(S, M, B)*
(6) You can be a success if only you try. *(S, T)*
(7) You will get a good bargain provided you get there early. *(B, E)*
(8) You cannot lead a happy life without friends. (Let H = "You can lead a happy life," and let F = "You have friends.")

▼ EXERCISE XII

Translate each of the following arguments into symbolic notation. Then (a) test the argument for validity using truth-table techniques and (b) comment on any violations of conversational rules.

Example: Harold is clever, so, if Harold isn't clever, then Anna isn't clever either. *(H, A)*

$$\frac{H}{\therefore \sim H \supset \sim A} \qquad \frac{p}{\therefore \sim p \supset \sim q}$$

(a)

Pr.				Cn.
p	*q*	~*p*	~*q*	~*p* ⊃ ~*q*
T	T	F	F	T
T	F	F	T	T
F	T	T	F	F
F	F	T	T	T

(b) The argument violates the rule of Relevance.

(1) Jones is brave, so Jones is brave or Jones is brave. (*J*)

(2) The Democrats will run either Jones or Borg. If Borg runs they will lose the South and if Jones runs they will lose the North. So the Democrats will lose either the North or South. (*J, B, S, N*)

(3) Although Brown will pitch, the Rams will lose. If the Rams lose, their manager will get fired, so their manager will get fired. (*B, L, F*)

(4) America will win the Olympics unless Russia does and Russia will win the Olympics unless East Germany does, so America will win the Olympics unless East Germany does. (*A, R, E*)

(5) If you dial 0, you will get the operator, so if you dial 0 and do not get the operator, then there is something wrong with the telephone. (*D, O, W*)

(6) The Republicans will carry either New Mexico or Arizona, but since they will carry Arizona they will not carry New Mexico. (*A, N*)

(7) John will play only if the situation is hopeless, but the situation will be hopeless, so John will play. (*P, H*)

(8) (a) Bush will win the election whether he wins Idaho or not, therefore Bush will win the election. (*R, I*)

(b) Bush will win the election, therefore Bush will win the election whether he wins Idaho or not. (*R, I*)

(c) Bush will win the election, therefore Bush will win the election whether he wins a majority or not. (*R, M*)

(9) If you flip the switch then the light will go on, but if the light goes on, then the generator is working; so if you flip the switch, then the generator is working. (*F, L, G*)
(This example is due to Charles L. Stevenson.)

NECESSARY AND SUFFICIENT CONDITIONS

Our discussion of conditionals can help us understand two important notions used in the analysis of many forms of argumentation: that of a sufficient condition and of a necessary condition. Later we will introduce a more general definition of both these notions, but we will begin by saying that *A* is sufficient condition for *B* just in case *B* is true if *A* is true. Thus the antecedent of a propositional conditional always lays down a sufficient condition for its consequent:

Sufficient Condition

$$\overbrace{A \supset B}$$

For example, if we say "If Joan is a mother, then Joan is female," we are indicating that Joan's being a mother is sufficient for her being female.

As an initial definition of a necessary condition, we will say that B is necessary condition for A just in case A is true *only if* B is true. We know that this is equivalent to:

$A \supset B$

Thus the consequent of any propositional conditional lays down a necessary condition for its antecedent:

$A \supset B$
$\underbrace{}$
     Necessary Condition

For example, if we say "If Joan is a mother, then Joan is female," we are indicating that Joan's being female is a necessary condition for her being a mother.

On the basis of these considerations, we can introduce the following principle relating sufficient conditions and necessary conditions:

I. If A is a sufficient condition for B, then B is a necessary condition for A.

It is important not to confuse sufficient and necessary conditions. Something can be a sufficient condition without being a necessary condition. For example, being a mother is a sufficient condition for being female, but it is not a necessary condition for being female. Furthermore, while being a female is a necessary condition for being a mother, it is not a sufficient condition for being a mother.

But even if necessary conditions and sufficient conditions are distinct notions, they are related in interesting ways. We can say that the car's being out of gas is *sufficient* to guarantee that it will *not* be able to run. Alternatively, we say that a car's having gasoline is *necessary* for its being *able* to run. We can express these ideas symbolically in the following way:

Let G = The car has gas.
Let R = The car can run.

We can then state that not having gas is a sufficient condition for the car's not running as follows:

(1) $\sim G \supset \sim R$ (If the car does not have gas, the car cannot run.)

The claim that having gas is a necessary condition for the car's running we state this way:

(2) $R \supset G$ (The car can run only if it has gas.)

But we know from the earlier discussion of conditionals that (1) and (2) are logically equivalent. This allows us to introduce two further principles relating necessary conditions and sufficient conditions:

II. If A is a sufficient condition for B, then $\sim A$ is a necessary condition for $\sim B$.

III. If A is a necessary condition for B, then $\sim A$ is a sufficient condition for $\sim B$.

This is guaranteed simply because of the equivalence between "$A \supset B$" and "$\sim B \supset \sim A$."

GENERAL CONDITIONALS

The subject matter of this chapter has been propositional logic: that branch of logic that deals with connectives like "and," "or," and "if . . . then . . ." which allow us to build up complex propositions from simpler propositions. In the last three sections we have examined some of the logical properties of propositional conditionals of the form "If p, then q." For example:

(1) If it is raining, then the ground is getting wet.

Here, "p" and "q" are replaced by complete sentences in the indicative mood: "It is raining" and "The ground is getting wet." Each sentence as it appears in this conditional is either true or false. We have called indicative conditionals of this kind *propositional conditionals*. So far in this chapter we have discussed only propositional conditionals.

The following sentence is superficially similar to (1):

(2) If it rains, then the ground gets wet.

The structure of (2) is, however, importantly different from the structure of (1). Notice that in (2) the words that formulate the antecedent and consequent of the conditional do not express propositions. Unlike (1), (2) does not introduce a relationship between propositions, but instead, it states a relationship between *kinds* of events. This becomes more clear if we paraphrase (2) in the following way:

(2') Whenever it rains, the ground gets wet.

Here we are not speaking of any specific occurrence of raining and the ground's getting wet, but instead we are making a general remark about the relationship between two kinds of phenomena.

In contrast to sentences like (1) which we have called *propositional conditionals*, we will call sentences like (2) *general conditionals*. We can usually tell whether we are dealing with a general conditional rather than a propositional conditional by asking whether the "if" can be replaced by such words as "whenever," "whoever," "whatever," and so on. These terms are marks of generality.

General conditionals often have the following form:

(3) For all x, if x has the feature F, then x has the feature G.[1]

For example:

(4) For all x, if x is mother, then x is female.

More naturally,

(4') If someone is a mother, then that person is female.

We can think of such general conditionals as providing a pattern—or a recipe—for an indefinitely large set of propositional conditionals fitting the pattern they present. Thus, if (4) is true, then so is the following propositional instance of it:

(5) If Joan is a mother, then Joan is female.

Notice that (5), unlike (4), is a propositional conditional. We can, of course, generate as many instances of (4) as we please simply by making different substitutions for the variable x in (4). If (4) is true, then each of the propositional conditionals we get through such substitutions will be true as well.

▼ EXERCISE XIII

Identify each of the following conditionals as either a propositional conditional or a general conditional.

(1) If Ohio State wins, Columbus goes crazy.
(2) If the bridge is closed, we will be late.
(3) If Jeff is here, Jody is not.
(4) If you play with pitch, you will be defiled.
(5) If there is a way out of this mess, I do not know about it.
(6) If you can't say anything nice, don't say anything at all.
      (This may take some thought.)

▼ EXERCISE XIV

The distinction between propositional and generalized conditionals is important because confusing them can lead to absurdities. The following argument is a case in point:

If everyone sits down, everyone will see better.

So: Everyone who sits down will see better.

---

[1] Logicians call the expression "for all x" a quantifier because it indicates the quantity or range of things we are referring to. The expression "for all x" provides a way of indicating that we are referring to *all* x's rather than, say, to *some* x's, *most* x's, and so on. Though important, these other quantifiers do not bear upon the present discussion, so we shall not be concerned with them here.

Here the premise expresses a propositional conditional which may well be true whereas the conclusion expresses a general conditional that is almost certainly false: sitting down will not help an individual to see better unless others sit down as well.

For each of the following arguments explain the source of absurdity by distinguishing propositional from generalized conditionals.

(1) When the pressure gets low, it always rains.
   If it always rains, the oceans flood.
   _____
So: When the pressure gets low, the oceans flood.

(2) Whenever the pitcher throws a curve, Joe always gets a hit.
   If Joe always gets a hit, he bats 1.000.
   _____
So: Whenever the pitcher throws a curve, Joe bats 1.000.

It is not hard to see why general conditionals are extremely useful means for communication. A teacher, for example, wishes to announce that anyone in the class with an average of 95 percent will be excused from the final. One way of communicating this would be to use a whole series of propositional conditionals, each laying down a sufficient condition for an individual student's being excused from the final:

If Abrams has an average of 95 percent, then Abrams will be excused from the final.
If Barnes has an average of 95 percent, then Barnes will be excused from the final. . . .
If Zazlovski has an average of 95 percent, then Zazlovski will be excused from the final.

It's a lot easier for the teacher just to say to the class:

If anyone has an average of 95 percent, then that person will be excused from the final.

Or more idiomatically:

Anyone who has an average of 95 percent will be excused from the final.

But not only do general conditionals provide a convenient way of packaging information, they also provide indispensable tools for dealing with the physical and social world around us. A great deal of our common knowledge about the world comes in the form of general conditionals stating either *sufficient* conditions, *necessary* conditions, or *both*. Our heads are packed with them, waiting for occasions to employ them. For example, to turn on a Macintosh computer, you must flip the switch in the back. This lays down a necessary condition for turning on a Mac, because, in effect, it tells us that a Macintosh computer will turn on only if the switch in the back is flipped. (It does not lay down a sufficient condition, for flipping the switch will not turn the computer on if, for example, it is not plugged in.) We carry this piece of information around with us all the time, for the most part not using it or even paying attention to it. But when the occasion comes to turn the computer on, we apply this general statement of a necessary condition to this *specific case*, recognizing that this computer will turn on right now only if we flip the switch in the back right now.

The use and evaluation of general statements of sufficient conditions and of necessary conditions will be examined again in detail in Chapter 9. Here we will simply note how the notions of sufficient conditions and necessary conditions can be extended from propositional conditionals to general conditionals. To see how to do this, we can look again at one of the basic patterns for general conditionals:

For all *x*, if *x* has the feature *F*, then *x* has the feature *G*.

Employing the same basic idea introduced for propositional conditionals, we will now say that a general conditional of this pattern claims that *x*'s having the feature *F* is a sufficient condition for its having the feature *G*, and that *x*'s having the feature *G* is a necessary condition for its having the feature *F*.

Sufficient Condition

If *x* has the feature *F*, then *x* has the feature *G*.

Necessary Condition

Finally, we can generalize our definitions even further by not limiting them to this particular conditional where we are saying that if *x* has a feature *F* then *x* itself must have the feature *G*. In many cases, if one thing possesses a feature *F*, then something *else* will possess the feature *G*. The following definitions capture this generality:

That *F* is a sufficient condition for *G* means that whenever *F* is present *G* is present.
That *F* is a necessary condition for *G* means that whenever *F* is absent *G* is absent.

▼ EXERCISE XV

Using this last definition, state whether the underlined words express a necessary or a sufficient condition. In some cases it will help to restate the sentence as an explicit general conditional.

Examples:

(a) It snows only when <u>the temperature is below forty degrees</u>.
The temperature being below forty degrees is a necessary condition for its snowing.

(b) <u>Hard work</u> guarantees success.
= If <u>one works hard</u>, one will succeed.
Working hard is sufficient for success.

(1) If litmus paper is put in acid, it turns red.

(2) A contract is binding only if there is no fraud.

(3) A contract is binding only if there is no fraud.

(4) Nothing ventured, nothing lost.

(5) If something is not worth doing, it is not worth doing well.

(6) All students are required to study a foreign language unless English is their second language.

(7) Students over 21 will be admitted, provided they have I.D. cards.

(8) No State shall deprive any person of life, liberty, or property without due process of law.

PROBLEMS IN DISTINGUISHING SUFFICIENT AND NECESSARY CONDITIONS

The difference between a sufficient condition and a necessary condition seems uncomplicated, but in practice they are easily confused. In dealing with propositional conditionals, we saw that the influence of conversational implications can often tempt us to treat conditionals as biconditionals, that is, we treat if-statements and only-if–statements as if they were if-and-only-if–statements. This itself can lead us to confuse sufficient conditions and necessary conditions with each other. Above we considered the statement:

(1) I'll clean the barn only if Hazel will help me.

Does this commit one to cleaning the barn if Hazel will help? We saw that the answer to this question is no, although in many contexts a person who makes this remark conversationally implies that he will. In other words, the sentence states that Hazel's helping is a necessary condition for my helping but not, as it stands, a sufficient condition.

Confusing sufficient conditions and necessary conditions is especially easy when dealing with general conditionals laying down complex conditions. Suppose, for example, that someone is told the following:

(2) If you have three tickets for speeding and one ticket for driving while intoxicated (DWI), you will lose your driver's licence.

This conditional has a conjunction for an antecedent and thus lays down a conjunctive sufficient condition for losing one's licence. Now suppose that, in fact, having three speeding tickets is *alone* sufficient for the loss of one's driver's licence, and so is having one ticket for DWI, what will we say about (2)? One temptation is to say that it is false, but that's wrong. To see this, suppose that someone with only two speeding tickets simultaneously gets two more tickets, one for speeding and one for DWI. This will certainly be sufficient—we might want to say, more than sufficient—for the loss of his licence. So strictly speaking, (1) is true. Yet in many contexts it can be misleading.

We can explain why it is misleading by appealing to the rule of Quantity discussed first in Chapter 1. Generally, people are interested in sufficient conditions because they are interested in what is needed to guarantee that something will happen. Given these practical concerns, what they want is a relevant list of *minimal* sufficient conditions. So even though (2) is, strictly speaking, true, the rule of Quantity demands that it be replaced by the following statement:

(2') If you have three speeding violations *or* one ticket for DWI, you will lose your driver's licence.

This statement, like (2), is true, but unlike (2) is not misleading. Specifically, (2) is misleading because it suggests that two things are necessary components of a sufficient condition when they are not.

Misunderstandings can run in the other direction as well: we are sometimes inclined to treat necessary conditions as sufficient conditions. Suppose the English department issues the following regulation:

(3) A student will be exempted from taking introductory English composition only if (i) the student has scored in the top twenty percentile in the English Composition Achievement Test and (ii) has studied four years of English in secondary school.

A student meeting these standards applies for exemption and then is told he or she must also present a writing sample to the English department for its approval before the exemption can be given. The student would feel cheated. Why? Let us suppose that the English department never gives this exemption to a student who has not both scored in the top twenty percentile in the English Composition Achievement Test and studied four years of English in secondary school. Sometimes, however, it refuses to give an exemption because of the quality of the writing sample. In this situation, (3) is literally true: it specifies conditions that are necessary for getting the exemption even if it does not specify all of them.

Yet even if (3) is strictly speaking true, it would be misleading for an English department to *publish* a regulation in this form; it would be misleading because it would violate the rule of Quantity as it concerns the statement of necessary conditions. In stating necessary conditions, we are expected to specify *all* those necessary conditions that are relevant in the given context, except, perhaps, those that are so obvious that they can be taken for granted.

Another factor can lead us to confuse necessary conditions with sufficient conditions. In a great many contexts, though perhaps not all, we assume that doing *everything necessary* to accomplish something is *sufficient* to accomplish it. If two parties do everything necessary to enter into a contract, then that is sufficient for them to have entered into a contract. If someone mixes all the ingredients necessary to make brownies, that person has mixed ingredients sufficient to make brownies, and so on. We usually assume that in doing everything necessary, we have done enough. Stated more carefully, we often assume that the total set of necessary conditions is also a sufficient condition.[2]

Now if we grant these points, it is easy to see how we can naturally treat a statement of necessary conditions as a statement of sufficient conditions.

(i)   The statement of necessary conditions often conversationally implies that all the necessary conditions are being stated (except perhaps those that can be taken for granted).

(ii) In many contexts, we assume that all necessary conditions taken together will be a sufficient condition.

(iii) Therefore, in many contexts the statement of necessary conditions will often be taken as the statement of a sufficient condition.

Seeing how it is natural for us to confuse sufficient conditions and necessary conditions can help us guard against doing so. It is important to keep these concepts straight; for, as we have seen, the rules concerning them are fundamentally different.

▼   SUMMARY

For the most part, this chapter had been dedicated to getting a clear conception of the notion of validity in one particular area. We have studied the logic of truth-functionally compound statements. These are arguments that depend for their validity on the logical properties of conjunction, disjunction, negation, and propositional conditionals. We have offered truth-table definitions of these notions and laid down a truth-table method for testing the validity of arguments that turn upon these connectives. Although we have not shown this, we have, in fact, developed a method for testing the validity of *all* arguments whose validity depends upon the character of these truth-functional connectives. At the close of the chapter we have gone beyond propositional logic to show how the notions of sufficient conditions and necessary conditions, which were first introduced for propositional conditionals, can be extended to general conditionals. Throughout we have tried to show how these abstract notions are related to everyday language.

---

[2] This principle may seem obviously true, but it might be false if there are genuinely indeterministic events—for example, at the subatomic level—or genuinely spontaneous acts of free will at the human level. In both cases it seems that everything necessary for an event to take place is present, yet the event need not take place.

▼ EXERCISE XVI

Decide whether each of the following claims is true or false, and then defend your answer:

(1) An argument that is a substitution instance of a valid argument form is always valid.

(2) An argument that is a substitution instance of an invalid argument form is always invalid.

(3) An invalid argument is always a substitution instance of an invalid argument form.

▼ DISCUSSION QUESTIONS

(1) If "not-*p* unless *q*" is translated as "*p* ⊃ *q*," then "*p* unless *q*" should be translated as "*p* v *q*." Why?

(2) Is a valid argument always a substitution instance of a valid argument form?

(3) Whatever its conclusion, an argument with inconsistent premises will always be valid. First of all, why is this true? Second, why doesn't this allow us to prove anything we please?

(4) As we have seen in Chapter 4, arguments are sometimes criticized for being circular. Are such arguments valid or invalid? Are they ever sound? In answering this question, pay close attention to the exact definitions of validity and soundness.

8

The Formal Analysis of Argument: Part Two

In Chapter 7 we saw how validity can depend on the external connections between propositions. By examining in detail the theory of *immediate inference* and the theory of the *categorical syllogism*, this chapter will demonstrate how validity can depend on the internal structure of propositions. Our interest in these two aspects of logic is mostly theoretical. Understanding the theory of the syllogism deepens our understanding of validity even if this theory is, in some cases, difficult to apply directly to complex arguments in daily life.

BEYOND PROPOSITIONAL LOGIC

Armed with the techniques developed in Chapter 7, we can look at the following argument:

> All squares are rectangles.
> All rectangles have parallel sides.
>
> ∴ All squares have parallel sides.

At a glance it is obvious that the conclusion follows from the premises—it is a valid argument. Furthermore, it seems to be valid in virtue of its form. To show the form of this argument, we might try something of the following kind:

$$p \supset q$$
$$q \supset r$$
$$\therefore p \supset r$$

But this is a mistake, and a bad mistake. We have used the letters "p," "q," and "r" as *propositional variables*—they stand for arbitrary propositions. But the proposition "All squares are rectangles" is not itself composed of two propositions. In fact, if we attempt to translate the above argument into the language of propositional logic, we get the following result:

$$p$$
$$q$$
$$\therefore r$$

This, of course, is not a valid argument form. But if we look back at the original argument we see that it is obviously valid. This shows that propositional logic—however adequate it is in its own areas—is not capable of explaining the validity of all valid arguments. There is more to logic than propositional logic. To broaden our understanding of the notion of validity, we will examine a modern version of a branch of logic first developed in ancient times, *the theory of the syllogism.*

CATEGORICAL PROPOSITIONS

In the argument above, the first premise asserts some kind of relationship between squares and rectangles; the second premise asserts some kind of relationship between rectangles and things with parallel sides; finally in virtue of these asserted relationships, the conclusion asserts a relationship between squares and things having parallel sides. Our task, now, is to understand these relationships as clearly as possible so that we can discover the *basis* for the validity of this argument. Again we shall adopt the strategy of starting from very simple cases and then use the insights gained there for dealing with more complicated cases.

A natural way to represent the relationships expressed by the propositions in an argument is through diagrams. Suppose we draw one circle standing for all things that are squares and another circle standing for all things that are rectangles. The claim that all squares are rectangles may be represented by placing the circle representing squares completely inside the circle representing rectangles.

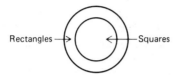

Another way of representing this relationship is to begin with overlapping circles.

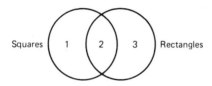

We then shade out the portions of the circles where there is nothing. Since all squares are rectangles, there is nothing that is a square that is not a rectangle—that is, there is nothing in region 1. So our diagram looks like this:

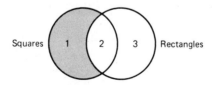

Either method of representation seems plausible. Perhaps the first seems more natural. We shall, however, use the system of overlapping circles because in the long run they actually work better. They are called Venn diagrams.

Having examined one relationship that can exist between two classes, it is natural to wonder what other relationships might exist. Going to the opposite extreme from our first example, two classes may share *nothing* in common. The proposition "No triangles are squares" expresses such a relationship. We diagram this by indicating that there is nothing in the overlapping region of things that are both triangles and squares:

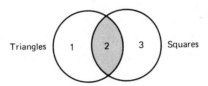

In these first two extreme cases we have indicated that one class is either completely included in another ("All squares are rectangles") or completely excluded from another ("No triangles are squares"). Sometimes, however, we only claim that two classes have at least *some* things in common. We say, for example, that "Some aliens are spies." How shall we indicate this on the following diagram?

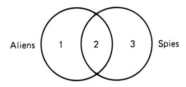

In this case, we do not want to cross out any whole region. We do not want to cross out region 1 because we are not saying that *all* aliens are spies. Plainly, we do not want to cross out region 2, for we are actually saying that some persons are both aliens and spies. Finally, we do not want to cross out region 3, for we are not saying that all spies are aliens. Saying that some aliens are spies does not rule out the possibility that some spies are homegrown. So we need some new device to represent claims that two classes have at least *some* members in common. We shall do this in the following way:

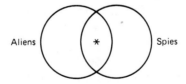

Here the asterisk indicates that there is at least one person who is both an alien and a spy. Notice, by the way, that we are departing a bit from an everyday way of speaking. "Some" is usually taken to mean *more than one;* here we let it mean *at least one.* In fact, this makes things simpler and will really cause no trouble.

Given this new method of diagramming class relationships, we can immediately think of other possibilities. The following diagram indicates that there is someone who is an alien but not a spy. In more natural language, it represents the claim that *some aliens are not spies.*

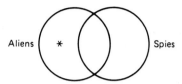

Next we can indicate that there is someone who is a spy but not an alien. More simply, we are representing the claim that *some spies are not aliens.*

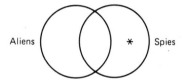

Finally, we can indicate that there is someone who is neither a spy nor an alien:

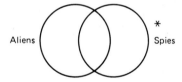

DOMAIN OF DISCOURSE

The last example raises a special problem. When we try to think of something that is neither a spy nor an alien, we naturally think of a person—say, Bill Cosby. But how about Mt. Whitney and the number seven? Neither of these things is either a spy or an alien. Yet is seems odd to say that Mt. Whitney is neither a spy nor an alien. Talk about spies and aliens typically concerns people. We can put it this way: Talk about spies and aliens normally *presupposes* that we are considering only persons. To reflect the notion of limiting our discussion to a certain kind of thing, we will make our diagrams a bit more elaborate. We will enclose the intersecting circles with a box that indicates *the domain of discourse* (DD). Some examples will make this clear:

1. All squares are rectangles (domain of discourse: plane figures):

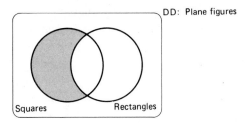

2. Some aliens are not spies (domain of discourse: people):

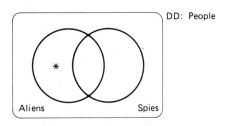

Deciding upon a domain of discourse is somewhat arbitrary. It depends on good sense and present interests. In the first example, we might have taken *four-sided figures* as the domain of discourse, and perhaps in the second example *people in the United States* might have done perfectly well. Actually, we will be quite casual about specifying a domain of discourse, and will only do so when it serves some useful purpose.

THE FOUR BASIC PROPOSITIONS

It is easy to see that two classes can be related in a great many different ways. Nonetheless, it is possible to examine all these relationships in terms of four basic propositions:

A: All *A* is *B*.   E: No *A* is *B*.
I: Some *A* is *B*.   O: Some *A* is not *B*.

The A and the E propositions are said to be *universal* propositions, and the I and the O propositions are said to be *particular* propositions. The A and the I propositions are said to be *affirmative* propositions, and the E and the O propositions are said to be *negative* propositions.

A: Universal Affirmative
E: Universal Negative
I: Particular Affirmative
O: Particular Negative

The four basic propositions are diagrammed as follows:

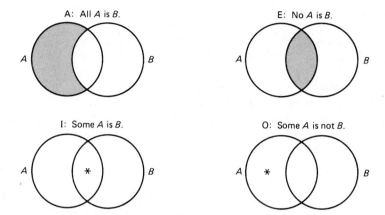

A: All A is B. E: No A is B.

I: Some A is B. O: Some A is not B.

These basic propositions, together with their labels, classification, and diagrams, should be memorized because they will be referred to constantly.

▼ EXERCISE I

Using just the four basic propositions, indicate what information is given in each of the following diagrams:

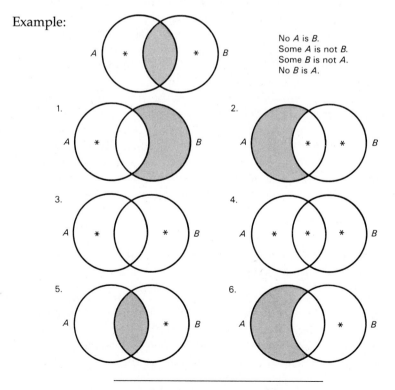

Example:

No A is B.
Some A is not B.
Some B is not A.
No B is A.

1.

2.

3.

4.

5.

6.

EXISTENTIAL IMPORT

Before developing our techniques for using Venn diagrams further, we must turn to a difficult problem that logicians have not fully settled. Usually when we make a statement, we are talking about certain things. If someone claims that all whales are mammals, that person is talking about whales and mammals and stating a relationship between them. That is, in making this statement, the person seems to be taking the *existence* of whales and mammals for granted. The remark seems to involve what logicians call *existential commitment* to the things referred to in the subject and predicate terms. Sometimes, however, we seem to use A propositions without committing ourselves to the existence of the things referred to in the subject and predicate terms. For example, if we say "All trespassers will be fined," we are not committing ourselves to the existence of trespassers; we are only saying, "*If* there are trespassers, then they will be fined." Given this one example of an A proposition that carries no commitment concerning things referred to, it is easy to think of many others. The question then arises whether we should include existential commitment in our treatment of categorical propositions or not.

Once more, then, we must make a decision. (Remember that we had to make decisions concerning the truth-table definitions of both disjunction and propositional conditionals.) Traditional logic was developed on the assumption that all the basic propositions carry existential import. Modern logic makes the opposite decision, treating the claim that all men are mortal as equivalent to the general conditional: if someone is a man, then that person is mortal. This way of speaking carries no commitment to the existence of men.

Which approach should we adopt? In the long run, the modern approach has proved a more powerful method. All the same, there is something beautiful about the classical approach and it is worth exploring in its own right. Our decision, then, is this: We will adopt the modern approach and *not* assign existential import to the A and E propositions. After this is done, we will show how to develop the classical theory by adding existential import to the modern theory.

VALIDITY FOR ARGUMENTS CONTAINING CATEGORICAL PROPOSITIONS

We have introduced Venn diagrams because they provide an efficient and illuminating way for testing the validity of arguments made up of categorical propositions. The basic idea is simple enough. We will say that an argument made up of categorical propositions is valid if all the information contained in the Venn diagram for the conclusion is contained in the Venn diagram for the premises. The procedure is efficient because there are only two ways that we can put information into a Venn diagram: we can either shade out an area or put an asterisk in an area. So to test the validity of an argument made up of categorical propositions, we need only examine the diagram of the conclusion for its information—its shading or asterisks—and then check to see whether the diagram for the premises contains this information as well. We will explain this procedure in more detail later on, but the following simple example will give a general idea of how it works.

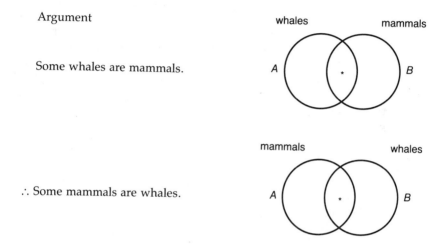

Argument

Some whales are mammals.

∴ Some mammals are whales.

Notice that the only information contained in the diagram for the conclusion is the asterisk in the overlap between A and B, and that information is also included for the diagram for the premise. Thus, the argument is valid.

THE THEORY OF IMMEDIATE INFERENCE

The theory of immediate inference concerns arguments with the following features:

(1) They have a single premise. (That is why the inference is called immediate.)
(2) They are constructed from the four basic A, E, I, O propositions.
(3) The same subject and predicate terms appear in both the premise and the conclusion.

Of course, there are all sorts of other arguments involving just one premise, but those involving the four basic propositions have been singled out for special attention. These inferences deserve special attention because they occur quite often in everyday reasoning.

We have, in fact, already examined a number of immediate inferences in the previous section. Here we shall make a systematic survey of three standard patterns of immediate inference: *conversion*, *obversion*, and *contraposition*.

Conversion

Conversion is the simplest immediate inference we shall consider. *We convert a proposition simply by reversing the subject term and the predicate term.* By the subject term, we simply mean the term that occurs as the grammatical subject; by the predicate term, we mean the term that occurs as the grammatical predicate. In the proposition "All spies are aliens," "spies" is the subject term and "aliens" is the predicate term. In this case identifying the predicate term is straightforward, since the grammatical predicate is a noun—a predicate nominative. Often, however, we have to change the grammatical predicate from an adjective to a noun phrase to get a noun that refers to a class of things. Though it is a bit artificial, we can always use this device. "All spies are dangerous" becomes "All spies are dangerous things." Here "spies" is the subject term and "dangerous things" is the predicate term. The reason we must make this change is that when we convert a proposition (that is, reverse the subject and predicate terms), we need a noun phrase to take the place of the grammatical subject. In English we cannot say "All dangerous are spies," but we can say "All dangerous things are spies."

Having explained what conversion is, we now want to know when this operation yields a *valid* immediate inference. To answer this question we use Venn diagrams to examine the relationship between each of the four basic propositions and its *converse*. If the immediate inference is valid, then the information contained in the conclusion must be contained in the premise: that is, any region that is shaded in the conclusion must be shaded in the premise, and any region that contains an asterisk in the conclusion must contain an asterisk in the premise.

Two cases are obvious at first sight. Both the I and the E propositions validly convert. From the I proposition, "Some S is P," we may validly infer "Some P is S."

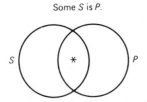

Some S is P.

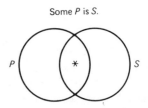

Some P is S.

From the E proposition "No S is P," we may validly infer "No P is S."

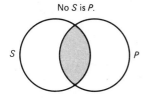

No S is P.

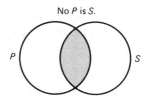

No P is S.

Notice that in both of these cases, the information is in the center of the original diagram, and the diagram for the converse flips over the original diagram. Thus the two diagrams contain the same information since the diagram for the converse has exactly the same markings as the original diagram. This shows that the E and I propositions not only *imply* their converses, but are implied by them. Since the implication runs both ways, they are said to be *logically equivalent*.

The use of a Venn diagram shows that the O proposition cannot, in general, be converted validly. From "Some S is not P," we may not, in general, infer "Some P is not S."[1]

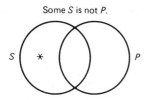

Some S is not P.

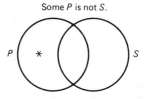

Some P is not S.

Finally, we can see that the A proposition does not validly convert, either. From "All S is P," we may not, in general, infer "All P is S."

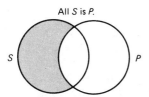

All S is P.

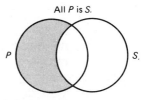

All P is S.

---

[1] There are some strange cases—logicians call them degenerate cases—where inferences of this pattern are valid. For example, from "Some men are not men," we may validly infer "Some men are not men." Here, by making the subject term and predicate term the same, we trivialize conversion. Keeping cases of this kind in mind, we must say that in general, but not always, the conversion of an O proposition does not yield a valid inference. In contrast, the set of valid inferences holds in all cases, including degenerate cases.

Obversion

Before we can deal with *obversion,* we must define the notion of a *complementary class.* The idea is simple enough. Given any class C, its complementary class is just all of those things that are not in C. One standard way of referring to a complementary class is to use the prefix "non." Here are some examples:

Class	Complementary class
Republicans	Non-Republicans
Voters	Nonvoters
Combatants	Noncombatants

If we look at the class of non-Republicans, we see that it is a mixed bag, for as we have defined the notion it includes everything that is not a Republican. This includes coyotes, subatomic particles, prime numbers, the top ten record hits, and the British royal family. Of course, in everyday life we certainly do not wish to include all these things in our notion of a non-Republican. When we speak about non-Republicans, the context will usually make it clear that we are referring to politicians, voters, or party members. We can capture this idea by using a notion introduced earlier, that of a *domain of discourse.* We might say that the domain of discourse here includes all those who are members of American political parties. A non-Republican is someone in this domain of discourse who is not a Republican. We can represent this using the following diagram:

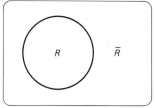

DD: Members of American political parties

A bar over a letter indicates a complementary class. In this case $\bar{R}$ means the class of non-Republicans. As indicated earlier, sometimes it is useful to specify the domain of discourse, sometimes it is not. In this book we will worry about the domain of discourse only when it serves some useful purpose.

We can now define the immediate inference called *obversion.* To pass from a basic proposition to its obverse:

(1) *We reverse the quality of the proposition, from affirmative to negative or negative to affirmative as the case may be.*

(2) *We replace the predicate term by its complementary term.*

Starting with "All men are mortal," this two-step process works as follows:

All men are mortal.

(1) Reversing the quality yields: No men are mortal.
(2) Replacing the predicate term by its complement yields: No men are nonmortal.

This final proposition is the obverse of "All men are mortal."

We now want to know when this operation of obversion is legitimate—that is, we want to know when obversion yields a valid immediate inference. The answer to this is that a proposition is always *logically equivalent* to its obverse. To show this, we can run through the four basic propositions. Since all these equivalences hold between a proposition and its *obverse*, there is no need to draw a diagram twice. The reader should, however, check to see whether the diagram is accurate for both propositions.

A: "All S is P" is logically equivalent to "No S is non-P."

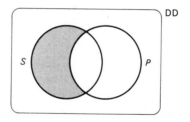

In this diagram, the class of things that are non-P includes all those things in the domain of discourse that are not in P. We can see that there is nothing in the class of things that are S that is also in the complementary class of P, because all the things in S are in the class P. This may sound a bit complicated, but with a very little thought the validity of inferences through obversion becomes quite obvious.

E: "No S is P" is logically equivalent to "All S is non-P."

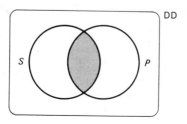

I: "Some *S* is *P*" is logically equivalent to "Some *S* is not non-*P*."

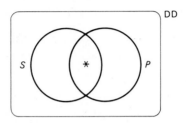

O: "Some *S* is not *P*" is logically equivalent to "Some *S* is non-*P*."

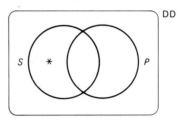

It is important to see that the final equivalence is a genuine equivalence and not a mere repetition. "Some *S* is not *P*" is an O proposition, whereas "Some *S* is non-*P*" is an I proposition. That is, the first proposition formulates a negative proposition—it indicates that there is at least one thing that is not in a certain class. The second proposition is an affirmative proposition, for it indicates that something is in a given class—in this case, a complementary class.

Contraposition

Contraposition is the final relationship we shall examine. We get the contrapositive of a proposition by the following two-step process:

(1) We convert the proposition.
(2) We replace both terms by their complementary terms.

For example, starting with "All men are mortal," this two-step process works as follows:

All men are mortal.
(1) Converted, this proposition becomes:
All mortal (things) are men.
(2) Replacing each term by its complementary term we get:
All nonmortal (things) are non-men.

This final proposition is the contrapositive of "All men are mortal."

Following our previous pattern, we must now ask when the contrapositive can be validly inferred from a given proposition. Here the situation is pretty much the reverse of what we discovered for conversion:

A: "All S is P" is logically equivalent to "All non-P is non-S."

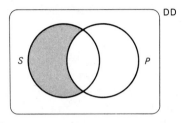

E: From "No S is P" we may not, in general, infer "No non-P is non-S."

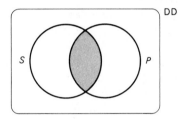
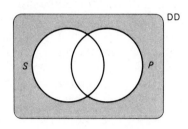

I: From "Some S is P," we may not, in general, infer "Some non-P is non-S."

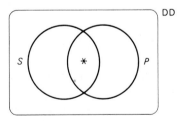
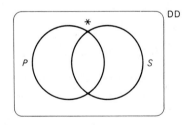

O: "Some S is not P" is logically equivalent to "Some non-P is not non-S."

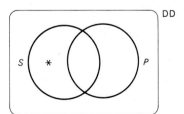
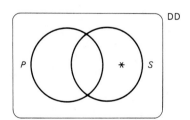

The following table summarizes all these equivalence relationships:

Proposition	Obversion	Conversion	Contraposition
A: All *S* is *P*.	No *S* is non-*P*.	XXXXXXX	All non-*P* is non-*S*.
E: No *S* is *P*.	All *S* is non-*P*.	No *P* is *S*.	XXXXXXX
I: Some *S* is *P*.	Some *S* is not non-*P*.	Some *P* is *S*.	XXXXXXX
O: Some *S* is not *P*.	Some *S* is non-*P*.	XXXXXXX	Some non-*P* is not non-*S*.

If we compare some of the propositions we have been studying with remarks that we make in everyday life, some of them, at least, will seem very artificial. It is hard to imagine a case where we would actually say "Some nonspies are not nonaliens." It would certainly be easier to say, "Some aliens are not spies," which is its equivalent by contraposition.

In fact, we do sometimes find ourselves in contexts where we use some of these complicated sentences. Discussing the voting patterns of nonresidents, we might find ourselves saying that some nonresidents are not nonvoters. Given the context, this remark loses much of its oddness. Usually, however, we choose simple, clear formulations; the ability to do this depends on an implicit understanding of the logical relationships within this system of propositions. Here we are trying to bring this implicit understanding to the surface so that we can understand it better. That is, we are trying to give clear rules for inferences that we make routinely in everyday life.

▼ EXERCISE II

For each of the following propositions, decide by using appropriate diagrams which of the above immediate inferences hold. For example:

All ministers are noncombatants.

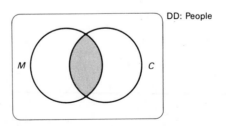

Obverse: No ministers are combatants.

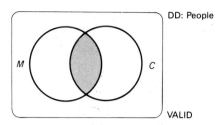

Converse: All noncombatants are ministers.

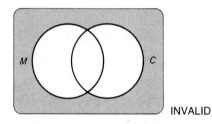

Contrapositive: All non-noncombatants are nonministers. Or more simply: All combatants are nonministers.

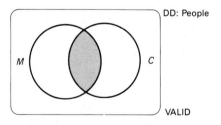

(1) Some dudes are not cowards.
(2) All nonresidents are taxpayers.
(3) Some nonaligned nations are wealthy (nations).
(4) No daughters are sons.
(5) No nonnegotiable stocks are safe (stocks).
(6) All that glitters is not gold.
(7) Some people cannot be bought.
(8) There is no such thing as a bad boy.

▼ EXERCISE III

Put the following sentences into plain, respectable English. Indicate the immediate inference or immediate inferences you have used to do so. (Be careful!)

(1) No noncombatant is a minister.
(2) Some nonresident is not a non-nonvoter.
(3) Not all snakes are not dangerous (things).
(4) No all-the-time losers are non-nonpersons.

THE CLASSICAL THEORY OF IMMEDIATE INFERENCE (OPTIONAL)

We saw earlier that the modern approach differs from the classical or traditional approach with respect to the assignment of existential import. We can think of the classical approach as a theory of reasoning for nonempty classes. The difference between the two approaches comes out in the treatment of the A and E propositions. On the modern approach, the A and E propositions do not presuppose existential import; on the classical approach, they do. The difference between these two approaches can be represented by Venn diagrams.

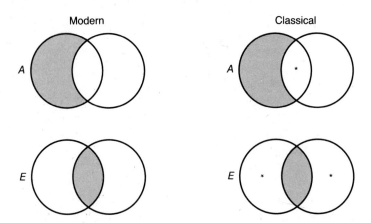

Since an asterisk is a sign of information, it is clear that the classical interpretation assigns more information to the A and E propositions than the modern interpretation does. For this reason, certain immediate inferences hold on the classical approach that do not hold on the modern approach. In particular, though conversion of the A proposition fails on both approaches, what is known as *conversion by limitation* holds on the classical approach (but not the modern). That is, from "All S is P" we may not validly infer that "All P is S" but, on the classical approach, we may validly infer that "Some P is S."

A second immediate inference that is valid on the classical approach that is not valid on the modern approach is known as *contraposition by limitation* for the E proposition. That is, on the classical approach, but not on the modern, the following is a valid immediate inference.

No *S* is *P*.
_____
∴ Some non-*P* is not non-*S*.

▼ EXERCISE IV

Using the Venn diagrams for the classical interpretation of the A and E propositions given above, show that conversion by limitation is classically valid for the A proposition and that contraposition by limitation is classically valid for the E proposition.

THE CLASSICAL SQUARE OF OPPOSITION (OPTIONAL)

Because of its historical importance, in this section we will examine an elegant set of relationships between the four basic propositions that holds on the classical approach to existential import, but not, for the most part, on the modern approach. This system of relationships form what has been called the *square of opposition*. Throughout the discussion, it is important to remember that the basic propositions are interpreted as carrying existential import.

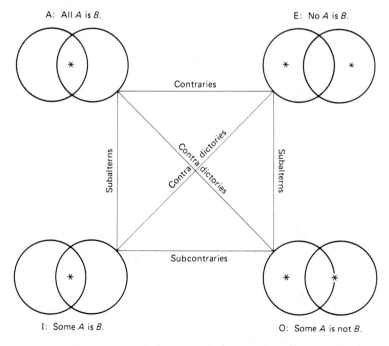

This diagram shows the relationship that each proposition has to the other three. All of these relationships have specific names which are explained below.

Contraries

Two basic propositions are said to be *contraries* of one another if they are so related that

(1) They cannot both be true.
(2) They can, however, both be false.

On the classical interpretation (but not the modern interpretation), the A and E propositions at the top of the square of oppositions are contraries of one another.

In common life, the relationship between the A and the E propositions is captured by the notion that one thing is the *complete opposite* of another. The complete opposite of "Everyone is here" is "No one is here." Clearly, such complete opposites cannot both be true at once. If we look at the diagrams for the A and E propositions, we see this at once. The middle region of the A proposition diagram shows the existence of something that is both A and B whereas the middle region of the E proposition diagram is shaded out, showing that nothing is both A and B. It should also be clear that both the A and E propositions may be false. Suppose that there is some A that is B and also some A that is not B:

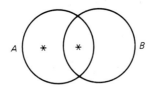

Going from left to right, the first asterisk shows that "All *A* is *B*" is false; the second asterisk shows that "No *A* is *B*" is false.

Contradictories

Two basic propositions are said to be *contradictories* of each other (or to contradict each other) when they are so related that

(1) They cannot both be true.
(2) They cannot both be false.

More simply, contradictory pairs of propositions always have opposite truth values. On the modern interpretation the A and O propositions are contradictories of one another and so are the E and I propositions.

Once more these relationships are reflected in the diagrams we have drawn for these propositions. Here we will only examine the A and O propositions.

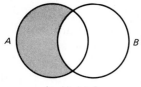

A: All A is B.

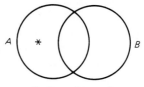

O: Some A is not B.

It is easy to see that these two propositions cannot both be true, for the second diagram has an asterisk in a region that is shaded out in the first diagram. But why must at least one of these propositions be true? Actually, it is rather easy to explain this in the modern approach, where there is no existential commitment for the A and E propositions.

On the modern approach we can represent the denial of a proposition by a simple procedure. The only information given in a Venn Diagram is represented either by *shading out* some region, thereby indicating that nothing exists in it, or by *putting an asterisk* in a region, thereby indicating that something does exist in it. We are given no information about regions that are unmarked. On the modern approach, to represent the denial of a proposition, we simply reverse the information in the diagram. That is, where there is an asterisk, we put in shading; where there is shading, we put in an asterisk. Everything else is left unchanged. Thus in the modern approach, we can see at once that the A and O propositions are denials of one another so that they must always take opposite truth values.

The situation in the classical interpretation is much less tidy. On the classical approach, the A and the O propositions are represented as follows:

A: All A is B.

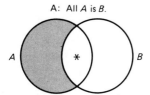

O: Some A is not B.

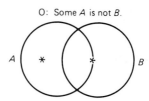

Notice that in the diagram for the O proposition, an asterisk is placed on a line. This indicates that something lies somewhere inside the B circle, but leaves it open whether anything lies in both the A and B circles.

Given these diagrams, it is clear that these propositions cannot both be true since one diagram contains a shaded area where the other contains an asterisk. Furthermore, they cannot both be false. There are only two ways that the O proposition can be false: (i) There might be nothing corresponding to the right-hand asterisk—the one on the line. But that would mean that the B circle is empty, which is not allowed in classical logic. (ii) There might be nothing corresponding to the left-hand asterisk in the diagram for the O proposition. But then that area should be shaded and, because the A circle cannot be empty in classical logic, an asterisk must be added to the remaining portion of the A circle, which makes the A proposition true. Thus, we see that the A and the O propositions that classical logic is willing to consider cannot both be true and cannot both be false. This makes them contradictories, but only because classical logic is not concerned with propositions dealing with empty classes. The same conclusion holds for the E and I propositions. When the classical presuppositions hold, they too are contradictories. (In passing, one reason for adopting the modern approach to categorical propositions is that it avoids this elaborate talk about presuppositions.)

Subcontraries

Basic propositions are *subcontraries* of one another when the following is the case:

(1) They can both be true.
(2) They cannot both be false.

On the classical approach (but not the modern approach), the I and O propositions are subcontraries. To see how this works out, compare the diagrams for the I and O propositions.

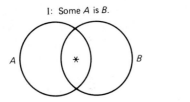

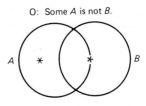

Consider just the left-hand side of the following diagram:

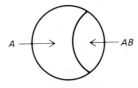

We know that in the classical approach, an asterisk must go into this diagram somewhere. But if the asterisk goes into the overlapping region *AB*, then the I proposition is true; if the asterisk goes into the nonoverlapping region of *A*, then, since *B* cannot be empty, the O proposition is true. So at least one of them is true. Finally, nothing rules out the possibility that there might be an asterisk in each region. In that case both the I and the O propositions would be true, and the situation would look like this:

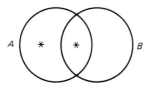

Subalterns

Subalternation is the relationship that holds down the sides of the classical square of opposition. Quite simply, the A proposition implies the I proposition and the E proposition implies the O proposition. Again, this relationship depends on the existential commitment found in the classical approach, and does not hold in the modern approach. We can use our diagrams for testing these implications in the following way: First diagram the premise, and then diagram the conclusion. If the inference from premise to conclusion is valid, then the information contained in the diagram for the conclusion must already be contained in the information given in the diagram for the premise. The validity for subalternation is illustrated by the following diagrams:

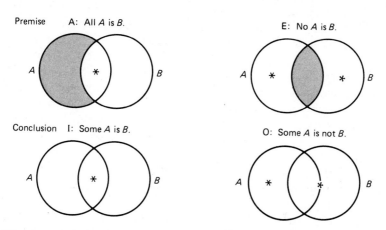

We can summarize the information given by the classical square of opposition using two charts. We shall ask two questions. First, for each proposition, what consequences follow from the assumption that it is true?

	A	E	I	O
A	T	F	T	F
Assumed true E	F	T	F	T
I	?	F	T	?
O	F	?	?	T

Secondly, for each proposition, what consequences follow from the assumption that it is false?

	A	E	I	O
A	F	?	?	T
Assumed false E	?	F	T	?
I	F	T	F	T
O	T	F	T	F

CONVERSATIONAL IMPLICATION AND THE SQUARE OF OPPOSITION (OPTIONAL)

As we have examined the classical treatment of the square of opposition, we have seen that at almost every turn the argument depended on the notion of existential commitment. We might say that the classical approach depends upon making it a logical feature of categorical propositions, that when we talk about things, we are committing ourselves to the existence of the things we are talking about.

We can now look at a different approach that is familiar to us from earlier discussions. Instead of saying that the A proposition *logically implies* the existence of things in its subject class, we can say that the *use* of an A proposition normally *conversationally implies* that there are some things in the subject class. We have to speak in this qualified way because there are times when the use of an A proposition has no such conversational implication. Remember the example of someone saying, "All trespassers will be fined." This does not conversationally imply that the person who says it believes that there will be trespassers. (Having announced this, he may now believe just the opposite.) Reflections of this kind lead to a different way of treating the square of opposition. We can take a logically simple approach of dropping the assumption that the A and E propositions carry existential import. On this modern approach, we get the result that only the relationships of contradictories holds for the square of opposition. All the other relationships now fail. This is all that is left of the traditional square of opposition in the modern approach.

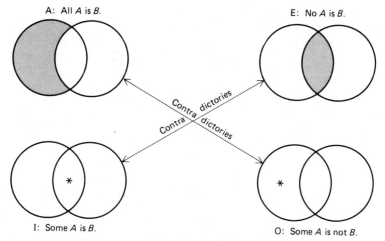

A: All A is B.

E: No A is B.

Contradictories

Contradictories

I: Some A is B.

O: Some A is not B.

We can, however, reflect more of the traditional relationships by adding to this square the conversational implications that arise in standard contexts:

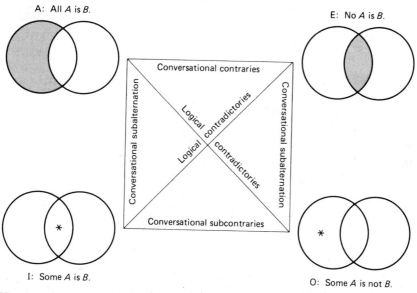

A: All A is B.

E: No A is B.

Conversational contraries

Conversational subalternation

Logical contradictories

Logical contradictories

Conversational subalternation

Conversational subcontraries

I: Some A is B.

O: Some A is not B.

Here only the relationship of contradictories is a logical one; all the other relationships depend on conversational implication and thus are labeled as conversational relationships.

Will it make much difference whether we adopt the classical or the modern approach to the propositions that form the square of opposition? For some purposes it will hardly make any difference at all. In the practical affairs of life it usually does not make any difference whether something is logically implied *by what is said* or conversationally implied by *the saying of it*. In fact, it is only relatively recently that philosophers have become aware of this difference in something like a clear-headed way. Yet from the point of view of logical theory, the distinction is crucial. When we mix up logical implications and conversational implications, our theory can become confused and perhaps incoherent.

This comes out first in the account of contraries on the classical square of opposition. Suppose a landowner posts a sign with an A proposition: All trespassers will be fined." This sign is successful in ensuring that nobody will trespass. Since there will be no trespassers, it certainly seems true that "No trespassers will be fined." But, in classical logic, this E proposition is contrary to the A proposition, so the truth of this E proposition logically implies the falsity of the A proposition on the sign. The sign has become so successful that what it says is false! The problem, of course, is that this E proposition only conversationally implies the falsity of the A proposition, and the absurdity arises when this conversational implication is confused with a logical implication.

Mixing up logical and conversational implication can actually lead to inconsistency. This can be illustrated by noticing another way that conversational rules apply to the use of the propositions on the square of opposition. The use of these propositions is governed by the rule of Strength; that is, where justified, we are expected to use the stronger A or E propositions rather than the weaker I or O propositions. Thus when we use either the I or O propositions, we conversationally imply that we are not in a position to use the stronger A or E propositions. A simple example will show how this works: Filled with greed, a person takes every last piece of candy from a box. When asked whether he has taken the candy, he replies, "I took some of the candy." Now, strictly speaking, this is true. The person did take some of the candy. Yet his remark plainly suggests that he took *only* some of it. Here the violation of the conversational rule is so extreme that it is tempting to call the person's reply an outright lie. In general, then, the use of an I proposition by a speaker conversationally implies that the speaker does not believe the A proposition to be true; sometimes it implies, even more strongly, that he knows the A proposition to be false. We get this stronger implication when the speaker is in a position to know whether the A proposition is true or not. For example, the person who took all the candy is obviously in a position to know what he has done. It is for this reason that his remark conversationally implies the *denial* of the assertion that he took all of the candy.

Now the very same relationship holds between the weak O proposition and the strong E proposition. The use of an O proposition by a speaker usually conversationally implies that the speaker does not believe the E proposition, and sometimes, even more strongly, that he knows it not to be true. This leads to a result that squares with our commonsense understanding of language: When someone says, "Some are . . . ," this conversationally implies "Some are not . . ."; conversely, when someone says, "Some are not . . . ," this conversationally implies "Some are . . ." In general, then, the use of one subcontrary conversationally implies that the use of the other subcontrary is also okay.

We are now in a position to see how mixing up conversational rules with logical rules can lead to lunacy. Consider the following line of reasoning:

> (1)   All aliens are spies.
> ∴ (2)   Some aliens are spies.
> ∴ (3)   Some aliens are not spies.

In this strange argument, we wind up with a proposition implying its own denial, a result we expect to get *only* when we start out from a self-contradictory proposition. It is not hard to see what has gone wrong here. The step from (1) to (2) is a logical implication in the classical approach, and a conversational implication in the modern approach. On the other hand, the step from (2) to (3) must be a conversational implication on either approach. In the argument as a whole, both steps are treated as logical implications, and disaster results.

This last example shows that mixing up logical implications with conversational implications can lead to unwanted results. This, however, does not settle the issue between the classical and the modern approach to the existential import of these basic propositions. A logician is free to argue that existential import is logically implied—not merely conversationally implied—by the A and E propositions. He can then develop his theory accordingly. There is nothing incoherent about such an approach. This text adopts the modern approach for three reasons:

(1)   It yields a simpler logical system.

(2)   It is part of a much wider system that has proved extraordinarily successful.

(3)   It fits in well with the general approach of distinguishing logical implications from conversational implications.

THE THEORY OF THE SYLLOGISM

In an immediate inference, we draw a conclusion directly from a single proposition. The theory of immediate inference explores such inferences as they arise for the basic A E I O propositions. The square of opposition answers the following question: Given the truth or falsity of one of these basic propositions, what, if anything, may we infer concerning the truth or falsity of the remaining basic propositions?

The next step in developing a theory concerning these basic propositions is to consider arguments containing two premises rather than just one. An important group of such arguments is called categorical syllogisms. The basic idea behind these arguments is commonsensical. Suppose you wish to prove that "All *S* is *P*"—whatever *S* or *P* might be. A proof should present some *link* or *connection* between *S* and *P*. This link can be some other term we shall label *M*. In a syllogism we establish a relationship between the terms *S* and *P* through some middle term *M*.

We can now define a categorical syllogism more carefully:

(1) A categorical syllogism is constructed from the basic A, E, I, and O propositions.
(2) Given that the conclusion will contain two terms *S* and *P*, we can place the following restrictions on the premises:
  (i) There are only two premises.
  (ii) One premise contains the term *S*. (This is called the minor premise.)
  (iii) One premise contains the term *P*. (This is called the major premise.)
  (iv) Each premise contains the middle term *M*.

Traditionally, the major premise is stated first, the minor premise second. Here are some examples of syllogisms:

All rectangles have four sides.	(Major premise)
All squares are rectangles.	(Minor premise)
∴ All squares have four sides.	(Conclusion)

Subject term   = Squares
Predicate term = Having four-sides
Middle term   = Rectangles

Schematically, the argument looks like this:

All *M* is *P*.
All *S* is *M*.

∴ All *S* is *P*.

Here is a syllogism containing a negative premise:

No ellipses have sides.
All circles are ellipses.

∴ No circles have sides.

Venn Diagrams for Syllogisms

In the previous section we used Venn diagrams to test the validity of immediate inferences. In a categorical syllogism, three terms appear; thus we are dealing with three classes. To reflect this, we will use diagrams of the following kind:

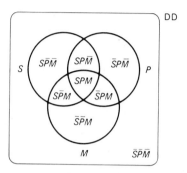

The diagram has eight different compartments:

S	P	$\overline{M}$
S	$\overline{P}$	M
S	$\overline{P}$	$\overline{M}$
$\overline{S}$	P	M
$\overline{S}$	P	$\overline{M}$
$\overline{S}$	$\overline{P}$	M
$\overline{S}$	$\overline{P}$	$\overline{M}$
S	P	M

Notice that if something is not an S or a P or an M, it falls completely outside the system of overlapping circles. In every other case, a thing is assigned to some compartment within the system of overlapping circles.

The Validity of Syllogisms on the Modern Approach

To test the validity of a syllogism using Venn diagrams, we first fill in the diagram to indicate the information contained in the premises. Remember, the only information contained in a Venn diagram is indicated either by shading out an area or putting an asterisk in it. If the argument is valid, then the information expressed by the conclusion will *already* be contained in the diagram. To see this, consider the diagrams for the examples already considered:

All rectangles have four sides.
All squares are rectangles.

∴ All squares have four sides.

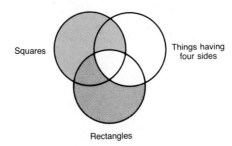

Notice that all the things that are squares are corralled into the region of things that are four-sided. So the argument is valid.

Now let's try a syllogism with a negative premise:

No ellipses have sides.
All circles are ellipses.

∴ No circles have sides.

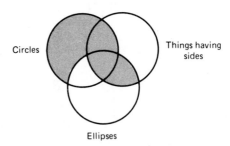

We diagram the conclusion "No circles have sides" as follows:

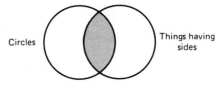

That information is already contained in the Venn diagram for the premises, so this syllogism is also valid.

Next, let's try a syllogism with a particular premise:

> All squares have equal sides.
> Some squares are rectangles.
> ∴ Some rectangles have equal sides.

It is a good strategy to diagram a universal proposition before we diagram a particular proposition. The diagram for the above argument looks like this:

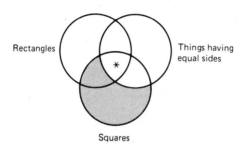

The conclusion—that there is something that is a rectangle that is equal-sided—appears in the diagram for the premises.

So far we have looked only at valid arguments. Here are some patterns for invalid arguments. The conclusion is diagrammed at the right. It is evident that this diagram is not already contained in the diagram for the premises. The arrows show differences in informational content.

> All *M* is *P*.
> All *M* is *S*.
> ∴ All *S* is *P*.

> All *S* is *P*.

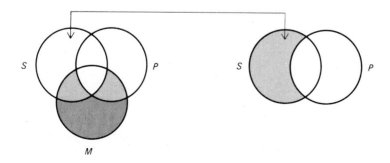

Some *M* is *P*.
Some *S* is *M*.
∴ Some *S* is *P*.

Some *S* is *P*.

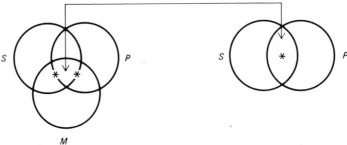

Examine this diagram closely. Notice that in saying "Some *M* is *P*," we had to put the asterisk *on* the boundary of *S*, since we were not given information saying whether anything falls into *S* or not. For the same reason we had to put the asterisk on the boundary of *P* when diagramming "Some *M* is *S*." The upshot was that we did not indicate that anything exists in the region of overlap between *S* and *P*. But this is what the conclusion demands, so the argument is invalid.

No *M* is *P*.
No *S* is *M*.
∴ No *S* is *P*.

No *S* is *P*.

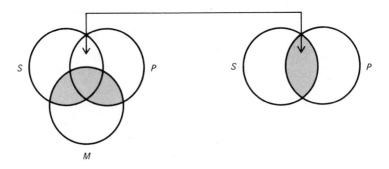

Again we see that this argument is invalid.

▼ EXERCISE V

Adopting the modern approach, test the following syllogisms for validity by using Venn diagrams.

(1)   All *M* is *P*.
      Some *M* is *S*.
    ∴ Some *S* is *P*.

(2)   No *M* is *P*.
      Some *S* is *M*.
    ∴ Some *S* is not *P*.

(3)   No *P* is *M*.
      Some *S* is not *M*.
    ∴ Some *S* is not *P*.

(4)   All *M* is *P*.
      Some *S* is not *M*.
    ∴ Some *S* is not *P*.

(5)   All *P* is *M*.
      No *S* is *M*.
    ∴ No *S* is *P*.

(6)   All *P* is *M*.
      Some *S* is *M*.
    ∴ Some *S* is *P*.

(7)   Some *P* is not *M*.
      Some *S* is *M*.
    ∴ Some *S* is not *P*.

(8)   No *P* is *M*.
      Some *M* is *S*.
    ∴ Some *S* is not *P*.

The Validity of Syllogisms on the Classical Approach

In the discussion of immediate inferences, we raised the question of whether the universal propositions—the A and the E propositions—carried existential import. That is, when we assert "All *S* is *P*" or assert "No *S* is *P*" are we committing ourselves to the existence of *S*s and *P*s? The ruling for the modern interpretation is no, the ruling for the classical interpretation is yes. The same rulings carry over to the theory of the syllogism. We have presented the modern theory of the syllogism by using Venn diagrams that do not assign an existential commitment to the A and E propositions. We get the classical interpretation simply by using diagrams that do indicate existential import for all of the basic propositions.

We can begin our study of this matter with an example that has had a curious history:

> All rectangles are four-sided.
> All squares are rectangles.
>
> ∴ *Some* squares are four-sided.

The argument is peculiar because the conclusion is weaker than it needs to be. We could, after all, conclude that *all* squares are four-sided. The argument thus violates the conversational rule of Quantity; perhaps for this reason, this syllogism was often not included in traditional lists of valid syllogisms. Yet the argument is valid on the traditional interpretation of existential import and our diagram should show this.

Step I

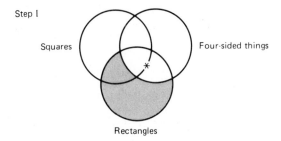

Squares   Four-sided things

Rectangles

Notice that the asterisk is placed on the line dividing regions SPM and $\overline{S}PM$ since we are not in a position to put it into one region rather than the other. We now draw in the second premise:

Step II

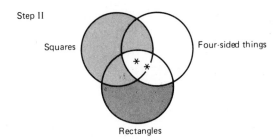

Squares   Four-sided things

Rectangles

As expected, the conclusion that some squares are four-sided is already diagrammed, so the argument is valid—provided that we commit ourselves to the existential import of A propositions.

Because classical logicians tended to ignore the previous argument, their writings did not bring out the importance of existential import in evaluating it. There is, however, an argument that did appear on the classical lists that makes clear the demand for existential commitment. These are syllogisms of the following kind:

$$\begin{array}{l} \text{All } M \text{ is } P. \\ \underline{\text{All } M \text{ is } S.} \\ \therefore \text{Some } S \text{ is } P. \end{array}$$

This is diagrammed as follows:

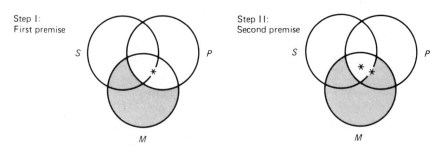

Step I:
First premise

S P

M

Step II:
Second premise

S P

M

Again we see that the conclusion follows, but only if we diagram the universal propositions to indicate existential import. This, then, is an argument that was declared valid in the classical approach, but invalid in the modern approach.

▼ SUMMARY

The method of Venn diagrams is adequate for deciding the formal validity or invalidity of all possible syllogisms. Furthermore, the use of Venn diagrams makes it easy to distinguish between syllogisms that are classically valid and those that are valid on the modern interpretation. To get the classical theory, we simply include existential commitment in our diagrams of all of the basic propositions; in the modern approach the A and E propositions are not assigned existential import.

Problems in Applying the Theory of the Syllogism

After students have mastered the techniques for evaluating syllogisms, they naturally turn to arguments that arise in daily life and attempt to use these newly acquired skills. They are often disappointed with the results. The formal theory of the syllogism seems to bear little relationship to everyday arguments, and there doesn't seem to be any easy way to bridge the gap.

This gap between formal theory and its application occurs for a number of reasons. First, as we saw in Chapter 1, our everyday discourse leaves much unstated. Many things are conversationally implied rather than explicitly asserted. Moreover, we do not feel called on to say many things that are matters of common agreement. Before we can apply the theory of the syllogism to everyday arguments, these things that are simply understood must be made explicit. This is often illuminating, and sometimes boring, but it usually involves a great deal of work. Second, the theory of the syllogism applies to statements only in a highly stylized form. Before we apply the theory of the syllogism to an argument, we must cast its premises and conclusion into the basic A, E, I, and O forms. This is not always easy. It may not always be possible. For these and related reasons, modern logicians have largely abandoned the project of reducing all reasoning to syllogisms.

Why study the theory of the syllogism at all, if it is hard to apply in some circumstances and perhaps impossible to apply in others? The answer to this question was given at the beginning of Chapter 7: The study of formal logic is important because it deepens our insight into the central notion of logic, *validity*. Furthermore, the argument forms we have studied do underlie much of our everyday reasoning, but so much else is going on in a normal conversational setting that this dimension is often hidden. By examining arguments in idealized forms, we can study their validity in isolation from all the other factors at work in a rich conversational setting.

There is a difference, then, between the techniques developed in Chapters 1 to 6 and the techniques developed in these last two chapters. The first six chapters presented methods of informal analysis that may be applied directly to the rich and complex arguments that arise in everyday life. These methods of analysis are not wholly rigorous, but they do provide practical guides for the analysis and evaluation of actual arguments. These two chapters concerning formal logic have the opposite tendency. In comparison with the first six chapters, the level of rigor is very high, but the range of application is correspondingly smaller. In general, the more rigor and precision you insist upon, the less you can talk about.

APPENDIX: A SYSTEM OF RULES FOR EVALUATING SYLLOGISMS

The method of Venn diagrams that we have used in this chapter is probably the most natural technique for analyzing syllogisms, because the relationship between overlapping figures is a clear analogy for the relationship between classes. Another method for evaluating syllogisms employs a system of rules. While this system has less intuitive appeal than Venn diagrams, it is easier to apply. The procedure is to lay down a set of rules such than any syllogism that satisfies all of the rules is valid and any syllogism that fails to satisfy any one of them is invalid. A concise summary of one such system is presented here.

Distribution. The central idea for one system of rules is that of the *distribution* or *extension* of a term. The basic idea is that a term is used distributively in a proposition if it is used to refer to the whole of a class or to all of the members in it. We shall first simply state the distributional properties for each of the basic A, E, I, and O propositions and then try to make sense out of this notion.

Proposition	Subject	Predicate
A	Distributed	Undistributed
E	Distributed	Distributed
I	Undistributed	Undistributed
O	Undistributed	Distributed

The two universal propositions A and E have distributed subject terms. In the I and O propositions we speak about *some S*, therefore the subject term is undistributed for these propositions.

The reasoning runs smoothly for the subject term, but the predicate term is not so easy to deal with. Notice that there is no word like "some" or "all" governing the predicate term.

The reasoning concerning the predicate term usually proceeds along the following lines: Suppose we assert that no squares are circles.

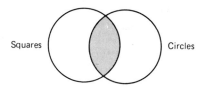

For this to be true, there can be no square that is identical with *any* circle. The appearance of the word "any" shows that the predicate term is distributed in the E proposition. Consider next the O proposition: Some *S* is not *P*. For this to be true, there must be some *S* that is not identical with *any P*. Again, the appearance of the word "any" shows that the predicate term is distributed. Our test for the distribution of terms is then to compare the basic A E I O proposition with a counterpart statement involving identity as follows:

A: All *S* is *P*.   For *any S* there is *some P* that is identical with it.
E: No *S* is *P*.   For *any S* there is not *any P* that is identical with it.
I: Some *S* is   For *some S* there is *some P* that is identical with it.
    P.
O: Some *S* is   For *some S* there is not *any P* that is identical with it.
    not *P*.

This comparison gives the pattern for the distribution of terms noticed earlier.

Quality. Along with the notion of distribution, the system of rules we are discussing here also uses the idea of the *quality* of a proposition—whether it is affirmative or negative. Recall that the A and I propositions are said to be *affirmative* propositions; the E and the O propositions are said to be *negative* propositions. The following rules are adequate for testing the validity of categorical syllogisms:

Quality:

(1) Nothing follows from two negative premises.
(2) If one premise is negative, then the conclusion must be negative as well.
(2') If the conclusion is negative, then one premise must be negative.[2]

---

[2] Rule 2' is not needed in the modern interpretation of existential import, because any syllogism that violates it will also violate a rule of distribution. It is, however, needed in the classical interpretation, which lacks Rule 6.

Distribution:

(3)   The middle term must be distributed at least once.
(4)   The subject term may not be distributed in the conclusion if it is not distributed in the premises.
(5)   The predicate term may not be distributed in the conclusion if it is not distributed in the premises.

The fallacies that result from violating these rules are called by the following names:

Quality:

(1)   The Fallacy of Two Negative Premises
(2)   The Fallacy of Drawing an Affirmative Conclusion from a Negative Premise
(2') The Fallacy of Drawing a Negative Conclusion from two Affirmative Premises

Distribution:

(3)   The Fallacy of the Undistributed Middle
(4)   The Fallacy of the Illicitly Distributed Subject
(5)   The Fallacy of the Illicitly Distributed Predicate

Quantity.   The rules of distribution and quality are adequate for the analysis of syllogisms in the classical interpretation. The modern interpretation requires a further rule of *quantity*. Recall that the A and the E propositions are said to be *universal* propositions; the I and the O propositions are said to be *particular* propositions.

Quantity:

(6)   A particular conclusion cannot be derived from two universal premises.

Corresponding to this there is, in the modern approach, a fallacy:

(6)   The Fallacy of Deriving a Particular Conclusion from Universal Premises

The following devises facilitate the application of these rules. Mark the propositions in the syllogism " + " or " − " to indicate quality. Circle all terms that are distributed, leaving all undistributed terms uncircled. This makes it easy to see if the first five rules of the syllogism have been satisfied, and so whether the syllogism is valid or invalid in the classical approach. No special devices are needed to check the additional sixth rule needed in the modern approach.

The following examples illustrate these methods:

(1)   +   All Ⓜ is P.
      +   All Ⓢ is M.   Valid
∴ +   All Ⓢ is P.

(2)   −   No Ⓜ is Ⓟ.
      +   Some M is S.   Valid
∴ −   Some S is not Ⓟ.

(3)   +   All Ⓜ is P.   Valid classically
      +   All Ⓜ is S.   Invalid in modern approach (Rule 6)
∴ +   Some S is P.

(4)   +   All Ⓜ is P.   Invalid—
      +   All Ⓜ is S.   Illicitly Distributed Subject
∴ +   All Ⓢ is P.

(5)   +   All Ⓟ is M.   Invalid—
      +   All Ⓢ is M.   Undistributed Middle
∴ +   All Ⓢ is P.

(6)   −   No Ⓟ is Ⓜ.   Invalid—
      −   No Ⓢ is Ⓜ.   Two Negatives Premises
∴ −   No Ⓢ is Ⓟ.

▼ EXERCISE VI

Using the system of rules we have developed, test the syllogisms given in Exercise V for validity. Where a fallacy occurs, give the name of that fallacy.

▼ EXERCISE VII

To a person familiar with computer programming, this system of rules immediately suggests that a program can be written for the evaluation of syllogisms. In fact, such a program can be written and is only moderately difficult. The first problem is to find some method for encoding all possible syllogisms. After this, the notions of distribution and quality must be given mathematical analogues. In writing such a program, there is a good chance that the programmer will discover on his or her own large portions of medieval logic.

▼ DISCUSSION QUESTIONS

(1) What are the chief differences between the logical procedures developed in this chapter and those developed in the previous chapter?

(2) If we evaluate arguments as they occur in everyday life by using the exact standards developed in these last two chapters, we discover that our everyday arguments rarely satisfy these standards, at least *explicitly*. Does this show that most of our ordinary arguments are illogical? What else might it show?

9

Inductive
Reasoning

This chapter begins by explaining the difference between *deductive* and *inductive* arguments. The difference depends on the relationship between the premises and conclusion of each type of argument. With a valid deductive argument, if the premises are true, then the conclusion *must* be true as well. This is not true for inductive arguments even when they place the conclusion beyond reasonable doubt.

Two kinds of inductive reasoning are examined in detail. First, the chapter describes *inductive generalizations,* where a statistical claim is made about a *population* on the basis of features of a *sample* of that population. The standard fallacies that can arise with such generalizations are examined in detail.

Second, the chapter examines *causal generalizations* and suggests ways they can be tested.

INDUCTION VS. DEDUCTION

Since Chapter 2 we have been concerned almost exclusively with *deductive* arguments, but many arguments (perhaps most arguments) encountered in daily life are not intended to be deductive. In particular, many arguments are said to be *inductive* in character. In this chapter we shall examine some of the chief forms that inductive arguments take.

The distinction between deductive arguments and inductive arguments can be drawn in a variety of ways, but the fundamental difference concerns the relationship that is claimed to hold between the premises and the conclusion for each type of argument. As we know, in a valid deductive argument, if the premises are true, then it is impossible for the conclusion to be false. For example, the following is a valid deductive argument:

> All ravens are black.
> _____
> ∴ If there is a raven on top of Pikes Peak, then it is black.

Since the premise lays down a universal principle governing all ravens, if it's true, then it *must* be true of all ravens (if any) on top of Pikes Peak. Of course, this same relationship does not hold for an *invalid* deductive argument. Still, if someone puts forward an argument as deductive, that person is committed to the claim that this relationship holds, that is, that the argument is valid, and can be criticized if it does not.

This same relationship between premises and conclusion is not even claimed to hold for inductive arguments. The following is an example of an inductive argument:

> All ravens we have observed are black.
> _____
> ∴ If there is a raven on top of Pikes Peak, then it is black.

Here we have drawn an inductive inference from the characteristics of ravens we have observed (the sample) to the characteristics of a raven we have not observed. We realize that the premise of this argument *could be* true, yet the conclusion turns out to be false. The raven on top of Pikes Peak may be an albino. We put forth the premise as offering strong support for the conclusion; we do not put it forth as necessitating it.

The fundamental difference between an inductive argument and a deductive argument can be brought out in another way. Suppose that we have a valid deductive argument of the following form:

$P_1, \ldots, P_n$, therefore Q.

Now a fundamental feature of a valid deductive argument is that its validity cannot be changed through the addition of further premises.

The definition of a valid deductive argument guarantees this: if an argument is valid, then the premises cannot be true without the conclusion being true as well, and that relationship between premises and conclusion cannot be cancelled or overridden by the introduction of further premises. Furthermore, if an argument is not only valid but sound, this property cannot be removed by adding further premises, as long as they are true. Additional information might, of course, lead us to question the truth of one of the premises that we previously accepted, and we might then reconsider whether the argument that we previously considered sound really is sound—but that's another matter.

The situation is strikingly different when we deal with inductive arguments. First, since the notion of validity was introduced for the assessment of deductive arguments, we will not use the term when dealing with inductive arguments, which, after all, are not put forward as being deductively valid. We will, instead, speak of inductive arguments as being *strong* or *weak*. Suppose we have an inductive argument that gives very strong support to its conclusion. To cite a famous example, before the time of Captain Cook's voyage to Australia, Europeans had observed a great many swans, and every last one of them was white. Thus, up to that time, Europeans had very strong inductive evidence to support the claim that all swans are white. Then Captain Cook discovered black swans in Australia. What happens if we add this new piece of information to the premises of the original inductive argument? Provided that we accept Captain Cook's report, we now have a sound deductive argument in behalf of the claim that *not* all swans are white, for, if some swans are black, then not all of them are white. This, then, is a feature of every inductive argument: no matter how strong an inductive argument is, the possibility remains open that further information can undercut it—perhaps *completely*. A valid deductive argument does not face a similar peril.[1]

Because of the strong relationship between the premises and conclusion of a valid deductive argument, it is sometimes said that the premises of valid deductive arguments (if true) provide conclusive support for their conclusions, whereas true premises in inductive arguments provide only partial support for their conclusions. In a way this is correct. Because the premises of a valid deductive argument (if true)

---

[1] In the technical literature on the subject, this difference between deductive arguments and inductive arguments is sometimes described by saying that deductive inferences are *monotonic*, whereas inductive inferences are nonmonotonic. These words are used on an analogy with mathematical curves. A (positive) monotonic curve rises, perhaps flattens out, but never changes direction. A nonmonotonic curve can change direction—for example, rise, then fall. Thus, in the white swan example, before Captain Cook's voyages, the evidence in behalf of the claim that all swans are white had become very strong. After his discovery of black swans, the evidential support collapsed.

necessitate the truth of the conclusion, they supply conclusive support for the conclusion. The same cannot be said for inductive arguments. But it would be altogether misleading to infer from this that inductive arguments are inherently inferior to deductive arguments in supplying a justification or ground for a conclusion. In the first place, inductive arguments often place matters beyond doubt. It is possible that the next pot of water will not boil at any temperature, however high, but this is not something we worry about—we do not take precautions against it.

Second, and more importantly, deductive arguments often enjoy no advantages over their inductive counterparts. We can see this by examining the two arguments just given:

Deductive	Inductive
All ravens are black.	All ravens so far observed have been black.
∴ If there is a raven on top of Pikes Peak, it will be black.	∴ If there is a raven on top of Pikes Peak, it will be black.

Of course, it is true for the deductive argument, and not true for the inductive argument, that if the premise is true, then the conclusion must be true, and this may seem to give an advantage to the deductive argument over the inductive argument. But before we can decide how much support a deductive argument gives its conclusion, we must ask whether its premises are, after all, true. That is not something we can just take for granted. Now if we examine the premises of these two arguments, we see that it is easier to establish the truth of the premise of the inductive argument than it is to establish the truth of the premises of the deductive argument. If we have observed carefully and kept good records, then we might be fully confident that all *observed* ravens have been black. On the other hand, how can we show that *all* ravens (observed and unobserved—past, present, and future) are black? The most obvious way, though there may be other ways, would be to observe ravens to see whether they are black or not. But this, of course, involves producing an inductive argument (called an inductive generalization) for the premise of the deductive argument. Here our confidence in the truth of the premise of the deductive argument should be no greater than our confidence in the strength of the inference in the inductive generalization. In this case—and it is not unusual—the deductive argument provides no stronger grounds in support of its conclusion than does its inductive counterpart, because any reservations we might have about the *strength* of the inductive inference will be paralleled by doubts concerning the *truth* of the premise of the deductive argument.

In passing, we will also avoid the common mistake of saying that deductive arguments always move from the general to the particular, whereas inductive arguments always move from the particular to the general. In fact, both sorts of arguments can move in either way. There are inductive arguments intended to establish particular matters of fact, and there are deductive arguments that involve generalizations from particulars.

For example, scientists are currently debating whether or not the extinction of the dinosaurs was caused by the impact of an asteroid. Their discussions are models of inductive reasoning because they are assembling empirical evidence to confirm or disconfirm this hypothesis. Yet they are not trying to establish a generalization or a scientific law; instead they are trying to determine whether a particular event occurred some 60 million years ago. Inductive reasoning concerning particular matters of fact occurs constantly in everyday life as well—for example, when we check to see whether someone using a computer is messing up our television reception. Deductive arguments from the particular to the general tend to be trivial, hence boring, but they do exist. Here's one: Benjamin Franklin was the first postmaster general; therefore, anyone identical with Benjamin Franklin was the first postmaster general.

Of course, many inductive arguments do move from particular premises to a general conclusion, and many deductive arguments move from the general to the particular. Again, however, this is not the *definitive* difference between these two kinds of arguments, and to suppose that it is can lead to serious misunderstandings. To repeat, the difference between inductive and deductive arguments consists in the *claimed* relationship between the premises and the conclusion.

Because inductive arguments involve different commitments than deductive arguments, it is a mistake to judge them by the same standards. What, then, are the standards appropriate for assessing inductive arguments? This question can be answered at various levels. At an informal level, we can lay down some general rules—or rules of thumb—that will allow us to avoid many of the more common errors of inductive reasoning. In complicated situations, however, our commonsense principles are often inadequate and can, in fact, let us down. When common sense gets out of its depth, we must turn to the procedures of mathematical statistics for help. Here we shall concern ourselves almost exclusively with informal procedures for the evaluation of inductive arguments, but we shall also examine cases where they are inadequate.

▼ EXERCISE I

Assuming a standard context, label each of the following arguments as deductive or inductive.

(1) The sun is coming out, so the rain should stop soon.

(2) It's going to rain tomorrow, so it is either going to rain or going to be clear tomorrow.

(3) Diet cola doesn't keep me awake at night; I drink it all the time without any problems.

(4) No one in Paris seems to understand me, so either my French is rotten or Parisians are unfriendly.

(5) If Harold is innocent, he would not go into hiding; but he is in hiding, so he is not innocent.

(6) The house is a mess, so Jeff must be home from college.

(7) No woman has ever been elected president of the United States; therefore, no woman will ever be elected president of the United States.

(8) There is no even number smaller than two, so one is not an even number.

INDUCTIVE GENERALIZATIONS

Inductive generalizations are a common (perhaps the most common) form of inductive reasoning. Here we cite characteristics of a sample of a population to support a claim about the character of the population as a whole. Opinion polls work this way. Suppose a candidate wants to know how popular she is with voters. Since it would be practically impossible to survey all voters, she takes a sample of voting opinions and then infers that the opinions of those sampled indicate the overall opinions of voters. Thus, if 60 percent of the voters sampled say that they will vote for her, she concludes that she will get more or less 60 percent of the vote in the actual election. As we shall see later on, inferences of this kind often go wrong, even when made by experts, but the general pattern of this reasoning is quite clear: statistical features of a sample are used to make statistical claims about the population as a whole.

How do we assess such inferences? To begin to answer this question, we can consider a simple example of an inductive generalization. On various occasions Harold has tried to use Canadian quarters in American telephones and found that they have not worked. From this he draws the conclusion that Canadian quarters do not work in American telephones. Harold's inductive reasoning looks like this:

In the past, when I have tried to use Canadian quarters in American telephones, they have not worked.

∴ Canadian quarters do not work in American telephones.

The force of the conclusion is that Canadian quarters never work in American telephones.

In evaluating this argument, what questions should we ask? As we proceed through the first half of this chapter, we will loosely frame some questions that can be applied to all inductive generalizations, and when we are through we should be able to restate those questions with greater accuracy. To start with, then, one question we should ask of any argument is about its premises:

(1) Should We Accept the Premises?

Perhaps Harold has a bad memory, or has kept bad records, or is a poor observer. For some obscure reason, he may even be lying. It is important to ask this question explicitly, because fairly often the premises, when challenged, will not stand up to scrutiny.

If we decide that the premises are acceptable, we can then shift our attention to the relationship between the premises and the conclusion and ask how much support the premises give to the conclusion. One commonsense question is this: "Just how many times has Harold tried to use Canadian quarters in American telephones?" If the answer comes back "Three or four times," then our confidence in his argument should drop to almost nothing. So for inductive generalizations, it is always appropriate to ask about the size of the sample:

(2) Is the Sample Large Enough to Avoid Bias?

One reason that we should be suspicious of small samples is that they can be affected by runs of luck. Suppose Harold flips a Canadian quarter four times and it comes up heads each time. From this, he can hardly conclude that Canadian quarters always come up heads when flipped. He could not even reasonably conclude that *this* Canadian quarter would always come up heads when flipped. The reason for this is obvious enough; if you spend a lot of time flipping coins, runs of four heads in a row are not all that unlikely (the odds are actually 1 in 16), and therefore samples of this size can easily be distorted by chance. On the other hand, if Harold flipped the coin 20 times and it continued to come up heads, he would have strong grounds for saying that this coin, at least, will always come up heads. In fact, he would have very strong grounds for thinking that he has a two-headed coin. Because an overly small sample can lead to erroneous conclusions, we can say that it is unfair or biased, simply on a statistical level.

How many is enough? On the assumption, for the moment, that our sampling has been fair in all other respects, how many samples do we need to provide the basis for a strong inductive argument? This is not always an easy question to answer, and sometimes answering it demands subtle mathematical techniques. Suppose your company is selling 100 million computer chips to the Department of Defense, and you have guaranteed that no more than 0.2 percent of them will be defective. It would be prohibitively expensive to test all the chips, and testing only a dozen would hardly be enough to reasonably guarantee that the total shipment of chips meet the required specifications. Because testing chips is expensive, you want to test as few as possible, but because meeting the specifications is crucial, you want to test enough to guarantee that you have done so. Answering questions of this kind demands sophisticated statistical techniques beyond the scope of this text.

Sometimes, then, it is difficult to decide how many samples are needed to give reasonable support to inductive generalizations; yet many times it is obvious, without going into technical details, that the sample is too small. Drawing an inductive conclusion from a sample that is too small can lead to the fallacy of *hasty generalization*, and it is surprising how common this fallacy is. We see a person two or three times and find him cheerful, and we immediately leap to the conclusion that he is a cheerful person. That is, from a few instances of cheerful behavior, we draw a general conclusion about his personality. When we meet him later and find him sad, morose, or grouchy, we then conclude that he has changed—thus swapping one hasty generalization for another.

This tendency toward hasty generalization was discussed more than two hundred years ago by the philosopher David Hume, who saw that we have a strong tendency to "follow general rules which we rashly form to ourselves, and which are the source of what we properly call prejudice." This tendency toward hasty generalization has been the subject of extensive psychological investigation. In an article titled "Belief in the Law of Small Numbers," cognitive psychologists Amos Tversky and Daniel Kahneman put the matter this way:

> We submit that people view a sample randomly drawn from a population as highly representative, that is, similar to the population in all essential characteristics. Consequently, they expect any two samples drawn from a particular population to be more similar to one another and to the population than sampling theory predicts, at least for small samples.[2]

To return to a previous example, we make our judgments of someone's personality on the basis of a very small sample of his or her behavior and expect this person to behave in similar ways in the future when we encounter further samples of behavior. We are surprised, some-

---

[2] Amos Tversky and Daniel Kahneman, "Belief in the Law of Small Numbers," *Psychological Bulletin*, Vol. 76, No. 2 (1971), p. 105.

times indignant, when the future behavior does not match our expectations.

By making our samples sufficiently large, we can guard against distortions due to "runs of luck," but even very large samples can give us a poor basis for an inductive generalization. Suppose that Harold has tried hundreds of times to use a Canadian quarter in an American telephone and it has never worked. This will increase our confidence in his inductive generalization, but size of sample alone is not a sufficient ground for a strong inductive argument. Suppose that Harold has tried the same coin in hundreds of different telephones, or tried a hundred different Canadian coins in the same telephone. In the first case, there might be something wrong with this particular coin; in the second case, there might be something wrong with this particular telephone. In neither case would he have good grounds for making the general claim that no Canadian quarters work in any American telephones. This leads us to the third question we should ask of any inductive generalization:

(3) Is the Sample Biased in Other Ways?

When the sample, however large, is not representative of the population, then again it is said to be unfair or biased. Here we can speak of the fallacy of *biased sampling*. One of the most famous examples of biased sampling was committed by a magazine named the *Literary Digest*. Before the presidential election of 1936, this magazine sent ten million questionnaires asking which candidate the recipient would vote for: Franklin Roosevelt or Alf Landon. They received two and a half million returns, and on the basis of the result confidently predicted that Landon would win by a landslide: 56 percent for Landon to only 44 percent for Roosevelt. When the election results came in, Roosevelt won by an even larger landslide in the opposite direction: 62 percent for Roosevelt to a mere 38 percent for Landon. What went wrong? The sample was certainly large enough; in fact, by contemporary standards it was much larger than needed. It was the way the sample was selected, not its size, that caused the problem: the sample was randomly drawn from names in telephone books and from club membership lists. Now in 1936 there were only 11 million telephones in the United States and many of the poor—especially the rural poor—did not have telephones. During the Great Depression there were more than nine million unemployed in America; they were almost all poor and thus under-represented in the magazine's sample. Finally, a very large percentage of this under-represented group voted for Roosevelt, the Democratic candidate. As a result of this bias in their sampling, along with some others as well, the *Literary Digest* underestimated Roosevelt's percentage of the vote by a whopping 18 percent.

Looking back, it may be hard to believe that intelligent observers could have done such a ridiculously bad job of sampling opinion, but the story repeats itself, though rarely on the grand scale of the *Literary Digest* fiasco. In 1948, for example, the Gallup Poll, which had correctly predicted Roosevelt's victory in 1936, predicted, along with other major polls, a clear victory for Dewey over Truman. Confidence was so high in this prediction that the *Chicago Tribune* published a banner headline declaring Dewey had won the election even before the votes were counted. What went wrong this time? The answer here is more subtle. Gallup (and others) went to great pains to make sure that their sample was representative of the voting population. Thus their interviewers were told to poll a certain number of people from particular social groups: rural poor, suburban middle class, urban middle class, ethnic minorities, and so on, so that the proportions of those interviewed matched, as closely possible, the proportions of those likely to vote. (The *Literary Digest* went bankrupt after its misprediction, so the pollsters were taking no chances.) Yet somehow bias crept into the sampling; the question was, how? One speculation was that a significantly large percentage of those sampled didn't tell the truth when they were interviewed; another was that a large number of people changed their minds at the last minute. So maybe the data collected were not very reliable. The explanation generally accepted was more subtle. Although Gallup's workers were told to interview specific numbers of people from particular classes (so many from the suburbs, for example), they were not instructed to choose people randomly from within each group. Without seriously thinking about it, they tended to go to "nicer" neighborhoods and interviewed "nicer" people. Because of this, they biased the sample in the direction of their own (largely) middle class preferences and, as a result, underrepresented constituencies that would give Truman his unexpected victory.

SOURCES OF BIAS

Because professionals using modern statistical analysis can make bad inductive generalizations through biased sampling, it is not surprising that our everyday, informal inductive generalizations are often inaccurate. It will be useful, then, to look at some of the main sources of bias in sampling. We have already examined two sources of bias: biases due to small samples and biases due to limited personal experience. Here are some other sources of bias.

Prejudice and Stereotypes

People who are prejudiced will find very little good and a great deal bad in those they despise, no matter how these people actually behave. In fact, most people are a mixture of good and bad qualities, and by ignoring the former and dwelling on the latter, it is easy enough for the prejudiced person to confirm his negative opinions. Similarly, stereotypes, which can be either positive or negative, often persist in the face of overwhelming counterevidence. Speaking of the beliefs common in Britain in his own day, David Hume remarked:

> An Irishman cannot have wit, and a Frenchman cannot have solidity; for which reason, though the conversation of the former in any instance be very agreeable, and of the latter very judicious, we have entertained such a prejudice against them, that they must be dunces and fops in spite of sense and reason.[3]

Informal Judgmental Heuristics

In daily life, we have to make a great many decisions, some of them important, most of them not. Furthermore, because we have to make a great many decisions, they often have to be made quickly without pausing to weigh evidence carefully. To deal with this overload of decisions, we commonly employ what cognitive psychologists call *judgmental heuristics*. Technically, a heuristic is a device that provides a general strategy for solving a problem or coming to a decision. (For example, a good heuristic for solving geometry problems is to start with the conclusion you are trying to reach and then work backwards.) Recent research in cognitive psychology has shown, first, that human beings rely very heavily on heuristics and, second, that we often put too much reliance on them. The result is that our inductive inferences often go badly wrong, and that sometimes our thinking gets utterly mixed up. In this regard, two heuristics are particularly interesting: the *representative heuristic* and the *availability heuristic*.

The Representative Heuristic.   A simple example illustrates how errors can arise from the representative heuristic. You are randomly dealt five-card hands from a standard deck. Which of the following two hands is more likely to come up?

(1)	(2)
Three of Clubs	Ace of Spades
Seven of Diamonds	Ace of Hearts
Nine of Diamonds	Ace of Clubs
Queen of Hearts	Ace of Diamonds
King of Spades	King of Spades

---

[3]   David Hume, *A Treatise of Human Nature,* 2nd ed. (London: Oxford University, 1978), pp. 146–47. This work was first published in 1739.

A surprisingly large number of people will automatically say that the second hand is much less likely than the first. Actually, if you think about it for a bit, it should be obvious that any two specific hands have exactly the same likelihood of being dealt. Here people get confused because the first hand is an ordinary hand, the kind that comes up all the time, a *representative* hand, whereas the second hand is extraordinary and looks unrepresentative. Here our reliance on representativeness blinds us to a simple and obvious point about probabilities: any specific hand is as likely to come up as any other.

A later set of experiments carried out by Tversky and Kahneman yielded an even more remarkable result.[4] Students were given the following description of a fictitious person named Linda:

> Linda is 31 years old, single, outspoken and very bright. She majored in philosophy. As a student, she was deeply concerned with issues of discrimination and social justice, and also participated in antinuclear demonstrations.

The students were then asked to rank the following statements with respect to the probability that they were also true of Linda:

> Linda is a teacher in elementary school.
> Linda works in a bookstore and takes yoga classes.
> Linda is active in the feminist movement.
> Linda is a psychiatric social worker.
> Linda is a member of the League of Women Voters.
> Linda is a bank teller.
> Linda is an insurance salesperson.
> Linda is a bank teller and is active in the feminist movement.

Not surprisingly, the students thought that it was most likely that Linda was a feminist, and least likely that she was a bank teller. What was surprising was that 89 percent of the subjects in one experiment thought that it was more likely that Linda was both a bank teller and a feminist than that she was simply a bank teller. Now, if you think about that for a moment, you will see that it cannot be right: the probability that two things are true can never be higher than the probability that just one of them is true. Presumably what happens here is something like this: unreflectively, people think that the claim that Linda is both a bank teller and a feminist at least says something plausible about her whereas the simple claim that she is a bank teller isn't plausible at all. But that is just bad reasoning, and here reliance on the representative heuristic doesn't merely give us an inaccurate estimate of a probability, it actually leads us into a logical blunder.

---

[4] Amos Tversky and Daniel Kahneman, "Extensional Versus Intuitive Reasoning: The Conjunction Fallacy in Probability Judgment," *Psychological Review*, Vol. 90, No. 4 (October 1983), p. 297.

The Availability Heuristic.   Because sampling and taking surveys is expensive, we often do it imaginatively—in our heads. If you ask a baseball fan which team has the better batting average, Detroit or San Diego, that person might just remember, might go look it up, or might think about each team and try to decide which one has the most good batters. The latter, needless to say, would be a risky business, but many baseball fans have remarkable knowledge of the batting averages of top hitters. Even with this knowledge, however, it is easy to go wrong. The players that naturally come to mind are the stars on each team: they are more *available* to our memory, and we are likely to make our judgment on the basis of them alone. Yet such a sample can easily be biased because *all* the batters contribute to the team average, not just the stars. (The fact that the weak batters on one team are much better than the weak batters on the other can swing the balance.)

Tversky and Kahneman conducted a further experiment that shows how the influence of the availability heuristic (like the influence of the representative heuristic) can lead to incoherent results. Subjects were asked the following question:

> In four pages of a novel (about 2,000 words), how many words would you expect to find that have the form ____ing (seven-letter words that end with *ing*)?
> Indicate your best estimate by circling one of the values below:
> 1–2 3–4 5–7 8–10 11–15 16+
> A second version of the question requested estimates for words of the form _____n_ The median estimates were 13.4 for *ing* words . . . and 4.7 for _____n_ words.

The result is again logically incoherent; there must be *at least* as many "____ing" words in the text as "_____n_" words, since every "____ing" word is also an "_____n_" word. Why didn't people think about this? The answer is that we rely on the availability heuristic and it is easy to think of "____ing" words: all sorts of verbs with "ing" endings pop into our minds at once. There is nothing similarly memorable about seven-letter words ending with "_n_". Thus, relying on what naturally pops into our heads will often produce biased samples that will lead us to draw false, even incoherent, conclusions.

The point of examining these two judgmental heuristics and noting the logical errors that they produce is *not* to suggest that we should cease relying on them. First, there is a good chance that this would psychologically not be possible, because the use of such heuristics seems to be built into our psychological makeup. Second, over a wide range of standard cases, these heuristics give *quick* and largely *accurate* estimates. Difficulties typically arise in using these heuristics when the situation is *nonstandard*, that is, when the situation is complex or out of the normal run of things. This suggests another question we should routinely ask about inductive generalizations:

Is the Situation Sufficiently Standard to Allow the Use of Informal Judgmental Heuristics?

Because this is a mouthful, we might ask, when appropriate, "Is this really the sort of thing that people can figure out in their heads?" When the answer to that question is no, as it often is, then we should turn to the formal procedures of statistical analysis for our answers.

SUMMARY

We should now be able to summarize and restate our questions with more accuracy. Confronted with inductive generalizations, there are five questions that we should routinely ask:

(1) Are the premises acceptable?
(2) Is the sample likely to be biased because it is too small?
(3) Is the sample likely to be biased in some other way?
(4) Is the sample likely to be biased because the sampling was affected by prejudice and stereotypes?
(5) Is the sample likely to be biased because it relies on informal heuristics in complex situations where they often prove unreliable?

▼ EXERCISE II

Ann Landers caused a stir when she announced the results of a mail poll that asked her women readers to respond to the following question:

> Would you be content to be held and treated tenderly, and forget about "the act"?

Her readers were instructed to answer yes or no and to indicate whether they were over or under 40 years of age.

The result was that 72 percent of the respondents answered yes and of those who answered yes, 40 percent indicated that they were under 40 years old.

What are we to make of these results? Ann Landers expressed surprise that so many of those who answered yes came from the under 40 group. But for her, "the greatest revelation" was "what the poll says about men as lovers. Clearly, there is trouble in paradise" (*Ask Ann Landers,* January 14, 15, 1985).

The poll, of course, did not employ scientific methods of sampling (nor did Ann Landers claim that it did), so it is important to look for sources of bias before drawing any conclusions from this poll. Discuss at least three possible sources of bias that could make the Landers sample unrepresentative of the opinions of the population of adult women in America.

STATISTICAL SYLLOGISMS

In a statistical generalization we draw inferences concerning a population from information concerning a sample of that population. From the fact that 60 percent of the population sampled said that they would vote for candidate X we might draw the conclusion that roughly 60 percent of the population will vote for candidate X. With a *statistical syllogism* we reason in the reverse direction: from information concerning a population, we draw a conclusion concerning a member of that population. Here is an example:

> 97 percent of the Republicans in California voted for Bush.
> Marvin is a Republican from California.
>
> ∴ Marvin voted for Bush.

Such arguments have the following general form:

> X percent of *F*s have the feature *G*.
> *a* is an *F*.
>
> ∴ *a* has the feature *G*.[5]

Obviously, when we evaluate the strength of a statistical syllogism, the percentage or the proportion of *F*s that have the feature *G* will be important. As the percentage approaches 100 percent, the statistical argument gains strength. Thus, our original argument concerning Marvin is quite strong. We can also note that we can get strong statistical syllogisms when the percentage approaches 0 percent. The following is also a strong inductive argument:

> 3 percent of the Socialists in California voted for Bush.
> Maureen is a Socialist from California.
>
> ∴ Maureen did *not* vote for Bush.

Statistical syllogism of the kind considered here will be strong only if the percentages are close to 100 percent or 0 percent. When the per-

---

[5] We can also have a *probabilistic* version of the statistical syllogism:

> 97 percent of the Republicans in California voted for Bush.
> Marvin is a Republican from California.
>
> ∴ There is a 97 percent chance that Marvin voted for Bush.

We will discuss arguments concerning probability in the next chapter.

centages are in the middle of this range, statistical syllogisms are weak.

A more interesting problem in evaluating the strength of a statistical syllogism concerns the *relevance* of the premises to the conclusion. In the above schematic representation of a statistical syllogism, F stands for what is called the *reference class*. In our first example, being a Republican from California is the reference class; in our second example, being a Socialist from California is the reference class. A striking feature of statistical syllogisms is that using different reference classes can yield incompatible results. To see this, consider the following statistical syllogism:

> 3 percent of Dukakis's relatives voted for Bush.
> Marvin is a relative of Dukakis.
> _____
>
> ∴ Marvin did not vote for Bush.

We now have a statistical syllogism that gives us strong support for the claim that Marvin did not vote for Bush, and this is incompatible with our first statistical syllogism that gave strong support to the claim that he did. To overlook this conflict between statistical syllogisms based on different reference classes would be a kind of fallacy. Which, if either, statistical syllogism should we trust? This will depend upon which of the reference classes we take to be more relevant. Which counts more, political affiliation or family ties? That might be hard to say.

One way of dealing with competing statistical syllogisms is to combine the reference classes. We could ask, for example, what percentage of Republicans from California who are relatives of Dukakis voted for Bush? The result might come out like this:

> 42 percent of Republicans from California who were relatives of Dukakis voted for Bush.
> Marvin is a Republican from California who is a relative of Dukakis.
> _____
>
> ∴ Marvin voted for Bush.

This statistical syllogism provides very weak support for its conclusion. It supplies stronger, but still weak, support for the denial of the conclusion, that is, that Marvin did not vote for Bush.

This series of arguments illustrates in a clear way what we earlier called the nonmonotonicity of inductive inferences: a strong inductive argument can be made weak by adding further information to the premises. Given that Marvin is a Republican from California, we seemed to have good reason to think that he voted for Bush. But when we added to this the additional piece of information that he was a relative of Dukakis, the original argument lost most of its force. And new information could produce another reversal. Suppose we discover that Marvin, though a relative of Dukakis, actively campaigned for Bush. Just about everyone who actively campaigns for a candidate votes for that candidate, so it seems that we again have good reason for thinking that Marvin voted for Bush.

It is clear, then, that the way we select our reference classes will affect the strength of a statistical syllogism. The general idea is that we should define our reference classes in a way that brings to bear all relevant evidence on the subject. But this raises difficulties. It is not always obvious what factors are relevant and what factors are not. In our example, party affiliation is relevant to how people voted in the 1988 election, shoe size presumably is not. Whether gender is significant, and, if so, how significant, is a matter for further statistical research.

These difficulties concerning the proper way to fix reference classes reflect a feature of all inductive reasoning: to be successful, such reasoning must take place within a broader framework that helps to determine what features are significant and what features are not. Without this background framework, there would be no reason not to consider shoe size when trying to decide how someone will vote. As we shall see, this reliance on a background framework is particularly important when dealing with causes.

▼ EXERCISE III

Carry the story of Marvin two steps further, producing two more reversals in the strength of the statistical syllogism with the conclusion that Marvin voted for Bush.

▼ EXERCISE IV

For each of the following statistical syllogisms, identify the reference class, and then evaluate the strength of the argument in terms of the percentages or proportions cited and the relevance of the reference class.

1. Less than 1 percent of the people in the world voted for Bush.
   Gale is a person in the world.

   ∴ Gale did not vote for Bush.
2. Very few teams repeat as Super Bowl champions.
   San Francisco was the last Super Bowl champion.

   ∴ San Francisco will not repeat as Super Bowl champion.
3. A very high percentage of people in the Senate are men.
   Nancy Katzenbaum is in the Senate.

   ∴ Nancy Katzenbaum is a man.

4. 3 percent of Socialists with blue eyes voted for Bush.
    Maureen is a Socialist with blue eyes.
    _____

∴ Maureen did not vote for Bush.

5. 98 percent of what John says is true.
    John says that the Giants are going to win.
    _____

∴ The Giants are going to win.

6. Half the time he doesn't know what he is doing.
    He is eating lunch.
    _____

∴ He does not know he is eating lunch.
    _____

REASONING ABOUT CAUSES

We often wonder why certain things have happened; why, for example, our car has gone dead in the middle of rush-hour traffic just after its 20,000-mile checkup. We think that there must be some reason for this happening—cars just don't stop for no reason at all—and reasons of this kind we commonly call *causes*. We could just as well have asked, "What caused the car to stop?" The answer might be that it has run out of gas. If you find, in fact, that it has run out of gas, then that will usually be the end of the matter; you will have discovered (or at least *think* you have discovered) why this particular car has stopped running. But even if your thinking is about a particular car on a particular occasion, your reasoning rests on certain *generalizations*. In particular, you are confident that *your* car stopped running when it ran out of gas because you believe that *all* cars stop running when they are out of gas. You probably did not think about this, but your causal reasoning in this particular case appealed to a commonly accepted *causal generalization*: cars won't go without gas. And what holds in this case, holds quite generally: when we offer a causal explanation of a particular event, we appeal, though not always explicitly, to causal generalizations.

A second important reason that we are interested in causal judgments is that we use them to *predict* the consequences of particular actions or events. A race-car driver might wonder, for example, what would happen if he added just a bit of nitroglycerine to his fuel mixture: would it give him better acceleration, blow him up, do very little, or what? In fact, the driver may not be in a position to answer this question straight off, but his thinking will be guided by the causal generalization that igniting nitroglycerine can cause a dangerous explosion.

So a similar pattern arises for both causal explanation and causal prediction. These inferences contain two essential elements:

(1) The facts in the particular case (For example, the car has stopped and the gas gauge says empty, or I have just put a pint of nitroglycerine in the gas tank of my Maserati and I am about to turn the ignition key.)

(2) Certain causal generalizations (For example, cars do not run without gasoline or that nitroglycerine explodes when ignited.)

The key idea, though this will turn out to be more complicated than these simple examples suggest, is that in drawing a causal inference we bring particular facts under causal generalizations. What, then, are *causal generalizations* and how are they established? We can take these questions up one at a time.

Causal Generalizations

Causal generalizations are obviously important, but what exactly are they? This remains a very controversial issue. Here we will treat them as a kind of *general conditional*. The idea of a general conditional was first introduced in Chapter 7 where it was said to have the following form:

For all x, if x has the feature F, then x has the feature G.[6]

There we said that x's having the feature F gives a *sufficient condition* for its having the feature G, and x's having the feature G lays down a necessary condition for its having the feature F.

Not every general conditional lays down *causal* conditions. For example, neither of these two general conditionals expresses a causal relationship.

If something is a square, then it is a rectangle.
If you are an 18-year-old male, you must register for the Selective Service.

The first tells us that being a square is sufficient for being a rectangle, but this is a mathematical (or *a priori*) relationship, not a causal relationship. The second statement tells us that being a male of 18 is sufficient to require registration. The relationship here is legal, not causal.

Although there are complications (and disagreements) in this area, general causal conditionals usually lay down sufficient and necessary conditions between *events*. It is important to know, for example, that if you put your finger in a light socket when the power is on, you are likely to receive a severe shock. In this case we recognize that a certain combination of factors is *sufficient* to bring about some effect. At other times we are interested in what factors are *necessary* to bring about an effect. This concern often arises when some expected event does not occur and you wonder why. You have dialed a telephone number and nothing happens. Of course, all sorts of things might account for this:

---

[6] It might be useful to review this material in Chapter 7 before proceeding.

perhaps the telephone lines are down, or the phone is disconnected, or you forgot to dial 1 before a long-distance number. In reflecting on these matters, you are concerned with a set of conditions that are causally necessary for completing a telephone call. Our common knowledge of the world consists, to a large extent, in having generalizations specifying those causal conditions that are necessary and those causal conditions that are sufficient for certain kinds of events to occur.

Our position, then, is that causal conditionals are a kind of general conditional. The picture looks like this:

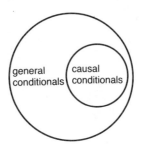

So if we are able to show that a particular general causal conditional is false just in virtue of its being a general conditional, we will have refuted it. This will serve our purposes well, for in what follows we will be almost exclusively concerned with finding reasons for *rejecting* causal generalizations.

Testing General Causal Conditionals

General causal conditionals are important for getting along in the world, but they will be helpful, of course, only if they are themselves correct and are also applied correctly. What is needed, then, are principles for testing and applying such generalizations. It is one of the central tasks of inductive logic to supply these principles.

In the past, very elaborate procedures have been developed for this purpose. The most famous set of such procedures was developed by John Stuart Mill and has come to be known as Mill's Methods.[7] Though inspired by Mill's Methods, the procedures introduced here involve a fundamental simplification: where Mill introduced five rules, or methods as he called them, here only two primary rules are introduced, one concerning sufficient conditions and the other concerning necessary conditions. Furthermore, the rules we will introduce for sufficient con-

---

[7] Mill's "methods of experimental enquiry" are found in Book 3, Chapter 7 of his *A System of Logic*, published in 1843. For a careful, but highly technical, examination and restatement of Mill's methods, see George Henrik von Wright's *A Treatise on Induction and Probability*, Chapters 3 through 6. A simpler version of von Wright's basic ideas is found in Brian Skyrms, *Choice and Chance*, Chapter 4.

ditions and for necessary conditions are *negative* in the sense that they only provide ways of showing that something is *not* a sufficient condition or *not* a necessary condition. They are rules for *eliminating* suggested candidates for either a sufficient condition or a necessary condition. We will call these two rules the Sufficient Condition Test (SCT) and the Necessary Condition Test (NCT).

SUFFICIENT CONDITIONS AND NECESSARY CONDITIONS

Our ultimate concern in this discussion is with causal conditions. Causality, however, is a complicated subject where significant disagreements still exist. We will therefore introduce the Sufficient Condition Test and the Necessary Condition Test first at an abstract level. Once it is clear how these rules work in general, we will apply them specifically to causal reasoning.

To keep our discussion as general as possible, we will adopt the definitions of sufficient conditions and necessary conditions first introduced at the end of Chapter 7.

> That *F* is a sufficient condition for *G* means that whenever *F* is present *G* is present.
> That *F* is a necessary condition for *G* means that whenever *F* is absent *G* is absent.

Not everything that is a sufficient condition or a necessary condition in these senses will be a *causally* necessary or sufficient condition, but anything that fails to be a necessary or sufficient condition in these senses will also fail to provide a necessary or sufficient condition in any more narrow sense of these terms. For this reason, these definitions will serve our purposes in formulating principles that *rule out* or *eliminate* proposed sufficient or necessary conditions of any kind, including those that are causal.[8]

The Sufficient Condition Test (SCT)[9]

It will simplify matters if we first state this test abstractly using letters. We will also begin with a very simple case where we consider only four *candidates—A B C D*—for sufficient conditions for a *target* feature G. "A" will indicate that the feature is present; "~A" will indicate

---

[8] Another advantage of introducing the notions of sufficient conditions and necessary conditions in this way is that it lays the foundation for discussing other kinds of sufficient and necessary conditions, for example, those that arise in legal and moral reasoning, the topics of Chapters 11 and 12.

[9] This procedure parallels, but is not identical with, Mill's Method of Difference.

that this feature is absent. Using these conventions, suppose that we are trying to decide whether any of the four features—A B C D—could be a sufficient condition for G. To this end we collect data of the following kind:

Table 1.

Case 1.	A	B	C	D	G
Case 2.	$\sim A$	B	C	$\sim D$	$\sim G$
Case 3.	A	$\sim B$	$\sim C$	$\sim D$	$\sim G$

We know by definition that for one thing to be a sufficient condition of another, when it is present, the other must be present as well. Thus, in applying SCT, we only have to examine cases where the target feature G is absent, and then check to see whether any of the candidate features are present.

> Any candidate that is present when G is absent is eliminated as a possible sufficient condition of G.

The test applies to Table 1 as follows: Case 1 need not be examined since G is present, so there can be no violation of SCT. Case 2 eliminates two of the candidates, B and C, for both are present in a situation where G is absent. Finally, Case 3 eliminates C, and we are thus left with D as our only remaining candidate for a sufficient condition for G.

Now let's consider D. Having survived the application of the sufficient condition test, can we conclude that D *is* a sufficient condition for G? No—at least not on the basis of what we have been told thus far. It remains entirely possible that the discovery of a further case will reveal an instance where D is present and G absent, thus showing that D is not a sufficient condition for G either. For example,

Case 4.	A	B	$\sim C$	D	$\sim G$

This reflects the fact that inductive inferences, however well confirmed, are always subject to refutation. (Remember Captain Cook's discovery of black swans.) Suppose, however, that we have good reason for thinking that A through D contain *all* the possible candidates for a sufficient condition of G, and suppose further that we have good reason for thinking that something must be a sufficient condition for G. Given this additional *background* information, we could reasonably conclude that D is a sufficient condition for G if we do not find any case (like Case 4) where D and ~G are present. As we shall see, in the actual application of the sufficient condition test, we can sometimes make a reasonable assignment of a sufficient condition in just this way.

The Necessary Condition Test (NCT)[10]

The necessary condition test is like the SCT, but works in reverse fashion. With SCT we eliminated a candidate F from being the sufficient condition for G, if F could be present and G absent. With NCT, we eliminate a candidate F from being a necessary condition for G if we can find a case where G is present, but F is not. This makes sense, because if G can be present when F is not, then F cannot be necessary for the occurrence of G. Thus, in applying NCT, we only have to examine cases where the target feature G is present, and then check to see whether any of the candidate features are absent.

Any candidate that is absent when G is present is eliminated as a possible necessary condition of G.

The following table gives an example of an application of this test

Table 2.					
Case 1.	A	B	C	D	$\sim G$
Case 2.	$\sim A$	B	C	D	G
Case 3.	A	$\sim B$	C	$\sim D$	G

Since Case 1 does not provide an instance where G is present, it can be ignored. Case 2 eliminates A, since it shows that G can be present without A being present. Case 3 eliminates both B and D, leaving only C as possible candidate for being a necessary condition for G. From this we cannot, of course, conclude that C *is* a necessary condition for G, for, as always, new cases may eliminate it as well. But if we have good reason to suppose that we have examined all of the possible candidates for being a necessary condition of G and eliminated all of them but C and, further, have good reason for thinking that something must be a necessary condition for G, then we may conclude that we have good reason to suppose that C is a necessary condition for G.

It is also possible to apply these rules simultaneously in the search for possible conditions that are both sufficient and necessary.[11] In Table 1, for example, D is a possible sufficient condition of G, since D is never present when G is absent, and it may also be a necessary condition for G, since G is never present when D is absent. In Table 2, C is the only possible necessary condition for G, but it is not also a possible sufficient condition, since in Case 1 it is present when G is absent.

---

[10] The procedure parallels, but is not identical with, Mill's Method of Agreement.

[11] This procedure parallels, but is not identical with, Mill's Joint Method of Agreement and Difference.

▼ EXERCISE V

For each of the following tables decide:

(a) Which, if any, of the candidates—*A B C D*—is not eliminated by the sufficient condition test?

(b) Which, if any, of the candidates—*A B C D*—is not eliminated by the necessary condition test?

(c) Which, if any, of the candidates—*A B C D*—is not eliminated by either test?

Examples:

Case 1.	*A*	*B*	~*C*	*D*	~*G*
Case 2.	~*A*	*B*	*C*	*D*	*G*
Case 3.	*A*	~*B*	*C*	*D*	*G*

a) Only *C* passes the SCT
b) *C* and *D* both pass the NCT
c) Only *C* passes both.

1. Case 1.	*A*	*B*	*C*	*D*	~*G*
Case 2.	~*A*	*B*	~*C*	*D*	*G*
Case 3.	*A*	~*B*	*C*	~*D*	*G*
2. Case 1.	*A*	*B*	*C*	~*D*	*G*
Case 2.	~*A*	*B*	*C*	*D*	*G*
Case 3.	*A*	~*B*	*C*	~*D*	*G*
3. Case 1.	*A*	*B*	*C*	*D*	~*G*
Case 2.	~*A*	*B*	*C*	*D*	*G*
Case 3.	*A*	~*B*	*C*	~*D*	*G*

Rigorous Testing

Going back to Table 1, it is easy to see that *A*, *B*, *C*, and *D* are not eliminated by NCT, since *G* is only present in one case (Case 1) and they are present there as well. So far so good, but if we wanted to test these features more rigorously, it would be important to find more cases where *G* was present and see whether these candidates are also present and thus continue to survive the NCT.

The following table gives a more extreme example of nonrigorous testing:

Table 3.					
Case 1.	*A*	~*B*	*C*	*D*	*G*
Case 2.	*A*	~*B*	~*C*	~*D*	~*G*
Case 3.	*A*	~*B*	*C*	~*D*	~*G*
Case 4.	*A*	~*B*	~*C*	*D*	*G*

Here, A is eliminated by SCT (in Cases 2 and 3) but is not eliminated by NCT, so A is a possible necessary condition, but not a possible sufficient condition. B is not eliminated by SCT, but is eliminated by NCT (in Cases 1 and 4), so it is a possible sufficient condition, but it is not a possible necessary condition. C is eliminated by both rules (in Cases 3 and 4). Only D is not eliminated by either test, so it is the only candidate for being both a necessary and a sufficient condition for G.

The peculiarity of this example is that A is always present whether G is present or not, and B is always absent whether G is absent or not. Now if something is always present, as A is, it cannot possibly fail the NCT, for there cannot be a case where the target is present and the candidate is absent if the candidate is *always* present. If we want to test A rigorously under the NCT, we should try to find cases where A is absent and then check to see whether G is absent as well. In reverse fashion, if we want to test B rigorously under the SCT, we should try to find cases where B is present and then check to see whether G is present as well. Similarly, if we restrict our attention to cases where G is always present, then no candidates can be tested by the SCT, and if we restrict our attention to cases where G is always absent, then no candidates can be tested by the NCT. For both rules, rigorous testing involves seeking out cases where failing the test is a live possibility. Passing the tests without this is rather like a person bragging that he has never struck out when, in fact, he has never come to bat.

Some Elaborations [Optional]

Our discussion of necessary and sufficient conditions has been overly simple in two important respects: (i) so far we have limited candidates to features that are present, and have not taken into account the fact that the absence of a feature can be a necessary condition or a sufficient condition. (ii) We have limited our attention to simple features and have not considered the possibility of necessary or sufficient conditions that are complex. We will consider these two matters one at a time.

(i) Negative Conditions. Sometimes the absence of a feature can serve as a sufficient condition for the presence or absence of something else. For example, if air is absent, then people will suffocate. Here the absence of air is a sufficient condition for suffocation. It is also true that wood will burn only if it is not wet. Here not having a trait—not being wet—is a necessary condition for wood's burning. Of course, it is often arbitrary whether we choose to describe things in positive or negative terms. In the last example we could just as well have said that being dry (rather than not being wet) is a necessary condition for wood burning. Even so, it is arbitrary to restrict the candidates for sufficient conditions and necessary conditions to features that are present.

To illustrate these points, we can look again at our first table:

Table 1
Case 1.	A	B	C	D	G
Case 2.	$\sim A$	B	C	$\sim D$	$\sim G$
Case 3.	A	$\sim B$	$\sim C$	$\sim D$	$\sim G$

Recall that in this set-up only D was not eliminated as a possible sufficient condition. It is also easy to see that A, B, C, and D all remain candidates for being necessary conditions of G. But if we allow the absence of a feature to be a candidate, we see from the table that $\sim D$ is a possible necessary condition for $\sim G$, since it is not eliminated by NCT. (There is no case where $\sim G$ is present but $\sim D$ is absent). $\sim D$ is also a possible sufficient condition of $\sim G$. (It gets by SCT because there is no case where $\sim D$ is present but $\sim G$ is absent.) In fact, $\sim A$, $\sim B$, and $\sim C$ are also possible sufficient conditions of $\sim G$. (They get by SCT because they are only present in Cases 2 and 3, and in those cases $\sim G$ is present as well.)

DISCUSSION QUESTION

The new batch of possible sufficient conditions and possible necessary conditions that arises when we introduce negative conditions is fully determined by the following two principles:

I. If presence of the property F is a necessary condition for the presence of property G, then the absence of property F is a sufficient condition for the absence of property G.

II. If the presence of the property F is a sufficient condition for the presence of property G, then the absence of property F is a necessary condition for the absence of property G.

Why do these principles hold?

_____

(ii) Complex conditions. Another way in which our discussion has been overly simple is that we have considered only simple conditions and have not taken into account the existence of complex conditions. Here are some examples of complex conditions.

If hydrogen and oxygen are combined and ignited, they will explode.

Here the conditional lays down a *conjunctive sufficient condition.*

If you eat mud or rocks, you will feel ill.

Here the conditional lays down a *disjunctive sufficient condition.*

A short circuit will cause a fire only if oxygen is present and combustible material is present.

Here the conditional lays down a *conjunctive necessary condition*.

▼ EXERCISE VI

(1) Give two examples of conditionals stating a true *disjunctive* necessary condition.

(2) Explain why if A is a sufficient condition for G, then A & B is a sufficient condition for G, for *any B*.

(3) Explain why if A is a necessary condition for G, then A v B is a necessary condition for G, for *any B*.

USING THESE TESTS TO FIND CAUSES

Our procedure thus far has been purely mechanical; we have simply stated two rules and then showed how they can be applied to abstract patterns of conditions. Applying these rules to actual concrete situations introduces a number of complicating factors.

Normality

First, it is important to keep in mind that in our ordinary understanding of causal conditions, we usually take it for granted that the setting is normal. It is part of common knowledge that if you strike a match, then it will light. Thus, we consider striking a match sufficient to make it light. But if someone has filled the room with carbon dioxide, then the match will not light no matter how it is struck. Here one may be inclined to say that, after all, striking a match is not sufficient to light it. We might try to be more careful and say that if a match is struck and the room is not filled with carbon dioxide, then it will light. But this new conditional overlooks other possibilities—for example, that the room has been filled with nitrogen, that the match has been fireproofed, that the wrong end of the match was struck, that the match has already been lit, etc., etc., etc. It now seems that the antecedent of our conditional will have to be endlessly long to specify a true or genuine sufficient condition. In fact, however, we usually feel quite happy with saying that if you strike a match, then it will light. We simply do not worry about the possibility that the room has been filled with carbon dioxide, the match has been fireproofed, and so on. Normally we think that things are normal, and give up this assumption only when some good reason appears for doing so.

These reflections suggest the following *contextualized* restatement of our original definitions of sufficient conditions and necessary conditions:

That *F* is a sufficient condition for *G* means that whenever *F* is present in a normal context, *G* is present there as well.

That *F* is a necessary condition for *G* means that whenever *F* is absent in a normal context, *G* is absent there as well.

What will count as a normal context will vary with the type and the aim of an investigation, but all investigations into causally sufficient conditions and causally necessary conditions take place against the background of many factors that are taken as fixed.

Background Assumptions

Along with a commitment to normality, our assessment of causal conditions takes place against a rich background of common knowledge and sometimes specialized technical knowledge of how things work. An investigator seeking the cause for a house burning down comes armed with a great deal of information of how this might have happened: through faulty wiring, a furnace explosion, spontaneous combustion of waste material, arson, and so on. The investigator will also have detailed knowledge of how to test for each of these possibilities. This background knowledge is crucial for the application of the two rules we have introduced because it suggests entries for the candidate list and also places limits on them. Thus, the investigator will routinely check to see whether the furnace has exploded, but will not check to see whether geese flew over the house, for it is part of his common understanding of fires that exploding furnaces can cause them, but overflying geese cannot.

A Detailed Example

To get a clearer idea of the complex interplay between the rules we have been examining and the reliance on background information, it will be helpful to look in some detail at the actual applications of these rules. For this purpose, we will examine an attempt to find the cause of a particular phenomenon—in particular, an outbreak of what came to be known as Legionnaires' Disease. The example not only shows how causal reasoning relies on background assumptions, it has another interesting feature as well: in the process of discovering the cause of Legionnaires' Disease the investigators were forced to abandon what was previously taken to be a well-established causal generalization. In fact, until it was discarded, this false background principle gave them no end of trouble.

The following account of the outbreak of Legionnaires' Disease and the subsequent difficulties in finding out what caused it is drawn from an article in *Scientific American*.[12]

---

[12] These excerpts are drawn from David W. Fraser and Joseph E. McDade, "Legionellosis," *Scientific American* (October 1977), pp. 82–99.

The 58th convention of the American Legion's Pennsylvania Department was held at the Bellevue-Stratford Hotel in Philadelphia from July 21 through 24, 1976. . . . Between July 22 and August 3, 149 of the conventioneers developed what appeared to be the same puzzling illness, characterized by fever, coughing and pneumonia. This, however, was an unusual, explosive outbreak of pneumonia with no apparent cause. . . . Legionnaires' Disease, as the illness was quickly named by the press, was to prove a formidable challenge to epidemiologists and laboratory investigators alike.

Notice that at this stage the researchers begin with the assumption that they are dealing with a single illness and not a collection of similar but different illnesses. That assumption could turn out to be wrong, but, if the symptoms of the various patients were sufficiently similar, this is a natural starting assumption. Another reasonable starting assumption is that this illness had a single causative agent. Again, this assumption could turn out to be false, though it didn't. The assumption that they were dealing with a single disease with a single cause was, at the very least, a good simplifying assumption, one to be held onto until there was good reason to give it up. In any case, we now have a clear specification of our target feature G—the occurrence of a carefully described illness that came to be known as Legionnaires' Disease. The situation concerning it was puzzling because people had contracted a disease with symptoms very much like pneumonia, yet they had not tested positive for any of the known agents that cause such diseases.

The narrative continues as follows:

The initial step in the investigation of any epidemic is to determine the character of the illness, who has become ill and just where and when. The next step is to find out what was unique about the people who became ill: where they were and what they did that was different from other people who stayed well. Knowing such things may indicate how the disease agent was spread and thereby suggest the identity of the agent and where it came from.

Part of this procedure involves a straightforward application of the NCT—was there any interesting feature that was always present in the history of people who came down with the illness? Progress was made almost at once on this front:

We quickly learned that the illness was not confined to Legionnaires. An additional 72 cases were discovered among people who had not been directly associated with the convention. They had one thing in common with the sick conventioneers: for one reason or another they had been in or near the Bellevue-Stratford Hotel.

Strictly speaking, of course, all these people who had contracted the disease had more than one thing in common. They were, for example, all alive at the time they were in Philadelphia, and being alive is, in fact, a necessary condition for getting Legionnaires' Disease. But the researchers were not interested in this necessary condition because it is a normal background condition for the contraction of any disease. Furthermore, it did not provide a condition that distinguished those who contracted the disease from those who did not. The overwhelming majority of people who were alive at the time did not contract Legionnaires' Disease. Thus, the researchers were not interested in this necessary condition because it would fail so badly when tested as a sufficient condition. On the basis of common knowledge and specialized medical knowledge, a great many other conditions were also kept off the candidate list.

The application of the NCT to presence at the Bellevue-Stratford was straightforward. Everyone who had contracted the disease had spent time in or near that hotel. The application of SCT was more complicated, for not everyone who stayed at the Bellevue-Stratford contracted the disease. Other factors made a difference:

> Older conventioneers had been affected at a higher rate than younger ones, men at three times the rate for women.

It is, however, part of medical background knowledge that susceptibility to disease often varies with age and sex. Giving these differences, some people who spent time at the Bellevue-Stratford were at higher risk of contracting the disease than others. The investigation so far suggested that, for some people, being at the Bellevue-Stratford was connected with a sufficient condition for contracting Legionnaires' Disease.

As soon as spending time at the Bellevue-Stratford became the focus of attention, other hypotheses naturally suggested themselves. Food poisoning was a reasonable suggestion, since it is part of medical knowledge that diseases are sometimes spread by food. It was put on the list of possible candidates, but failed.

> The obvious possibility that the disease might have been spread by food or drink was ruled out. Conventioneers who became ill were shown to be no more likely than those who remained well to have eaten at particular restaurants, to have attended particular functions where food and drink were served or to have drunk water or used ice in the hotels.

Thus, the food/drink hypothesis was eliminated by both NCT and SCT.

Further investigation turned up another important clue to the cause of the illness.

> Certain observations suggested that the disease might have been spread through the air. Legionnaires who became ill had spent on the average about 60 percent more time in the lobby of the Bellevue-Stratford than those who remained well; the sick Legionnaires' had also spent more time on the sidewalk in front of the hotel than their unaffected fellow conventioneers. . . . It appeared, therefore, that the most likely mode of transmission was airborne.

Again, appealing to background medical knowledge, there seemed to be three main candidates for the airborne agents that could have caused the illness: "heavy metals, toxic organic substances and infectious organisms." However, examination of tissues taken from patients who had died from the disease revealed "no unusual levels of metallic or toxic organic substances that might be related to the epidemic," so this left an infectious organism as the remaining candidate. Once more we have an application of NCT. If the disease had been caused by heavy metals or toxic organic substances, then there would have been unusually high levels of these substances in the tissue of those who had contracted the disease. Since this was not so, these candidates were eliminated.

Again appealing to background knowledge, it seemed that a bacterium would be the most likely source of an airborne disease with the symptoms of Legionnaires' Disease. But researchers had already made a routine check for bacteria that cause pneumonia-like diseases and they had found none. For this reason, attention was "directed to the possibility that some unknown organism had been responsible, but had somehow escaped detection."

It turned out that it was an undetected and previously unknown bacterium that caused the illness, but it took more than four months to find this out. The difficulties encountered in this effort show another important fact about the reliance on a background assumption: sometimes it turns out to be *false*. To simplify, the standard way to test for the presence of bacteria is to try to grow them in culture dishes—flat dishes containing nutrient that bacteria can live on. If, after a reasonable number of tries, a colony of a particular kind of bacterium does not appear, then it is concluded that the bacterium is not present. As it turned out, the bacterium that caused Legionnaires' Disease would not grow in the cultures commonly used to detect the presence of bacteria. Thus, an important background assumption turned out to be false.

After a great deal of work, a suspicious bacterium was detected using a live tissue culture rather than the standard synthetic culture. The task, then, was to show that this particular bacterium in fact caused the disease. Again to simplify, when people are infected by a particular organism, they often develop antibodies that are specifically aimed at these organisms. In the case of Legionnaires' Disease, these antibodies were easier to detect than the bacterium itself. They also remained in the patient's body after the infection had run its course. We thus have another chance to apply NCT: if Legionnaires' Disease was caused by this particular bacterium, then whenever the disease was present, this antibody should be present as well. The suspicious bacterium passed this test with flying colors and was named, appropriately enough *Legionella pneumophila*.

The story of the search for the cause of Legionnaires' Disease brings out two important features of the use of inductive methods in the sciences: (i) it involves a complicated interplay between what is already established and what is being tested. Confronted with a new problem, established principles can be used to suggest theoretically significant hypotheses to be tested. The tests then eliminate some hypotheses, leave others. If at the end of the investigation a survivor remains that fits in well with our previously established principles, then the stock of established principles is increased. (ii) The second thing that this example shows is that the inductive method is fallible. Without the background of established principles, the application of inductive principles like NCT and SCT would be undirected, yet sometimes these established principles let us down, for they can turn out to be false. The discovery of the false background principle that hindered the search for the cause of Legionnaires' Disease led to important revisions in laboratory techniques. The discovery that more fundamental background principles are false can lead to revolutionary changes in science. This topic is discussed in Chapter 13 where the nature of scientific frameworks is examined.

Calling Things Causes

After their research was finally completed, with the bacterium identified, described, and named, it was then said that Legionella pneumophila was the *cause* of Legionnaires' Disease. What was meant by this? To simplify a bit, suppose L. pneumophila (as it is abbreviated) entered the bodies of *all* those who contracted the disease: whenever the disease was present, L. pneumophila was present. Thus, L. pneumophila passes the NCT. We will further suppose, as is common in bacterial infections, that some people's immune systems were successful in combatting L. pneumophila and never actually developed the disease. Thus, the presence of L. pneumophila would not pass the SCT. This suggests that we *sometimes* call something a cause if it passes the NCT, even if it does not pass the SCT.

But even if we sometimes consider necessary conditions to be causes, we certainly do not consider *all* necessary conditions to be causes. We have already noted that to get Legionnaires' Disease, one has to be alive, yet no one thinks that being alive is the cause of Legionnaires' Disease. To cite another example, this time one that is not silly, it might be that another necessary condition for developing Legionnaires' Disease is that the person be in a run-down condition—healthy people might always be able to resist L. pneumophila. Do we then want to say that being in a run-down condition is the cause of Legionnaires' Disease? As we have described the situation, almost certainly not, but we might want to say that it is an important causal *factor* or *causally relevant factor*.

Although the matter is far from clear, what we call *the* cause rather than simply *a* causal factor or causally relevant factor seems to depend upon a number of things. We tend to reserve the expression "the cause" for *changes* that occur prior to the effect, and describe *permanent* or *standing* features of the context as causal factors instead. That's how we speak about Legionnaires' Disease. Being exposed to L. pneumophila, which was a specific event that occurred before the onset of the disease, *caused it*. Being run-down, which was a feature that patients possessed for some time before they contracted the disease, was not the cause, but, instead, a causal factor. It is not clear, however, that we always draw the distinction between what we call the cause and what we call a causal factor along the lines of prior event as opposed to standing condition. For example, if we are trying to explain why certain people who came in contact with L. pneumophila contracted the disease whereas others did not, then we might say that the former group contracted the disease because they were in a run-down condition. Thus, by limiting our investigation only to those who came in contact with L. pneumophila, our perspective has changed. Within that group we want to know why some contracted the disease and others did not. Citing the run-down condition of those who contracted the disease as the cause now seems entirely natural. These examples suggest that we call something *the* cause when it plays a particularly important role relative to the purposes of our investigation. Usually this will be an event or change taking place against the background of fixed necessary conditions; sometimes not.

Sometimes we call sufficient conditions causes. We say that short circuits cause fires because in many normal contexts a short circuit is sufficient to cause a fire. Of course, short circuits are not necessary to cause a fire, since, in the same normal contexts, fires can be caused by a great many other things. With sufficient conditions, as with necessary conditions, we often draw a distinction between what we call *the cause* as opposed to what we call a *causal factor,* and we seem to draw it along similar lines. Speaking very loosely, we might say that we sometimes call the *key* components of sufficient conditions causes. Then, holding background conditions fixed, we can use the SCT to evaluate such a causal claim.

In sum, we can use the NCT to eliminate proposed necessary causal conditions. We can use the SCT to eliminate proposed sufficient causal conditions. Those candidates that survive these tests may be called *causal* conditions or *causal* factors if they fit in well with our system of other causal generalizations. Finally, some of these causal conditions or causal factors will be called *causes* if they play a key role in our causal investigations. Typically, though not always, we call something the cause of an event if it is a prior event or change that stands out against the background of fixed conditions.

CONCOMITANT VARIATION

The use of the Sufficient Condition Test and the Necessary Condition Test depend upon the fact that certain features of the world are sometimes present and sometimes absent. However, certain features of the world are always present to some degree. Since they are always present, the NCT will never eliminate them as a possible necessary condition of any event, and the SCT will never eliminate anything as sufficient conditions for them. Yet the *extent* or *degree* to which a feature exists in the world is often a significant phenomenon that demands causal explanation.

An example will make this clear. In recent years a controversy has raged over the impact of acid rain on the environment of the northeastern United States and Canada. Part of the controversy involves the proper interpretation of the data that have been collected. The controversy has arisen for the following reason: the atmosphere always contains a certain amount of acid, much of it from natural sources. It is also known that an excess of acid in the environment can have severe effects on both plants and animals. Lakes are particularly vulnerable to the effects of acid rain. Finally, it is also acknowledged that industries, mostly in the Midwest, discharge large quantities of sulphur dioxide (SO_2) into the air, and this increases the acidity of water in the atmosphere. The question, and here the controversy begins, is whether the contribution of acid from these industries is the cause of the environmental damage downwind from them.

How can we settle such a dispute? The two rules we have introduced provide no immediate help, for, as we have seen, they provide a rigorous test of a causal hypothesis only when we can find contrasting cases of the presence or the absence of a feature. The NCT provides a rigorous test for a necessary condition only if we can find cases where the feature does not occur and then check to make sure that that target feature does not occur either. The SCT provides a rigorous test for a sufficient condition only when we can find cases where the target phenomenon is absent and then check whether the candidate sufficient condition is absent as well. In this case, however, neither test applies, for there is always a certain amount of acid in the atmosphere, so it is not possible to check what happens when atmospheric acid is completely absent. Similarly, environmental damage, which is the target phenomenon under investigation, is so widespread in our modern industrial society that it is also hard to find a case where it is completely absent.

So, if there is always acid in the atmosphere, and environmental damage always exists at least to some extent, how can we determine whether the SO_2 released into the atmosphere is *significantly* responsible for the environmental damage in the affected areas? Here we use what John Stuart Mill called *the method of concomitant variation*. We ask whether the amount of environmental damage varies directly in proportion to the amount of SO_2 released into the environment. If environmental damage increases with the amount of SO_2 released into the environment and drops when the amount of SO_2 is lowered, then it seems reasonable to suppose that the level of SO_2 in the atmosphere is *positively correlated* with environmental damage. We would have good reason to believe that lowering SO_2 emissions would lower the level of environmental damage, at least to some extent.

Arguments relying on the method of concomitant variation are difficult to evaluate, especially when there is no generally accepted background theory that makes sense of the concomitant variation. Some such variations are well understood. For example, everyone knows that the faster you drive, the more gasoline you consume. (Gasoline consumption varies *inversely* with speed.) Why? There is a good theory here; it takes more energy to drive at a high speed than at a low speed, and this energy is derived from the gasoline consumed in the car's engine. Other correlations are less well understood. There seems to be a correlation between the cholesterol level in the blood and the chances of heart attack. First of all, the correlation here is not nearly as good as the gasoline consumption–speed correlation, for many people with high cholesterol levels do not suffer heart attacks, and many people with low cholesterol levels do. Furthermore, no generally accepted background theory has been found that explains the positive correlation that does seem to exist.

This reference to background theory is important, because two sets of phenomena can be correlated to a very high degree, even with no direct causal relationship between them. A favorite example that appears in many statistics text is the discovered positive correlation in boys between foot size and quality of handwriting. It is hard to imagine causal correlation holding in either direction. Having big feet should not make you write better and, just as obviously, writing well should not give you big feet. The correct explanation is that both foot size and handwriting ability are positively correlated with age. Here a noncausal correlation between two phenomena (foot size and handwriting ability) is explained by a third common correlation (maturation) that *is* causal.

At times, it is possible to get causal correlations *backwards*. For example, a few years ago, sports statisticians discovered a negative correlation between forward passes thrown and winning. That is, the more forward passes that a team threw, the less chance it had of winning. This suggests that passing is not a good strategy, since the more you do it, the more likely you are to lose. Closer examination showed, however, that the causal relationship, in fact, went in the other direction. Toward the end of a game, losing teams tend to throw a great many passes in an effort to catch up. In other words, teams throw a lot of passes because they are losing, rather than the other way around.

Finally, some correlations seem inexplicable. For example, a strong positive correlation holds between the birthrate in Holland and the number of storks nesting in chimneys. There is, of course, a background theory that would explain this—storks bring babies—but that theory is not favored by modern science. For the lack of any better background theory, the phenomenon just seems weird.

So, given a strong correlation between phenomena of types *A* and *B*, four possibilities exist:

(1) *A* is the cause of *B*.
(2) *B* is the cause of *A*.
(3) Some third thing is the cause of both.
(4) The correlation is simply accidental.

Before we accept any one of these possibilities, we must have good reasons for preferring it over the other three.

▼ EXERCISE VII

In each of the following examples a strong correlation, either negative or positive, holds between two sets of phenomena *A* and *B*. Try to decide whether *A* is the cause of *B*, *B* is the cause of *A*, both are caused by some third factor *C*, or the correlation is simply accidental. Explain your choice.

(1) At one time there was a strong negative correlation between the number of mules in a state (*A*) and the salaries paid to professors at the state university (*B*). In other words, the more mules, the lower professorial salaries.[13]

(2) It has been claimed that there is a strong positive correlation between those students who take sex education courses (*A*) and those who contract venereal disease (*B*).

(3) "LOCKED DOORS NO BAR TO CRIME, STUDY SAYS

"Washington (UPI)—Rural Americans with locked doors, watchdogs or guns may face as much risk of burglary as neighbors who leave doors unlocked, a federally financed study says.

"The study, financed in part by a three-year $170,000 grant from the Law Enforcement Assistance Administration, was based on a survey of nearly 900 families in rural Ohio.

"Sixty percent of the rural residents surveyed regularly locked doors [*A*], but were burglarized more often than residents who left doors unlocked [*B*]."[14]

---

[13] From Gregory A. Kimble, *How to Use (and Misuse) Statistics* (Englewood Cliffs, N.J.: Prentice-Hall, 1978).

[14] "Locked Doors No Bar to Crime, Study Says," *Santa Barbara* [California] *Newspress*, Wednesday, Feb. 16, 1977.

(4) There is a high positive correlation between the number of fire engines in a particular borough in New York City (A) and the number of fires that occur there (B).[15]

(5) For a particular United States president, there is a negative correlation between the number of hairs on his head (A) and the population of China (B).

▼ DISCUSSION QUESTIONS

(1) Many defenders of nuclear deterrence have relied on an inductive argument to the effect that World War III has been avoided because of the balance of power between West and East. What evidence has been offered in support of this conclusion? How strong is the argument?

(2) Now that it seems beyond doubt that smoking is dangerous to people's health, a new debate has arisen concerning the possible health hazards of smoke on nonsmokers. Collect statements pro and con on this issue and evaluate the strength of the inductive arguments on each side.

(3) Although both in science and in daily life, we rely heavily on the methods of inductive reasoning, a number of perplexing problems exist concerning the legitimacy of this kind of reasoning. The most famous problem concerning induction was formulated by the eighteenth-century philosopher David Hume, first in his *Treatise of Human Nature* and then later in his *Enquiry Concerning Human Understanding*. A simplified version of Hume's skeptical argument goes as follows: Our inductive generalizations seem to rest on the assumption that *unobserved* cases will follow the patterns that we discovered in *observed* cases. That is, our inductive generalizations seem to presuppose that nature operates uniformly: the way things are observed to behave here and now are accurate indicators of how things behave anywhere and at any time. But by what right can we assume that nature is uniform? Because this claim itself asserts a matter of fact, it could only be established by inductive reasoning. But because all inductive reasoning presupposes the principle that nature is uniform, any inductive justification of this principle would seem to be circular. It seems, then, that we have no ultimate justification for our inductive reasoning at all. Is this a good or bad argument?

(4) In mathematics, proofs are sometimes employed using the method of *mathematical induction*. If you are familiar with these procedures, decide whether these proofs are inductive or deductive in character.

---

[15] Also from *How to Use (and Misuse) Statistics.*

10

Taking Chances

This chapter offers an elementary discussion of reasoning about choices when outcomes involve risk. It shows how the related notions of *probability*, *expected value*, and *relative value* bear on choices of this kind. The chapter concludes with an examination of two common mistakes in reasoning about probabilities, committing the so-called *gambler's fallacy*, and failing to understand the phenomenon of *regression to the mean*.

THE LANGUAGE OF PROBABILITY

In everyday life we express various degrees of certainty about the world around us. Looking out the window we might say that there is a fifty-fifty chance of rain. More vividly, someone might have remarked that the Dodgers didn't have the chance of a pound of butter in hell of repeating the 1988 World Championship. In each case, the speaker is indicating the relative strength of the evidence for the occurrence or nonoccurrence of some event. To say that there is a fifty-fifty chance that it will rain indicates that we hold that the evidence is equally strong that it will rain rather than not rain. Each event strikes us as being equally likely. The metaphor in the second statement indicates that the person who uttered it believed that the probability of the Dodgers repeating as World Champions was essentially nonexistent.

Our common language provides various ways of expressing probabilities. The guarding terms discussed in Chapter 2 provide examples of informal ways of expressing probability commitments. Thus someone might say that it is very likely that Edward Kennedy will seek the Democratic presidential nomination without saying precisely *how* likely it is. We can make our probability claims more precise by using numbers. Sometimes we use percentages; for example, the weather bureau might say that there is a 75 percent chance of snow tomorrow. This can naturally be changed to a fraction: the probability is 3/4 that it will snow tomorrow. Finally, this fraction can be changed into a decimal expression: there is a .75 probability that it will snow tomorrow.

The probability scale has two endpoints: the absolute certainty that the event will occur and the absolute certainty that it will not occur. Because you cannot do better than absolute certainty, a probability can neither rise above 100 percent nor drop below 0 percent (neither above 1, nor below 0). (This should sound pretty obvious, but it is possible to become confused when combining percentages and fractions, as when Yogi Berra was supposed to have said that success is one-third talent and 75 percent hard work.) Of course, what we normally call *probability* claims usually fall between these two endpoints. For this reason it sounds somewhat peculiar to say that there is a 100 percent chance of rain and just plain weird to say the chance of rain is 1 out of 1. Even so, these peculiar ways of speaking cause no procedural difficulties and rarely come up in practice.

ESTABLISHING PROBABILITY CLAIMS

When people make probability claims, we have a right to ask why they assign the probability they do. In the previous chapter, we saw how statistical procedures can be used for establishing probability claims.

Here we will examine the so called *a priori* approach to probabilities. A simple example will bring out the differences between these two approaches. We might wonder what the probability is of drawing an ace from a standard deck of 52 cards. Using the procedure discussed in the previous chapter, we could make a great many random draws from the deck (replacing the cards each time) and then form a statistical generalization concerning the results. Using this approach we would discover that an ace *tends* to come up roughly 1/13 of the time. From this we could draw the conclusion that chances of drawing an ace are 1 in 13.

But we do not have to go to all this trouble. We can assume that each of the 52 cards has an equal chance of being selected. Given this, an obvious *a priori* line of reasoning runs as follows: there are 4 aces in a standard 52-card deck, so the probability of selecting one randomly is 4 in 52. That reduces to 1 chance in 13. Here the set of favorable outcomes is a subset of the total number of equally likely (equi-likely) outcomes, and to compute the probability that the favorable outcome will occur, we merely divide the number of favorable outcomes by the total number of possible outcomes. This fraction gives us the probability that the event will occur on a random draw.

Since all outcomes here are equally likely:

$$\text{Probability} = \frac{\text{favorable outcomes}}{\text{total outcomes}} = \frac{4}{52} = \frac{1}{13}$$

Notice that in coming to our conclusion that there is 1 chance in 13 of randomly drawing an ace from a 52-card deck, we simply used mathematical reasoning. This illustrates the *a priori* approach to probabilities. It is called the *a priori* approach because we arrive at the result simply by reasoning about the circumstances.

A Priori Probability

In calculating the probability of drawing an ace from a 52-card deck, we took the ratio of favorable equi-likely outcomes to total equi-likely outcomes. Generally, then, the probability of a hypothesis h, symbolized "$\Pr(h)$," when all outcomes are equally likely, is expressed as follows:

$$\Pr(h) = \frac{\text{favorable outcomes}}{\text{total outcomes}}$$

We can illustrate this principle with a slightly more complicated example. What is the probability of throwing an 8 on the cast of two dice? Here are all the equi-likely ways in which two dice can turn up on a single cast:

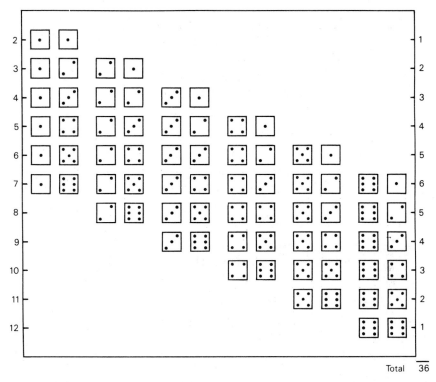

Total 36

As indicated, 5 of the 36 possible outcomes produce an 8, so the probability of throwing an 8 is 5/36.

▼ EXERCISE I

Using the above chart, answer the following questions:

(1) Which is more likely, throwing a 5 or an 8?
(2) What is the probability of throwing either a 5 or an 8?
(3) Which is more likely, to throw a 5 or an 8, or a 2 or a 7?
(4) What is the probability of throwing a 10 or above?
(5) What is the probability of throwing a value from 4 to 6?

Some Laws of Probability

Suppose that you have determined the probability that certain simple events will occur, how do you go about applying this to complicated combinations of events? This is a complex question, and one that can be touched on only lightly in this text. There are, however, some simple rules of probability that are worth knowing because they can guide us in making choices where outcomes are uncertain.

By convention, events are assigned probabilities between 0 and 1 (inclusive). Now an event is either going to occur or not occur; that, at least, is certain (that is, it has a probability of 1). From this it is easy to see how to calculate the probability that the event will not occur given the probability that it will occur: we simply subtract the probability that it will occur from 1. This is our first rule:

Rule 1. The probability that an event will not occur is 1 minus the probability that it will occur. Symbolically:

$$\text{Pr}(\text{not } h) = 1 - \text{Pr}(h)$$

For example, the probability of drawing an ace from a standard deck is 1 in 13, so the probability of *not* drawing an ace is 12 in 13. (This makes sense because there are 48 out of 52 ways of not drawing an ace, and this reduces to 12 chances in 13.)

Rule 2. Given two independent events, the probability of their both occurring is the product of their individual probabilities. Symbolically (where h_1 and h_2 are independent):

$$\text{Pr}(h_1 \text{ \& } h_2) = \text{Pr}(h_1) \times \text{Pr}(h_2)$$

Here the word "independent" needs explanation. Suppose you randomly draw a card from the deck, then put it back (shuffle) and draw again. In this case the outcome of the first draw provides no information about the outcome of the second draw, so it is *independent* of it. What is the probability of drawing two aces in a row using this system? Using Rule 2, we see that the answer is $1/13 \times 1/13$ or 1 chance in 169.

The situation is different if we do not replace the card after the first draw. Rule 2 does not apply to this case because the two events are no longer independent. The chances of getting an ace on the first draw are still 1 in 13, but if an ace is drawn (and not returned to the pack) then there is one less ace in the deck, so the chances of drawing an ace on the next draw are reduced to 3 in 51. Thus the probability of drawing two consecutive aces (without returning the first draw to the deck) are $4/52 \times 3/51$ or 1 in 221, which is considerably lower than 1 in 169.

If we want to extend Rule 2 to cover cases where the events are not independent, we will have to speak of the probability of one event occurring *given that another has occurred*. The probability that h_2 will occur given that h_1 has occurred is called the *conditional* probability of h_2 on h_1, and is usually symbolized: $\text{Pr}(h_2/h_1)$. Rule 2 can be modified to deal with cases where events need not be independent as follows:

Rule 2G. Given two events, the probability of their both occurring is the probability of the first occurring times the probability of the second occurring, given that the first has occurred.

$$\text{Pr}(h_1 \text{ \& } h_2) = \text{Pr}(h_1) \times \text{Pr}(h_2/h_1)$$

Notice that in the event that h_1 and h_2 are independent, the probability of h_2 is not related to the occurrence of h_1, so the probability of h_2 on h_1 is simply the probability of h_2. Thus, Rule 2 is simply a special case of the more general Rule 2G.

We can extend these rules to cover more than two events. For example, with Rule 2 however many events we might consider, provided that they are independent of each other, the probability of all of them occurring is the product of each one of them occurring. For example, the chances of flipping a coin and having it come up heads is 1 chance in 2. What are the chances of flipping a coin 8 times and having it come up heads every time? The answer is:

$$1/2 \times 1/2 \times 1/2 \times 1/2 \times 1/2 \times 1/2 \times 1/2 \times 1/2$$

which equals 1 chance in 256.

Our next rule allows us to answer questions of the following kind: What are the chances of either an 8 or a 2 coming up on a single throw of the dice? Going back to the chart, we saw that we could answer this question by counting the number of ways that a 2 can come up (which is 1) and adding this to the number of ways that an 8 can come up (which is 5). We could then conclude that the chances of one or the other of them coming up is 6 chances in 36 or 1/6. The principle involved in this calculation can be stated as follows:

Rule 3. The probability that at least one of two mutually exclusive events will occur is the sum of the probabilities that each of them will occur. Symbolically (where h_1 and h_2 are mutually exclusive):

$$\Pr(h_1 \text{ or } h_2) = \Pr(h_1) + \Pr(h_2)$$

To say that events are *mutually exclusive* means that they can't both occur. You cannot, for example, get both a 10 and an 8 on the same cast of two dice. You might, however, throw neither one of them.

When events are not mutually exclusive, the rule for calculating disjunctive probabilities becomes more complicated. Suppose, for example, that exactly half of the class is female and exactly half of the class is over 19 and the age distribution is the same for females and males. What is the probability that a randomly selected student will be either a female or over 19? If we simply add the probabilities ($1/2 + 1/2 = 1$) we would get the result that we are certain to pick a female over 19. But that answer is wrong, since a quarter of the class is male and not over 19, and one of them might have been randomly selected. The correct answer is that the chances are 3/4 of randomly selecting a female over 19.

We can see that this is the correct answer, by examining the following table, which looks something like a truth table:

Female	Over 19	Percentage of Class
Yes	Yes	25
Yes	No	25
No	Yes	25
No	No	25

It is easy to see that in 75 percent of the cases a randomly selected student will be either female or over 19.

A general formulation for the rule governing the calculation of disjunctive probabilities is stated as follows:

Rule 3G. The probability that at least one of two events will occur is the sum of the probabilities that each of them will occur, minus the probability that they both occur.

$$Pr(h_1 \text{ or } h_2) = Pr(h_1) + Pr(h_1) - Pr(h_1 \& h_2)$$

If h_1 and h_2 are mutually exclusive, then $Pr(h_1 \& h_2) = 0$, and Rule 3G is reduced to Rule 3.

Before stating Rule 4, we can think about a particular example. What is the probability of tossing at least 1 head in 8 tosses of a coin? Here it is tempting to reason in the following way. There is a 50 percent chance of getting a heads on the first toss and a 50 percent chance of getting a heads on the second toss, so after 2 tosses it is already certain that we will toss at least 1 head, and, thus, after 8 tosses there should be a 400 percent chance. In other words, you just can't miss. There are two good reasons for thinking that this argument is fishy. First, probability can never exceed 100 percent and, secondly, there must be some chance, however small, that we could toss a coin 8 times and not have it come up heads.

The best way to look at this question is to restate it so that the first two rules can be used. Instead of asking what the probability is that a head will come up at least once, we can ask what the probability is that it will *not* come up at least once. Now to say that heads will not come up even once is equivalent to saying that tails will come up 8 times in a row. Now by Rule 2 we know how to compute that probability: it's just 1/2 multiplied by itself 8 times, and that, as we saw, is 1/256. Finally, by Rule 1 we know that the probability that this will not happen (that heads will come up at least once) is 1 − 1/256. In other words, the probability of tossing heads at least once in 8 tosses is 255/256. That comes pretty close to a certainty, but not quite.

We can generalize these results as follows:

Rule 4. The probability that an event will occur at least once in a series of independent trials is simply 1 minus the probability that it will *not* occur in that number of trials. Symbolically (where n is the number of independent trials):

The probability that h will occur at least once in n trials =

$$1 - Pr(\text{not } h)^n$$

Strictly speaking, Rule 4 is unnecessary since it can be derived from Rules 1 and 2, but it is important to know about because it blocks a common misunderstanding about probabilities. *People often think that they have sure things when they do not.*

▼ EXERCISE II

Compute the probability of making the following draws from a standard 52-card deck:

(1) Drawing either a 7 or a 5 on a single draw.
(2) Drawing neither a 7 nor a 5 on a single draw.
(3) Drawing a 7 and then, without returning the first card to the deck, drawing a 5 on the next draw.
(4) Same as (3), but the first card is returned to the deck and the deck is shuffled after the first draw.
(5) Drawing at least 1 spade in a series of 4 consecutive draws, where the card drawn is not returned to the deck.
(6) Same as (5), but the card is returned to the deck after each draw and the deck is reshuffled.

EXPECTED VALUE

It is obvious that having some sense of probable outcomes is important for running our lives. If we hear that there is a 95 percent chance of rain, this usually provides good enough reason for calling off a picnic. But the exact relationship between probabilities and decisions is complex and often misunderstood. The best way to illustrate these misunderstandings is through looking at lotteries where the numbers are fixed and clear.

A dollar bet in a lottery might make you as much as $10 million. That sounds good; why not take a shot at $10 million for only a dollar? Of course, there isn't much chance of winning the lottery—only 1 chance in 20 million—and that sounds bad. Why throw $1 away on nothing? So we are torn in two directions. What we want to know is just how good the bet is. Is it, for example, better or worse than a wager in some other lottery? To answer questions of this kind, we need to introduce the notion of *expected value*.

The idea of expected value takes into account three features that determine whether a bet is financially good or not: the probability of winning, the amount you get if you win, and the amount you lose if you lose. Suppose that on a $1 ticket there is 1 chance in 20 million of winning the New York State Lottery, and you will get $10 million from the state if you do. First, it is important to remember that if the state pays you $10 million, what you have actually won or gained on your $1 ticket is $9,999,999. The state, after all, still has your original $1. So the amount won equals the payoff minus the cost of betting. This is not something that those who win huge lotteries worry about, but taking into account the cost of betting can become important when this cost becomes high relative to the size of the payoff. There is nothing complicated about the amount you will lose when you lose on a $1 ticket: it's $1.

We compute the *expected value* or *financial worth* of a bet in the following way: Expected Value equals

> The probability of winning times the amount one gains by winning,
> minus
> the probability of losing times the amount one loses by losing.

In the example we are looking at, a person who buys a $1 ticket in the lottery has 1 chance in 20 million of gaining $9,999,999, and 19,999,999 chances in 20 million of losing a dollar. So the expected value of this wager equals:

> (1/20,000,000 × $9,999,999)
> minus
> ((19,999,999/20,000,000 × $1))

That comes out to minus $.50.

What does this mean? One way of looking at it is as follows: if you could somehow buy up all of the lottery tickets and thus ensure that you would win, your $20 million investment would net you $10 million, or $.50 on the dollar—certainly a bad investment. Another way of looking at the situation is as follows: if you invested a great deal of money in the lottery over many millions of years, you could expect to win eventually but, in the long run, you would be losing fifty cents on every ticket you bought. One last way of looking at the situation is this: you go down to your local drugstore and buy a *blank* lottery ticket for $.50. Since it is blank, you have no chance of winning, with the result that you lose $.50 every time you bet. Although almost no one looks at the matter in this way, this is, in effect, what you are doing *over the long run* when you buy lottery tickets.

We are now in a position to draw a distinction between a favorable expected value and an unfavorable expected value. The expected value is favorable when it is greater than zero. Changing our example, suppose the chances of hitting a $20 million payoff on a $1 bet are 1 in 10 million. In this case, the state still has the $1 you paid for the ticket, so your winnings or gain are actually $19,999,999. The expected value is calculated as follows:

(1/10 million × $19,999,999)
minus
(9,999,999/10,000,000 × $1)

That comes to $1. So financially this is a good bet. For *in the long run* you will gain $1 for every $1 you bet in such a lottery.

The rule, then, is this: if the expected value of the bet is more than zero, then the expected value is *favorable;* if the expected value of the bet is less than zero, then the expected value is *unfavorable.* If the expected value of the bet is zero, then the bet is *neutral*—financially, a waste of time.

▼ EXERCISE III

Compute the probability and the expected value for the following bets. Each time, you bet that a certain card will be drawn from a standard 52-card deck. If you win, you get the sum indicated; if you lose, of course, you lose a dollar:

Example: Draw a seven of spades. Win $26.
Probability of winning = 1/52
Expected value: $(1/52 \times \$26) - (51/52 \times \$1) = -\$.48$

(1) Draw a 7 of spades or a 7 of clubs. Win: $26.
(2) On two consecutive draws (without returning the first card to the deck), draw a 7 of spades, then a 7 of clubs. Win: $2000.
(3) On two consecutive draws (without returning the first card to the deck), do not draw a club. Win: $.78.
(4) Same as in (3), but this time the card is returned to the deck and the deck is shuffled before the second draw. Win: $.78.

RELATIVE VALUE

Given the fact that actual lotteries usually have extremely unfavorable expected payoffs, why do millions of people invest billions of dollars in them each year? Part of the answer is that some people are stupid, superstitious, or both. People will sometimes reason, "Somebody has to win, why not me?" They can also convince themselves that their lucky day has come. But that is not the whole story, for most people who put down money on lottery tickets realize that the bet is a bad bet, but think that it is worth doing anyway. People fantasize about what they will do with the money if they win, and that's fun. Furthermore, if the bet is only $1, and the person making the bet is not desperately poor, losing isn't going to hurt much. Even if the expected value on the lottery ticket is the loss of fifty cents, this might strike someone as a reasonable price for the fun of thinking about winning. So a bet that is bad from a purely monetary point of view might be acceptable when other factors are considered.

The reverse situation can also arise: a bet may be unreasonable, even though it has a positive expected value. Suppose, for example, that you are allowed to participate in a lottery where a $1 ticket gives you one chance in 10 million of getting a payoff of $20 million. Here, as noted above, the expected value of a $1 bet is a profit of $1, so from the point of view of expected value it is a good bet. This makes it sound reasonable to bet in this lottery, and a small bet probably is reasonable. But under these circumstances would it be reasonable for people to sell everything they owned to buy lottery tickets? The answer to this is almost certainly no, for even though the expected value is positive, the odds of winning are still extremely low, and the loss of someone's total resources would be personally catastrophic.

When we examine the effects that success or failure will have on a *particular* person relative to his or her own needs, resources, preferences, and so on, we are then examining what we shall call the *relative value* or the *utility* of a choice. Considerations of this kind often force us to make adjustments in weighing the significance of costs and payoffs. In the examples that we have just examined, the immediate catastrophic consequences of a loss outweigh the long-term gains that one can expect from participating in the lottery.

Another factor that *typically* affects the relative value of a bet is the phenomenon known as *diminishing marginal value* or *diminishing marginal utility* of a payoff as it gets larger. Diminishing marginal value is illustrated by the following example. Suppose someone offers to pay a debt by buying you a hamburger. Provided that the debt matches the cost of a hamburger and you feel like having one, you might go along with this. But suppose this person offers to pay off a debt ten times larger by buying you ten hamburgers? The chances are that you will reject the offer, for even though ten hamburgers *cost* ten times as much as one hamburger, they are not *worth* ten times as much to you. At some point you will get stuffed and not want any more. The notion of marginal value applies to money as well. If you are starving, $10 will mean a lot to you. You might be willing to work hard to get it. If you are wealthy, $10 more or less makes very little difference; losing $10 might only be an annoyance.

Because of this phenomenon of diminishing marginal value, betting on lotteries is even a worse bet than most people suppose. A lottery with a payoff of $20 million sounds attractive, but it doesn't seem to be 20 times more attractive than a payoff of $1 million. So even if the expected value of your $1 bet in a lottery is the loss of $.50, the actual value to you is really something less than this, and so the bet is worse even than it seemed at first.

In general, then, when payoffs are large, the relative value of the payoff to someone is reduced because of the effects of diminishing marginal value. But not always. It is possible to think of exotic cases where relative value increases with size of the payoff. Suppose a witch told you that she would turn you into a toad if you did not give her $10 million by tomorrow. You believe her, because you know for a fact that she has turned others into toads. You have $1 to your name and you are given the opportunity to participate in the first lottery described above, where a $1 ticket gives you one chance in 20 million of hitting a $10 million payoff. We saw that the expected value of that wager was an unfavorable minus $.50. But now consider the relative value or utility value of $1 to you if you are turned into a toad. Toads have no use for money, so to you, as a toad, the value of the one dollar would drop to nothing. Thus, unless some other more attractive alternatives are available, it would be reasonable to buy a lottery ticket, despite the unfavorable expected value of the wager.

▼ EXERCISE IV

(1) Though the situation is somewhat farfetched, suppose that you are going to the drugstore to buy medicine for a friend who will die without it. You have only $10—exactly what the medicine costs. Outside the drugstore a young man is playing *three-card monte*, a simple game where the dealer shows you three cards, turns them over, shifts them briefly from hand to hand, and then lays them out, face down, on the top of a box. You are supposed to identify a particular card (usually the ace of spades), and if you do, you are paid even money. You yourself are a magician and know the sleight-of-hand trick that fools most people, and you are sure that you can guess the card right 9 times out of 10. First, what is the expected payoff of a bet of $10? In this context, would it be reasonable to make this bet? Why?

(2) In the witch example, considerations of relative value made a bet reasonable even when the expected payoff of the bet was unfavorable. In the three-card monte example, the reverse happened; a bet is unreasonable even though the expected payoff is favorable. Think of an example of your own illustrating one of these possibilities.

THE GAMBLER'S FALLACY

In assessing probabilities, a little knowledge can be a dangerous thing. Ordinary people often refer to something called the Law of Averages. "In the long run," they say, "things will even out (or average out)." Interpreted one way, this amounts to what mathematicians call the Law of Large Numbers, and it is perfectly correct. For example, when flipping a coin, we expect it to come up heads half the time, so with 10 flips, it should come up heads 5 times. But if we actually check this out, we discover that the number of times it comes out heads in 10 flips varies significantly from this predicted value, sometimes coming up heads more than 5 times, sometimes coming up less. What the Law of Large Numbers tell us is that the actual percentage of heads will tend to come closer to the theoretically predicted percentage of heads the more trials we make. If you flipped a coin a million times, it would be very surprising if the percentage of heads were more than 1 percent away from the predicted 50 percent.

When interpreted as the Law of Large Numbers, the so-called Law of Averages contains an important truth, but it is often interpreted in a way that involves a fundamental fallacy. People sometimes reason in the following way: If they have had a run of bad luck, they should increase their bets because they are due for a run of good luck to even things out. Gambling systems are sometimes based on this fallacious idea. People keep track of the numbers that come up on a roulette wheel trying to discover a number that has not come up for a long time. They then pile their money on that number on the assumption that it is due.

To see that this is a fallacy, we can go back to flipping coins again. Toss a coin until it comes up 3 heads in a row. (This will take less time than you might imagine.) What is the probability that it will come up heads a forth time? Put crudely, some people think that the probability of it coming up heads again must be very small because a string of tails is needed to *even things out*. Less crudely, but just as mistakenly, someone might use Rule 2 and argue that the chances of a coin coming up 4 times in a row equal $1/2 \times 1/2 \times 1/2 \times 1/2$, or 1 chance in 16, so the chance of it coming up heads again after 3 occurrences of heads is also 1 in 16. But that's just wrong. Our assumption is that the chances of getting heads on any given toss is 1/2. This is true whatever happened on the preceding tosses. So the probability from the start of tossing heads 4 times in a row is 1 in 16, but the probability of tossing another head after tossing heads 3 times in a row is just 1/2.

REGRESSION TO THE MEAN

The notion of *regression to the mean* is somewhat subtle, but an illustration should help make this notion clear. In a famous example, Israeli flight instructors claimed to notice the following phenomenon: when cadet pilots were praised for their good flying, they tended to do worse the next time up, whereas those cadets who were criticized for poor flying tended to do better. The explanation seemed obvious: the good flyers who were praised got cocky and overconfident and thus didn't fly as well, while the bad flyers who were criticized knuckled down and did better. It seemed, then, that bad flying should be criticized, but good flying should not be praised.

Now it is possible that the explanation and the moral drawn from it are correct. Another possibility is that the observed phenomenon has nothing to do with praise and blame but is simply the result of statistical variation. The statistical explanation runs as follows: in early flight training performance varies considerably from flight to flight. Sometimes the student pilot does well, sometimes not. Given this variation, a good many of those who did well on one flight will not do as well on the next. Of course, the reverse will also be true: as a matter of chance, a good many who flew badly one time will fly well the next. Consequently, statistical variation alone may explain why a good number of those who did well and were praised will do worse on their next flight, and a good number of those who did badly and were criticized will do better. It could well be that the praise and criticism had nothing to do with these results. The results might have been exactly the same if none of the student pilots was either praised or blamed.

Most people don't know about the phenomenon of regression to the mean, and when they hear about it, they are often not impressed. Here is a simple experiment that illustrates its significance. Suppose that you decide that coming up heads is good for a coin, whereas coming up tails is bad. You now take a jug with 100 pennies in it and spill them out on the table. You "praise" the coins that came up heads by putting a red dot of paint on each of them. You "criticize" coins that came up tails by putting a blue dot of paint on them. You put the coins back in the jug, shake them up, and pour them back on the table. When you examine the coins you find that they fall into four (roughly equal) groups:

(1)   Heads with red dots on them
(2)   Tails with blue dots on them
(3)   Heads with no dots on them
(4)   Tails with no dots on them

In the first group, we have coins that were "praised" without making them worse. In the second group we have coins that were "criticized" without making them better. But the last two groups are more interesting. If a coin shows heads with no dot, it must have a blue dot on its other side; that is, it is a coin that was previously criticized for being tails. Furthermore, if a coin shows tails with no dot, it must have a red dot on the other side; that is, it must have been previously praised for coming up heads. In other words, roughly half of the coins exhibit the phenomenon attributed to the Israeli cadet pilots: they either got worse after praise or got better after blame. On the assumption that little dots of paint would not significantly affect the way a coin will come up, it is obvious that the so-called praise and blame had nothing to do with the matter: the distribution into these four groups can be explained on statistical grounds alone. It is entirely possible that the actual praise and blame bestowed on the student pilots had no more effect on their performance than the make-believe praise and blame had on the performance of these pennies.

There is a moral to be drawn from this: when trying to understand a phenomenon, we should always ask whether it can be explained simply on probabilistic grounds. To use commonsense language, we should always entertain the possibility that the phenomenon is just a matter of luck—good or bad. More carefully, we should always entertain the possibility that regression to the mean is a significant component in accounting for some phenomenon.

▼ EXERCISE V

Illustrate the phenomenon of regression to the mean by having, say, ten people take two successive simple true-false exams—answering all the questions by flipping a coin.

STRANGE THINGS HAPPEN

What are the chances of tossing a fair coin and having it come up heads 19 times in a row? The answer is 1/2 multiplied by itself 19 times, which equals 1 chance in 524,288. Now those chances are so remote that you might think it could never really happen. You'd be wrong. Of course, if you sat flipping a single coin, you might spend a very long time before you hit a sequence of 19 consecutive heads, but there is a way of getting this result (with some help from friends) in a single afternoon. First of all, you start out with $5,242.88 worth of pennies and put them in a large truck. (Actually, the truck would not be all that large.) Dump the coins out and then pick up all the coins that come up heads. Put them back in the truck and repeat the procedure. Do that over and over again, always returning those that come up heads to the truck. With tolerably good luck, on the nineteenth dump of the coins you will get at least one coin that comes up heads again. Any such coin will have come up heads 19 times in a row.[1]

---

[1] According to our colleague J. Laurie Snell, starting with 524,288 pennies gives you a 63.2 percent chance of having at least one of the pennies come up heads 19 times in a row. If this seems too risky, you could get more pennies and find more friends to help you with the experiment.

What's the point of this example? Specifically, it is intended to show that we often attribute abilities or the lack of abilities to people when, in fact, their performances may be statistically insignificant. When people invest with stock brokers, they tend to shift when they lose money. When they hit upon a broker who earns them money, they stay and praise this broker's abilities. In fact, some financial advisers seem to be better than others—they have a long history of sound financial advice—but the financial community is, in many ways, like the truckload of pennies we have just examined. There are a great many brokers giving all sorts of different advice and, by chance alone, some of them are bound to give good advice. Furthermore, some of them are bound to have runs of success, just as some of the pennies dumped from the truck will have long strings of coming up heads. Thus, in some cases, what appears to be brilliance in predicting stock prices may be nothing more than a run of statistically expected good luck.

The gambling casinos of the world are like the truck full of pennies as well. With roulette wheels spinning in a great many places over a great deal of time, startling long runs are bound to occur. For example in 1918, black came up 26 consecutive times on a roulette wheel in Monte Carlo. The odds against this are staggering. But before we can decide what to make of this event, we would have to judge it in the context of the vast number of times that the game of roulette has been played.

Honors Project

Students familiar with computer programming should not find it difficult to write a program that will simulate a Monte Carlo roulette wheel and keep track of long runs of black and long runs of red. On a Monte Carlo wheel, the odds of coming up black are (18/37). The same odds hold for coming up red. Write such a program; run it for a day; then report back the longest runs.

SOME PUZZLES CONCERNING PROBABILITY

We will conclude the chapter with several puzzles that will draw on your understanding of many of the concepts we have just discussed.

(1) You are presented with two bags, one containing two ham sandwiches and the other containing a ham sandwich and a cheese sandwich. You reach in one bag and draw out a ham sandwich. What is the probability that the other sandwich in the bag is also a ham sandwich?

(2) You are presented with three bags: two contain a chicken fat sandwich and one contains a cheese sandwich. You are asked to guess

which bag contains the cheese sandwich. You do so, and the bag you have selected is set aside. (You obviously have one chance in three of guessing correctly.) From the two remaining bags, one containing a chicken fat sandwich is then removed. You are now given the opportunity to switch your selection to the remaining bag. Will such a switch increase, decrease, or leave unaffected your chances of correctly selecting the bag with the cheese sandwich in it?

(3) Fogelin's Palace in Border, Nevada, offers the following unusual bet. If you win, then you make a 50 percent profit on your bet; if you lose, you take a 40 percent loss. That is, if you bet $1 and win, you get back $1.50; if you bet $1 and lose, you get back $.60. The chances of winning are fifty-fifty. This sounds like a marvelous opportunity, but there is one hitch: in order to play, you must let your bet ride with its winnings, or losses, for four plays. For example, starting with $100, a four bet sequence might look like this:

	Win	Win	Lose	Win
Total	$150	$225	$135	$202.50

At the end of this sequence, you can pick up $202.50, and thus make a $102.50 profit.

Now it seems that Fogelin's Palace is a good place to gamble, but consider the following argument on the other side. Because the chances of winning are fifty-fifty, you will, on the average, win half the time. But notice what happens in such a case:

	Win	Lose	Lose	Win
Total	$150	$90	$54	$81

So, even though you have won half the time, you have come out $19 behind.

Surprisingly, it doesn't matter what order the wins and losses come in; if two are wins and two are losses, you come out behind. (You can check this.) So, because you are only going to win roughly half the time, and when you win half the time you actually lose money, it now seems to be a bad idea to gamble at Fogelin's Palace. What should you do, gamble at Fogelin's Palace or not?

Answers to these puzzles appear in the Appendix at the end of this book.

▼ DISCUSSION QUESTIONS

1. In a remarkable study, Gilovich, Vallone, and Tversky found striking instance of people's tendency to treat things as statistically significant when they are not. In professional basketball certain players have the reputation of being *streak shooters*. Streak shooters seem to score points in batches, then go cold and cannot buy a basket. Stated more precisely, in streak shooting "the performance of a player during a particular period is significantly better than expected on the basis of the player's overall record." (295–96)

   To test whether streak shooting really exists, the authors made a detailed study of a year's shooting record for the players on the Philadelphia 76ers. This team included Andrew Toney, noted around the league as being a streak shooter. The authors found no evidence for streak shooting, not even for Andrew Toney. How would you go about deciding whether streak shooting exists or not? If, as Gilovich, Vallone, and Tversky have argued, belief in this phenomenon is a "cognitive illusion," why do so many people, including most professional athletes, believe that it does exist?[2]

2. The idea discussed earlier—that in making decisions under uncertainty we should consider the prospective gains and losses together with relevant probabilities—was clearly stated in the *Port-Royal Logic,* a very influential work on logic published by the French writers Arnauld and Nicole in 1662. Speaking of the majority of mankind, these writers tell us that they

   > fall into an illusion which is more deceptive in proportion as it appears to them to be reasonable; it is, that they regard only the greatness or importance of the advantage which they hope for, or of the disadvantage which they fear, without considering at all the probability which there is of that advantageous or disadvantageous event befalling.
   >
   > Thus, when they apprehend any great evil, as the loss of their livelihood or their fortune, they think it the part of prudence to neglect no precaution for preserving these; and if it is some great good, as the gain of a hundred thousand crowns, they think that they act wisely in seeking to obtain it, if the hazard is a small amount, however little likelihood there may be of a success.

   To correct this defect in reasoning, these authors suggest that

   > it is necessary to consider not only the good and evil in themselves, but also the probability of their happening and not happening.

---

2. For more on this see, Thomas Gilovich, Robert Vallone, and Amos Tversky, "The Hot Hand in Basketball: On the Misperception of Random Sequences," *Cognitive Psychology* 17 (1985), pp. 295–314.

This is sound advice, for it will prevent us from taking excessive precautions against large evils that are hardly likely to occur and from squandering money (for example, in lotteries) seeking enormous gains that we have only a minute chance of obtaining.

These authors conclude their discussion with a striking remark concerning the reverse situation that obtains concerning *salvation*.

> It belongs to infinite things alone, as eternity and salvation, that they cannot be equalled by any temporal advantage; and thus we ought never to place them in the balance with any of the things of the world. This is why the smallest degree of facility for the attainment of salvation is of higher value than all the blessings of the world put together; and why the slightest peril of being lost is more serious than all temporal evils, considered simply as evils.[3]

The authors conclude that we ought to spend all of our efforts, however great, in an attempt to attain salvation.

This is obviously an argument concerning what we have called *expected value* and *relative value*. State it clearly and evaluate it.

3. The following, recent article raises another interesting problem with dealing with eternity. How would you answer it?

▼ *Playing Games With Eternity: The Devil's Offer*[4]
BY EDWARD J. GRACELY

Suppose Ms C dies and goes to hell, or to a place that seems like hell. The devil approaches and offers to play a game of chance. If she wins, she can go to heaven. If she loses, she will stay in hell forever; there is no second chance to play the game. If Ms C plays today, she has a 1/2 chance of winning. Tomorrow the probability will be 2/3. Then 3/4, 4/5, 5/6, etc., with no end to the series. Thus every passing day increases her chances of winning. At what point should she play the game?

The answer is not obvious: after any given number of days spent waiting, it will still be possible to improve her chances by waiting yet another day. And any increase in the probability of winning a game with infinite stakes has an infinite utility. For example, if she waits a year, her probability of winning the game would be approximately .997268; if she waits one more day, the probability would increase to .997275, a difference of only .000007. Yet even .000007 multiplied by infinity is infinite.

On the other hand, it seems reasonable to suppose the cost of delaying for a day to be finite—a day's more suffering in hell. So the infinite expected benefit from a delay will always exceed the cost.

---

3 These passages come from the final chapter of *The Port-Royal Logic*, generally thought to be by Arnauld and Nicole, translated by Thomas Spencer Baynes (Edinburgh: Sutherland and Knox, 1851), pp. 365 ff.

4 Edward J. Gracely, "Playing Games With Eternity: The Devil's Offer," *Analysis* 48.3 (1988), p. 113.

This logic might suggest that Ms C should wait forever, but clearly such a strategy would be self-defeating: why should she stay forever in a place in order to increase her chances of leaving it? So the question remains: what should Ms C do?*

*I would like to thank Janet Fleetwood for her very helpful comments on the first version of this paper.

AREAS OF
ARGUMENTATION

11

Legal Reasoning

One area where arguments are very important is the law. Legal decisions have concrete effects on people's lives. In criminal cases, judges can deprive people of their freedom or even their lives. In civil cases, judges often take away large sums of money, the custody of one's children, and so on. These decisions are made because certain legal arguments are accepted, and others are rejected.

Unfortunately, it is sometimes difficult to find any good reason for a legal decision. Important facts may not be known, and the law is sometimes unclear or inconsistent. Some cases "fall between the cracks" so that no law seems to apply. Human beings have a remarkable ability to produce weird cases that would tax even the wisdom of Solomon.

Even in the toughest cases, judges must reach *some* decision. Outside the law, we can often just let matters ride—we can postpone a decision until further facts are established, or even declare that the issues are too vague to admit of any decision. This is rarely an option in a legal case. If A sues B, either A or B must win. The judge cannot say, "This case is too tough for me. I'm not going to rule on it." Throwing the case out of court amounts to ruling in favor of the defendant. A decision must be made, and usually in a relatively short period of time.

These pressures have led lawyers and judges to develop many ingenious ways to argue. Lawyers cite statutes, precedents, and their historical contexts. They claim the authority of common sense and science, and they cite scholarly articles, even some by philosophers. They deploy metaphors and rhetorical devices—almost anything to convince the judge or jury to decide in favor of their clients. The variety of these arguments makes legal reasoning complex and also fascinating.

Despite this variety, some rough generalizations can be made. A decision in a legal case usually depends upon two kinds of questions: (1) questions of fact and (2) questions of law. These questions are handled differently in different kinds of cases.

COMPONENTS OF LEGAL REASONING

Questions of Fact

A *criminal law* prohibits a certain kind of behavior and assigns a punishment to those who violate it. When a person is accused of violating this law, a trial is held to determine whether *in fact* he or she has done so. The judge instructs the jury on the law bearing on the case. If the jury then decides that the accused has violated the law, they find him or her guilty, and the judge usually hands down the punishment stated in the statute.

In a *civil* suit, one party sues another, say, for breach of contract. Because states have laws governing contracts, once more a trial is held to decide whether *in fact* there was a contract (instead of some other speech act) and whether *in fact* it was breached. If a breach of contract is found, the judge or jury awards damages as the law specifies.

Although questions of fact arise in all cases, criminal and civil cases do differ in *the burden of proof*—in who is required to establish the facts and to what degree of certainty. In a criminal procedure, the prosecution must establish its case *beyond a reasonable doubt* (an inherently vague expression). In a civil case, the burden of proof is less. Generally, the case is won by the party who shows that the *preponderance* of evidence favors his or her side of the case. Although this is a bit too simple, it is sometimes said that if the scales tip ever so slightly in favor of A rather than B, then A wins the case. The complicated rules that govern civil procedure are supposed to give each party a fair chance to show that the preponderance of evidence falls on his or her side of the case.

The only way to carry the burden of proof is to present *evidence*. This evidence can contain conflicts and unclarities, which make it hard to prove the facts. Sleazy Sam is accused of murder. The prosecution presents eyewitnesses who saw Sam enter the victim's hotel room just before the body was found and expert witnesses who identify the fingerprints on the murder weapon as Sam's. And, of course, Sam had a fight in public with the victim on the day before the murder. Perry Mason defends Sam by arguing that the victim could have been killed hours earlier, and Sam's fingerprints got on the weapon when he found the body. In the movies, the next step is for the real murderer to confess in the courtroom. But real life is rarely that easy, so juries often have a hard job.

Sometimes the facts are so complex that they simply cannot be proven one way or the other, and sometimes the distinction between facts and law is not so clear. These problems arise often in cases that raise larger social issues. For example, in the case of *Brown v. Board of Education* (excerpted below), the Supreme Court answered the question of law by saying, "the opportunity of an education . . . is a right which must be available to all on equal terms." The Court next asked: "Does segregation of children in public schools solely on the basis of race . . . deprive the children of the minority group of equal educational opportunities?" (301–302) This question was presented as a question of fact. The Court answered in the affirmative and tried to justify its answer by citing various psychological studies of the performance of minority children from segregated schools. This answer would be accepted by most people today, but the studies used as proof were controversial and inconclusive, so the Court had to decide whether studies of this kind were reliable enough to serve as evidence in this case. Moreover, the answer to the above question also depends on what count as "equal educational opportunities" for the purposes of the law. For example, the studies cited by the Court found that segregated schools "affect the motivation of a child to learn," (302) but these factual studies could not determine whether lowered *motivation* to learn counts as lowered *opportunity* to learn. The Court had to decide this issue because it in effect determines what the law is—what it prohibits and what it allows. Thus, what was presented as a question of fact turns out to be at least partly a question of law. In such cases, it is not clear where law ends and facts begin.

Questions of Law

Even after the facts are determined, no decision can be reached without determining what the law is. The law varies from place to place and from time to time, so we have to know what the law is at the right time and place. This is determined mainly by looking at the legal institutions that actually exist. In our legal system, there are three main sources of the law: statutes, the Constitution, and precedents.

Statutes

Roughly, statutes are general rules of law passed by legislatures. Statutes are made at various levels (federal, state, and local), and they cover various subjects, including crimes as well as property, contracts, and other areas of civil law. There are also statutes governing the procedures and kinds of evidence that can be presented in court.

When a general statute is applied to a particular case, the legal argument is often primarily deductive. For example, Sally drove 95 miles per hour in front of Hanover High School at 4:00 P.M. on a school day. It is illegal to drive over 15 m.p.h. in front of any school at 4:00 P.M. on a school day. Therefore, Sally's driving was illegal. Of course, there are lots of suppressed premises, such as that 95 m.p.h. is over 15 m.p.h. Even in this simple case, other assumptions are much trickier. Sally might not be found guilty if she had an excuse or justification, such as that a terrorist had a gun to her head. It is very difficult to give a complete and precise list of all possible excuses and justifications. It is at least as hard to say exactly when an excuse or justification is adequate. Nonetheless, it might be obvious that Sally had no excuse or justification. If we add this claim as a premise, then the legal argument against Sally is deductively sound. She might as well plead guilty.

Such simple cases are common, but they are also boring. Things get much more difficult and interesting when a statute is *vague*, so that it is not clear whether the statute applies to the case at issue. Then the statute must be *interpreted*. We need some way to tell more exactly what the law prohibits and what it allows. There is much disagreement about how to interpret statutes and about how to show that one interpretation is correct, but we can say which factors are commonly used in these arguments.

The first step in interpreting a statute is to look carefully at the *words* in the statute and their literal *meanings*. But the courts must often look beyond the mere words of the statute. This need arises when the words are unclear and when they lead to absurd results. For example, suppose a city council passes an ordinance requiring zoos to provide clean, dry cages for all mammals. This works fine until one zoo puts a whale in its aquarium. The whale would be in trouble if the courts stuck to the words of the ordinance. Fortunately, the courts can also consider the *intentions* of the legislators, which can be gleaned from their debates about the law. Of course, the city council might not have thought at all about whales, or they might have thought that whales are fish instead of mammals. Thus, if their intentions are what the legislators consciously had in mind, then we also need to consider the deeper, more general *purpose* of the legislators—the goal they were trying to reach or the moral outlook they were trying to express. This purpose is revealed by the wider historical context and by other laws of the same legislature. In our example, the purpose of the statute was obviously to provide a healthy environment for mammals in zoos. This purpose is best served by interpreting the ordinance so that it does not require dry cages for whales. Most judges would conclude that this interpretation is best, even if it does go against the words of the statute and beyond any conscious intentions of the legislators.

In addition to words, intentions, and purposes, *moral beliefs* are also often used to interpret statutes. Judges often argue that a statute should be interpreted one way by claiming that any other interpretation would lead to some kind of practical difficulty or moral unfairness. Such arguments are effective when everyone agrees about what is immoral or unfair, but judges often depend on more controversial moral beliefs. Critics claim that judges should not use their own moral views in this way, but there is no doubt that judges do in fact reason from such moral premises.

It should be clear that none of these methods of interpretation is mechanical, and none guarantees a single best interpretation of every statute. Part of the legal controversy is often over which factors can or should be used to argue for an interpretation. When all is said and done, legal reasoning from statutes is often far from the straightforward deduction which it appears to be in simple cases.

The Constitution

Even when a statute has been interpreted, it is sometimes not clear whether the statute is *valid*—whether it has any legal force. This is determined by the Constitution. The Constitution occupies a special place in the legal system of the United States. If any statute conflicts with the Constitution, including its amendments, that statute has no legal force. Generally it is not the role of courts to enact laws, but the courts do have the power to strike down laws if they conflict with provisions in our Constitution.

It is easy to imagine clear cases of laws that violate constitutional provisions. If the State of Rhode Island began printing its own money, that would plainly violate the constitutional provision that reserves this right to the federal government. But, typically, those constitutional questions that reach the courts are not clear-cut. Even more so than statutes, provisions in the Constitution are very general and sometimes vague. This vagueness serves a purpose. The framers of the Constitution recognized that they could not foresee every eventuality, so they wanted to allow future courts to interpret the Constitution as cases arose. But the vagueness of the Constitution also creates problems. Interpretations can often conflict and become the source of controversy. As with statutes, arguments for and against interpretations of the Constitution usually refer to the words of the Constitution, the intentions and purposes of the framers of the Constitution, the effects of adopting an interpretation, moral beliefs, and so on. Such arguments are often inconclusive. The Supreme Court is then the final arbiter on questions of constitutionality.

Precedents

Our legal system is not only a constitutional system; it is also partly a system of common law. This means that lawyers and judges often cite precedents as arguments for present decisions. A *precedent* is simply a past case or decision which is supposed to be similar to the present case.

The practice of citing precedents might seem strange at first sight. Why should one case provide any reason for a decision in a different case? The answer is that the cases resemble each other in important respects. Of course, when there is an important enough difference between the cases, they should be *distinguished* and then the precedent provides no argument in the present case. But, when there is no important enough difference, like cases should be treated alike. If similar precedents were not followed, the legal system would lack continuity, and this would make it unfair and ineffective. Of course, past decisions that were mistaken or immoral should not be continued. That is why precedents can be *overturned*. Nonetheless, our legal system assumes that, if there is no adequate reason to overturn a precedent or to distinguish the precedent from the present case, then the precedent provides some reason to decide the present case in the same way as the precedent. This general doctrine of precedent is often called *"stare decisis"* (to adhere to previous decisions).

Precedents are used for many different purposes. When a statute is vague, precedents are often used to argue for one interpretation over another. When no statute applies directly, precedents are often used to argue about what the law is. Precedents can also be used in arguments for general questions of fact, or just as sources of persuasive rhetoric.

The form of arguments from precedents also varies. Often a judge or lawyer merely quotes part of the opinion in the precedent and treats that quotation as an authoritative pronouncement of the law. Arguments from precedents are then similar to arguments from legislative statutes, and there often arises a similar need to interpret the judicial pronouncement in the precedent. In other precedents, the judge chooses to make the decision without explicitly formulating any general rule of law. The precedent can still be used to argue for future decisions by emphasizing analogies and discounting differences between the precedent and the present case.

One relatively simple example occurs in the case of *Plessy v. Ferguson* (1896) (excerpted below). Louisiana passed a statute which required blacks and whites to use "separate but equal" cars in trains. Plessy refused to comply, because he claimed that the Louisiana law violated the Fourteenth Amendment to the Constitution, which forbids states to deprive anyone of "the equal protection of the laws."

In his argument for this claim, Plessy cited the precedent of *Yick Wo v. Hopkins* (1886). That case was about an ordinance in San Francisco that required a permit from the Board of Supervisors for any public laundry not operated in a brick or stone building. On its face, this ordinance was supposed simply to prevent fires. In practice, however, the Board of Supervisors granted permits to all but one of the non-Chinese applicants and denied permits to all of the Chinese applicants. Because of this practice, Yick Wo claimed that the ordinance violated the equal protection clause. The Supreme Court agreed and declared the ordinance unconstitutional, at least insofar as it gave the city power to grant and refuse permits "without regard to the competency of the persons applying, or the propriety of the places selected for the carrying on of business" (from *Plessy*, 297).

The argument from a precedent to a decision in a present case is often presented as an argument from *analogy*.[1] In this form, the argument emphasizes similarities between the cases, and then concludes that the decision in the present case should be the same as in the precedent. Plessy's argument then appears to run something like this:

(1) The ordinance in *Yick Wo* was declared unconstitutional.
(2) The ordinance in *Yick Wo* is similar to the statute in *Plessy* in several respects.

(Conclusion) The statute in *Plessy* also ought to be declared unconstitutional.

This argument is not very good as it stands, so we need to add some suppressed premises.

The first step is to construct a list of the respects in which the cases are similar. That is not always so easy. When we are evaluating someone else's argument, we can focus on the similarities that he or she mentions. But when we are constructing our own legal arguments, we have to be more creative; we have to formulate the respects in which the cases are supposed to be similar.

The crucial point to realize is that it is not enough to list just any similarities. Some similarities do not matter. It is clearly irrelevant that the laws in *Yick Wo* and *Plessy* both contain more than ten words or that both apply to large cities. This much is assumed by both sides in the case, and legal reasoning would be impossible without assuming that many such similarities are irrelevant.

It is also obvious that there are always some differences between the precedent and the present case. This might seem to suggest that no precedent can give any reason for a similar decision in the present case. However, not all differences matter. It is not important, even if true, that Yick Wo was married and over 50 years old, but Plessy was not. To discount or distinguish the precedent, one must show that some

---

[1] For an elegant discussion of the role of analogical reasoning in the law, *see* Edward Levi, *An Introduction to Legal Reasoning* (Chicago: University of Chicago Press, 1963).

difference between *Yick Wo* and *Plessy* is important enough to justify reaching different decisions in these cases.

The central question, then, asks which factors (similarities and differences) *do* matter. The point of the argument in our example is that the factor which justified the decision in *Yick Wo* also justifies a similar decision in *Plessy*. Consequently, the only similarities and differences that matter concern the factors that were needed to justify the decision in the precedent, *Yick Wo*. These are often called the *ratio decidendi*—the reason for the decision.

Using the doctrine of precedents as a suppressed premise, the argument can be reconstructed as follows:

(1) The ordinance in *Yick Wo* was declared unconstitutional.
(2) The ordinance in *Yick Wo* is similar to the statute in *Plessy* in several respects (A, B, C, D, and so on).
(3) These are the features that justified declaring the ordinance in *Yick Wo* unconstitutional.
(4) There are no important enough differences between *Yick Wo* and *Plessy* to justify distinguishing the precedent.
(5) *Yick Wo* ought not to be overturned.
(6) If a precedent is similar to a present case in the respects that justified the decision in the precedent, and if the precedent ought not to be either overturned or distinguished, then the present case ought to be decided in the same way as the precedent.

(Conclusion) The statute in *Plessy* ought to be declared unconstitutional.

This argument is now valid, but this does not get us very far. We still need to know whether its premises are true.

Clearly, the crucial question is this: How do we determine which features of the precedent are needed to justify that decision? What we need to do is to extract a general rule of law which provides the best justification for the precedent decision. There is no simple way to extract this rule of law, but some rough guidelines can be given.

The most obvious way to argue that a certain feature is important is to look at the written opinion in the precedent and see what the court said—more specifically, what reasons it gave for its decision. In *Yick Wo*, the Court wrote:

> whatever may have been the intent of the ordinances as adopted, . . . [t]hough the law itself be fair on its face and impartial in appearance, yet, if it is applied and administered by public authority with an evil eye and an unequal hand, so as practically to make unjust and illegal discriminations between persons in similar circumstances, material to their rights, the denial of equal justice is still within the prohibition of the Constitution.

Here the Court explicitly announces that the intent of the ordinance and its appearance (for example, whether the ordinance explicitly mentions race or ethnic background) did not matter to their decision. The

Court also declares that it did matter that the ordinance in practice creates inequalities in rights. Such official pronouncements by a court have considerable force for future courts in legal arguments.

Another way to determine which factors matter is to use the necessary condition test or the sufficient condition test from Chapter 9. These tests had to be passed by each side in the *Plessy* case. Plessy claimed that a sufficient condition of unconstitutionality is that a law has a discriminatory *effect* on the rights of a particular racial or ethnic group. This claim would fail the sufficient condition test if there were any precedent still in force where a law was found to have a discriminatory effect but the law was not found unconstitutional. Since there was no such precedent, the sufficient condition test does not exclude Plessy's claim that discriminatory effect is sufficient by itself to make a law unconstitutional.

On the other side, the Court claimed that discriminatory effect is not sufficient, because discriminatory *motive* is a necessary condition for a law to be unconstitutional under the equal protection clause. For this claim to pass the necessary condition test, there must have been no precedent still in force where a law was held unconstitutional under the equal protection clause but the Court did not find any discriminatory motive. Plessy claimed that *Yick Wo* was such a case, but the Court responded that, even if those who passed the ordinance had no discriminatory motive, the administration of the ordinance in *Yick Wo* "was held to be a covert attempt on the part of the municipality to make an arbitrary and unjust discrimination against the Chinese race." If so, the necessary condition test does not rule out the Court's claim that discriminatory motive is necessary for unconstitutionality in this case.

This disagreement reveals the limits on the tests of necessary conditions and sufficient conditions. These tests are useful when there is a rich body of coherent precedents. But when there are not enough precedents of the right kinds, and when the precedents are not coherent, the necessary condition test and the sufficient condition test cannot be used to rule out conflicting interpretations of the precedents.

When the actual precedents are not enough, judges sometimes refer to *hypothetical cases*. In *Plessy*, a judge might imagine a law with discriminatory effect but no discriminatory motive. If the judge can show why this law should be found unconstitutional, this would suggest that a discriminatory motive is not really necessary for a violation of the equal protection clause. This takes some imagination, and it also requires judges to apply their moral beliefs about which laws should be allowed. Some critics deny that moral arguments should have any legal force, because they are so controversial. Nonetheless, there is no doubt that judges often do in fact assume such moral beliefs in arguments from precedents.

One common example of such an argument can be called a *"parade of horrors."* The goal in a parade of horrors is to show that harmful or immoral consequences would follow if the courts reached a certain decision, because this decision would operate as a precedent in future cases. These arguments often seem like slippery-slope arguments, but there is no need for a continuum of horrors. For example, in response to an argument for the Louisiana law, the lawyers for Plessy claimed that

> . . . the same argument that will justify the state legislature in requiring railways to provide separate accommodations for the two races will also authorize them to require separate cars to be provided for people whose hair is of a certain color, or who are aliens, or who belong to certain nationalities, or to enact laws requiring colored people to walk upon one side of the street, and white people upon the other, or requiring white men's houses to be painted white, and colored men's black, or their vehicles or business signs to be of different colors, upon the theory that one side of the street is as good as another, or that a house or vehicle of one color is as good as one of another color. (297)

One question which must be asked about any parade of horrors is whether the results really are so horrible. Sometimes a lawyer will show that a certain decision leads to certain results, but the opponent responds, "Yes, isn't it wonderful?" However, this response is not available here. Most people, including the Court in *Plessy*, agree that the results cited above would be terrible, mainly because such laws would restrict people's freedom for no good reason.

The next issue is whether these results would in fact follow. Sometimes one can respond to a parade of horrors by showing that no legislature really would pass such silly laws. Then there is supposed to be nothing to be afraid of.

However, even if such laws would never in fact be passed, there is still something wrong with a decision that would *permit* such laws. The *Plessy* decision would establish an unjust standard if it allowed such horrible laws, but does it? That depends on the reasons that are given for the precedent. The Court denies that the *Plessy* decision would justify these results, because these horrible laws would serve no good purpose, so they would have to be passed out of a discriminatory motive, whereas there is supposed to be no discriminatory motive in the *Plessy* statute. This is hard to believe, but it illustrates that one way to respond to a parade of horrors is to show that the decision would not lead to the horrors.

A final point to remember is that arguments from precedents are usually inconclusive, like other inductive arguments. (*See* Chapter 9.) One reason is that more precedents might be found, and these new precedents might conflict with the precedents in the original argument. Another reason is that any precedent can be overturned. Precedents are not supposed to be overturned unless they are very badly mistaken or immoral, but this is always a possibility. Nonetheless, even though arguments from precedents always might be refuted in such ways, precedents can still provide some reasons for legal decisions.

So far we have looked at arguments from precedents as ways to determine what is necessary or sufficient to violate the law. Even after this is determined, the law still must be applied to the facts in the present case. In *Plessy*, the Court held that there was no intent to discriminate, because the statute in *Plessy* was "reasonable" and "enacted in good faith for the promotion of the public good and not for the annoyance or oppression of a particular class." This claim is very questionable. In his famous dissent, Justice Harlan denies it when he writes,

> Everyone knows that the statute in question had its origin in the purpose, not so much to exclude white persons from railroad cars occupied by blacks, as to exclude colored people from coaches occupied by or assigned to white persons. . . . No one would be so wanting in candor as to assert the contrary.

If Harlan is right, the Court's argument has a false premise, so the statute in *Plessy* should have been found unconstitutional even if the Court was right about what was necessary to find a law unconstitutional.

We can summarize this discussion by listing various ways in which arguments from precedents can fail:

(1) The precedent and the present case might not *truly* resemble each other in the ways that the argument claims.

(2) The respects in which the cases resemble each other might not be *important* enough to justify the same decision in the present case.

(3) The precedent and the present case might also *differ* from each other in important respects which justify distinguishing the precedent.

(4) The precedent might be mistaken or immoral enough to be *overturned*.

(5) There might be other, stronger precedents that *conflict* with the precedent in the argument.

Whenever you evaluate or present any argument from a precedent, you need to ask whether the argument fails in any of these ways.

THE LAW OF DISCRIMINATION

These general methods of legal reasoning can be seen at work in a particular area of constitutional law—the law of discrimination. To understand the cases in this area, some background will be helpful.

The provision of the Constitution which governs discrimination is the equal protection clause of the Fourteenth Amendment. It provides that:

> No state shall make or enforce any law which shall . . . deny to any person within its jurisdiction the equal protection of the laws.

The clearest thing about this clause is that it is not clear. Whatever it means, it cannot mean that laws cannot ever treat people unequally. Criminal laws treat those who commit crimes quite differently from those who do not. The general idea behind the clause seems to be that like cases should be treated in like ways. Put negatively, the clause prohibits unequal treatment when there is no significant difference. This, however, is still both general and vague, for we need principles that determine what sorts of likenesses matter and what kinds of differences are significant.

Going back to the historical context in which the Fourteenth Amendment was adopted, we know that it was intended to prohibit unequal treatment on the basis of "race, color, or previous condition of servitude" (a phrase which occurs in the companion Fifteenth Amendment on voting rights). More specifically, it was one of those constitutional provisions intended to protect the newly emancipated slaves. This was the primary purpose of these provisions, but the language is more general, giving like protection to all citizens of the United States.

After the Fourteenth Amendment was adopted, many questions arose concerning its interpretation and application. The amendment explicitly refers only to state laws, but the state does many things besides pass laws, so the courts had to determine what counts as a *state action*. In a series of cases, the amendment was interpreted to mean that only positive actions of the state fell under the amendment. Thus, when thugs broke up a black political rally, with the police standing by doing nothing to protect the demonstrators, the Supreme Court ruled that this was not a violation of the equal protection clause because the state itself had not participated in the action (*U.S. v. Cruikshank*). On this view, the state was forbidden to aid discrimination, but it was not required to protect anyone against it.

Another issue which arose concerned what the state has to do to justify treating people differently. Here the courts decided that it was not their business to examine the details of legislation to make sure that the laws were as equitable as possible. The task of making laws, they held, falls to legislatures, and the courts gave legislatures wide latitude in formulating these laws. Flagrant violations of the equal protection clause could lead to the decision that the law was unconstitutional, but only if the law failed what became known as *the rational relation test*. This test required only that the unequal treatment of individuals be reasonably likely to achieve some legitimate end.

A final issue was whether the Fourteenth Amendment protected only the civil rights of citizens or also rights of other kinds. In *Strauder v. West Virginia* (1880), a law which made blacks ineligible for jury duty was struck down on the grounds that the equal protection clause prohibits discrimination in areas of civil rights. In *Yick Wo v. Hopkins* (1886), the Court applied the equal protection clause to discrimination in areas of economic rights. *Yick Wo* also established that the equal protection clause protects not only blacks but also other groups (such as Chinese), and that laws which do not explicitly mention racial or ethnic groups can violate the equal protection clause if they are applied unequally in practice.

In 1896, the Supreme Court decided the case of *Plessy v. Ferguson*, about a Louisiana statute enforcing racial segregation in public transportation. This was clearly a state action, and the Court continued to apply the rational relation test; so the main issues were whether the equal protection clause extends to social rights, whether the segregation law served any reasonable purpose, and whether the separate facilities were truly equal. The Court held that the segregation statute did not violate the equal protection clause as long as the facilities were equal. This became known as *the separate but equal doctrine*.

▼ Plessy v. Ferguson (163 U.S. 537, 1896)

Mr. Justice Brown delivered the opinion of the Court.

This case turns upon the constitutionality of an act of the general assembly of the state of Louisiana, passed in 1890, providing for separate railway carriages for the white and colored races.

The 1st section of the statute enacts "that all railway companies carrying passengers in their coaches in this state shall provide equal but separate accommodations for the white and colored races, by providing two or more passenger coaches for each passenger train, or by dividing the passenger coaches by a partition so as to secure separate accommodations: *Provided*, That this section shall not be construed to apply to street railroads. No person or persons shall be permitted to occupy seats in coaches other than the ones assigned to them, on account of the race they belong to."

By the 2d section it was enacted "that the officers of such passenger trains shall have power and are hereby required to assign each passenger to the coach or compartment used for the race to which such passenger belongs; any passenger insisting on going into a coach or compartment to which by race he does not belong, shall be liable to a fine of $25 or in lieu thereof to imprisonment for a period of not more than twenty days in the parish prison, and any officer of any railroad insisting on assigning a passenger to a coach or compartment other than the one set aside for the race to which said passenger belongs, shall be liable to a fine of $24, or in lieu thereof to imprisonment for a period of not more than twenty days in the parish prison; and should any passenger refuse to occupy the coach or compartment to which he or she is assigned by the officer of such railway, said officer shall have power to refuse to carry such passenger on his train, and for such refusal neither he nor the railway company which he represents shall be liable for damages in any of the courts of this state." . . .

The information filed in the criminal district court charged in substance that Plessy, being a passenger between two stations within the state of Louisiana, was assigned by officers of the company to the coach used for the race to which he belonged, but he insisted upon going into a coach used by the race to which he did not belong. Neither in the information nor plea was his particular race or color averred.

The petition for the writ of prohibition averred that petitioner was seven-eighths Caucasian and one-eighth African blood; that the mixture of colored blood was not discernible in him, and that he was entitled to every right, privilege, and immunity secured to citizens of the United States of the white race; and that, upon such theory, he took possession of a vacant seat in a coach where passengers of the white race were accommodated, and was ordered by the conductor to vacate said coach and take a seat in another assigned to persons of the colored race, and having refused to comply with such demand he was forcibly ejected with the aid of a police officer, and imprisoned in the parish jail to answer a charge of having violated the above act.

The constitutionality of this act is attacked upon the ground that it conflicts both with the 13th Amendment of the Constitution, abolishing slavery, and the 14th Amendment, which prohibits certain restrictive legislation on the part of the states.

1. That it does not conflict with the 13th Amendment, which abolished slavery and involuntary servitude, except as a punishment for crime, is too clear for argument. . . .

. . . Indeed, we do not understand that the 13th Amendment is strenuously relied upon by the plaintiff in error in this connection.

2. By the 14th Amendment, all persons born or naturalized in the United States, and subject to the jurisdiction thereof, are made citizens of the United States and of the state wherein they reside; and the states are forbidden from making or enforcing any law which shall abridge the privileges or immunities of citizens of the United States, or shall deprive any person within their jurisdiction the equal protection of the laws. . . .

The object of the amendment was undoubtedly to enforce the absolute equality of the two races before the law, but in the nature of things it could not have been intended to abolish distinctions based upon color, or to enforce social, as distinguished from political, equality, or a commingling of the two races upon terms unsatisfactory to either. Laws permitting, and even requiring their separation in places where they are liable to be brought into contact do not necessarily imply the inferiority of either race to the other, and have been generally, if not universally, recognized as within the competency of the state legislatures in the exercise of their police power. The most common instance of this is connected with the establishment of separate schools for white and colored children, which have been held to be a valid exercise of the legislative power even by courts of states where the political rights of the colored race have been longest and most earnestly enforced. . . .

[Justice Brown next reviews a whole series of cases where statutes similar to the one in question have been upheld as constitutional.]

It is . . . suggested by the learned counsel for the plaintiff in error that the same argument that will justify the state legislature in requiring railways to provide separate accommodations for the two races will also authorize them to require separate cars to be provided for people whose hair is of a certain color, or who are aliens, or who belong to certain nationalities, or to enact laws requiring colored people to walk upon one side of the street, and white people upon the other, or requiring white men's houses to be painted white, and colored men's black, or their vehicles or business signs to be of different colors, upon the theory that one side of the street is as good as the other, or that a house or vehicle of one color is as good as one of another color. The reply to all this is that every exercise of the police power must be reasonable, and extend only to such laws as are enacted in good faith for the promotion of the public good, and not for the annoyance or oppression of a particular class. Thus in *Yick Wo v. Hopkins* it was held by this court that a municipal ordinance of the city of San Francisco to regulate the carrying on of public laundries within the limits of the municipality violated the provisions of the Constitution of the United States if it conferred upon the municipal authorities arbitrary power, at their own will, and without regard to discretion, in the legal sense of the term, to give or withhold consent as to persons or places, without regard to the competency of the persons applying, or the propriety of the places selected for the carrying on of the business. It was held to be a covert attempt on the part of the municipality to make an arbitrary and unjust discrimination against the Chinese race. While this was the case of a municipal ordinance a like principle has been held to apply to acts of a state legislature passed in the exercise of the police power.

So far, then, as a conflict with the 14th Amendment is concerned, the case reduces itself to the question whether the statute of Louisiana is a reasonable regulation, and with respect to this there must necessarily be a large discretion on the part of the legislature. In determining the question of reasonableness it is at liberty to act with reference to the established usages, customs, and traditions of the people, and with a view to the promotion of their comfort, and the preservation of the public peace and good order. Gauged by this standard, we cannot say that a law which authorizes or even requires the separation of the two races in public conveyances is unreasonable or more obnoxious to the 14th Amendment than the acts of Congress requiring separate schools for colored children in the District of Columbia, the constitutionality of which does not seem to have been questioned, or the corresponding acts of state legislatures.

We consider the underlying fallacy of the plaintiff's argument to consist in the assumption that the enforced separation of the two races stamps the colored race with a badge of inferiority. If this be so, it is not by reason of anything found in the act, but solely because the colored race chooses to put that construction upon it. The argument necessarily assumes that if, as has been more than once the case, and is not unlikely to be so again, the colored race should become the dominant power in the state legislature, and should enact a law in precisely similar terms, it would thereby relegate the white race to an inferior position. We imagine that the white race, at least, would not acquiesce in this assumption. The argument also assumes that social prejudices may be overcome by legislation, and that equal rights cannot be secured to the Negro except by an enforced commingling of the two races. We cannot accept this proposition. If the two races are to meet on terms of social equality, it must be the result of natural affinity, a mutual appreciation of each other's merits and a voluntary consent of individuals. As was said by the court of appeals of New York in *People v. Gallagher*, "this end can neither be accomplished nor promoted by laws which conflict with the general sentiment of the community upon whom they are designed to operate. When the government, therefore, has secured to each of its citizens equal rights before the law and equal opportunities for improvement and progress, it has accomplished the end for which it is organized and performed all of the functions respecting social advantages with which it is endowed." Legislation is powerless to eradicate racial instincts or to abolish distinctions based upon physical differences, and the attempt to do so can only result in accentuating the difficulties of the present situation. If the civil and political rights of both races be equal, one cannot be inferior to the other civilly or politically. If one race be inferior to the other socially, the Constitution of the United States cannot put them upon the same plane. . . .

> The judgment of the Court below is therefore affirmed.

From *Plessy* to *Brown*

As soon as *Plessy* was decided, southern and some border states rapidly passed a whole series of segregation laws. These were subsequently upheld by the courts on the precedent of *Plessy* and its separate but equal doctrine. The result was the introduction of a system of racial segregation throughout much of the country.

The doctrine of the rational relation test remained basically unchanged until the 1940s. During World War II, the Supreme Court had to decide whether it was constitutional to relocate Japanese Americans away from Pacific ports. In *Korematsu v. United States* (1944), the Court announced that

> [A]ll legal restrictions which curtail the rights of a single racial group are immediately suspect. That is not to say that all such restrictions are unconstitutional. It is to say that the courts must subject them to the most rigid scrutiny.

It is ironic that the Court did not strike down the Japanese relocation orders, but these cases established a new interpretation of equal protection which eventually greatly increased the power of the courts to strike down discriminatory laws.

On this new interpretation of the equal protection clause, most laws still need to pass only the rational relation test, but there are two features of a law which serve as *triggers* of strict scrutiny. A law must pass *strict scrutiny* if the law either restricts a *fundamental right* or employs a *suspect classification*. Fundamental rights concern such things as the right to vote or the right to procreate. A classification is suspect if it concerns race, religion, national origin, and so on. Under the new interpretation of the equal protection clause, states could still pass laws restricting fundamental rights, and these laws could still employ suspect classifications, but, when they did so, a heavy burden of proof fell on them. To justify such a law, the state had to show that (1) the legislation serves a *legitimate* and *compelling* state interest, and also that (2) it does so in the *least intrusive* way possible. This is the strict scrutiny test.

It should be clear that the rational relation test is very easy to meet, whereas the test of strict scrutiny is nearly impossible to satisfy. It is not hard to show that a piece of legislation has some chance of serving some legitimate goal—that's the rational relation test. It is very difficult to show that the purpose of a law is compelling, that is, of overwhelming importance; and it is even more difficult to show that the stated purpose cannot be achieved by any less intrusive means. Thus, in adopting this new test, the Court no longer showed great deference to state legislatures, as it did in *Plessy*, when it applied the rational relation test. Instead, the heaviest burden was shifted to the states in areas which involved what the Court declared to be suspect classifications or fundamental rights.

This new test is implicit in the decision of *Brown v. Board of Education* (1954), which declared segregation in public schools unconstitutional. The *Brown* opinion does not directly mention strict scrutiny, but this test looms in the background. Segregation clearly involved a suspect classification, but the court emphasized that "the opportunity of an education . . . is a *right* which must be available to all on equal terms" (our emphasis). The next step was to argue that segregated schools violate this right by their very nature, even if all "tangible" factors were equal. This violation of a fundamental right triggers strict scrutiny, and the *Brown* opinion then simply assumes that segregation in education will fail this test. Separate but equal is thus found unconstitutional, at least in education, and *Plessy* is in effect overturned.

▼ Brown v. Board of Education (347 U.S. 483, 1954)

Mr. Chief Justice Warren delivered the opinion of the Court.

These cases come to us from the States of Kansas, South Carolina, Virginia, and Delaware. They are premised on different facts and different local conditions, but a common legal question justifies their consideration together in this consolidated opinion.

In each of the cases, minors of the Negro race, through their legal representatives, seek the aid of the courts in obtaining admission to the public schools of their community on a nonsegregated basis. In each instance, they had been denied admission to schools attended by white children under laws requiring or permitting segregation according to race. This segregation was alleged to deprive the plaintiffs of the equal protection of the laws under the Fourteenth Amendment. In each of the cases other than the Delaware case, a three-judge federal district court denied relief to the plaintiffs on the so-called "separate but equal" doctrine announced by this Court in *Plessy* v. *Ferguson*. Under that doctrine, equality of treatment is accorded when the races are provided substantially equal facilities, even though these facilities be separate. In the Delaware case, the Supreme Court of Delaware adhered to that doctrine, but ordered that the plaintiffs be admitted to the white schools because of their superiority to the Negro schools.

The plaintiffs contend that segregated public schools are not "equal" and cannot be made "equal," and that hence they are deprived of the equal protection of the laws. Because of the obvious importance of the question presented, the Court took jurisdiction. Argument was heard in the 1952 Term, and reargument was heard this Term on certain questions propounded by the Court.

Reargument was largely devoted to the circumstances surrounding the adoption of the Fourteenth Amendment in 1868. It covered exhaustively consideration of the Amendment in Congress, ratification by the states, then existing practices in racial segregation, and the views of proponents and opponents of the Amendment. This discussion and our own investigation convince us that, although these sources cast some light, it is not enough to resolve the problem with which we are faced. At best, they are inconclusive. The most avid proponents of the post-War Amendments undoubtedly intended them to remove all legal distinctions among "all persons born or naturalized in the United States." Their opponents, just as certainly, were antagonistic to both the letter and the spirit of the Amendments and wished them to have the most limited effect. What others in Congress and the state legislatures had in mind cannot be determined with any degree of certainty.

An additional reason for the inconclusive nature of the Amendment's history, with respect to segregated schools, is the status of public education at that time. In the South, the movement toward free common schools, supported by general taxation, had not yet taken hold. Education of white children was largely in the hands of private groups. Education of Negroes was almost nonexistent, and practically all of the race were illiterate. In fact, any education of Negroes was forbidden by law in some states. Today, in contrast, many Negroes have achieved outstanding success in the arts and sciences as well as in the business and professional world. It is true that public school education at the time of the Amendment had advanced further in the North, but the effect of the Amendment on northern states was generally ignored in the congressional debates. Even in the North, the conditions of public education did not approximate those existing today. The curriculum was usually rudimentary; ungraded schools were common in rural areas; the school term was but three months a year in many states; and compulsory school attendance was virtually unknown. As a consequence, it is not surprising that there should be so little in the history of the Fourteenth Amendment relating to its intended effect on public education.

In the first cases in this Court construing the Fourteenth Amendment, decided shortly after its adoption, the Court interpreted it as proscribing all state-imposed discriminations against the Negro race. The doctrine of "separate but equal" did not make its appearance in this Court until 1896 in the case of *Plessy* v. *Ferguson* involving not education but transportation. American courts have since labored with the doctrine for over half a century. In this Court, there have been six cases involving the "separate but equal" doctrine in the field of public education. In *Cumming* v. *County Board of Education* and *Gong Lum* v. *Rice* the validity of the doctrine itself was not challenged. In more recent cases, all on the graduate school level, inequality was found in that specific benefits enjoyed by white students were denied to Negro students of the same educational qualifications. In none of these cases was it necessary to re-examine the doctrine to grant relief to the Negro plaintiff. And in *Sweatt* v. *Painter* the Court expressly reserved decision on the question whether *Plessy* v. *Ferguson* should be held inapplicable to public education.

In the instant cases, that question is directly presented. Here, unlike *Sweatt* v. *Painter,* there are findings below that the Negro and white schools involved have been equalized, or are being equalized, with respect to buildings, curricula, qualifications and salaries of teachers, and other "tangible" factors. Our decision, therefore, cannot turn on merely a comparison of these tangible factors in the Negro and white schools involved in each of the cases. We must look instead to the effect of segregation itself on public education.

In approaching this problem, we cannot turn the clock back to 1868 when the Amendment was adopted, or even to 1896 when *Plessy* v. *Ferguson* was written. We must consider public education in the light of its full development and its present place in American life throughout the Nation. Only in this way can it be determined if segregation in public schools deprives these plaintiffs of the equal protection of the laws.

Today, education is perhaps the most important function of state and local governments. Compulsory school attendance laws and the great expenditures for education both demonstrate our recognition of the importance of education to our democratic society. It is required in the performance of our most basic public responsibilities, even service in the armed forces. It is the very foundation of good citizenship. Today it is a principal instrument in awakening the child to cultural values, in preparing him for later professional training, and in helping him to adjust normally to his environment. In these days, it is doubtful that any child may reasonably be expected to succeed in life if he is denied the opportunity of an education. Such an opportunity, where the state has undertaken to provide it, is a right which must be made available to all on equal terms.

We come then to the question presented: Does segregation of children in public schools solely on the basis of race, even though the physical facilities and other "tangible" factors may be equal, deprive the children of the minority group of equal educational opportunities? We believe that it does.

In *Sweatt* v. *Painter* in finding that a segregated law school for Negroes could not provide them equal educational opportunities, this Court relied in large part on "those qualities which are incapable of objective measurement but which make for greatness in a law school." In *McLaurin* v. *Oklahoma State Regents* the Court, in requiring that a Negro admitted to a white graduate school be treated like all other students, again resorted to intangible considerations: ". . . his ability to study, to engage in discussions and exchange views with other students, and, in general, to learn his profession." Such considerations apply with added force to children in grade and high schools. To separate them from others of similar age and qualifications solely because of their race generates a feeling of inferiority as to their status in the community that may affect their hearts and minds in a way unlikely ever to be undone. The effect of this separation on their educational opportunities was well stated by a finding in the Kansas case by a court which nevertheless felt compelled to rule against the Negro plaintiffs:

> Segregation of white and colored children in public schools has a detrimental effect upon the colored children. The impact is greater when it has the sanction of the law; for the policy of separating the races is usually interpreted as denoting the inferiority of the Negro group. A sense of inferiority affects the motivation of a child to learn. Segregation with the sanction of law, therefore, has a tendency to [retard] the education and mental development of Negro children and to deprive them of some of the benefits they would receive in a racial[ly] integrated school system.

Whatever may have been the extent of psychological knowledge at the time of *Plessy* v. *Ferguson,* this finding is amply supported by modern authority. Any language in *Plessy* v. *Ferguson* contrary to this finding is rejected.

We conclude that in the field of public education the doctrine of "separate but equal" has no place. Separate educational facilities are inherently unequal. Therefore, we hold that the plaintiffs and others similarly situated for whom the actions have been brought are, by reason of the segregation complained of, deprived of the equal protection of the laws guaranteed by the Fourteenth Amendment. . . .

▼ DISCUSSION QUESTIONS

1. Can *Brown* be used as a precedent to argue against the constitutionality of racial segregation in *public transportation?* Why or why not? Be sure to consider the similarities and differences between education and transportation.

2. Can *Brown* be used as a precedent to argue against the constitutionality of segregation by *gender* in public schools (for example, in sports)? Why or why not? Be sure to consider the similarities and differences between gender and race, and whether gender should

be a suspect classification for the purposes of the strict scrutiny test.

3. What should count as a *state action?* Apply your views to the case of *Moose Lodge v. Irvis* (407 U.S. 163, 1972), where Pennsylvania granted a liquor license to a private club that refused to serve blacks, but some blacks complained that they were deprived because only a limited number of liquor licenses were available.

From *Brown* to *Bakke*

After *Brown,* the Supreme Court struck down segregation in many other areas—transportation, parks, libraries, and so on—as well as laws against racial intermarriage (in 1967). Another string of decisions required busing to end segregation in school systems. The Court also required some employers to hire or promote minimum percentages of minorities to overcome the effects of illegal discrimination in employment.

In response to these court decisions, some schools and companies voluntarily took steps to overcome what they saw as the effects of past discrimination. These steps required them to use racial classifications, and that raised the issue of reverse discrimination.

Part of the issue was about what to call such programs. Their opponents describe them as "reverse discrimination," but their defenders refer to them as "affirmative action." Both descriptions involve evaluation, so neither should be used without an argument. A more neutral description is "preferential treatment," so we will use this label.

The most important case in this area is *Regents of the University of California v. Bakke* (1978) (hereafter *Bakke*). The basic situation was that the medical school of the University of California at Davis had very few minority students, so they created a special admissions program which gave preferential treatment to minorities who were disadvantaged. Bakke applied to the school but was rejected even though he had higher scores on admissions tests than some minority members who were admitted under the special admissions program.

Bakke claimed that Davis's special admissions program violated the equal protection clause of the United States Constitution, the California Constitution, and Title VI of the Civil Rights Act of 1964, which provides, "No person in the United States shall, on the ground of race, color, or national origin, be excluded from participation in, be denied the benefits of, or be subjected to discrimination under any program or activity receiving Federal financial assistance." The Supreme Court was thus asked to rule on four main issues:

(1) Did the Davis special admissions program violate the equal protection clause of the Constitution?

(2) Does reference to race without judicial findings of particular past discrimination violate this constitutional guarantee?

(3) Did the Davis special admissions program violate Title VI of the Civil Rights Act?

(4) Should Davis be required to admit Bakke into its medical school?

The decision of the Supreme Court on these issues is so complicated that it takes a scorecard to follow it:

	Brennan, Marshall, Blackmun, and White	Powell	Burger, Stewart, Stevens, and Rehnquist	The majority
(1)	No	Yes	No decision	No decision
(2)	No	No	No decision	No
(3)	No	Yes	Yes	Yes
(4)	No	Yes	Yes	Yes

Since the justices split into two groups of four, the remaining justice, Powell, determined the majority on most issues. However, Powell was the only justice who argued that the Davis program was unconstitutional. Four others (Brennan, Marshall, Blackmun, and White) dissented. The remaining four (Burger, Stevens, Stewart, and Rehnquist) chose not to address this constitutional issue, because they had already ruled out the Davis program under Title VI. Since a majority did not join Powell in his opinion, the Court did *not* explicitly declare the Davis program *unconstitutional*. But the Davis program was held to violate Title VI and Davis was ordered to admit Bakke, because Burger, Stevens, Stewart, and Rehnquist did join Powell on these issues. Despite Davis's loss, the Court took the opposite position on the second issue. Powell argued that it was not always unconstitutional for the state to refer to race, and he created a majority when he was joined by Brennan, Marshall, Blackmun, and White. Thus, each group of justices got part of what they wanted.

The constitutional issues are raised most directly in the opinions of Powell and Brennan (excerpted below). These opinions differ not only in their conclusions but also in their interpretations of the equal protection clause. Powell argued that the Davis program and any consideration of race must be subjected to the test of strict scrutiny. He held that the Davis program did not meet the high standards of this test, but some other consideration of race might.

In contrast, Brennan argued for a new interpretation of the equal protection clause. On this new interpretation, strict scrutiny would still be applied to most racial classifications, but, when certain conditions were met, the courts would apply a less exacting test—often called *middle level scrutiny.* The test of middle level scrutiny requires the state to show that (1) the state action serves a *legitimate* and *important* state interest, (2) it does not *stigmatize* or inflict any pervasive injury on those who are excluded, and (3) there is no *significantly* less intrusive means to serve the purpose. Brennan argued that this more lenient test should be applied when the state uses a racial classification to serve a *benign, remedial purpose.* The purpose of a racial classification is benign when it was not adopted out of any discriminatory motive, and it is remedial if the state used the racial classification because the state found that, without the racial classification, an underprivileged group would suffer harm or differential impact because of past discrimination in society at large.

The conditions under which to apply middle level scrutiny are the heart of the controversy. Powell criticized Brennan's conditions on the grounds that the notion of stigma is too vague and that it is not groups but individuals who are protected by the equal protection clause. Brennan responded by distinguishing stigma from other harms and by emphasizing the importance of groups. Powell also argued that some kinds of preferential treatment (which use *goals,* as in the Harvard admissions program) are less intrusive than other kinds of preferential treatment (which use *quotas,* as in the Davis program). Brennan responded that this difference is not significant, because both kinds of preferential treatment produce the same result for those who are excluded. These and many other disputes were not settled by this case. They are still alive today.

Regents of the University of California v. Bakke (438 U.S. 268, 1978)

Summary by the Reporter of Decisions:

[The Medical School of the University of California at Davis (hereinafter Davis) had two admissions programs for the entering class of 100 students—the regular admissions program and the special admissions program. Under the regular procedure, candidates whose overall undergraduate grade point averages fell below 2.5 on a scale of 4.0 were summarily rejected. About one out of six applicants was then given an interview, following which he was rated on a scale of 1 to 100 by each of the committee members (five in 1973 and six in 1974), his rating being based on the interviewers' summaries, his overall grade point average, his science courses grade point average, and his Medical College Admissions Test (MCAT) scores, letters of recommendation, extracurricular activities, and other biographical data, all of which resulted in a total "benchmark score." The full admissions committee then made offers of admission on the basis of their review of the applicant's file and his score, considering and acting upon applications as they were received. The committee chairman was responsible for placing names on the waiting list and had discretion to include persons with "special skills." A separate committee, a majority of whom were members of minority groups, operated the special admissions program. The 1973 and 1974 application forms, respectively, asked candidates whether they wished to be considered as "economically and/or educationally disadvantaged" applicants and members of a "minority group" (blacks, Chicanos, Asians, American Indians). If an applicant of a minority group was found to be "disadvantaged," he would be rated in a manner similar to the one employed by the general admissions committee. Special candidates, however, did not have to meet the 2.5 grade point cut-off and were not ranked against candidates in the general admissions process. About one-fifth of the special applicants were invited for interviews in 1973 and 1974, following which they were given benchmark scores, and the top choices were then given to the general admissions committee, which could reject special candidates for failure to meet course requirements or other specific deficiencies. The special committee continued to recommend candidates until 16 special admission selections had been made. During a four-year period 63 minority students were admitted to Davis under the special program and 44 under the general program. No disadvantaged whites were admitted under the special program, though many applied.

Respondent, a white male, applied to Davis in 1973 and 1974, in both years being considered only under the general admissions program. Though he had a 468 out of 500 score in 1973, he was rejected since no general applicants with scores less than 470 were being accepted after respondent's application, which was filed late in the year, had been processed and completed. At that time four special admission slots were still unfilled. In 1974 respondent applied early, and though he had a total score of 549 out of 600, he was again rejected. In neither year was his name placed on the discretionary waiting list. In both years special applicants were admitted with significantly lower scores than respondent's. After his second rejection, respondent filed this action in state court for mandatory injunctive and declaratory relief to compel his admission to Davis, alleging that the special admissions program operated to exclude him on the basis of his race in violation of the Equal Protection Clause of the Fourteenth Amendment, a provision of the California Constitution, and §601 of Title VI of the Civil Rights Act of 1964, which provides, inter alia, that no person shall on the ground of race or color be excluded from participating in any program receiving federal financial assistance. Petitioner cross-claimed for a declaration that its special admissions program was lawful. The trial court found that the special program operated as a racial quota, because minority applicants in that program were rated only against one another, and 16 places in the class of 100 were reserved for them. Declaring that petitioner could not take race into account in making admissions decisions, the program was held to violate the Federal and State Constitutions and Title VI. Respondent's admission was not ordered, however, for lack of proof that he would have been admitted but for the special program.

The California Supreme Court, applying a strict-scrutiny standard, concluded that the special admissions program was not the least intrusive means of achieving the goals of the admittedly compelling state interests of integrating the medical profession and increasing the number of doctors willing to serve minority patients. Without passing on the state constitutional or federal statutory grounds the court held that petitioner's special admissions program violated the Equal Protection Clause. Since petitioner could not satisfy its burden of demonstrating that respondent, absent the special program, would not have been admitted, the court ordered his admission to Davis.]

Excerpts from Justice Powell's Opinion:

III

Racial and ethnic classifications . . . are subject to stringent examination without regard to . . . additional characteristics. We declared as much in the first cases explicitly to recognize racial distinctions as suspect:

". . . [A]ll legal restrictions which curtail the rights of a single racial group are immediately suspect. That is not to say that all such restrictions are unconstitutional. It is to say that courts must subject them to the most rigid scrutiny" (*Korematsu,* 323 U.S. at 216).

The Court has never questioned the validity of those pronouncements. Racial and ethnic distinctions of any sort are inherently suspect and thus call for the most exacting judicial examination. . . .

Petitioner urges us to adopt for the first time a more restrictive view of the Equal Protection Clause and hold that discrimination against members of the white "majority" cannot be suspect if its purpose can be characterized as "benign." The clock of our liberties, however, cannot be turned back to 1868. It is far too late to argue that the guarantee of equal protection to *all* persons permits the recognition of special wards entitled to a degree of protection greater than that accorded others.

Moreover, there are serious problems of justice connected with the idea of preference itself. First, it may not always be clear that a so-called preference is in fact benign. Courts may be asked to validate burdens imposed upon individual members of particular groups in order to advance the group's general interest. . . . Nothing in the Constitution supports the notion that individuals may be asked to suffer otherwise impermissible burdens in order to enhance the societal standing of their ethnic groups. Second, preferential programs may only reinforce common stereotypes holding that certain groups are unable to achieve success without special protection based on a factor having no relationship to individual worth . . . . Third, there is a measure of inequity in forcing innocent persons in respondent's position to bear the burdens of redressing grievances not of their making.

Petitioner contends that on several occasions this Court has approved preferential classifications without applying the most exacting scrutiny. Most of the cases upon which petitioner relies are drawn from three areas: School desegregation, employment discrimination, and sex discrimination. Each of the cases cited presented a situation materially different from the facts of this case.

The school desegregation cases are inapposite. Each involved remedies for clearly determined constitutional violations . . . . Racial classifications thus were designed as remedies for the vindication of constitutional entitlement. Here, there was no judicial determination of constitutional violation as a predicate for the formulation of a remedial classification.

The employment discrimination cases also do not advance petitioner's cause. For example, in *Franks v. Bowman Transportation Co.*, 424 U.S. 747 (1975), we approved a retroactive award of seniority to a class of Negro truck drivers who had been the victims of discrimination—not just by society at large, but by the respondent in that case. While this relief imposed some burdens on other employees, it was held necessary " 'to make [the victims] whole for injuries suffered on account of unlawful employment discrimination.' " . . . The courts of appeals have fashioned various types of racial preferences as remedies for constitutional or statutory violations resulting in identified, race-based injuries to individuals held entitled to the preference. . . . Such preferences also have been upheld where a legislative or administrative body charged with the responsibility made determinations of past discrimination by the industries affected, and fashioned remedies deemed appropriate to rectify the discrimination.

But we have never approved preferential classifications in the absence of proven constitutional or statutory violations.

Nor is petitioner's view as to the applicable standard supported by the fact that gender-based classifications are not subjected to this level of scrutiny. E.g. *Califano v. Webster* . . . (1977); e.g. *Craig v. Boren* . . . (1976). . . . Gender-based distinctions are less likely to create the analytical and practical problems present in preferential programs premised on racial or ethnic criteria. With respect to gender there are only two possible classifications. The incidence of the burdens imposed by preferential classifications is clear. There are no rival groups who can claim that they, too, are entitled to preferential treatment. Classwide questions as to the group suffering previous injury and groups which fairly can be burdened are relatively manageable for reviewing courts. . . . The resolution of these same questions in the context of racial and ethnic preferences presents far more complex and intractable problems than gender-based classifications. More importantly, the perception of racial classifications as inherently odious stems from a lengthy and tragic history that gender-based classifications do not share. In sum, the Court has never viewed such classification as inherently suspect or as comparable to racial or ethnic classifications for the purpose of equal-protection analysis.

Petitioner also cites *Lau v. Nichols*, 414 U.S. 563 (1974), in support of the proposition that discrimination favoring racial or ethnic minorities has received judicial approval without the exacting inquiry ordinarily accorded "suspect" classifications. In *Lau*, we held that the failure of the San Francisco school system to provide remedial English instruction for some 1,800 students of oriental ancestry who spoke no English amounted to a violation of Title VI of the Civil Rights Act of 1964, 42 U.S.C. § 2000d, and the regulations promulgated thereunder. Those regulations required remedial instructions where inability to understand English excluded children of foreign ancestry from participation in educational programs. . . . Because we found that the students in *Lau* were denied "a meaningful opportunity to participate in the educational program," . . . we remanded for the fashioning of a remedial order.

Lau provides little support for petitioner's argument. The decision rested solely on the statute, which had been construed by the responsible administrative agency to reach educational practices "which have the effect of subjecting individuals to discrimination." We stated: "Under these state-imposed standards there is no equality of treatment merely by providing students with the same facilities, textbooks, teachers and curriculum; for students who do not understand English are effectively foreclosed from any meaningful education." . . . Moreover, the "preference" approved did not result in the denial of the relevant benefit—"meaningful participation in the educational program"—to anyone else. No other student was deprived by that preference of the ability to participate in San Francisco's school system, and the applicable regulations required similar assistance for all students who suffered similar linguistic deficiencies. . . .

In a similar vein, petitioner contends that our recent decision in *United Jewish Organizations v. Carey*, 430 U.S. 144 (1977), indicates a willingness to approve racial classifications designed to benefit certain minorities, without denominating the classifications as "suspect." The State of New York had redrawn its reapportionment plan to meet objections of the Department of Justice under § 5 of the Voting Rights Act of 1965, 42 U.S.C. § 1973c. Specifically, voting districts were redrawn to enhance the electoral power of certain "nonwhite" voters found to have been the victims of unlawful "dilution" under the original reapportionment plan. *United Jewish Organizations*, like *Lau*, properly is viewed as a case in which the remedy for an administrative finding of discrimination encompassed measures to improve the previously disadvantaged group's ability to participate, without excluding individuals belonging to any other group from enjoyment of the relevant opportunity—meaningful participation in the electoral process.

In this case, unlike *Lau* and *United Jewish Organizations*, there has been no determination by the legislature or a responsible administrative agency that the University engaged in a discriminatory practice requiring remedial efforts. Moreover, the operation of petitioner's special admissions program is quite different from the remedial measures approved in those cases. It prefers the designated minority groups at the expense of other individuals who are totally foreclosed from competition for the 16 special admissions seats in every medical school class. Because of that foreclosure, some individuals are excluded from enjoyment of a state-provided benefit—admission to the medical school—they otherwise would receive. When a classification denies an individual opportunities or benefits enjoyed by others solely because of his race or ethnic background, it must be regarded as suspect. . . .

IV

We have held that in "order to justify the use of a suspect classification, a State must show that its purpose or interest is both constitutionally permissible and substantial, and that its use of the classification is 'necessary . . . to the accomplishment' of its purpose or the safeguarding of its interest." The special admissions program purports to serve the purposes of: (i) "reducing the historic deficit of traditionally disfavored minorities in medical schools and the medical profession"; (ii) countering the effects of societal discrimination; (iii) increasing the number of physicians who will practice in communities currently underserved; and (iv) obtaining the educational benefits that flow from an ethnically diverse student body. It is necessary to decide which, if any, of these purposes is substantial enough to support the use of a suspect classification. . . .

If petitioner's purpose is to assure within its student body some specified percentage of a particular group merely because of its race or ethnic origin, such a preferential purpose must be rejected not as insubstantial but as facially invalid. Preferring members of any one group for no reason other than race or ethnic origin is discrimination for its own sake. This the Constitution forbids. . . .

The State certainly has a legitimate and substantial interest in ameliorating, or eliminating where feasible, the disabling effects of identified discrimination. The line of school desegregation cases, commencing with *Brown,* attests to the importance of this state goal and the commitment of the judiciary to affirm all lawful means towards its attainment. In the school cases, the States were required by court order to redress the wrongs worked by specific instances of racial discrimination. That goal was far more focused than the remedying of the effects of "societal discrimination," an amorphous concept of injury that may be ageless in its reach into the past.

We have never approved a classification that aids persons perceived as members of relatively victimized groups at the expense of other innocent individuals in the absence of judicial, legislative or administrative findings of constitutional or statutory violations. . . . After such findings have been made, the governmental interest in preferring members of the injured groups at the expense of others is substantial, since the legal rights of the victims must be vindicated. . . . Without such findings of constitutional or statutory violations, it cannot be said that the government has any greater interest in helping one individual than in refraining from harming another. Thus, the government has no compelling justification for inflicting such harm.

Petitioner does not purport to have made, and is in no position to make, such findings. Its broad mission is education, not the formulation of any legislative policy or the adjudication of particular claims of illegality. . . .

Hence, the purpose of helping certain groups whom the faculty of the Davis Medical School perceived as victims of "societal discrimination" does not justify a classification that imposes disadvantages upon persons like respondent, who bear no responsibility for whatever harm the beneficiaries of the special admissions program are thought to have suffered.

Petitioner identifies, as another purpose of its program, improving the delivery of health care services to communities currently underserved. It may be assumed that in some situations a State's interest in facilitating the health care of its citizens is sufficiently compelling to support the use of a suspect classification. But there is virtually no evidence in the record indicating that petitioner's special admissions program is either needed or geared to promote that goal. The court below addressed this failure of proof: "The University concedes it cannot assure that minority doctors who entered under the program, all of whom express an 'interest' in participating in a disadvantaged community, will actually do so. . . ."

[Thus the petitioner] simply has not carried its burden of demonstrating that it must prefer members of particular ethnic groups over all other individuals in order to promote better health care delivery to deprived citizens. Indeed, petitioner has not shown that its preferential classification is likely to have any significant effect on the problem. . . .

The fourth goal asserted by petitioner is the attainment of a diverse student body. This clearly is a constitutionally permissible goal for an institution of higher education. Academic freedom, though not a specifically enumerated constitutional right, long has been viewed as a special concern of the First Amendment. The freedom of a university to make its own judgments as to education includes the selection of its student body. . . . Thus, in arguing that its universities must be accorded the right to select those students who will contribute the most to the "robust exchange of ideas," petitioner invokes a countervailing constitutional interest, that of the First Amendment. In this light, petitioner must be viewed as seeking to achieve a goal that is of paramount importance in the fulfillment of its mission. . . .

It may be assumed that the reservation of a specified number of seats in each class for individuals from the preferred ethnic groups would contribute to the attainment of considerable ethnic diversity in the student body. But petitioner's argument that this is the only effective means of serving the interest of diversity is seriously flawed. In a most fundamental sense the argument misconceives the nature of the state interest that would justify consideration of race or ethnic background. It is not an interest in simple ethnic diversity, in which a specific percentage of the student body is in effect guaranteed to be members of selected ethnic groups, with the remaining percentage an undifferentiated aggregation of students. The diversity that furthers a compelling state interest encompasses a far broader array of qualifications and characteristics of which racial or ethnic origin is but a single though important element. Petitioner's special admissions program, focused *solely* on ethnic diversity, would hinder rather than further attainment of genuine diversity.

The experience of other university admissions programs, which take race into account in achieving the educational diversity valued by the First Amendment, demonstrates that the assignment of a fixed number of places to a minority group is not a necessary means toward that end. An illuminating example is found in the Harvard College program:

> In recent years Harvard College has expanded the concept of diversity to include students from disadvantaged economic, racial and ethnic groups. Harvard College now recruits not only Californians or Louisianans but also blacks and Chicanos and other minority students.

In practice, this new definition of diversity has meant that race has been a factor in some admission decisions. When the Committee on Admissions reviews the large middle group of applicants who are 'admissible' and deemed capable of doing good work in their courses, the race of an applicant may tip the balance in his favor just as geographic origin or a life spent on a farm may tip the balance in other candidates' cases. A farm boy from Idaho can bring something to Harvard College that a Bostonian cannot offer. Similarly, a black student can usually bring something that a white person cannot offer. . . .

In Harvard college admissions the Committee has not set target-quotas for the number of blacks, or of musicians, football players, physicists or Californians to be admitted in a given year. . . . But that awareness [of the necessity of including more than a token number of black students] does not mean that the Committee sets the minimum number of blacks or of people from west of the Mississippi who are to be admitted. It means only that in choosing among thousands of applicants who are not only 'admissible' academically but have other strong qualities, the Committee, with a number of criteria in mind, pays some attention to distribution among many types and categories of students. (Brief for Columbia University, Harvard University, Stanford University, and the University of Pennsylvania, as *Amici Curiae*, App. 2, 3.)

In such an admissions program, race or ethnic background may be deemed a "plus" in a particular applicant's file, yet it does not insulate the individual from comparison with all other candidates for the available seats. The file of a particular black applicant may be examined for his potential contribution to diversity without the factor of race being decisive when compared, for example, with that of an applicant identified as an Italian-American if the latter is thought to exhibit qualities more likely to promote beneficial educational pluralism. Such qualities could include exceptional personal talents, unique work or service experience, leadership potential, maturity, demonstrated compassion, a history of overcoming disadvantage, ability to communicate with the poor, or other qualifications deemed important. In short, an admissions program operated in this way is flexible enough to consider all pertinent elements of diversity in light of the particular qualifications of each applicant, and to place them on the same footing for consideration, although not necessarily according them the same weight. Indeed, the weight attributed to a particular quality may vary from year to year depending upon the "mix" both of the student body and the applicants for the incoming class.

This kind of program treats each applicant as an individual in the admissions process. The applicant who loses out on the last available seat to another candidate receiving a "plus" on the basis of ethnic background will not have been foreclosed from all consideration for that seat simply because he was not the right color or had the wrong surname. It would mean only that his combined qualifications, which may have included similar nonobjective factors, did not outweigh those of the other applicant. His qualifications would have been weighed fairly and competitively, and he would have no basis to complain of unequal treatment under the Fourteenth Amendment.

It has been suggested that an admissions program which considers race only as one factor is simply a subtle and more sophisticated—but no less effective—means of according racial preference than the Davis program. A facial intent to discriminate, however, is evident in petitioner's preference program and not denied in this case. No such facial infirmity exists in an admissions program where race or ethnic background is simply one element—to be weighed fairly against other elements—in the selection process. "A boundary line," as Mr. Justice Frankfurter remarked in another connection, "is none the worse for being narrow." And a Court would not assume that a university, professing to employ a facially nondiscriminatory admissions policy, would operate it as a cover for the functional equivalent of a quota system. In short, good faith would be presumed in the absence of a showing to the contrary in the manner permitted by our cases.

In summary, it is evident that the Davis special admission program involves the use of an explicit racial classification never before countenanced by this Court. It tells applicants who are not Negro, Asian, or "Chicano" that they are totally excluded from a specific percentage of the seats in an entering class. No matter how strong their qualifications, quantitative and extracurricular, including their own potential for contribution to educational diversity, they are never afforded the chance to compete with applicants from the preferred groups for the special admission seats. At the same time, the preferred applicants have the opportunity to compete for every seat in the class.

The fatal flaw in petitioner's preferential program is its disregard of individual rights as guaranteed by the Fourteenth Amendment. Such rights are not absolute. But when a State's distribution of benefits or imposition of burdens hinges on the color of a person's skin or ancestry, that individual is entitled to a demonstration that the challenged classification is necessary to promote a substantial state interest. Petitioner has failed to carry this burden. For this reason, that portion of the California court's judgment holding petitioner's special admissions program invalid under the Fourteenth Amendment must be affirmed.

Excerpts from Justice Brennan's Opinion:

The assertion of human equality is closely associated with the proposition that differences in color or creed, birth or status, are neither significant nor relevant to the way in which persons should be treated. Nonetheless, the position that such factors must be "[c]onstitutionally an irrelevance," summed up by the shorthand phrase "[o]ur Constitution is color-blind," has never been adopted by this Court as the proper meaning of the Equal Protection Clause. Indeed, we have expressly rejected this proposition on a number of occasions.

We conclude, therefore, that racial classifications are not per se invalid under the Fourteenth Amendment. Accordingly, we turn to the problem of articulating what our role should be in reviewing state action that expressly classifies by race. . . .

Respondent argues that racial classifications are always suspect and, consequently, that this Court should weigh the importance of the objectives served by Davis' special admissions program to see if they are compelling. In addition, he asserts that this Court must inquire whether, in its judgment, there are alternatives to racial classifications which would suit Davis' purposes. Petitioner, on the other hand, states that our proper role is simply to accept petitioner's determination that the racial classifications used by its program are reasonably related to what it tells us are its benign purposes. We reject petitioner's view, but, because our prior cases are in many respects inapposite to that before us now, we find it necessary to define with precision the meaning of that inexact term, "strict scrutiny." . . .

Unquestionably we have held that a government practice or statute which restricts "fundamental rights" or which contains "suspect classifications" is to be subjected to "strict scrutiny" and can be justified only if it furthers a compelling government purpose and, even then, only if no less restrictive alternative is available. . . . But no fundamental right is involved here. . . . Nor do whites as a class have any of the "traditional indicia of suspectness: the class is not saddled with such disabilities, or subjected to such a history of purposeful unequal treatment, or relegated to such a position of political powerlessness as to command extraordinary protection from the majoritarian political process."

[The] fact that this case does not fit neatly into our prior analytic framework for race cases does not mean that it should be analyzed by applying the very loose rational-basis standard of review that is the very least that is always applied in equal protection cases. " '[T]he mere recitation of a benign, compensatory purpose is not an automatic shield which protects against any inquiry into the actual purposes underlying a statutory scheme.' " Instead, a number of considerations—developed in gender discrimination cases but which carry even more force when applied to racial classifications—lead us to conclude that racial classifications designed to further remedial purposes " 'must serve important governmental objectives and must be substantially related to achievement of those objectives.' "

First, race, like "gender-based classifications too often [has] been inexcusably utilized to stereotype and stigmatize politically powerless segments of society." While a carefully tailored statute designed to remedy past discrimination could avoid these vices, we nonetheless have recognized that the line between honest and thoughtful appraisal of the effects of past discrimination and paternalistic stereotyping is not so clear and that a statute based on the latter is patently capable of stigmatizing all women with a badge of inferiority. State programs designed ostensibly to ameliorate the effects of past racial discrimination obviously create the same hazard of stigma, since they may promote racial separatism and reinforce the views of those who believe that members of racial minorities are inherently incapable of succeeding on their own.

Second, race, like gender and illegitimacy, is an immutable characteristic which its possessors are powerless to escape or set aside. While a classification is not per se invalid because it divides classes on the basis of an immutable characteristic, it is nevertheless true that such divisions are contrary to our deep belief that "legal burdens should bear some relationship to individual responsibility or wrongdoing," and that advancement sanctioned, sponsored, or approved by the State should ideally be based on individual merit or achievement, or at the least on factors within the control of an individual. . . .

In sum, because of the significant risk that racial classifications established for ostensibly benign purposes can be misused, causing effects not unlike those created by invidious classifications, it is inappropriate to inquire only whether there is any conceivable basis that might sustain such a classification. Instead, to justify such a classification an important and articulated purpose for its use must be shown. In addition, any statute must be stricken that stigmatizes any group or that singles out those least well represented in the political process to bear the brunt of a benign program. Thus our review under the Fourteenth Amendment should be strict—not " 'strict' in theory and fatal in fact," because it is stigma that causes fatality—but strict and searching nonetheless. . . .

Davis' articulated purpose of remedying the effects of past societal discrimination is, under our cases, sufficiently important to justify the use of race-conscious admissions programs where there is a sound basis for concluding that minority underrepresentation is substantial and chronic, and that the handicap of past discrimination is impeding access of minorities to the medical school.

[In the school desegregation cases, the Court] held both that courts could enter desegregation orders which assigned students and faculty by reference to race, *Swann* v. *Charlotte-Mecklenberg Board of Ed.*, 402 U.S. 1 (1971), and that local school boards could *voluntarily* adopt desegregation plans which made express reference to race if this was necessary to remedy the effects of past discrimination. *McDaniel* v. *Barresi* (1971). Moreover, we stated that school boards, even in the absence of a judicial finding of past discrimination, could voluntarily adopt plans which assigned students with the end of creating racial pluralism by establishing fixed ratios of black and white students in each school. *Charlotte-Mecklenburg,* supra, at 16. In each instance, the creation of unitary school systems, in which the effects of past discrimination had been "eliminated root and branch," . . . was recognized as a compelling social goal justifying the overt use of race.

These cases cannot be distinguished simply by the presence of judicial findings of discrimination, for race-conscious remedies have been approved where such findings have not been made. *McDaniel* v. *Barresi,* supra; *UJO*, supra; see *Califano* v. *Webster*, supra; *Kahn* v. *Shevin*, 416 U.S. 351 (1974). See also *Katzenbach* v. *Morgan*, 384 U.S. 641 (1967). Indeed, the requirement of a judicial determination of a constitutional or statutory violation as a predicate for race-conscious remedial actions would be self-defeating. Such a requirement would severely undermine efforts to achieve voluntary compliance with the requirements of law. And, our society and jurisprudence have always stressed the value of voluntary efforts to further the objectives of the law. Judicial intervention is a last resort to achieve cessation of illegal conduct or the remedying of its effects rather than a prerequisite to action. . . .

Moreover, the presence or absence of past discrimination by universities or employers is largely irrelevant to resolving respondent's constitutional claims. The claims of those burdened by the race-conscious actions of a university or employer who has never been adjudged in violation of an antidiscrimination law are not any more or less entitled to deference than the claims of the burdened nonminority workers in *Franks* v. *Bowman*, 424 U.S. 747 (1976), in which the employer had violated Title VII, for in each case the employees are innocent of past discrimination.

Properly construed, therefore, our prior cases unequivocally show that a state government may adopt race-conscious programs if the purpose of such programs is to remove the disparate racial impact its actions might otherwise have and if there is reason to believe that the disparate impact is itself the product of past discrimination, whether its own or that of society at large. There is no question that Davis' program is valid under this test.

Certainly, on the basis of the undisputed factual submissions before this Court, Davis had a sound basis for believing that the problem of underrepresentation of minorities was substantial and chronic and that the problem was attributable to handicaps imposed on minority applicants by past and present racial discrimination. Until at least 1973, the practice of medicine in this country was, in fact, if not in law, largely the prerogative of whites. In 1950, for example, while Negroes comprised 10% of the total population, Negro physicians constituted only 2.2% of the total number of physicians. The overwhelming majority of these, moreover, were educated in two predominantly Negro medical schools, Howard and Meharry. By 1970, the gap between the proportion of Negroes in medicine and their proportion in the population had widened: The number of Negroes employed in medicine remained frozen at 2.2% while the Negro population had increased to 11.1%. The number of Negro admittees to predominantly white medical schools, moreover, had declined in absolute numbers during the years 1955 to 1964.

Moreover, Davis had a very good reason to believe that the national pattern of underrepresentation of minorities in medicine would be perpetuated if it retained a single admissions standard. For example, the entering classes in 1968 and 1969, the years in which such a standard was used, included only one Chicano and two Negroes out of 100 admittees. Nor is there any relief from this pattern of underrepresentation in the statistics for the regular admissions program in later years.

Davis clearly could conclude that the serious and persistent underrepresentation of minorities in medicine depicted by these statistics is the result of handicaps under which minority applicants labor as a consequence of a background of deliberate, purposeful discrimination against minorities in education and in society generally, as well as in the medical profession. . . .

The second prong of our test—whether the Davis program stigmatizes any discrete group or individual and whether race is reasonably used in light of the program's objectives—is clearly satisfied by the Davis program.

It is not even claimed that Davis' program in any way operates to stigmatize or single out any discrete and insular, or even any identifiable, nonminority group. Nor will harm comparable to that imposed upon racial minorities by exclusion or separation on grounds of race be the likely result of the program. It does not, for example, establish an exclusive preserve for minority students apart from and exclusive of whites. Rather, its purpose is to overcome the effects of segregation by bringing the races together. True, whites are excluded from participation in the special admissions program, but this fact only operates to reduce the number of whites to be admitted in the regular admissions program in order to permit admission of a reasonable percentage—less than their proportion of the California population—of otherwise underrepresented qualified minority applicants.

Nor was Bakke in any sense stamped as inferior by the Medical School's rejection of him. . . . Unlike discrimination against racial minorities, the use of racial preferences for remedial purposes does not inflict a pervasive injury upon individual whites in the sense that wherever they go or whatever they do there is a significant likelihood that they will be treated as second-class citizens because of their color. This distinction does not mean that the exclusion of a white resulting from the preferential use of race is not sufficiently serious to require justification; but it does mean that the injury inflicted by such a policy is not distinguishable from disadvantages caused by a wide range of government actions, none of which has ever been thought impermissible for that reason alone.

In addition, there is simply no evidence that the Davis program discriminates intentionally or unintentionally against any minority group which it purports to benefit. The program does not establish a quota in the invidious sense of a ceiling on the number of minority applicants to be admitted. Nor can the program reasonably be regarded as stigmatizing the program's beneficiaries or their race as inferior. The Davis program does not simply advance less qualified applicants; rather, it compensates applicants, whom it is uncontested are fully qualified to study medicine, for educational disadvantage which it was reasonable to conclude was a product of state-fostered discrimination. Once admitted, these students must satisfy the same degree requirements as regularly admitted students; they are taught by the same faculty in the same classes; and their performance is evaluated by the same standards by which regularly admitted students are judged. Under these circumstances, their performance and degrees must be regarded equally with the regularly admitted students with whom they compete for standing. Since minority graduates cannot justifiably be regarded as less well qualified than nonminority graduates by virtue of the special admissions program, there is no reasonable basis to conclude that minority graduates at schools using such programs would be stigmatized as inferior by the existence of such programs.

Finally, Davis' special admissions program cannot be said to violate the Constitution simply because it has set aside a predetermined number of places for qualified minority applicants rather than using minority status as a positive factor to be considered in evaluating the applications of disadvantaged minority applicants. For purposes of constitutional adjudication, there is no difference between the two approaches. In any admissions program which accords special consideration to disadvantaged racial minorities, a determination of the degree of preference to be given is unavoidable, and any given preference that results in the exclusion of a white candidate is no more or less constitutionally acceptable than a program such as that at Davis. Furthermore, the extent of the preference inevitably depends on how many minority applicants the particular school is seeking to admit in any particular year so long as the number of qualified minority applicants exceeds that number. There is no sensible, and certainly no constitutional, distinction between, for example, adding a set number of points to the admissions rating of disadvantaged minority applicants as an expression of the preference with the expectation that this will result in the admission of an approximately determined number of qualified minority applicants and setting a fixed number of places for such applicants as was done here.

Accordingly, we would reverse the judgment of the Supreme Court of California holding the Medical School's special admissions program unconstitutional and directing respondent's admission, as well as that portion of the judgment enjoining the Medical School from according any consideration to race in the admissions process.

▼ SUMMARY

We have now seen the three main interpretations of the equal protection clause. They are summarized in the following chart:

	Segregation	Antidiscrimination	Affirmative Action
State Action	Only (1) the state is forbidden to do positive acts of discrimination	(1) and also (2) the state is required to protect its citizens against future discrimination	(1), (2), & (3) the state is allowed or required to remedy the effects of past discrimination
Separation	Separation is not inherently unequal	Separation is inherently unequal	Same as Antidiscrimination
Levels of Scrutiny	Single-tier: (1) the rational relation test	Two-tier: (1) except (2) strict scrutiny when suspect classification or fundamental right	Three-tier: (1) & (2) except (3) middle level scrutiny when a benign, remedial purpose
Bearers of Rights	Individuals Only	Individuals Only	Individuals and Groups
Found in	*Plessy v. Ferguson* (majority opinion)	*Brown* (court opinion) *Bakke* (part of Powell)	*Bakke* (Brennan opinion)

Burden of Proof

A remarkable feature of the line of cases from *Plessy* through *Bakke* is the extent to which these interpretations of equal protection turn on the matter of *burden of proof*. Under the rational relation test that governed *Plessy*, the state bears a very light burden when it is asked to show that its actions do not conflict with the equal protection clause. In contrast, the strict scrutiny test which governed *Brown,* and which Powell applied in *Bakke,* places a very heavy burden on the state to justify any use of suspect classification or any interference with fundamental rights. The middle-level test advocated by Brennan in *Bakke* is an effort to lighten the burden of strict scrutiny so as to permit legislation that explicitly tries to aid those who have been disadvantaged by past discrimination.

It may seem peculiar that an important legal decision can turn on such a technical and procedural matter as burden of proof. But the question of burden of proof often plays a decisive role in a legal decision, so it is worth knowing something about it.

The two basic questions concerning burden of proof are (1) *who* bears this burden and (2) how *heavy* is the burden. In our system of criminal justice, the rules governing burden of proof are fairly straightforward. The state has the burden of establishing the guilt of the accused. The defendant has no obligation to establish his or her innocence. That is what is meant by saying that the defendant is *innocent until proven guilty.* The burden of proof is also very heavy on the state in criminal procedures, for it must show *beyond a reasonable doubt* that the accused is guilty. If the prosecution shows only that it is more likely than not that the accused has committed a crime, then the jury should vote for acquittal.

Turning to civil law, there is no simple way of explaining burden of proof. Very roughly, the plaintiff (the one who brings the suit) has an initial burden to establish a *prima facie* case, that is, a case that is strong enough that it needs to be rebutted, in behalf of his or her complaint. The burden then shifts to the respondent (the one against whom the suit is being brought) to answer these claims. The burden may then shift back and forth depending on the nature of the procedure. Provided that both sides have met their legally required burdens of proof, the case is then decided on the basis of the *preponderance of evidence;* that is, the judge or jury decides which side has made the stronger case.

Burden of proof is primarily a legal notion, but it is sometimes used, often very loosely, outside the law. The notion of burden of proof is needed within the law because law cases are adversarial and the court has to come to a decision. Outside the law, people have a very general burden to *have* good reasons for what they say. That's the second part of Grice's rule of Quality. More specifically, people have a burden to *present* some reasons when they make accusations or statements that run counter to common opinion.

The important thing to see is that you cannot establish the truth of something through an appeal to the burden of proof. The following argument is perfectly weird:

There is life in other parts of the universe, because you can't prove otherwise.

Of course, no one can prove that there *isn't* life elsewhere in the universe, but this has no tendency to show that there *is*. Attempts to prove the truth of something through appeals to burden of proof—often called arguments from ignorance—are another example of a *fallacy of relevance.*

Nonetheless, the importance of burden of proof in the law does give force to another kind of argument. In a criminal case, the following argument would be perfectly fine:

The defendant ought to be found not guilty, because the prosecution has not proven beyond a reasonable doubt that she is guilty.

This argument would also be a fallacy of relevance if the burden of proof were not so important. But the relevant burden of proof makes this argument very strong in a court of law.

Who bears the burden of proof and how heavy the burden is determine which legal arguments work. Consider the following argument:

This law uses a suspect classification, and the state has not shown that it serves any compelling purpose, so we ought to find the law unconstitutional.

This argument is strong if the strict scrutiny interpretation is accepted (assuming the premises are true). However, this argument fails if a weaker burden of proof is required, as in the middle level scrutiny interpretation. When one chooses between interpretations of equal protection and between different burdens of proof, one also chooses which arguments will have force in courts of law. This is another example of a general phenomenon that has been stressed throughout this book—that background assumptions can determine whether an argument is any good.

▼ DISCUSSION QUESTIONS

1. Evaluate Brennan's and Powell's uses of precedents in their opinions. Be sure to consider similarities and differences between *Bakke* and the precedents cited.

2. Consider the *Bakke* case as a precedent and argue for or against the constitutionality of the laws in these cases:

   a. *Fullilove v. Klutznik* (1980) concerned a congressional spending program that required 10 percent of the federal funds granted for local public works projects to be used to procure services or supplies from businesses owned and controlled by members of minority groups. (Be sure to consider any differences between employment and education.)

b. *California Federal Savings and Loan Association et al. v. Guerra, Director, Department of Fair Employment and Housing et al.* (1987) concerned a California law requiring employers to provide leave and reinstatement to employees who are pregnant.

c. *Morton v. Mancari* (1974) concerned a federal statute that gave members of federally recognized tribes a preference for employment in the Bureau of Indian Affairs. (Does the purpose of the bureau justify this statute?)

3. Find out what kinds of preferential treatment programs exist in your own school or town, and then argue either that these programs are constitutional or that they are not.

12

Moral Arguments

People often disagree on moral questions. When these disagreements arise, it is often difficult—sometimes impossible—to resolve them. At times these disagreements turn on questions of fact. If one person thinks that an action will have a particular consequence, and another thinks that it will not, they might well disagree on the moral worth of that action. For example, those who have defended the United States' decision to drop atomic bombs on Japan have often claimed that, in fact, this saved lives by forcing Japan to surrender. Many critics of this decision have denied this factual claim.

Moral disagreements can also arise from disagreements about moral principles. To many people, it is immoral to have sex outside marriage. To others, it is immoral to interfere with such acts. Despite such disagreements, it is surprising how much agreement there is on general moral principles. In our society, most people accept a great many moral principles as a matter of course. If a policy has no other consequence but to produce widespread misery, it is rejected out of hand. We share a conception of justice which includes, among other things, equality of opportunity and equality before the law. Most people also have a conception of human dignity: a human being is not a thing to be used and disposed of for personal advantage.

With all this agreement, how does moral disagreement arise at all? The answer is that in certain circumstances, our moral principles *conflict* with one another, and people are inclined to resolve this conflict in different ways. People often agree on principles about welfare, justice, and human dignity, and yet, by weighing these principles differently or seeing the situation in a different light, they arrive at opposing moral conclusions.

Another kind of moral disagreement concerns the *range* or *scope* of moral principles. Even if everyone agrees that death and suffering are bad, they often disagree about *whose* death and suffering counts. With few exceptions, it is thought to be wrong to inflict death and suffering on human beings. Most people have a similar attitude toward their pet dogs or cats. Some, however, go further and claim that it is also immoral to kill any animals—including cows, chickens, and fish—just to produce tasty food for humans.

The very hardest problems combine issues of *range* with *conflicts of principles*. It is a disagreement of this complex kind that we will focus on in this chapter. The problem is abortion. The main issues are (i) whether fetuses lie within the range of a standard moral principle against killing, and (ii) how to resolve conflicts between the principles that protect the fetus and other principles concerning, for example, human welfare and a woman's control over her body.

THE PROBLEM OF ABORTION

What Is the Problem?

When faced with a moral problem, it often seems clear what the problem is, but this assumption can be mistaken. Sometimes a problem is formulated so vaguely that there is no way even to begin to solve it. People can argue for hours or even years without realizing that they are really talking about different things.

To clarify a moral problem, the first step is to specify precisely what is being judged—which action or kind of action is at issue. In the problem of abortion, the first step is to specify exactly what counts as an abortion. It is common to define abortion as the termination of a pregnancy. This includes spontaneous abortions or miscarriages, but these raise no moral problems because they are not the result of human action. Furthermore, the moral problem of abortion arises only when the death of the fetus is an expected consequence of terminating the pregnancy. To focus on these problematic cases, from now on we will take "abortion" to mean the intentional termination of a pregnancy with the expected consequence that the fetus will die as a result.

After the class of actions is picked out, we need to determine what is being asked about this class of actions—what kind of moral judgment is at stake. It is one thing to ask whether abortion is *morally wrong*, another thing to ask whether abortion *should be illegal*. These are both moral questions (since the second asks what the law should be and not what it is), but they can be answered differently. It is not uncommon for people to claim that abortion is morally wrong but should not be made illegal, because it is a matter of personal, not public, morality. It is also important to distinguish the question of whether abortion is or is not morally *wrong* from the separate question of whether abortion is or is not *good*. People who deny that abortion is morally wrong do not hold that abortion is a positive good. They do not, for example, recommend that people get pregnant so that they can have abortions. So, from now on, we will focus on the issue of the moral wrongness of abortion.

The Conservative Argument

We can begin to understand this problem if we reconstruct the main argument against abortion, using the method discussed in Chapter 4. Most opponents of abortion call themselves "pro-life" and base their position on an appeal to a moral principle involving the "right to life." Of course, most opponents of abortion are not opposed to killing weeds, germs, or even fish. What they have in mind, then, is probably a principle like this:

It is always wrong to kill a human being.

This principle by itself does not rule out abortion. To reach this conclusion, we need further premises of the following kind:

Abortion involves killing a human fetus.
A human fetus is a human being.

With these premises, the antiabortion argument will have the following form:

(1) Abortion involves killing a human fetus.
(2) A human fetus is a human being.
(3) It is always wrong to kill a human being.

(4) Therefore, abortion is wrong.

This argument is valid and reasonably charitable, so we have completed the first stage of reconstruction.

We next ask if the premises of this argument are true. The first premise is not controversial, given our definition of abortion above. However, the second premise raises many problems. Much of the debate concerning abortion turns on the question of whether a fetus is a human being, and we will examine this question later on. For now, we will assume for the sake of argument that a fetus is a human being.

Some people—for example, strong pacifists—accept the third premise, but most people who adopt strong antiabortion positions do not. This comes out in the following way. Many of those who oppose abortion are in favor of the death penalty for certain crimes. Therefore, they do not accept the general principle that it is always wrong to take a human life. What they need, then, is a principle that allows taking a human life in some instances but not in others. In an effort to achieve this, those who oppose abortion could reformulate the third premise in these words:

It is always wrong to kill an innocent human being.

Here the word "innocent" allows an exception for the death penalty being imposed on those who are guilty of certain crimes. Even stated this way, however, the principle seems to admit of counterexamples. If someone's life is threatened by a madman, it is generally thought that the person has the right to use whatever means are necessary against the madman to prevent being killed. This may include killing the madman, even though the insane are usually thought to be morally innocent of their deeds. If so, the principle must be modified again, and then we get something like this:

It is always wrong to kill an innocent human being except in certain cases of self-defense.

It is still possible to find difficulties with this principle that will lead some to add further modifications or clarifications. Children, for example, are often the innocent victims of bombing raids, yet the raids are often thought to be justified, because these deaths are not intended, even though they are foreseeable. At this point it is common to modify the principle again by including a reference to intentions. We shall not, however, pursue this complex line of reasoning here.[1]

We have arrived, then, at a principle that seems to make sense out of a position that is against abortion but in favor of the death penalty and self-defense. With these modifications included, the argument now looks like this:

(1*) Abortion involves killing a human fetus.
(2*) A human fetus is a human being.
(3*) A human fetus is innocent.
(4*) It is always wrong to kill an innocent human being except in certain cases of self-defense.

(5) Therefore, abortion is always wrong.

But, having made the premises more plausible, we confront a new problem: the argument is invalid as it stands, since the qualification "except in certain cases of self-defense" has been dropped from the conclusion. The proper conclusion of the argument should be:

---

[1] For a discussion of this approach, and for a model of how to argue about a moral principle, see Philippa Foot, "The Problem of Abortion and the Doctrine of Double Effect," reprinted in *Virtues and Vices and Other Essays in Moral Philosophy* (Berkeley and Los Angeles: University of California Press, 1978), pp. 19–32.

(5*) Abortion is always wrong except in certain cases of self-defense.

Rewriting the conclusion in this way has an important consequence: the argument no longer leads to a conclusion that abortion is *always* wrong. This qualified conclusion could permit abortion in those cases in which it is needed to defend the life of the pregnant woman who bears the fetus. In fact, this is the position that many people who are generally opposed to abortion adopt: abortion is wrong except in those cases in which it is necessary to save the life of the mother. Although this does not lay down an absolute prohibition, it is a strong antiabortion position, since it would condone abortion in only a few exceptional cases.

Liberal Responses

We can now examine the way that those who adopt the liberal or "pro-choice" position will respond to the conservative argument as it has just been spelled out. The first premise should not be a subject for controversy. Nor does it seem likely that the third premise will be attacked on the ground that the fetus is not innocent. How could a fetus be guilty of anything?

This leaves three strategies for the liberal: (i) Further modify the moral principle in the fourth premise to allow more exceptions. (ii) Deny the second premise—that the fetus is a human being. (iii) Oppose this conservative argument with a different argument based on a different moral principle.

(i) Further Modifications Even if it is agreed that abortion is justified when it saves the mother's life, we still need to ask whether this is the only exception or whether abortion is justified in other cases as well. Many conservatives admit that abortion is also justified when the pregnancy results from rape or incest. It is not easy to see how to modify the moral principle against killing to allow an exception in cases of rape and incest, so this exception is controversial. We will return to this issue later in this discussion. But even if exceptions are made both for life-threatening pregnancies and for pregnancies due to rape and incest, the range of morally permissible abortions will still be very small.

Liberals can, however, argue for a wider range of morally permissible abortions by extending the self-defense exception. It can be argued that a woman has a right to defend not only her life but also her physical and psychological well-being. Liberals can also argue that the exception of rape shows that abortion is allowed when the woman is not responsible for her pregnancy, and this might include cases where the woman tried to prevent pregnancy by using contraceptives. Granting exceptions of this kind does not provide the basis for an absolute right to an abortion, but it does move things away from a conservative "pro-life" position in the direction of a liberal "pro-choice" position.

(ii) The Status of the Fetus So far we have assumed for the sake of argument that a human fetus is a human being. However, liberals often deny this premise. It may seem hard to deny that a human fetus is human. After all, it is not an aardvark. However, liberals claim that the real issue is not about biological species. The real issue is whether a human fetus is covered by the moral principle against killing, and whether it is protected to the same extent as an adult human. Anything that is protected to this extent is said to have a "right to life" and will be called a "person." The issue, then, is whether a human fetus is a person. If a fetus *is* a person, the burden of proof is on those who maintain the liberal position to show why the moral principle against killing should be set aside or modified. If a fetus is *not* a person, this moral principle cannot show that there is anything wrong with abortion for any reason—with what is called "abortion on demand."

Any argument that a fetus either is a person or is not a person must proceed from some idea of which properties make something a person—which properties warrant the protection of moral principles. To argue that a fetus is not a person, liberals need to find some feature that fetuses lack and that is necessary for personhood. In response, conservatives need to find some feature that fetuses have and that is sufficient for personhood.

Many conditions of personhood have been suggested. This list is not complete:

(a)   genetic code (which determines biological species)
(b)   ensoulment (when a soul enters the body)
(c)   brain activity (first detected around eight weeks)
(d)   capacity to feel pain and pleasure
(e)   viability (when the fetus can survive outside the womb)
(f)   rationality (and other related capacities)

Conservatives usually emphasize tests such as genetic code, which is formed at conception, or ensoulment, which is supposed to occur at or shortly after conception. In contrast, liberals usually employ tests such as viability, which is reached during the second trimester, or rationality, which comes sometime after birth (depending on what counts as rationality—ability to choose and plan, self-consciousness, and so on). Thus, the personhood of fetuses during the first trimester is usually asserted by conservatives and denied by liberals on this issue.

How can we determine whether a feature is necessary or sufficient for personhood? We can start by rejecting any test of personhood that leads to *implausible* results. Many conservatives argue that rationality is not necessary for personhood, because, whatever rationality is, newborn babies and severely retarded adults are not rational, but it is still morally wrong to kill them. Other tests of personhood are ruled out because they do not seem *important* enough. Many liberals argue that a certain genetic code is not sufficient to make something a person, because there is no reason to favor one genetic code over another except that it later produces other important features, such as rationality. It is also common to rule out a test of personhood if we cannot *know* when the test is passed. For example, some people reject ensoulment as a criterion of personhood, because they see no way to tell when, if ever, a fetus has a soul. And tests of personhood are also often rejected if they depend on factors which are *extraneous*. Conservatives often argue that viability cannot be a test of personhood because the point when a fetus can survive outside the womb depends on what technology happens to be available to doctors at the time.

In addition to features which fetuses have when they are fetuses, they also seem to have the *potential* to develop much more, including rationality. Conservatives often use this premise to argue that fetuses are persons and have a right to life. The first problem with this argument is that it seems to assume that something has a right if it has the potential to come to have that right. But this is clearly too strong. A three-year-old child does not have the right to vote even though it has the potential to develop into someone who will have the right to vote. Furthermore, the notion of a potential is not clear. If the fetus has the potential, why doesn't the egg and/or sperm? This does not refute potentiality as a test of personhood, but much more must be done to show what potentiality is and why it is sufficient to make something a person even before the potential is realized.

All of these positions on personhood are controversial, and many people feel uncertain about which is the correct one. A major issue in many moral problems is how to deal with uncertainties such as this.

One reaction is a position called "gradualism".[2] We have assumed so far that the fetus either has or does not have a right to life, but rights sometimes come in various strengths. Gradualists claim that a fetus slowly develops a right to life which is at first very weak. As pregnancy progresses, this right gets stronger, so it takes more to justify abortion. Late abortions still might be permitted, but only in extreme circumstances. This position is still vague, but it is attractive to some people who want to avoid placing too much emphasis on any single point in fetal development.

Uncertainty is also exploited in many other ways. We discussed slippery slope arguments already in Chapter 5. Another way to exploit uncertainty is to put the burden on the other side to produce a reason for drawing a line at some point. For example, Reagan says, "anyone who doesn't feel sure whether we are talking about a second human

---

[2] Gradualism is discussed in more detail by Joel Feinberg, "Abortion," in *Matters of Life and Death*, 2nd ed., ed. Tom Regan (New York: Random House, 1986), pp. 256–93.

life should clearly give life the benefit of the doubt" (352). However, the same kind of argument is also available to liberals: Since we are not sure whether the fetus is a person, but we are sure that the pregnant woman has rights over her body, we should give the benefit of the doubt to the pregnant woman. We should always suspect that there is something wrong with an argument that can be used equally well in opposing directions.

(iii) Conflicting Principles   A third kind of liberal response is to invoke another principle which conflicts with the conservative principle against killing. Liberals often emphasize two such principles: one about the rights of the pregnant woman to control her own body and another about overall human welfare. We will focus on human welfare.

Those who adopt a liberal position on abortion often argue that abortion can sometimes be justified in terms of the welfare of the woman who bears the fetus, or in terms of the welfare of the family into which it will be born, or even in terms of the welfare of the child itself, if it were to be born with a severe disability or into an impoverished situation. This argument, when spelled out, looks like this:

(1)   An action that best increases overall human welfare is not morally wrong.
(2)   Abortion sometimes is the best way of increasing overall human welfare.

(3)   Therefore, abortion is sometimes not morally wrong.

What are we to say about this argument? It seems valid in form, so we can turn to the premises themselves and ask whether they are acceptable. The first (and leading) premise of the argument is subject to two immediate criticisms. First of all, it is vague. Probably what a person who uses this kind of argument has in mind by speaking of human welfare is a certain level of material and psychological well-being. Of course, this is still vague, but it is clear enough to make the premise a target of the second, more important, criticism. While maximizing human welfare may, in general, be a good thing, it is not the only relevant consideration in deciding how to act. To cite a previous example (in Chapter 6), it might be true that our society would be much more prosperous on the whole if 10 percent of the population were designated slaves who would do all menial work. Yet, even if a society could be made generally happy in this way, most people would reject such a system on the grounds that it is unfair to the slave class. For reasons of this kind, most people would modify the first premise of the argument we are now examining in the following way:

(1*)   An action that best increases human welfare is not morally wrong, provided that it is fairly applied.

But if the first premise is modified in this way, then the entire argument must be restated to reflect this revision. It will now look like this:

(1*)   An action that best increases human welfare is not morally wrong, provided that it is fairly applied.
(2*)   Abortion is sometimes an action that best increases human welfare.

(3*)   Therefore, abortion is sometimes not morally wrong, provided that it is fairly applied.

It should be obvious how conservatives on abortion will reply to this argument. They will maintain that abortion almost always involves unfairness, namely, to the fetus, so abortion is still wrong in almost all cases, as the conservative argument claimed. Once more we have encountered a standard situation: given a strong premise (Premise 1), it is possible to derive a particular conclusion, but this strong premise is subject to criticism and therefore must be modified. When the premise is modified, it no longer supports the original conclusion that the person presenting the argument wishes to establish.

The argument does not stop here. A person who holds a liberal position on abortion might reply in a number of ways. Some theory of fairness might be developed to argue that many abortions are not unfair to the fetus, since the fetus has no right to use the pregnant woman's body. The burden of the argument may shift to the question of whether or not a human fetus is a human being and therefore possessed of a right to fair treatment. It might also be argued that questions of human welfare are sometimes more important than issues of equal or even fair treatment. During war and some emergencies, for example, members of a certain segment of the population are called upon to risk their lives for the good of the whole in ways that might seem unfair to them.

When the argument is put on this new basis, the question then becomes this: Are there circumstances in which matters of welfare become so urgent that the rights of the fetus (here assuming that the fetus has rights) are overriden? The obvious case in which this might happen is when the life of the bearer of the fetus is plainly threatened. For many conservatives on abortion, this does count as a case in which abortion is permitted. Those who hold a liberal position will maintain that severe psychological, financial, or personal losses to the pregnant woman may also take precedence over the life of the fetus. Furthermore, if not aborted, many fetuses would live in very deprived circumstances, and some would not develop very far or live very long, because they have deadly diseases, such as Tay-Sachs. How severe must these losses, deprivations, and diseases be? From our previous discussion of slippery slope arguments, we know that we should not expect any sharp lines to exist here, and, indeed, people will tend to be spread out in their opinions along a continuum ranging from a belief in complete prohibition to no prohibition.

ANALOGICAL REASONING IN ETHICS

Using the method for reconstructing arguments, we now have a fairly clear idea of the main options on the abortion issue. But understanding the structure of the debate—though essential for dealing with it intelligently—does not settle it. If the reasons on all sides are fully spelled out and disagreement remains, what is to be done?

At this stage, those who do not simply turn to abuse often appeal to *analogical arguments*. The point of an analogical argument is to reach a conclusion in a controversial case by comparing it to a similar situation where it is clearer what is right or wrong. In fact, a great deal of ethical reasoning uses such analogies. We have already seen one simple analogy between an abortion to save the life of the mother and self-defense against an insane person. To get a better idea of how analogical reasoning works in ethics, we will concentrate on a more complex analogy which raises the issue of whether abortion is morally permissible in cases of pregnancy due to rape.

A classic analogical argument is given by Judith Jarvis Thomson in "A Defense of Abortion" (reprinted below) in which she tells the following story:

> You wake up in the morning and find yourself back to back in bed with an unconscious violinist. A famous unconscious violinist. He has been found to have a fatal kidney ailment, and the Society of Music Lovers has canvassed all of the available medical records and found that you alone have the right blood type to help. They have therefore kidnapped you, and last night the violinist's circulatory system was plugged into yours, so that your kidneys can be used to extract poisons from his blood as well as your own. The director of the hospital now tells you, "Look, we're sorry the Society of Music Lovers did this to you—we would never have permitted it if we had known. But still, they did it, and the violinist is now plugged into you. To unplug you would be to kill him. But never mind, it's only for nine months. By then he will have recovered from his ailment, and can safely be unplugged from you."

Thomson claims that it is not wrong for you to unplug yourself from the violinist in this situation, and most people seem to agree with her judgment in this case. By analogy, abortion after rape is not wrong either.

The basic assumption to this analogical argument is that we should not make different moral judgments in cases which do not differ. More positively:

(1) If two actions are similar in all morally relevant respects, and if one of the acts is not morally wrong, then the other act is also not morally wrong.

Now we can apply this principle to Thomson's story:

(2) It is not morally wrong for you to unplug the violinist in Thomson's example.
(3) To unplug the violinist and to abort a pregnancy due to rape are similar in all morally relevant respects.

(Conclusion) It is not morally wrong for a woman to abort a pregnancy due to rape.

This argument is valid, so, following the normal procedure, we can ask whether the premises are true. The first premise seems plausible, and it is accepted in most moral theories. Most people also accept the second premise. Consequently, the discussion usually focusses on the third premise—on the similarities and differences between Thomson's story and abortion in a pregnancy due to rape.

First consider these similarities between Thomson's story and abortion after rape:

(a) Both the fetus and the violinist are on or near the surface of the earth.
(b) Kidnapping is immoral and illegal, like rape.
(c) The hospital stay lasts nine months, like pregnancy.
(d) The violinist is innocent and a human being, like the fetus (given our present assumption).
(e) Unplugging the violinist is supposed to be killing, like an abortion.

Now here are some differences between the situations:

(f) The fetus cannot play the violin, but the violinist can.
(g) The person who is plugged into the violinist might not be female.
(h) The person who is plugged into the violinist cannot leave the hospital room, but pregnant women can still move around, even if they have some difficulty.
(i) Abortion involves killing, but unplugging the violinist is merely refusing to save.

It is obvious that some of these similarities and differences are not relevant. It does not matter whether killing occurs near the earth. Killing is usually wrong even on the Starship Enterprise. It is also accepted that differences in musical talent and in sex cannot justify killing. The other similarities and differences on our list do seem important. They each concern harm and responsibility, matters that must be considered in reaching a moral judgment about these actions. The force of Thompson's analogical argument is that the very features that lead us to conclude that it would not be wrong to unplug the violinist are also found in the case of pregnancy due to rape. Furthermore, there are no relevant differences that are important enough to override the significance of these similarities. These considerations, if correct, provide a reason for treating the two cases in the same way. If we then agree, as Thomson thinks we will, that it is not wrong to unplug the violinist, we have a reason to conclude that abortion after rape is not wrong either.

Responses to Thomson's argument have largely turned on emphasizing the differences between the two situations. Baruch Brody, for example, in "The Morality of Abortion" (reprinted below), claims that Thomson's argument fails because abortion involves *killing*, whereas unplugging does not. If you stay plugged to the violinist, this will save the violinist, so to unplug yourself is to *fail to save* the violinist. But Brody denies that to unplug yourself from the violinist is the same as to *kill* the violinist, or to take the violinist's life. And Brody argues that there is a crucial difference between killing and failing to save, because a negative duty not to kill is much stronger than any positive duty to save another person's life.

To determine whether unplugging the violinist is more like acts of killing or more like other acts of refusing to save, we might consider more analogies. Thomson also introduces additional analogies which seem more like abortions where the pregnancy is not due to rape. In the end, our sense of which features seem most important will determine how we evaluate all such analogical arguments. The analogies bring certain features to our attention, but we have to decide which features are important, and how important they are.

WEIGHING FACTORS

Our discussion has brought us to the following point: disagreements concerning abortion in general cannot be reduced to a yes-no dispute. Most conservatives on abortion acknowledge that it is permissible in some (though very few) cases. Most liberals on abortion admit that there are some (though not restrictively many) limitations on its use. The way people place themselves on this continuum does not depend on any simple acceptance of one argument over another, but instead on the *weight* they give certain factors. To what extent does a fetus have rights? The conservative position we examined earlier grants the fetus a full (or close to full) right to life. The liberal position usually grants little or no rights to the fetus. In what areas do questions of welfare override certain individual rights? The conservative in this matter usually restricts this to those cases in which the very life of the mother is plainly threatened. As the position on abortion becomes more liberal, the more extensive becomes the range of cases in which the rights, if any, of the fetus are set aside in favor of the rights of the bearer of the fetus. Where a particular person strikes this balance is not only a function of basic moral beliefs but also a function of different weights assigned to them.

How can one deal with such bedrock disagreements? The first thing to see is that logic alone will not settle them. Starting from a certain conception of persons, it is possible to argue coherently for a liberal view on abortion; starting from another point of view, it is possible to argue coherently for a conservative view on abortion. The important thing to see is that it is possible to *understand* an opposing view, that is, get a genuine feeling for its inner workings, even if you disagree with it completely. Logical analysis may show that particular arguments are unsound or have unnoticed and unwanted implications. This may force clarification and modification. But the most important service that logical analysis can perform is to lay bare the fundamental principles that lie beneath surface disagreements. Analysis will sometimes show that these disagreements are fundamental and perhaps irreconcilable. Dealing with such irreconcilable differences in a humane way is one of the fundamental tasks of a society dedicated to freedom and a wide range of civil liberties.

▼ A Defense of Abortion *[1]

JUDITH JARVIS THOMSON

Most opposition to abortion relies on the premise that the fetus is a human being, a person, from the moment of conception. The premise is argued for, but, as I think, not well. Take, for example, the most common argument. We are asked to notice that the development of a human being from conception through birth into childhood is continuous; then it is said that to draw a line, to choose a point in this development and say "before this point the thing is not a person, after this point it is a person" is to make an arbitrary choice, a choice for which in the nature of things no good reason can be given. It is concluded that the fetus is, or anyway that we had better say it is, a person from the moment of conception. But this conclusion does not follow. Similar things might be said about the development of an acorn into an oak tree, and it does not follow that acorns are oak trees, or that we had better say they are. Arguments of this form are sometimes called "slippery slope arguments"— the phrase is perhaps self-explanatory—and it is dismaying that opponents of abortion rely on them so heavily and uncritically.

---

* *Philosophy and Public Affairs*, Vol. 1, No. 1 (Fall 1971), pp. 47–66.
[1] I am very much indebted to James Thomson for discussion, criticism, and many helpful suggestions.

I am inclined to agree, however, that the prospects for "drawing a line" in the development of the fetus look dim. I am inclined to think also that we shall probably have to agree that the fetus has already become a human person well before birth. Indeed, it comes as a surprise when one first learns how early in its life it begins to acquire human characteristics. By the tenth week, for example, it already has a face, arms and legs, fingers and toes; it has internal organs, and brain activity is detectable.[2] On the other hand, I think that the premise is false, that the fetus is not a person from the moment of conception. A newly fertilized ovum, a newly implanted clump of cells, is no more a person than an acorn is an oak tree. But I shall not discuss any of this. For it seems to me to be of great interest to ask what happens if, for the sake of argument, we allow the premise. How, precisely, are we supposed to get from there to the conclusion that abortion is morally impermissible? Opponents of abortion commonly spend most of their time establishing that the fetus is a person, and hardly any time explaining the step from there to the impermissibility of abortion. Perhaps they think the step too simple and obvious to require much comment. Or perhaps instead they are simply being economical in argument. Many of those who defend abortion rely on the premise that the fetus is not a person, but only a bit of tissue that will become a person at birth; and why pay out more arguments than you have to? Whatever the explanation, I suggest that the step they take is neither easy nor obvious, that it calls for closer examination than it is commonly given, and that when we do give it this closer examination we shall feel inclined to reject it.

I propose, then, that we grant that the fetus is a person from the moment of conception. How does the argument go from here? Something like this, I take it. Every person has a right to life. So the fetus has a right to life. No doubt the mother has a right to decide what shall happen in and to her body; everyone would grant that. But surely a person's right to life is stronger and more stringent than the mother's right to decide what happens in and to her body, and so outweighs it. So the fetus may not be killed; an abortion may not be performed.

It sounds plausible. But now let me ask you to imagine this. You wake up in the morning and find yourself back to back in bed with an unconscious violinist. A famous unconscious violinist. He has been found to have a fatal kidney ailment, and the Society of Music Lovers has canvassed all the available medical records and found that you alone have the right blood type to help. They have therefore kidnapped you, and last night the violinist's circulatory system was plugged into yours, so that your kidneys can be used to extract poisons from his blood as well as your own. The director of the hospital now tells you, "Look, we're

---

[2] Daniel Callahan, *Abortion: Law, Choice and Morality* (New York, 1970), p. 373. This book gives a fascinating survey of the available information on abortion. The Jewish tradition is surveyed in David M. Feldman, *Birth Control in Jewish Law* (New York, 1968), Part 5; the Catholic tradition in John T. Noonan, Jr., "An Almost Absolute Value in History," in *The Morality of Abortion*, ed. John T. Noonan, Jr. (Cambridge, Mass., 1970).

sorry the Society of Music Lovers did this to you—we would never have permitted it if we had known. But still, they did it, and the violinist now is plugged into you. To unplug you would be to kill him. But never mind, it's only for nine months. By then he will have recovered from his ailment, and can safely be unplugged from you." Is it morally incumbent on you to accede to this situation? No doubt it would be very nice of you if you did, a great kindness. But do you *have* to accede to it? What if it were not nine months, but nine years? Or longer still? What if the director of the hospital says, "Tough luck, I agree, but you've now got to stay in bed, with the violinist plugged into you, for the rest of your life. Because remember this. All persons have a right to life, and violinists are persons. Granted you have a right to decide what happens in and to your body, but a person's right to life outweighs your right to decide what happens in and to your body. So you cannot ever be unplugged from him." I imagine you would regard this as outrageous, which suggests that something really is wrong with that plausible-sounding argument I mentioned a moment ago.

In this case, of course, you were kidnapped; you didn't volunteer for the operation that plugged the violinist into your kidneys. Can those who oppose abortion on the ground I mentioned make an exception for a pregnancy due to rape? Certainly. They can say that persons have a right to life only if they didn't come into existence because of rape; or they can say that all persons have a right to life, but that some have less of a right to life than others, in particular, that those who came into existence because of rape have less. But these statements have a rather unpleasant sound. Surely the question of whether you have a right to life at all, or how much of it you have, shouldn't turn on the question of whether or not you are the product of a rape. And in fact the people who oppose abortion on the ground I mentioned do not make this distinction, and hence do not make an exception in the case of rape.

Nor do they make an exception for a case in which the mother had to spend the nine months of her pregnancy in bed. They would agree that would be a great pity, and hard on the mother; but all the same all persons have a right to life, the fetus is a person, and so on. I suspect, in fact, that they would not make an exception for a case in which, miraculously enough, the pregnancy went on for nine years or even the rest of the mother's life.

Some won't even make an exception for a case in which continuation of the pregnancy is likely to shorten the mother's life; they regard abortion as impermissible even to save the mother's life. Such cases are nowadays very rare, and many opponents of abortion do not accept this extreme view. All the same, it is a good place to begin: a number of points of interest come out in respect to it.

1. Let us call the view that abortion is impermissible even to save the mother's life "the extreme view." I want to suggest first that it does not issue from the argument I mentioned earlier without the addition of some fairly powerful premises. Suppose a woman has become pregnant, and now learns that she has a cardiac condition such that she will die if she carries the baby to term. What may be done for her? The fetus, being a

person, has a right to life, but as the mother is a person too, so has she a right to life. Presumably they have an equal right to life. How is it supposed to come out that an abortion may not be performed? If mother and child have an equal right to life, shouldn't we perhaps flip a coin? Or should we add to the mother's right to life her right to decide what happens in and to her body which everybody seems to be ready to grant—the sum of her rights now outweighing the fetus' right to life?

The most familiar argument here is the following. We are told that performing the abortion would be directly killing[3] the child, whereas doing nothing would not be killing the mother, but only letting her die. Moreover, in killing the child, one would be killing an innocent person, for the child has committed no crime, and is not aiming at his mother's death. And then there are a variety of ways in which this might be continued. (1) But as directly killing an innocent person is always and absolutely impermissible, an abortion may not be performed. Or, (2) as directly killing an innocent person is murder, and murder is always and absolutely impermissible, an abortion may not be performed.[4] Or, (3) as one's duty to refrain from directly killing an innocent person is more stringent than one's duty to keep a person from dying, an abortion may not be performed. Or, (4) if one's only options are directly killing an innocent person or letting a person die, one must prefer letting the person die, and thus an abortion may not be performed.[5]

Some people seem to have thought that these are not further premises which must be added if the conclusion is to be reached; but that they follow from the very fact that an innocent person has a right to life.[6] But this seems to me to be a mistake, and perhaps the simplest way to show

---

[3] The term "direct" in the arguments I refer to is a technical one. Roughly what is meant by "direct killing" is either killing as an end by itself, or killing as a means to some end, for example, the end of saving someone else's life. See note 6, below, for an example of its use.

[4] Cf. *Encyclical Letter of Pope Pius XI on Christian Marriage*, St. Paul Editions (Boston, n.d.), p. 32: "however much we may pity the mother whose health and even life is gravely imperiled in the performance of the duty allotted to her by nature, nevertheless what could ever be a sufficient reason for excusing in any way the direct murder of the innocent? This is precisely what we are dealing with here." Noonan (*The Morality of Abortion*, p. 43) reads this as follows: "What cause can ever avail to excuse in any way the direct killing of the innocent? For it is a question of that."

[5] The thesis in (4) is in an interesting way weaker than those in (1), (2), and (3): they rule out abortion even in cases in which both mother *and* child will die if the abortion is not performed. By contrast, one who held the view expressed in (4) could consistently say that one needn't prefer letting two persons die to killing one.

[6] Cf. the following passage from Pius XII, *Address to the Italian Catholic Society of Midwives*: "The baby in the maternal breast has the right to life immediately from God—Hence there is no man, no human authority, no science, no medical, eugenic, social, economic or moral 'indication' which can establish or grant a valid juridical ground for a direct deliberate disposition of an innocent human life, that is a disposition which looks to its destruction either as an end or as a means in another end perhaps in itself not illicit. The baby, still not born, is a man in the same degree and for the same reason as the mother" (quoted in Noonan, *The Morality of Abortion*, p. 45).

this is to bring out that while we must certainly grant that innocent persons have a right to life, the theses in (1) through (4) are all false. Take (2), for example. If directly killing an innocent person is murder, and thus is impermissible, then the mother's directly killing the innocent person inside her is murder, and thus is impermissible. But it cannot seriously be thought to be murder if the mother performs an abortion on herself to save her life. It cannot seriously be said that she *must* refrain, that she *must* sit passively by and wait for her death. Let us look again at the case of you and the violinist. There you are, in bed with the violinist, and the director of the hospital says to you, "It's all most distressing, and I deeply sympathize, but you see this is putting an additional strain on your kidneys, and you'll be dead within the month. But you *have* to stay where you are all the same. Because unplugging you would be directly killing an innocent violinist, and that's murder, and that's impermissible." If anything in the world is true, it is that you do not commit murder, you do not do what is impermissible, if you reach around to your back and unplug yourself from that violinist to save your life.

The main focus of attention in writings on abortion has been on what a third party may or may not do in answer to a request from a woman for an abortion. This is in a way understandable. Things being as they are, there isn't much a woman can safely do to abort herself. So the question asked is what a third party may do, and what the mother may do, if it is mentioned at all, is deduced, almost as an afterthought, from what it is concluded that third parties may do. But it seems to me that to treat the matter in this way is to refuse to grant to the mother that very status of person which is so firmly insisted on for the fetus. For we cannot simply read off what a person may do from what a third party may do. Suppose you find yourself trapped in a tiny house with a growing child. I mean a very tiny house, and a rapidly growing child—you are already up against the wall of the house and in a few minutes you'll be crushed to death. The child on the other hand won't be crushed to death; if nothing is done to stop him from growing he'll be hurt, but in the end he'll simply burst open the house and walk out a free man. Now I could well understand it if a bystander were to say, "There's nothing we can do for you. We cannot choose between your life and his, we cannot be the ones to decide who is to live, we cannot intervene." But it cannot be concluded that you too can do nothing, that you cannot attack it to save your life. However innocent the child may be, you do not have to wait passively while it crushes you to death. Perhaps a pregnant woman is vaguely felt to have the status of house, to which we don't allow the right of self-defense. But if the woman houses the child, it should be remembered that she is a person who houses it.

I should perhaps stop to say explicitly that I am not claiming that people have a right to do anything whatever to save their lives. I think, rather, that there are drastic limits to the right of self-defense. If someone threatens you with death unless you torture someone else to death, I think you have not the right, even to save your life to do so. But the case under consideration here is very different. In our case there are only two people involved, one whose life is threatened, and one who threatens it.

Both are innocent: the one who is threatened is not threatened because of any fault, the one who threatens does not threaten because of any fault. For this reason we may feel that we bystanders cannot intervene. But the person threatened can.

In sum, a woman surely can defend her life against the threat to it posed by the unborn child, even if doing so involves its death. And this shows not merely that the theses in (1) through (4) are false; it shows also that the extreme view of abortion is false, and so we need not canvass any other possible ways of arriving at it from the argument I mentioned at the outset.

2. The extreme view could of course be weakened to say that while abortion is permissible to save the mother's life, it may not be performed by a third party, but only by the mother herself. But this cannot be right either. For what we have to keep in mind is that the mother and the unborn child are not like two tenants in a small house which has, by an unfortunate mistake, been rented to both: the mother *owns* the house. The fact that she does adds to the offensiveness of deducing that the mother can do nothing from the supposition that third parties can do nothing. But it does more than this: it casts a bright light on the supposition that third parties can do nothing. Certainly it lets us see that a third party who says "I cannot choose between you" is fooling himself if he thinks this is impartiality. If Jones has found and fastened on a certain coat, which he needs to keep him from freezing, but which Smith also needs to keep him from freezing, then it is not impartiality that says "I cannot choose between you" when Smith owns the coat. Women have said again and again "This body is *my* body!" and they have reason to feel angry, reason to feel that it has been like shouting into the wind. Smith, after all, is hardly likely to bless us if we say to him, "Of course it's your coat; anybody would grant that it is. But no one may choose between you and Jones who is to have it."

We should really ask what it is that says "no one may choose" in the face of the fact that the body that houses the child is the mother's body. It may be simply a failure to appreciate this fact. But it may be something more interesting, namely the sense that one has a right to refuse to lay hands on people, even where it would be just and fair to do so, even where justice seems to require that somebody do so. Thus justice might call for somebody to get Smith's coat back from Jones, and yet you have a right to refuse to be the one to lay hands on Jones, a right to refuse to do physical violence to him. This, I think, must be granted. But then what should be said is not "no one may choose," but only "*I* cannot choose," and indeed not even this, but "*I* will not *act*," leaving it open that somebody else can or should, and in particular that anyone in a position of authority, with the job of securing people's rights, both can and should. So this is no difficulty. I have not been arguing that any given third party must accede to the mother's request that he perform an abortion to save her life, but only that he may.

I suppose that in some views of human life the mother's body is only on loan to her, the loan not being one which gives her any prior claim to it. One who held this view might well think it impartiality to say "I cannot choose." But I shall simply ignore this possibility. My own view is that if a human being has any just, prior claim to anything at all, he has a just, prior claim to his own body. And perhaps this needn't be argued for here anyway, since, as I mentioned, the arguments against abortion we are looking at do grant that the woman has a right to decide what happens in and to her body.

But although they do grant it, I have tried to show that they do not take seriously what is done in granting it. I suggest the same thing will reappear even more clearly when we turn away from cases in which the mother's life is at stake, and attend, as I propose we now do, to the vastly more common cases in which a woman wants an abortion for some less weighty reason than preserving her own life.

3. Where the mother's life is not at stake, the argument I mentioned at the outset seems to have a much stronger pull. "Everyone has a right to life, so the unborn person has a right to life." And isn't the child's right to life weightier than anything other than the mother's own right to life, which she might put forward as ground for an abortion?

This argument treats the right to life as if it were unproblematic. It is not, and this seems to me to be precisely the source of the mistake.

For we should now, at long last, ask what it comes to, to have a right to life. In some views having a right to life includes having a right to be given at least the bare minimum one needs for continued life. But suppose that what in fact *is* the bare minimum a man needs for continued life is something he has no right at all to be given? If I am sick unto death, and the only thing that will save my life is the touch of Henry Fonda's cool hand on my fevered brow, then all the same, I have no right to be given the touch of Henry Fonda's cool hand on my fevered brow. It would be frightfully nice of him to fly in from the West Coast to provide it. It would be less nice, though no doubt well meant, if my friends flew out to the West Coast and carried Henry Fonda back with them. But I have no right at all against anybody that he should do this for me. Or again, to return to the story I told earlier, the fact that for continued life that violinist needs the continued use of your kidneys does not establish that he has a right to be given the continued use of your kidneys. He certainly has no right against you that *you* should give him continued use of your kidneys. For nobody has any right to use your kidneys unless you give him such a right; and nobody has the right against you that you shall give him this right—if you do allow him to go on using your kidneys, this is a kindness on your part, and not something he can claim from you as his due. Nor has he any right against anybody else that *they* should give him continued use of your kidneys. Certainly he had no right against the Society of Music Lovers that they should plug him into you in the first place. And if you now start to unplug yourself, having learned that you will otherwise have to spend nine years in bed with him, there is nobody in the world who must try to prevent you, in order to see to it that he is given something he has a right to be given.

Some people are rather stricter about the right to life. In their view, it does not include the right to be given anything, but amounts to, and only to, the right not to be killed by anybody. But here a related difficulty arises. If everybody is to refrain from killing that violinist then everybody must refrain from doing a great many different sorts of things. Everybody must refrain from slitting his throat, everybody must refrain from shooting him—and everybody must refrain from unplugging you from him. But does he have a right against everybody that they shall refrain from unplugging you from him? To refrain from doing this is to allow him to continue to use your kidneys. It could be argued that he has a right against us that *we* should allow him to continue to use your kidneys. That is, while he had no right against us that we should give him the use of your kidneys, it might be argued that he anyway has a right against us that we shall not now intervene and deprive him of the use of your kidneys. I shall come back to third-party interventions later. But certainly the violinist has no right against you that *you* shall allow him to continue to use your kidneys. As I said, if you do allow him to use them, it is a kindness on your part, and not something you owe him.

The difficulty I point to here is not peculiar to the right to life. It reappears in connection with all the other natural rights; and it is something which an adequate account of rights must deal with. For present purposes it is enough just to draw attention to it. But I would stress that I am not arguing that people do not have a right to life—quite to the contrary, it seems to me that the primary control we must place on the acceptability of an account of rights is that it should turn out in that account to be a truth that all persons have a right to life. I am arguing only that having a right to life does not guarantee having either a right to be given the use of or a right to be allowed continued use of another person's body—even if one needs it for life itself. So the right to life will not serve the opponents of abortion in the very simple and clear way in which they seem to have thought it would.

4. There is another way to bring out the difficulty. In the most ordinary sort of case, to deprive someone of what he has a right to is to treat him unjustly. Suppose a boy and his small brother are jointly given a box of chocolates for Christmas. If the older boy takes the box and refuses to give his brother any of the chocolates, he is unjust to him, for the brother has been given a right to half of them. But suppose that, having learned that otherwise it means nine years in bed with that violinist, you unplug yourself from him. You surely are not being unjust to him, for you gave him no right to use your kidneys, and no one else can have given him any such right. But we have to notice that in unplugging yourself, you are killing him; and violinists, like everybody else, have a right to life, and thus in the view we were considering just now, the right not to be killed. So here you do what he supposedly has a right you shall not do, but you do not act unjustly to him in doing it.

The emendation which may be made at this point is this: the right to life consists not in the right not to be killed, but rather in the right not to be killed unjustly. This runs a risk of circularity, but never mind: it would enable us to square the fact that the violinist has a right to life with the fact that you do not act unjustly toward him in unplugging yourself, thereby killing him. For if you do not kill him unjustly, you do not violate his right to life, and so it is no wonder you do him no injustice.

But if this emendation is accepted, the gap in the argument against abortion stares us plainly in the face: it is by no means enough to show that the fetus is a person, and to remind us that all persons have a right to life—we need to be shown also that killing the fetus violates its right to life, i.e., that abortion is unjust killing. And is it?

I suppose we may take it as a datum that in a case of pregnancy due to rape the mother has not given the unborn person a right to the use of her body for food and shelter. Indeed, in what pregnancy could it be supposed that the mother has given the unborn person such a right? It is not as if there were unborn persons drifting about the world, to whom a woman who wants a child says, "I invite you in."

But it might be argued that there are other ways one can have acquired a right to the use of another person's body than by having been invited to use it by that person. Suppose a woman voluntarily indulges in intercourse, knowing of the chance it will issue in pregnancy, and then she does become pregnant; is she not in part responsible for the presence, in fact the very existence, of the unborn person inside her? No doubt she did not invite it in. But doesn't her partial responsibility for its being there itself give it a right to the use of her body?[7] If so, then her aborting it would be more like the boy's taking away the chocolates, and less like your unplugging yourself from the violinist—doing so would be depriving it of what it does have a right to, and thus would be doing it an injustice.

And then, too, it might be asked whether or not she can kill it even to save her own life: If she voluntarily called it into existence, how can she now kill it, even in self-defense?

The first thing to be said about this is that it is something new. Opponents of abortion have been so concerned to make out the independence of the fetus, in order to establish that it has a right to life, just as the mother does, that they have tended to overlook the possible support they might gain from making out that the fetus is *dependent* on the mother, in order to establish that she has a special kind of responsibility for it, a responsibility that gives it rights against her which are not possessed by any independent person—such as an ailing violinist who is a stranger to her.

On the other hand, this argument would give the unborn person a right to its mother's body only if her pregnancy resulted from a voluntary act, undertaken in full knowledge of the chance a pregnancy might result from it. It would leave out entirely the unborn person whose existence is due to rape. Pending the availability of some further argument, then, we would be left with the conclusion that unborn persons whose existence is due to rape have no right to the use of their mothers' bodies, and thus

---

[7] The need for a discussion of this argument was brought home to me by members of the Society for Ethical and Legal Philosophy, to whom this paper was originally presented.

that aborting them is not depriving them of anything they have a right to and hence is not unjust killing.

And we should also notice that it is not at all plain that this argument really does go even as far as it purports to. For there are cases and cases, and the details make a difference. If the room is stuffy, and I therefore open a window to air it, and a burglar climbs in, it would be absurd to say, "Ah, now he can stay, she's given him a right to the use of her house—for she is partially responsible for his presence there, having voluntarily done what enabled him to get in, in full knowledge that there are such things as burglars, and that burglars burgle." It would be still more absurd to say this if I had had bars installed outside my windows, precisely to prevent burglars from getting in, and a burglar got in only because of a defect in the bars. It remains equally absurd if we imagine it is not a burglar who climbs in, but an innocent person who blunders or falls in. Again, suppose it were like this: people-seeds drift about in the air like pollen, and if you open your windows, one may drift in and take root in your carpets or upholstery. You don't want children, so you fix up your windows with fine mesh screens, the very best you can buy. As can happen, however, and on very, very rare occasions does happen, one of the screens is defective; and a seed drifts in and takes root. Does the person-plant who now develops have a right to the use of your house? Surely not—despite the fact that you voluntarily opened your windows, you knowingly kept carpets and upholstered furniture, and you knew that screens were sometimes defective. Someone may argue that you are responsible for its rooting, that it does have a right to your house, because after all you *could* have lived out your life with bare floors and furniture, or with sealed windows and doors. But this won't do—for by the same token anyone can avoid a pregnancy due to rape by having a hysterectomy, or anyway by never leaving home without a (reliable!) army.

It seems to be that the argument we are looking at can establish at most that there are *some* cases in which the unborn person has a right to the use of its mother's body, and therefore *some* cases in which abortion is unjust killing. There is room for much discussion and argument as to precisely which, if any. But I think we should side-step this issue and leave it open, for at any rate the argument certainly does not establish that all abortion is unjust killing.

5. There is room for yet another argument here, however. We surely must all grant that there may be cases in which it would be morally indecent to detach a person from your body at the cost of his life. Suppose you learn that what the violinist needs is not nine years of your life, but only one hour: all you need do to save his life is to spend one hour in that bed with him. Suppose also that letting him use your kidneys for that one hour would not affect your health in the slightest. Admittedly you were kidnapped. Admittedly you did not give anyone permission to plug him into you. Nevertheless it seems to me plain you *ought* to allow him to use your kidneys for that hour—it would be indecent to refuse.

Again, suppose pregnancy lasted only an hour, and constituted no threat to life or health. And suppose that a woman becomes pregnant as a result of rape. Admittedly she did not voluntarily do anything to bring about the existence of a child. Admittedly she did nothing at all which would give the unborn person a right to the use of her body. All the same it might well be said, as in the newly emended violinist story, that she *ought* to allow it to remain for that hour—that it would be indecent in her to refuse.

Now some people are inclined to use the term "right" in such a way that it follows from the fact that you ought to allow a person to use your body for the hour he needs, that he has a right to use your body for the hour he needs, even though he has not been given that right by any person or act. They may say that it follows also that if you refuse, you act unjustly toward him. This use of the term is perhaps so common that it cannot be called wrong; nevertheless it seems to me to be an unfortunate loosening of what we would do better to keep a tight rein on. Suppose that box of chocolates I mentioned earlier had not been given to both boys jointly, but was given only to the older boy. There he sits, stolidly eating his way through the box, his small brother watching enviously. Here we are likely to say "You ought not to be so mean. You ought to give your brother some of those chocolates." My own view is that it just does not follow from the truth of this that the brother has any right to any of the chocolates. If the boy refuses to give his brother any, he is greedy, stingy, callous—but not unjust. I suppose that the people I have in mind will say it does follow that the brother has a right to some of the chocolates, and thus that the boy does act unjustly if he refuses to give his brother any. But the effect of saying this is to obscure what we should keep distinct, namely the difference between the boy's refusal in this case and the boy's refusal in the earlier case, in which the box was given to both boys jointly, and in which the small brother thus had what was from any point of view clear title to half.

A further objection to so using the term "right" that from the fact that A ought to do a thing for B, it follows that B has a right against A that A do it for him, is that it is going to make the question of whether or not a man has a right to a thing turn on how easy it is to provide him with it; and this seems not merely unfortunate, but morally unacceptable. Take the case of Henry Fonda again. I said earlier that I had no right to the touch of his cool hand on my fevered brow, even though I needed it to save my life. I said it would be frightfully nice of him to fly in from the West Coast to provide me with it, but that I had no right against him that he should do so. But suppose he isn't on the West Coast. Suppose he has only to walk across the room, place a hand briefly on my brow—and lo, my life is saved. Then surely he ought to do it, it would be indecent to refuse. Is it to be said "Ah, well, it follows that in this case she has a right to the touch of his hand on her brow, and so it would be an injustice in him to refuse"? So that I have a right to it when it is easy for him to provide it, though no right when it's hard? It's rather a shocking idea that anyone's rights should fade away and disappear as it gets harder and harder to accord them to him.

So my own view is that even though you ought to let the violinist use your kidneys for the one hour he needs, we should not conclude that he has a right to do so—we should say that if you refuse, you are, like the boy who owns all the chocolates and will give none away, self-centered and callous, indecent in fact, but not unjust. And similarly, that even supposing a case in which a woman pregnant due to rape ought to allow the unborn person to use her body for the hour he needs, we should not conclude that he has a right to do so; we should conclude that she is self-centered, callous, indecent, but not unjust, if she refuses. The complaints are no less grave; they are just different. However, there is no need to insist on this point. If anyone does wish to deduce "he has a right" from "you ought," then all the same he must surely grant that there are cases in which it is not morally required of you that you allow that violinist to use your kidneys, and in which he does not have a right to use them, and in which you do not do him an injustice if you refuse. And so also for mother and unborn child. Except in such cases as the unborn person has a right to demand it—and we were leaving open the possibility that there may be such cases—nobody is morally *required* to make large sacrifices, of health, of all other interests and concerns, of all other duties and commitments, for nine years, or even for nine months, in order to keep another person alive.

6. We have in fact to distinguish between two kinds of Samaritan: the Good Samaritan and what we might call the Minimally Decent Samaritan. The story of the Good Samaritan, you will remember, goes like this:

> A certain man went down from Jerusalem to Jericho, and fell among thieves, which stripped him of his raiment, and wounded him, and departed, leaving him half dead.
>
> And by chance there came down a certain priest that way; and when he saw him, he passed by on the other side.
>
> And likewise a Levite, when he was at the place, came and looked on him, and passed by on the other side.
>
> But a certain Samaritan, as he journeyed, came where he was and when he saw him he had compassion on him.
>
> And went to him, and bound up his wounds, pouring in oil and wine, and set him on his own beast, and brought him to an inn, and took care of him.
>
> And on the morrow, when he departed, he took out two pence, and gave them to the host, and said unto him, "Take care of him: and whatsoever thou spendest more, when I come again, I will repay thee."
>
> (Luke 10:30–35)

The Good Samaritan went out of his way, at some cost to himself, to help one in need of it. We are not told what the options were, that is, whether or not the priest and the Levite could have helped by doing less than the Good Samaritan did, but assuming they could have, then the fact they did nothing at all shows they were not even Minimally Decent Samaritans, not because they were not Samaritans, but because they were not even minimally decent.

These things are a matter of degree, of course, but there is a difference, and it comes out perhaps most clearly in the story of Kitty Genovese, who, as you will remember, was murdered while thirty-eight people watched or listened, and did nothing at all to help her. A Good Samaritan would have rushed out to give direct assistance against the murderer.

Or perhaps we had better allow that it would have been a Splendid Samaritan who did this, on the ground that it would have involved a risk of death for himself. But the thirty-eight not only did not do this, they did not even trouble to pick up a phone to call the police. Minimally Decent Samaritanism would call for doing at least that, and their not having done it was monstrous.

After telling the story of the Good Samaritan, Jesus said "Go, and do thou likewise." Perhaps he meant that we are morally required to act as the Good Samaritan did. Perhaps he was urging people to do more than is morally required of them. At all events it seems plain that it was not morally required of any of the thirty-eight that he rush out to give direct assistance at the risk of his own life, and that it is not morally required of anyone that he give long stretches of his life—nine years or nine months—to sustaining the life of a person who has no special right (we were leaving open the possibility of this) to demand it.

Indeed, with one rather striking class of exceptions, no one in any country in the world is *legally* required to do anywhere near as much as this for anyone else. The class of exceptions is obvious. My main concern here is not the state of the law in respect to abortion, but it is worth drawing attention to the fact that in no state in this country is any man compelled by law to be even a Minimally Decent Samaritan to any person; there is no law under which charges could be brought against the thirty-eight who stood by while Kitty Genovese died. By contrast, in most states in this country women are compelled by law to be not merely Minimally Decent Samaritans, but Good Samaritans to unborn persons inside them. This doesn't by itself settle anything one way or the other, because it may well be argued that there should be laws in this country— as there are in many European countries—compelling at least Minimally Decent Samaritanism.[8] But it does show that there is a gross injustice in the existing state of the law. And it shows also that the groups currently working against liberalization of abortion laws, in fact working toward having it declared unconstitutional for a state to permit abortion, had better start working for the adoption of Good Samaritan laws generally, or earn the charge that they are acting in bad faith.

I should think, myself, that Minimally Decent Samaritan laws would be one thing, Good Samaritan laws quite another, and in fact highly improper. But we are not here concerned with the law. What we should ask is not whether anybody should be compelled by law to be a Good Samaritan, but whether we must accede to a situation in which somebody is being compelled—by nature, perhaps—to be a Good Samaritan. We have, in other words, to look now at third-party interventions. I have been arguing that no person is morally required to make large sacrifices to sustain the life of another who has no right to demand them, and this even where the sacrifices do not include life itself; we are not morally required to be Good Samaritans or anyway Very Good Samaritans to one another. But what if a man cannot extricate himself from such a situa-

---

[8] For a discussion of the difficulties involved, and a survey of the European experience with such laws, see *The Good Samaritan and the Laws*, ed. James M. Ratcliffe (New York, 1966).

tion? What if he appeals to us to extricate him? It seems to me plain that there are cases in which we can, cases in which a Good Samaritan would extricate him. There you are, you were kidnapped, and nine years in bed with that violinist lie ahead of you. You have your own life to lead. You are sorry, but you simply cannot see giving up so much of your life to the sustaining of his. You cannot extricate yourself, and ask us to do so. I should have thought that—in light of his having no right to the use of your body—it was obvious that we do not have to accede to your being forced to give up so much. We can do what you ask. There is no injustice to the violinist in our doing so.

7. Following the lead of the opponents of abortion, I have throughout been speaking of the fetus merely as a person, and what I have been asking is whether or not the argument we began with, which proceeds only from the fetus being a person, really does establish its conclusion. I have argued that it does not.

But of course there are arguments and arguments, and it may be said that I have simply fastened on the wrong one. It may be said that what is important is not merely the fact that the fetus is a person, but that it is a person for whom the woman has a special kind of responsibility issuing from the fact that she is its mother. And it might be argued that all my analogies are therefore irrelevant—for you do not have that special kind of responsibility for that violinist, Henry Fonda does not have that special kind of responsibility for me. And our attention might be drawn to the fact that men and women both *are* compelled by law to provide support for their children.

I have in effect dealt (briefly) with this argument in section 4 above; but a (still briefer) recapitulation now may be in order. Surely we do not have any such "special responsibility" for a person unless we have assumed it, explicitly or implicitly. If a set of parents do not try to prevent pregnancy, do not obtain an abortion, and then at the time of birth of the child do not put it out for adoption, but rather take it home with them, then they have assumed responsibility for it, they have given it rights, and they cannot *now* withdraw support from it at the cost of its life because they now find it difficult to go on providing for it. But if they have taken all reasonable precautions against having a child, they do not simply by virtue of their biological relationship to the child who comes into existence have a special responsibility for it. They may wish to assume responsibility for it, or they may not wish to. And I am suggesting that if assuming responsibility for it would require large sacrifices, then they may refuse. A Good Samaritan would not refuse—or anyway, a Splendid Samaritan, if the sacrifices that had to be made were enormous. But then so would a Good Samaritan assume responsibility for that violinist; so would Henry Fonda, if he is a Good Samaritan, fly in from the West Coast and assume responsibility for me.

8. My argument will be found unsatisfactory on two counts by many of those who want to regard abortion as morally permissible. First, while I do argue that abortion is not impermissible, I do not argue that it is always permissible. There may well be cases in which carrying the child to term requires only Minimally Decent Samaritanism of the mother, and this is a standard we must not fall below. I am inclined to think it a merit

of my account precisely that it does *not* give a general yes or a general no. It allows for and supports our sense that, for example, a sick and desperately frightened fourteen-year-old schoolgirl, pregnant due to rape, may *of course* choose abortion, and that any law which rules this out is an insane law. And it also allows for and supports our sense that in other cases resort to abortion is even positively indecent. It would be indecent in the woman to request an abortion, and indecent in a doctor to perform it, if she is in her seventh month, and wants the abortion just to avoid the nuisance of postponing a trip abroad. The very fact that the arguments I have been drawing attention to treat all cases of abortion, or even all cases of abortion in which the mother's life is not at stake, as morally on a par ought to have made them suspect at the outset.

Secondly, while I am arguing for the permissibility of abortion in some cases, I am not arguing for the right to secure the death of the unborn child. It is easy to confuse these two things in that up to a certain point in the life of the fetus it is not able to survive outside the mother's body; hence removing it from her body guarantees its death. But they are importantly different. I have argued that you are not morally required to spend nine months in bed, sustaining the life of that violinist; but to say this is by no means to say that if, when you unplug yourself, there is a miracle and he survives, you then have a right to turn around and slit his throat. You may detach yourself even if this costs him his life; you have no right to be guaranteed his death by some other means, if unplugging yourself does not kill him. There are some people who will feel dissatisfied by this feature of my argument. A woman may be utterly devastated by the thought of a child, a bit of herself, put out for adoption and never seen or heard of again. She may therefore want not merely that the child be detached from her, but more, that it die. Some opponents of abortion are inclined to regard this as beneath contempt—thereby showing insensitivity to what is surely a powerful source of despair. All the same, I agree that the desire for the child's death is not one which anybody may gratify, should it turn out to be possible to detach the child alive.

At this place, however, it should be remembered that we have only been pretending throughout that the fetus is a human being from the moment of conception. A very early abortion is surely not the killing of a person, and so is not dealt with by anything I have said here.

▼ *The Morality of Abortion**
BARUCH BRODY

In a recent article,[1] Professor Judith Thomson has, in effect, argued that [a simple view of abortion] is mistaken. How does Professor Thomson

---

* From Baruch Brody, *Abortion and the Sanctity of Human Life: A Philosophical View* (Cambridge, Mass.: MIT Press, 1975), pp. 27–30.

[1] J. Thomson, "A Defense of Abortion," *Philosophy and Public Affairs*, Vol. 1 (1971), pp. 47–66. [This is the same article, of course, just reprinted in these pages. Brody's page references will be to the journal in which it first appeared.]

defend her claim that the mother has a right to abort the fetus, even if it is a human being, whether or not her life is threatened and whether or not she has consented to the act of intercourse in which the fetus is conceived? At one point,[2] discussing just the case in which the mother's life is threatened, she makes the following suggestion:

> In [abortion], there are only two people involved, one whose life is threatened and one who threatens it. Both are innocent: the one who is threatened is not threatened because of any fault, the one who threatens does not threaten because of any fault. For this reason, we may feel that we bystanders cannot intervene. But the person threatened can.

But surely this description is equally applicable to the following case: A and B are adrift on a lifeboat, B has a disease that he can survive, but A, if he contracts it, will die, and the only way that A can avoid that is by killing B and pushing him overboard. Surely, A has no right to do this. So there must be some special reason why the mother has, if she does, the right to abort the fetus.

There is, to be sure, an important difference between our lifeboat case and abortion, one that leads us to the heart of Professor Thomson's argument. In the case that we envisaged, both A and B have equal rights to be in the lifeboat, but the mother's body is hers and not the fetus's, and she has first rights to its use. The primacy of these rights allow an abortion whether or not her life is threatened. Professor Thomson summarizes this argument in the following way:[3]

> I am arguing only that having a right to life does not guarantee having either a right to be given the use of, or a right to be allowed continued use of, another person's body—even if one needs it for life itself.

One part of this claim is clearly correct. I have no duty to X to save X's life by giving him the use of my body (or my life savings, or the only home I have, and so on), and X has no right, even to save his life, to any of those things. Thus, the fetus conceived in the laboratory that will perish unless it is implanted into a woman's body has in fact no right to any woman's body. But this portion of the claim is irrelevant to the abortion issue, for in abortion of the fetus that is a human being the mother must kill X to get back the sole use of her body, and that is an entirely different matter.

This point can also be put as follows: . . . we must distinguish the taking of X's life from the saving of X's life, even if we assume that one has a duty not to do the former and to do the latter. Now that latter duty, if it exists at all, is much weaker than the first duty; many circumstances may relieve us from the latter duty that will not relieve us from the former one. Thus, I am certainly relieved from my duty to save X's life by the fact that fulfilling it means the loss of my life savings. It may be noble for me to save X's life at the cost of everything I have, but I certainly have no duty to do that. And the same observation may be made about cases in which I can save X's life by giving him the use of

[2] Ibid., p. 53.
[3] Ibid., p. 56.

my body for an extended period of time. However, I am not relieved of my duty not to take *X*'s life by the fact that fulfilling it means the loss of everything I have and not even by the fact that fulfilling it means the loss of my life. . . . Something more is required before rights like self-defense become applicable. A fortiori, it would seem that I am not relieved of the duty not to take life by the fact that its fulfillment means that some other person, who is innocently occupying my body, continues to do so.

At one point in her paper,[4] Professor Thomson does consider this objection. She has previously imagined the following case: a famous violinist, who is dying from a kidney ailment, has been, without your consent, plugged into you for a period of time so that his body can use your kidneys:

> Some people are rather stricter about the right to life. In their view, it does not include the right to be given anything, but amounts to, and only to, the right not to be killed by anybody. But here a related difficulty arises. If everybody is to refrain from killing that violinist, then everybody must refrain from doing a great many different sorts of things . . . everybody must refrain from unplugging you from him. But does he have a right against everybody that they shall refrain from unplugging you from him? To refrain from doing this is to allow him to continue to use your kidneys . . . certainly the violinist has no right against you that you shall allow him to continue to use your kidneys.

Applying this argument to the case of abortion, we can see that Professor Thomson's argument would run as follows:

a. Assume that the fetus's right to life includes the right not to be killed by the woman carrying him.

b. But to refrain from killing the fetus is to allow him the continued use of the woman's body.

c. So our first assumption entails that the fetus's right to life includes the right to the continued use of the woman's body.

d. But we all grant that the fetus does not have the right to the continued use of the woman's body.

e. Therefore, the fetus's right to life cannot include the right not to be killed by the woman in question.

And it is also now clear what is wrong with this argument. When we granted that the fetus has no right to the continued use of the woman's body, all that we meant was that he does not have this right merely because the continued use saves his life. But, of course, there may be

---

[4] Ibid., pp. 55–56. It was, therefore, wrong of me to say, as I did in my article, "Thomson on Abortion," *Philosophy and Public Affairs*, Vol. 1 (1972), pp. 335–340, that "she has not attended to the distinction between our duty to save *X*'s life and our duty not to take it." My argument is rather that she has not sufficiently attended to it, to the point that she could discover that, for example, her whole discussion of Henry Fonda's flying in from the West Coast to save my life is, of course, entirely irrelevant.

other reasons why he has this right. One would be that the only way to take the use of the woman's body away from the fetus is by killing him, and that is something that neither she nor we have the right to do. So, I submit, the way in which Assumption d is true is irrelevant, and cannot be used by Professor Thomson, for Assumption d is true only in cases where the saving of the life of the fetus is at stake and not in cases where the taking of his life is at stake.

I conclude therefore that Professor Thomson has not established the truth of her claims about abortion, primarily because she has not sufficiently attended to the distinction between our duty to save X's life and our duty not to take it. Once one attends to that distinction, it would seem that the mother, in order to regain control over her body, has no right to abort the fetus from the point at which it becomes a human being.

▼ ## *Abortion and the Conscience of the Nation**
RONALD REAGAN

The 10th anniversary of the Supreme Court decision in *Roe v. Wade* is a good time for us to pause and reflect. Our nationwide policy of abortion-on-demand through all nine months of pregnancy was neither voted for by our people nor enacted by our legislators—not a single State had such unrestricted abortion before the Supreme Court decreed it to be national policy in 1973. But the consequences of this judicial decision are now obvious: since 1973, more than 15 million unborn children have had their lives snuffed out by legalized abortions. That is over ten times the number of Americans lost in all our nation's wars.

Make no mistake, abortion-on-demand is not a right granted by the Constitution. No serious scholar, including one disposed to agree with the Court's result, has argued that the framers of the Constitution intended to create such a right. Shortly after the *Roe v. Wade* decision, Professor John Hart Ely, now Dean of Stanford Law School, wrote that the opinion "is not constitutional law and gives almost no sense of an obligation to try to be." Nowhere do the plain words of the Constitution even hint at a "right" so sweeping as to permit abortion up to the time the child is ready to be born. Yet that is what the Court ruled.

As an act of "raw judicial power" (to use Justice White's biting phrase), the decision by the seven-man majority in *Roe v. Wade* has so far been made to stick. But the Court's decision has by no means settled the debate. Instead, *Roe v. Wade* has become a continuing prod to the conscience of the nation.

Abortion concerns not just the unborn child, it concerns every one of us. The English poet, John Donne, wrote: ". . . any man's death diminishes me, because I am involved in mankind; and therefore never send to know for whom the bell tolls; it tolls for thee."

---

* President Reagan published this essay in 1983.

We cannot diminish the value of one category of human life—the un-born—without diminishing the value of all human life. We saw tragic proof of this truism last year when the Indiana courts allowed the starvation death of "Baby Doe" in Bloomington because the child had Down's Syndrome.

Many of our fellow citizens grieve over the loss of life that has followed *Roe v. Wade*. Margaret Heckler, soon after being nominated to head the largest department of our government, Health and Human Services, told an audience that she believed abortion to be the greatest moral crisis facing our country today. And the revered Mother Teresa, who works in the streets of Calcutta ministering to dying people in her world-famous mission of mercy, has said that "the greatest misery of our time is the generalized abortion of children."

Over the first two years of my Administration I have closely followed and assisted efforts in Congress to reverse the tide of abortion—efforts of Congressmen, Senators and citizens responding to an urgent moral crisis. Regrettably, I have also seen the massive efforts of those who, under the banner of "freedom of choice," have so far blocked every effort to reverse nationwide abortion-on-demand.

Despite the formidable obstacles before us, we must not lose heart. This is not the first time our country has been divided by a Supreme Court decision that denied the value of certain human lives. The *Dred Scott* decision of 1857 was not overturned in a day, or a year, or even a decade. At first, only a minority of Americans recognized and deplored the moral crisis brought about by denying the full humanity of our black brothers and sisters; but that minority persisted in their vision and finally prevailed. They did it by appealing to the hearts and minds of their countrymen, to the truth of human dignity under God. From their example, we know that respect for the sacred value of human life is too deeply engrained in the hearts of our people to remain forever suppressed. But the great majority of the American people have not yet made their voices heard, and we cannot expect them—any more than the public voice arose against slavery—*until* the issue is clearly framed and presented.

What, then, is the real issue? I have often said that when we talk about abortion, we are talking about two lives—the life of the mother and the life of the unborn child. Why else do we call a pregnant woman a mother? I have also said that anyone who doesn't feel sure whether we are talking about a second human life should clearly give life the benefit of the doubt. If you don't know whether a body is alive or dead, you would never bury it. I think this consideration itself should be enough for all of us to insist on protecting the unborn.

The case against abortion does not rest here, however, for medical practice confirms at every step the correctness of these moral sensibilities. Modern medicine treats the unborn child as a patient. Medical pioneers have made great breakthroughs in treating the unborn—for genetic problems, vitamin deficiencies, irregular heart rhythms, and other medical conditions. Who can forget George Will's moving account of the little boy who underwent brain surgery six times during the nine weeks before he was born? Who is the *patient* if not that tiny unborn human being who can feel pain when he or she is approached by doctors who come to kill rather than to cure?

The real question today is not when human life begins, but, *What is the value of human life?* The abortionist who reassembles the arms and legs of a tiny baby to make sure all its parts have been torn from its mother's body can hardly doubt whether it is a human being. The real question for him and for all of us is whether that tiny human life has a God-given right to be protected by the law—the same right we have.

What more dramatic confirmation could we have of the real issue than the Baby Doe case in Bloomington, Indiana? The death of that tiny infant tore at the hearts of all Americans because the child was undeniably a live human being—one lying helpless before the eyes of the doctors and the eyes of the nation. The real issue for the courts was *not* whether Baby Doe was a human being. The real issue was whether to protect the life of a human being who had Down's Syndrome, who would probably be mentally handicapped, but who needed a routine surgical procedure to unblock his esophagus and allow him to eat. A doctor testified to the presiding judge that, even with his physical problem corrected, Baby Doe would have a "non-existent" possibility for "a minimally adequate quality of life"—in other words, that retardation was the equivalent of a crime deserving the death penalty. The judge let Baby Doe starve and die, and the Indiana Supreme Court sanctioned his decision.

Federal law does not allow Federally-assisted hospitals to decide that Down's Syndrome infants are not worth treating, much less to decide to starve them to death. Accordingly, I have directed the Departments of Justice and HHS to apply civil rights regulations to protect handicapped newborns. All hospitals receiving Federal funds must post notices which will clearly state that failure to feed handicapped babies is prohibited by Federal Law. The basic issue is whether to value and protect the lives of the handicapped, whether to recognize the sanctity of human life. This is the same basic issue that underlies the question of abortion.

The 1981 Senate hearings on the beginning of human life brought out the basic issue more clearly than ever before. The many medical and scientific witnesses who testified disagreed on many things, but not on the *scientific* evidence that the unborn child is alive, is a distinct individual, or is a member of the human species. They did disagree over the *value* question, whether to give value to a human life at its early and most vulnerable stages of existence.

Regrettably, we live at a time when some persons do *not* value all human life. They want to pick and choose which individuals have value. Some have said that only those individuals with "consciousness of self" are human beings. One such writer has followed this deadly logic and concluded that "shocking as it may seem, a newly born infant is not a human being."

A Nobel Prize winning scientist has suggested that if a handicapped child "were not declared fully human until three days after birth, then all parents could be allowed the choice." In other words, "quality control" to see if newly born human beings are up to snuff.

Obviously, some influential people want to deny that every human life has intrinsic, sacred worth. They insist that a member of the human race must have certain qualities before they accord him or her status as a "human being."

Events have borne out the editorial in a California medical journal which explained three years before *Roe v. Wade* that the social acceptance of abortion is a "defiance of the long-held Western ethic of intrinsic and equal value for every human life regardless of its stage, condition, or status."

Every legislator, every doctor, and every citizen needs to recognize that the real issue is whether to affirm and protect the sanctity of all human life, or to embrace a social ethic where some human lives are valued and others are not. As a nation, we must choose between the sanctity of life ethic and the quality of life ethic.

I have no trouble identifying the answer our nation has always given to this basic question, and the answer that I hope and pray it will give in the future. America was founded by men and women who shared a vision of the value of each and every individual. They stated this vision clearly from the very start in the Declaration of Independence, using words that every schoolboy and schoolgirl can recite:

> We hold these truths to be self-evident, that all men are created equal,
> that they are endowed by their Creator with certain inalienable rights, that
> among these are life, liberty, and the pursuit of happiness.

We fought a terrible war to guarantee that one category of mankind—black people in America—could not be denied the inalienable rights with which their Creator endowed them. The great champion of the sanctity of all human life in that day, Abraham Lincoln, gave us his assessment of the Declaration's purpose. Speaking of the framers of that noble document, he said:

> This was their majestic interpretation of the economy of the Universe. This
> was their lofty, and wise, and noble understanding of the justice of the
> Creator to His creatures. Yes, gentlemen, to all His creatures, to the whole
> great family of man. In their enlightened belief, nothing stamped with the
> divine image and likeness was sent into the world to be trodden on . . .
> They grasped not only the whole race of man then living, but they
> reached forward and seized upon the farthest posterity. They erected a
> beacon to guide their children and their children's children, and the
> countless myriads who should inhabit the earth in other ages.

He warned also of the danger we would face if we closed our eyes to the value of life in any category of human beings:

> I should like to know if taking this old Declaration of Independence,
> which declares that all men are equal upon principle and making excep-
> tions to it where will it stop. If one man says it does not mean a Negro,
> why not another say it does not mean some other man?

When Congressman John A. Bingham of Ohio drafted the Fourteenth Amendment to guarantee the rights of life, liberty, and property to all human beings, he explained that *all* are "entitled to the protection of

American law, because its divine spirit of equality declares that all men are created equal." He said the rights guaranteed by the amendment would therefore apply to "any human being." Justice William Brennan, writing in another case decided only the year before *Roe v. Wade*, referred to our society as one that "strongly affirms the sanctity of life."

Another William Brennan—not the Justice—has reminded us of the terrible consequences that can follow when a nation rejects the sanctity of life ethic:

> The cultural environment for a human holocaust is present whenever any society can be misled into defining individuals as less than human and therefore devoid of value and respect.

As a nation today, we have *not* rejected the sanctity of human life. The American people have not had an opportunity to express their view on the sanctity of human life in the unborn. I am convinced that Americans do not want to play God with the value of human life. It is not for us to decide who is worthy to live and who is not. Even the Supreme Court's opinion in *Roe v. Wade* did not explicitly reject the traditional American idea of intrinsic worth and value in all human life; it simply dodged this issue.

The Congress has before it several measures that would enable our people to reaffirm the sanctity of human life, even the smallest and the youngest and the most defenseless. The Human Life Bill expressly recognizes the unborn as human beings and accordingly protects them as persons under our Constitution. This bill, first introduced by Senator Jesse Helms, provided the vehicle for the Senate hearings in 1981 which contributed so much to our understanding of the real issue of abortion.

The Respect Human Life Act, just introduced in the 98th Congress, states in its first section that the policy of the United States is "to protect innocent life, both before and after birth." This bill, sponsored by Congressman Henry Hyde and Senator Roger Jepsen, prohibits the Federal government from performing abortions or assisting those who do so, except to save the life of the mother. It also addresses the pressing issue of infanticide which, as we have seen, flows inevitably from permissive abortion as another step in the denial of the inviolability of innocent human life.

I have endorsed each of these measures, as well as the more difficult route of constitutional amendment, and I will give these initiatives my full support. Each of them, in different ways, attempts to reverse the tragic policy of abortion-on-demand imposed by the Supreme Court ten years ago. Each of them is a decisive way to affirm the sanctity of human life.

We must all educate ourselves to the reality of the horrors taking place. Doctors today know that unborn children can feel a touch within the womb and that they respond to pain. But how many Americans are aware that abortion techniques are allowed today, in all 50 states, that burn the skin of a baby with a salt solution, in an agonizing death that can last for hours?

Another example: two years ago, the *Philadelphia Inquirer* ran a Sunday special supplement on "The Dreaded Complication." The "dreaded complication" referred to in the article—the complication feared by doctors who perform abortions—is the *survival* of the child despite all the painful attacks during the abortion procedure. Some unborn children *do survive the late-term abortions* the Supreme Court has made legal. Is there any question that these victims of abortion deserve our attention and protection? Is there any question that those who *don't* survive were living human beings before they were killed?

Late-term abortions, especially when the baby survives, but is then killed by starvation, neglect, or suffocation, show once again the link between abortion and infanticide. The time to stop both is now. As my Administration acts to stop infanticide, we will be fully aware of the real issue that underlies the death of babies before and soon after birth.

Our society has, fortunately, become sensitive to the rights and special needs of the handicapped, but I am shocked that physical or mental handicaps of newborns are still used to justify their extinction. This Administration has a Surgeon General, Dr. C. Everett Koop, who has done perhaps more than any other American for handicapped children, by pioneering surgical techniques to help them, by speaking out on the value of their lives, and by working with them in the context of loving families. You will not find his former patients advocating the so-called quality of life ethic.

I know that when the true issue of infanticide is placed before the American people, with all the facts openly aired, we will have no trouble deciding that a mentally or physically handicapped baby has the same intrinsic worth and right to life as the rest of us. As the New Jersey Supreme Court said two decades ago, in a decision upholding the sanctity of human life, "a child need not be perfect to have a worthwhile life."

Whether we are talking about pain suffered by unborn children, or about late-term abortions, or about infanticide, we inevitably focus on the humanity of the unborn child. Each of these issues is a potential rallying point for the sanctity of life ethic. Once we as a nation rally around any one of these issues to affirm the sanctity of life, we will see the importance of affirming this principle across the board.

Malcolm Muggeridge, the English writer, goes right to the heart of the matter: "Either life is always and in all circumstances sacred, or intrinsically of no account; it is inconceivable that it should be in some cases the one, and in some the other." The sanctity of innocent human life is a principle that Congress should proclaim at every opportunity.

It is possible that the Supreme Court itself may overturn its abortion rulings. We need only recall that in *Brown v. Board of Education* the Court reversed its own earlier "separate-but-equal" decision. I believe if the Supreme Court took another look at *Roe v. Wade*, and considered the real issue between the sanctity of life ethic and the quality of life ethic, it would change its mind once again.

As we continue to work to overturn *Roe v. Wade*, we must also continue to lay the groundwork for a society in which abortion is not the accepted answer to unwanted pregnancy. Pro-life people have already taken heroic steps, often at great personal sacrifice, to provide for unwed mothers. I recently spoke about a young pregnant woman named Victoria, who said, "In this society we save whales, we save timber wolves and bald eagles and Coke bottles. Yet, everyone wanted me to throw away my baby." She has been helped by Sav-a-Life, a group in Dallas, which provides a way for unwed mothers to preserve the human life within them when they might otherwise be tempted to resort to abortion. I think also of House of His Creation in Coatesville, Pennsylvania, where a loving couple has taken in almost 200 young women in the past ten years. They have seen, as a fact of life, that the girls are *not* better off having abortions than saving their babies. I am also reminded of the remarkable Rossow family of Ellington, Connecticut, who have opened their hearts and their home to nine handicapped adopted and foster children.

The Adolescent Family Life Program, adopted by Congress at the request of Senator Jeremiah Denton, has opened new opportunities for unwed mothers to give their children life. We should not rest until our entire society echoes the tone of John Powell in the dedication of his book, *Abortion: The Silent Holocaust,* a dedication to every woman carrying an unwanted child: "Please believe that you are not alone. There are many of us that truly love you, who want to stand at your side, and help in any way we can." And we can echo the always-practical woman of faith, Mother Teresa, when she says, "If you don't want the little child, that unborn child, give him to me." We have so many families in America seeking to adopt children that the slogan "every child a wanted child" is now the emptiest of all reasons to tolerate abortion.

I have often said we need to join in prayer to bring protection to the unborn. Prayer and action are needed to uphold the sanctity of human life. I believe it will not be possible to accomplish our work, the work of saving lives, "without being a soul of prayer." The famous British Member of Parliament, William Wilberforce, prayed with his small group of influential friends, the "Clapham Sect," for *decades* to see an end to slavery in the British empire. Wilberforce led that struggle in Parliament, unflaggingly, because he believed in the sanctity of human life. He saw the fulfillment of his impossible dream when Parliament outlawed slavery just before his death.

Let his faith and perseverance be our guide. We will never recognize the true value of our own lives until we affirm the value in the life of others, a value of which Malcolm Muggeridge says: ". . . however low it flickers or fiercely burns, it is still a Divine flame which no man dare presume to put out, be his motives ever so humane and enlightened."

Abraham Lincoln recognized that we could not survive as a free land when some men could decide that others were not fit to be free and should therefore be slaves. Likewise, we cannot survive as a free nation when some men decide that others are not fit to live and should be abandoned to abortion or infanticide. My Administration is dedicated to the preservation of America as a free land, and there is no cause more important for preserving that freedom than affirming the transcendent right to life of all human beings, the right without which no other rights have any meaning.

Is Abortion Really a "Moral Dilemma"?*
BARBARA EHRENREICH

Quite apart from blowing up clinics and terrorizing patients, the anti-abortion movement can take credit for a more subtle and lasting kind of damage: It has succeeded in getting even pro-choice people to think of abortion as a "moral dilemma," an "agonizing decision" and related code phrases for something murky and compromising, like the traffic in infant formula mix. In liberal circles, it has become unstylish to discuss abortion without using words like "complex," "painful" and the rest of the mealy-mouthed vocabulary of evasion. Regrets are also fashionable, and one otherwise feminist author writes recently of mourning, each year following her abortion, the putative birthday of her discarded fetus.

I cannot speak for other women, of course, but the one regret I have about my own abortions is that they cost money that might otherwise have been spent on something more pleasurable, like taking the kids to movies and theme parks. Yes, that is abortions, plural (two in my case)—a possibility that is not confined to the promiscuous, the disorderly or the ignorant. In fact, my credentials for dealing with the technology of contraception are first rate: I have a Ph.D. in biology that is now a bit obsolescent but still good for conjuring up vivid mental pictures of zygotes and ova, and I was actually paid, at one point in my life, to teach other women about the mysteries of reproductive biology.

●　　　●　　　●

Yet, as every party to the abortion debate should know, those methods of contraception that are truly safe are not absolutely reliable no matter how reliably they are used. Many women, like myself, have felt free to choose the safest methods because legal abortion is available as a backup to contraception. Anyone who finds that a thoughtless, immoral choice should speak to the orphans of women whose wombs were perforated by Dalkon shields or whose strokes were brought on by high-estrogen birth-control pills.

I refer you to the orphans only because it no longer seems to be good form to mention women themselves in discussions of abortion. In most of the antiabortion literature I have seen, women are so invisible that an uninformed reader might conclude that fetuses reside in artificially warm tissue culture flasks or similar containers. It must be enormously difficult for the antiabortionist to face up to the fact that real fetuses can only

---

* This essay appeared in the "Hers" column of *The New York Times*, February 7, 1984.

survive inside women, who, unlike any kind of laboratory apparatus, have thoughts, feelings, aspirations, responsibilities and, very often, checkbooks. Anyone who thinks for a moment about women's role in reproductive biology could never blithely recommend "adoption, not abortion," because women have to go through something unknown to fetuses or men, and that is pregnancy.

From the point of view of a fetus, pregnancy is no doubt a good deal. But consider it for a moment from the point of view of the pregnant person (if "woman" is too incendiary and feminist a term) and without reference to its potential issue. We are talking about a nine-month bout of symptoms of varying severity, often including nausea, skin discolorations, extreme bloating and swelling, insomnia, narcolepsy, hair loss, varicose veins, hemorrhoids, indigestion and irreversible weight gain, and culminating in a physiological crisis which is occasionally fatal and almost always excruciatingly painful. If men were equally at risk for this condition—if they knew that their bellies might swell as if they were suffering from end-stage cirrhosis, that they would have to go for nearly a year without a stiff drink, a cigarette or even an aspirin, that they would be subject to fainting spells and unable to fight their way onto commuter trains—then I am sure that pregnancy would be classified as a sexually transmitted disease and abortions would be no more controversial than emergency appendectomies.

Adding babies to the picture does not make it all that much prettier, even if you are, as I am, a fool for short, dimpled people with drool on their chins. For no matter how charming the outcome of pregnancy that is allowed to go to term no one is likely to come forth and offer to finance its Pampers or pay its college tuition. Nor are the opponents of abortion promising a guaranteed annual income, subsidized housing, national health insurance and other measures that might take some of the terror out of parenthood. We all seem to expect the individual parents to shoulder the entire burden of supporting any offspring that can be traced to them, and, in the all-too-common event that the father cannot be identified or has skipped town to avoid child-support payments, "parent" means mother.

When society does step in to help out a poor woman attempting to raise children on her own, all that it customarily has to offer is some government-surplus cheese, a monthly allowance so small it would barely keep a yuppie male in running shoes, and the contemptuous epithet "welfare cheat." It would be far more reasonable to honor the survivors of pregnancy in childbirth with at least the same respect and special benefits that we give, without a second thought, to veterans of foreign wars.

But, you will object, I have greatly exaggerated the discomforts of pregnancy and the hazards of childbearing, which many women undergo quite cheerfully. This is true, at least to an extent. In my own case, the case of my planned and wanted pregnancies, I managed to interpret morning sickness as a sign of fetus tenacity and to find, in the hypertrophy of my belly, a voluptuousness ordinarily unknown to the skinny. But this only proves my point: A society that is able to make a good thing out of pregnancy is certainly free to choose how to regard abortion. We can treat it as a necessary adjunct to contraception, or as a vexing moral dilemma, or as a form of homicide—and whichever we choose, this is how we will tend to experience it.

•   •   •

So I will admit that I might not have been so calm and determined about my abortions if I had had to cross a picket line of earnest people yelling "baby killer," or if I felt that I might be blown to bits in the middle of a vacuum aspiration. Conversely, though, we would be hearing a lot less about ambivalence and regrets if there were not so much liberal head-scratching going on. Abortions will surely continue, as they have through human history, whether we approve or disapprove or hem and haw. The question that worries me is: How is, say, a 16-year-old girl going to feel after an abortion? Like a convicted sex offender, a murderess on parole? Or like a young woman who is capable, as the guidance counselors say, of taking charge of her life?

This is our choice, for biology will never have an answer to that strange and cabalistic question of when a fetus becomes a person. Potential persons are lost every day as a result of miscarriage, contraception or someone's simple failure to respond to a friendly wink. What we can answer, with a minimum of throat-clearing and moral agonizing, is the question of when women themselves will finally achieve full personhood: And that is when we have the right, unquestioned and unabrogated, to *choose* not to be pregnant when we decide not to be pregnant.

▼ DISCUSSION QUESTIONS

1. Exactly what is Thomson trying to show with her examples of the burglar and the people-seeds? Reconstruct and evaluate these arguments from analogy. Remember to say which similarities and differences are important, and why.

2. Brody compares abortion in self-defense to killing someone on a lifeboat. Reconstruct and evaluate his argument from analogy. If you find important differences between this case and abortion, remember to ask whether this case can be modified so as to make it more analogous to abortion.

3. Reagan gives many arguments to show that fetuses should be treated as persons, including these:
   (a) "We cannot diminish the value of one category of human life—the unborn—without diminishing the value of all human life" (352).
   (b) "I have also said that anyone who doesn't feel sure whether we are talking about a second human life should surely give life the benefit of the doubt" (352).
   (c) "Modern medicine treats the unborn child as a patient" (352).

(d) "I am convinced that Americans do not want to play God with the value of human life" (355).

(e) "Likewise, we cannot survive as a free nation when some men decide that others are not fit to live and should be abandoned to abortion and infanticide" (357).

Reconstruct and evaluate the arguments which use these claims.

4. Determine whether you think abortion is morally wrong in the following cases:

(a) where the mother is in danger of dying if she does not have an abortion,

(b) where the pregnancy is due to rape,

(c) where contraception was used, but it failed,

(d) where the fetus has a disease which usually causes death within a year or two,

(e) where the fetus has a disease which usually causes severe mental retardation,

(f) where the pregnant woman is mentally or physically unable to be a good mother,

(g) where the mother will suffer severe personal losses if the pregnancy continues.

Now try to formulate principles and analogies to justify your positions in these controversial cases.

5. What underlying principles, if any, could protect human lives with only a few exceptions, yet allow us to take lives of:

(a) contract killers sentenced to capital punishment?

(b) humans who are in irreversible comas?

(c) ourselves in suicide?

(d) animals for food, clothing, and entertainment?

6. Describe a moral problem that you have faced in your personal life, and apply the methods of moral reasoning that you have learned in this chapter.

13

Scientific Reasoning

The products of science are all around us. We depend on science when we drive cars, listen to compact discs, and burn food in a microwave. Still, few people understand how science operates. To some, the scientific enterprise seems to consist of nothing more than amassing huge quantities of data to prove or disprove some hypothesis. Of course, careful observation and experimental data are the final court of appeal in much scientific research, but there is more to science than just collecting and organizing data. One way to see this is to look closely at the ways scientists talk. When scientists praise each other's work, they sometimes say that the analysis of some phenomenon is profound and far-reaching, or even elegant, beautiful, and tasteful. This kind of praise would be out of place if the point of science were simply to amass data and test hypotheses. Such praise is appropriate because one important point of scientific theory is to make sense out of nature, to explain it, to make it more intelligible. To choose among conflicting scientific theories, we have to decide which theory makes the most sense and provides the best explanations. It is in its explanatory power that a scientific theory can be elegant, beautiful, or even tasteful.

STANDARD SCIENCE

The beginning of science still lies in observation. When we look at the world around us, we see that many things happen. Apples fall off of trees, the leaves of some trees change color in the autumn, the tides come in and go out, chickens lay eggs, and so on. One job of scientists is to describe and classify what happens and what exists. But scientists also wonder *why* some things happen rather than others. Maple trees change color in the fall, and spruce trees do not, but why? Chickens lay eggs, and monkeys do not, but why? A sphere of wood floats in water, and a gold sphere does not, but why? And why does gold float when pressed into the shape of a boat? These questions ask for *explanations*.

To provide an explanation, scientists often give arguments of the kind discussed in Chapter 6. The event to be explained is derived from a general principle plus a statement of initial conditions or particular facts. For example, given the general principle that a sphere floats in water if and only if it is less dense than water, and also given the particular facts that wood is less dense than water, whereas gold is more dense than water, we can explain why a wooden sphere floats in water and a gold sphere does not.

Scientists often seek *deeper* explanations by asking why certain general principles themselves are true. The principle that a sphere floats in water only when it is less dense than water can be explained as an instance of the more general principle that *anything* floats only when it displaces more than its own weight in water. This broader principle not only explains why a wooden sphere floats in water but also why a piece of gold will float when molded into the form of a boat. This broader principle is in turn explained by deriving it from even more basic principles about gravity and the mutual repulsion of molecules. A larger scientific theory is thus used to explain not only why particular things happen but also why certain general principles hold.

Of course, scientists often put forward conflicting theories, so we need some way to test which theory is correct. One simple method is to use the theory to make *predictions*. Since an explanation depends on principles that are general, these principles have implications beyond the particular phenomenon that they were orginally intended to explain. The theory thus predicts what will happen in circumstances that the scientist has not yet observed. We can then test the theory by seeing whether these predictions hold true. For example, we can make spheres out of a wide variety of materials, calculate their densities, then see which ones float. If any sphere floats which is denser than water, then we have to give up our principle that a sphere floats in water *only if* it is less dense than water. (This is an application of the necessary condition test discussed in Chapter 9.) If we find a sphere that is less dense than water but does not float, then we have to give up the principle that a sphere floats *if* it is less dense than water. (This is an application of the sufficient condition test discussed in Chapter 9.) These methods help us to rule out certain scientific principles, but the fact that a principle implies true predictions does not, by itself, prove that the principle is true. That argument would commit something like the fallacy of affirming the consequent. (*See* Chapter 7.) Nonetheless, we can still say that a theory is *confirmed* if it yields true predictions, and it is confirmed more strongly if it yields more, more varied, and more unexpected true predictions.

Scientific method is actually much more complex than this simple example suggests. This becomes apparent when we encounter *anomalies*. Suppose we have confirmed and explained the principle that a sphere floats in water if and only if it is less dense than water. Suppose also that another principle is well confirmed: a substance gets smaller and more dense as it gets colder. Taken together, these principles predict that a sphere of ice should sink in water. Ice is colder than water, so, according to the second principle, ice should be more dense than water, and that, given the first principle, means that it should not float in water. Of course, our prediction is wrong, since spheres of ice do float in water. What do we do now? The obvious solution is to modify the principle that a substance gets smaller and more dense as it gets colder. This holds for most substances, but not for water. Water expands and thus gets less dense as it freezes.

We could have tried another solution. We could have denied the other principle: that a sphere floats in water if and only if it is less dense than water. Why don't scientists go this way? One reason is that we have independent evidence that water expands when it freezes. That is why jars of water burst when they are left in a freezer. Another reason is that we could not give up this principle alone, since it follows from more basic principles about gravity and the mutual repulsion of molecules. Thus, many other areas of science would be affected if we gave up the principle that a sphere floats in water if and only if it is less dense than water. The fact that all of these other scientific theories are not only well confirmed but useful is what makes scientists give up one principle rather than another when an anomaly arises.

At this point we might seek an even deeper explanation and ask why water expands when it freezes. In fact, to this day, nobody seems to have a fully adequate explanation of this phenomenon. There are various theories but no agreement about how to explain the expansion of water. Does this show that certain phenomena are beyond scientific understanding? Probably not. But it does suggest that science may never be complete. More questions arise as science progresses, and there may always be questions that remain unanswered. As scientists discover and explain more and more phenomena and see connections among principles in different areas, every new step gives rise to more questions that need to be answered. That is one way that science makes progress.

CONFLICTING SCIENTIFIC INTERPRETATIONS

Another type of scientific development is more radical—knowledge is not simply extended, but, instead, one scientific framework is replaced (or largely replaced) by another. In biology, the Germ Theory of Disease and the Theory of Evolution through Natural Selection are examples of such revolutionary developments. Einstein's Theory of Relativity and the rise of Quantum Mechanics are also revolutionary developments. Indeed, every branch of science has undergone at least one such revolutionary change during the past few centuries.

There are some important differences between scientific progress within a framework and the replacement of one framework by another.[1] In the first place, such changes in framework usually meet with strong resistance. A new conceptual framework will be unfamiliar and hard to understand, and may even seem absurd or unintelligible. Even today, for example, the thought that the earth is spinning on its axis and revolving around the sun seems completely counter to our commonsense view of the world. Also, arguments on behalf of a new framework will be very different from arguments that occur *within* a framework. Disputes over conceptual frameworks cannot be settled by a straightforward appeal to facts. The long debate between Albert Einstein and Niels Bohr concerning Quantum Theory did not turn upon matters of fact, but upon their interpretation. Einstein could not accept the indeterminacy involved in the Quantum Theory's interpretation of the world, and he worked until the end of his life to find some alternative to it. At present, almost no scientist shares Einstein's reservations.

The selection given below illustrates a clash between two such scientific frameworks. It is taken from Galileo's *Dialogue Concerning the Two World Systems—Ptolemaic and Copernican*. The interlocutors are Salviati, Sagredo, and Simplicio. Salviati represents the Copernican system; Simplicio, the Ptolemaic system; Sagredo acts as a moderator, forcing the other two participants in the dialogue to clarify and defend their positions. In attacking the Copernican system, Simplicio lists various arguments from Aristotle that are supposed to show that the earth does not move. Some of these arguments are taken, he says,

---

[1] Thomas Kuhn gives prominence to this difference in his important work, *The Structure of Scientific Revolutions*, 2nd ed. (Chicago: University of Chicago Press, 1970).

from experiments with heavy bodies which, falling from a height, go perpendicularly to the surface of the earth. Similarly, projectiles thrown vertically upward come down again perpendicularly by the same line, even though they have been thrown to immense height. These arguments are necessary proofs that their motion is toward the center of the earth, which, without moving in the least, awaits and receives them.[2]

Salviati replies that these phenomena do not show that the Ptolemaic system is correct and the Copernican system incorrect, since they can be explained in either world system. More generally, Salviati argues that no terrestrial phenomenon—that is, no phenomenon observable on the earth—can be cited to show that one of these systems is true and the other false. For that matter, no celestial phenomena will settle this issue either, since both world systems provide interpretations of the motions of heavenly bodies. That proponents of each of these systems can agree on particular facts yet disagree profoundly on their correct interpretation shows that we are dealing with a conflict between general frameworks, or general world systems. Arguments of this kind are very different from those that take place within a given scientific framework.

▼ *Dialogue Concerning the Two World Systems— Ptolemaic and Copernican* *

GALILEO GALILEI

SALVIATI: Aristotle says, then, that a most certain proof of the earth's being motionless is that things projected perpendicularly upward are seen to return by the same line to the same place from which they were thrown, even though the movement is extremely high. This, he argues, could not happen if the earth moved, since in the time during which the projectile is moving upward and then downward it is separated from the earth, and the place from which the projectile began its motion would go a long way toward the east, thanks to the revolving of the earth, and the falling projectile would strike the earth that distance away from the place in question. Thus we can accommodate here the argument of the cannon ball as well as the other argument, used by Aristotle and Ptolemy, of seeing heavy bodies falling from great heights along a straight line perpendicular to the surface of the earth. Now, in order to begin to untie these knots, I ask Simplicio by what means he would prove that freely falling bodies go along straight and perpendicular lines directed toward the center, should anyone refuse to grant this to Aristotle and Ptolemy.

* Galileo Galilei, *Dialogue Concerning the Two World Systems—Ptolemaic and Copernican*, Stillman Drake, trans. (Berkeley: University of California Press, 1953), pp. 125.
* Ibid., pp. 139–49.

SIMPLICIO: By means of the senses, which assure us that the tower is straight and perpendicular, and which show us that a falling stone goes along grazing it, without deviating a hairsbreadth to one side or the other, and strikes at the foot of the tower exactly under the place from which it was dropped.

SALV: But if it happened that the earth rotated, and consequently carried along the tower, and if the falling stone were seen to graze the side of the tower just the same, what would its motion then have to be?

SIMP: In that case one would have to say "its motions," for there would be one with which it went from top to bottom, and another one needed for following the path of the tower.

SALV: The motion would then be a compound of two motions: the one with which it measures the tower, and the other with which it follows it. From this compounding it would follow that the rock would no longer describe that simple straight perpendicular line, but a slanting one, and perhaps not straight.

SIMP: I don't know about its not being straight, but I understand well enough that it would have to be slanting, and different from the straight perpendicular line it would describe with the earth motionless.

SALV: Hence just from seeing the falling stone graze the tower, you could not say for sure that it described a straight and perpendicular line, unless you first assumed the earth to stand still.

SIMP: Exactly so; for if the earth were moving, the motion of the stone would be slanting and not perpendicular.

SALV: Then here, clear and evident, is the paralogism of Aristotle and of Ptolemy, discovered by you yourself. They take as known that which is intended to be proved.

SIMP: In what way? It looks to me like a syllogism in proper form, and not a *petitio principii*.

SALV: In this way: Does he not, in his proof, take the conclusion as unknown?

SIMP: Unknown, for otherwise it would be superfluous to prove it.

SALV: And the middle term; does he not require that to be known?

SIMP: Of course; [otherwise it would be an attempt to prove *ignotum per aeque ignotum*.]

SALV: Our conclusion, which is unknown and is to be proved; is this not the motionlessness of the earth?

SIMP: That is what it is.

SALV: Is not the middle term, which must be known, the straight and perpendicular fall of the stone?

SIMP: That is the middle term.

SALV: But wasn't it concluded a little while ago that we could not have any knowledge of this fall being straight and perpendicular unless it was first known that the earth stood still? Therefore in your syllogism, the certainty of the middle term is drawn from the uncertainty of the conclusion. Thus you see how, and how badly, it is a paralogism.

SAGREDO: On behalf of Simplicio I should like, if possible, to defend Aristotle, or at least to be better persuaded as to the force of your deduction. You say that seeing the stone graze the tower is not enough to assure us that the motion of the rock is perpendicular (and this is the middle term of the syllogism) unless one assumes the earth to stand still (which is the conclusion to be proved). For if the tower moved along with the earth and the rock grazed it, the motion of the rock would be slanting, and not perpendicular. But I reply that if the tower were moving, it would be impossible for the rock to fall grazing it; therefore, from the scraping fall is inferred the stability of the earth.

SIMP: So it is. For to expect the rock to go grazing the tower if that were carried along by the earth would be requiring the rock to have two natural motions; that is, a straight one toward the center, and a circular one about the center, which is impossible.

SALV: So Aristotle's defense consists in its being impossible, or at least in his having considered it impossible, that the rock might move with a motion mixed of straight and circular. For if he had not held it to be impossible that the stone might move both toward and around the center at the same time, he would have understood how it could happen that the falling rock might go grazing the tower whether that was moving or was standing still, and consequently he would have been able to perceive that this grazing could imply nothing as to the motion or rest of the earth.

Nevertheless this does not excuse Aristotle, not only because if he did have this idea he ought to have said so, it being such an important point in the argument, but also, and more so, because it cannot be said either that such an effect is impossible or that Aristotle considered it impossible. The former cannot be said because, as I shall shortly prove to you, this is not only possible but necessary; and the latter cannot be said either, because Aristotle himself admits that fire moves naturally upward in a straight line and also turns in the diurnal motion which is imparted by the sky to all the element of fire and to the greater part of the air. Therefore if he saw no impossibility in the mixing of straight-upward with circular motion, as communicated to fire and to the air up as far as the moon's orbit, no more should he deem this impossible with regard to the rock's straight-downward motion and the circular motion natural to the entire globe of the earth, of which the rock is a part.

SIMP: It does not look that way to me at all. If the element of fire goes around together with the air, this is a very easy and even a necessary thing for a particle of fire, which, rising high from the earth, receives that very motion in passing through the moving air, being so tenuous and light a body and so easily moved. But it is quite incredible that a very heavy rock or a cannon ball which is dropped without restraint should let itself be budged by the air or by anything else. Besides which, there is the very appropriate experiment of the stone dropped from the top of the mast of a ship, which falls to the foot of the mast when the ship is standing still, but falls as far from that same point when the ship is sailing as the ship is perceived to have advanced during the time of the fall, this being several yards when the ship's course is rapid. . . .

SALV: Tell me, Simplicio: Do you feel convinced that the experiment on the ship squares so well with our purpose that one may reasonably believe that whatever is seen to occur there must also take place on the terrestrial globe?

SIMP: So far, yes; . . .

SALV: Rather, I hope that you will stick to it, and firmly insist that the result on the earth must correspond to that on the ship, so that when the latter is perceived to be prejudicial to your case you will not be tempted to change your mind.

You say, then, that since when the ship stands still the rock falls to the foot of the mast, and when the ship is in motion it falls apart from there, then conversely, from the falling of the rock at the foot it is inferred that the ship stands still, and from its falling away it may be deduced that the ship is moving. And since what happens on the ship must likewise happen on the land, from the falling of the rock at the foot of the tower one necessarily infers the immobility of the terrestrial globe. Is that your argument?

SIMP: That is exactly it, briefly stated, which makes it easy to understand.

SALV: Now tell me: If the stone dropped from the top of the mast when the ship was sailing rapidly fell in exactly the same place on the ship to which it fell when the ship was standing still, what use could you make of this falling with regard to determining whether the vessel stood still or moved?

SIMP: Absolutely none; just as by the beating of the pulse, for instance, you cannot know whether a person is asleep or awake, since the pulse beats in the same manner in sleeping as in waking.

SALV: Very good. Now, have you ever made this experiment of the ship?

SIMP: I have never made it, but I certainly believe that the authorities who adduced it had carefully observed it. Besides, the cause of the difference is so exactly known that there is no room for doubt.

SALV: You yourself are sufficient evidence that those authorities may have offered it without having performed it, for you take it as certain without having done it, and commit yourself to the good faith of their dictum. Similarly it not only may be, but must be that they did the same thing too—I mean, put faith in their predecessors, right on back without ever arriving at anyone who had performed it. For anyone who does will find that the experiment shows exactly the opposite of what is written: that is, it will show that the stone always falls in the same place on the ship: whether the ship is standing still or moving with any speed you please. Therefore, the same cause holding good on the earth as on the ship, nothing can be inferred about the earth's motion or rest from the stone falling always perpendicularly to the foot of the tower.

SIMP: If you had referred me to any other agency than experiment, I think that our dispute would not soon come to an end; for this appears to me to be a thing so remote from human reason that there is no place in it for credulity or probability.

SALV: For me there is, just the same.

SIMP: So you have not made a hundred tests, or even one? And yet you so freely declare it to be certain? I shall retain my incredulity, and my own confidence that the experiment has been made by the most important authors who make use of it, and that it shows what they say it does.

SALV: Without experiment, I am sure that the effect will happen as I tell you, because it must happen that way; and I might add that you yourself also know that it cannot happen otherwise, no matter how you may pretend not to know it—or give that impression. But I am so handy at picking people's brains that I shall make you confess this in spite of yourself. . . .

Now tell me: Suppose you have a plane surface as smooth as a mirror and made of some hard material like steel. This is not parallel to the horizon, but somewhat inclined, and upon it you have placed a ball which is perfectly spherical and of some hard and heavy material like bronze. What do you believe this will do when released? Do you think, as I do, that it will remain still?

SIMP: If that surface is tilted?

SALV: Yes, that is what was assumed.

SIMP: I do not believe that it would stay still at all; rather, I am sure that it would spontaneously roll down. . . .

SALV: Now how long would the ball continue to roll, and how fast? Remember that I said a perfectly round ball and a highly polished surface, in order to remove all external and accidental impediments. Similarly I want you to take away any impediment of the air caused by its resistance to separation, and all other accidental obstacles, if there are any.

SIMP: I completely understood you, and to your question I reply that the ball would continue to move indefinitely, as far as the slope of the surface extended, and with a continually accelerated motion. For such is the nature of heavy bodies, which *vires acquirunt eundo;* and the greater the slope, the greater would be the velocity.

SALV: But if one wanted the ball to move upward on this same surface, do you think it would go?

SIMP: Not spontaneously, no; but drawn or thrown forcibly, it would.

SALV: And if it were thrust along with some impetus impressed forcibly upon it, what would its motion be, and how great?

SIMP: The motion would constantly slow down and be retarded, being contrary to nature, and would be of longer or shorter duration according to the greater or lesser impulse and the lesser or greater slope upward.

SALV: Very well: up to this point you have explained to me the events of motion upon two different planes. On the downward inclined plane, the heavy moving body spontaneously descends and continually accelerates, and to keep it at rest requires the use of force. On the upward slope, force is needed to thrust it along or even to hold it still, and motion which is impressed upon it continually diminishes until it is entirely annihilated. You say also that a difference in the two instances arises from the greater or lesser upward or downward slope of the plane, so that from a greater slope downward there follows a greater speed, while on the contrary upon the upward slope a given movable body thrown with a given force moves farther according as the slope is less.

Now tell me what would happen to the same movable body placed upon a surface with no slope upward or downward.

SIMP: Here I must think a moment about my reply. There being no downward slope, there can be no natural tendency toward motion; and there being no upward slope, there can be no resistance to being moved, so there would be an indifference between the propensity and the resistance to motion. Therefore it seems to me that it ought naturally to remain stable. But I forgot; it was not so very long ago that Sagredo gave me to understand that this is what would happen.

SALV: I believe it would do so if one set the ball down firmly. But what would happen if it were given an impetus in any direction?

SIMP: It must follow that it would move in that direction.

SALV: But with what sort of movement? One continually accelerated, as on the downward plane, or increasingly retarded as on the upward one?

SIMP: I cannot see any cause for acceleration or deceleration, there being no slope upward or downward.

SALV: Exactly so. But if there is no cause for the ball's retardation, there ought to be still less for its coming to rest; so how far would you have the ball continue to move?

SIMP: As far as the extension of the surface continued without rising or falling.

SALV: Then if such a space were unbounded, the motion on it would likewise be boundless? That is, perpetual?

SIMP: It seems so to me, if the movable body were of durable material.

SALV: That is of course assumed, since we said that all external and accidental impediments were to be removed, and any fragility on the part of the moving body would in this case be one of the accidental impediments.

Now tell me, what do you consider to be the cause of the ball moving spontaneously on the downward inclined plane, but only by force on the one tilted upward?

SIMP: That the tendency of heavy bodies is to move toward the center of the earth, and to move upward from its circumference only with force; now the downward surface is that which gets closer to the center, while the upward one gets farther away.

SALV: Then in order for a surface to be neither downward nor upward, all its parts must be equally distant from the center. Are there any such surfaces in the world?

SIMP: Plenty of them; such would be the surface of our terrestrial globe if it were smooth, and not rough and mountainous as it is. But there is that of the water, when it is placid and tranquil.

SALV: Then a ship, when it moves over a calm sea, is one of these movables which courses over a surface that is tilted neither up nor down, and if all external and accidental obstacles were removed, it would thus be disposed to move incessantly and uniformly from an impulse once received?

SIMP: It seems that it ought to be.

SALV: Now as to that stone which is on top of the mast: does it not move, carried by the ship, both of them going along the circumference of a circle about its center? And consequently is there not in it an ineradicable motion, all external impediments being removed? And is not this motion as fast as that of the ship?

SIMP: All this is true, but what next?

SALV: Go on and draw the final consequence by yourself, if by yourself you have known all the premises.

SIMP: By the final conclusion you mean that the stone, moving with an indelibly impressed motion, is not going to leave the ship, but will follow it, and finally will fall at the same place where it fell when the ship remained motionless. And I, too, say that this would follow if there were no external impediments to disturb the motion of the stone after it was set free. But there are two such impediments; one is the inability of the movable body to split the air with its own impetus alone, once it has lost the force from the oars which it shared as part of the ship while it was on the mast; the other is the new motion of falling downward, which must impede its other, forward, motion.

SALV: As for the impediment of the air, I do not deny that to you, and if the falling body were of very light material, like a feather or a tuft of wool, the retardation would be quite considerable. But in a heavy stone it is insignificant, and if, as you yourself just said a little while ago, the force of the wildest wind is not enough to move a large stone from its place, just imagine how much the quiet air could accomplish upon meeting a rock which moved no faster than the ship! All the same, as I said, I concede to you the small effect which may depend upon such an impediment, just as I know you will concede to me that if the air were moving at the same speed as the ship and the rock, this impediment would be absolutely nil.

As for the other, the supervening motion downward, in the first place it is obvious that these two motions (I mean the circular around the center and the straight motion toward the center) are not contraries, nor are they destructive of one another, nor incompatible. As to the moving body, it has no resistance whatever to such a motion, for you yourself have already granted the resistance to be against motion which increases the distance from the center, and the tendency to be toward motion which approaches the center. From this it follows necessarily that the moving body has neither a resistance nor a propensity to motion which does not approach toward or depart from the center, and in consequence no cause for diminution in the property impressed upon it. Hence the cause of motion is not a single one which must be weakened by the new action, but there exist two distinct causes. Of these, heaviness attends only to the drawing of the movable body toward the center, and impressed force only to its being led around the center, so no occasion remains for any impediment.

EVOLUTION-SCIENCE VERSUS CREATION-SCIENCE

Debates in the philosophy of science rarely gain public attention, but recent controversies stirred by the demand for *balanced treatment* for creation-science and evolution-science in school science curricula has changed this. Discussions of the nature of science have not only caught the public's attention, they have found their way into our courtrooms. What follows is an attempt at a balanced treatment of those who think that creation-science is a science and those who think it is not.

Background: In 1981, the State of Arkansas adopted legislation mandating a "balanced treatment for Creation-Science and Evolution-Science." The first section of this act (called Act 590 of 1981) reads as follows:

> *Requirement for Balanced Treatment.* Public Schools within this State shall give balanced treatment to creation-science and to evolution-science. Balanced treatment to these two models shall be given in classroom lectures taken as a whole for each course, in textbook materials taken as a whole for each course, in library materials taken as a whole for the sciences and taken as a whole for the humanities, and in other educational programs in public schools, to the extent that such lectures, textbooks, library materials, or educational programs deal in any way with the subject of the origin of man, life, the earth, or the universe.

In response to this legislation, twenty-three individuals and organizations (representing religious, scientific, and educational interests) brought suit, claiming that this bill was unconstitutional on the grounds that it violated the First Amendment doctrine of the separation of church and state. Early in 1982 the U.S. District Court (in *McLean v. Arkansas*) ruled that the plaintiffs were correct in holding that Act 590 violated the First Amendment. It was therefore struck down as unconstitutional.

McLean v. Arkansas could have been argued on a number of grounds. One possible position is that explicit religious instruction does not violate the Constitution's doctrine of the separation of church and state. Those defending the Arkansas bill did not, however, adopt this approach, but instead argued that creation-science is a genuine *scientific* alternative to the theory of evolution through natural selection. As such, it can be presented and evaluated in the same manner that any scientific theory is presented and evaluated. Thus defenders of instruction in creation-science deny that teaching this subject matter amounts to introducing religious instruction into public education. The opponents of teaching creation-science in public schools argue that creation-science is not a science, and therefore has no place in a science curriculum. (They further argue that it has no place in any other part of a public school curriculum, because its purposes are clearly religious and thus violate the First Amendment's principle of separation of church and state.) The issue, then, is sharply drawn.

More specifically, proponents of a balanced treatment for creation-science have maintained that creation-science and evolution-science provide alternative *models* for the explanation of the origin of the world and its life. The creation-science model, they argue, is no less scientific than the evolution-science model. Henry M. Morris, Ph.D., has been a forceful defender of the view that creationism should be taught as a *scientific* alternative to Darwin's theory of evolution. The following excerpts from his writings defend the scientific legitimacy of creation-science. Morris's views are then criticized by Stephen J. Gould, a prominent biologist. In *McLean v. Arkansas*, Judge Overton concluded that creation-science is not really a science at all, but you have to decide for yourself whether you agree with his conclusion.

▼ *Scientific Creationism**
HENRY M. MORRIS

IMPOSSIBILITY OF SCIENTIFIC PROOF OF ORIGINS

It must . . . be emphasized that it is impossible to *prove* scientifically any particular concept of origins to be true. This is obvious from the fact that the essence of the scientific method is experimental observation and repeatability. A scientific investigator, be he ever so resourceful and brilliant, can neither observe nor repeat *origins!*

This means that, though it is important to have a philosophy of origins, it can only be achieved by faith, not by sight. That is no argument against it, however. Every step we take in life is a step of faith. Even the pragmatist who insists he will only believe what he can see, *believes* that his pragmatism is the best philosophy, though he can't prove it! He also believes in invisible atoms and in such abstractions as the future.

As a matter of observation, belief in something is necessary for true mental health. A philosophy of life is a philosophy, not a scientific ex-

---

* From Henry M. Morris, *Scientific Creationism* (San Diego: Creation-Life Publishers, 1974), pp. 5–13.

periment. A life based on the whim of the moment, with no rationale, is "a tale told by an idiot, full of sound and fury, signifying nothing."

Thus, one must *believe,* at least with respect to ultimate origins. However, for optimally beneficial application of that belief, his faith should be a reasoned faith, not a credulous faith or a prescribed faith.

To illustrate more exactly what we mean when we say origins cannot be proved, a brief discussion is given below on each of the two basic concepts of origins, creation and evolution:

A. *Creation cannot be proved*

1. Creation is not taking place now, so far as can be observed. Therefore, it was accomplished sometime in the past, if at all, and thus is inaccessible to the scientific method.

2. It is impossible to devise a scientific experiment to describe the creation process, or even to ascertain whether such a process *can* take place. The Creator does not create at the whim of a scientist.

B. *Evolution cannot be proved*

1. If evolution is taking place today, it operates too slowly to be measurable, and, therefore, is outside the realm of empirical science. To transmute one kind of organism into a higher kind of organism would presumably take millions of years, and no team of scientific observers is available to make measurements on any such experiment.

2. The small variations in organisms which are observed to take place today . . . are irrelevant to this question, since there is no way to prove that these changes within present kinds eventually change the kinds into different, higher kinds. Since small variations (including mutations) are as much to be expected in the creation model as in the evolution model, they are of no value in discriminating between the two models.

3. Even if modern scientists should ever actually achieve the artificial creation of life from non-life, or of higher kinds from lower kinds, in the laboratory, this would not *prove* in any way that such changes did, or even could, take place in the past by random natural processes.

Since it is often maintained by evolutionists that evolution is scientific, whereas creationism is religious, it will be well at this point to cite several leading evolutionists who have recognized that evolution also is incapable of being proved.[1]

---

[1] It is interesting and encouraging to note that, in the Foreword to the most recent edition of Darwin's *Origin of Species,* a leading British evolutionary biologist, Professor L. Harrison Matthews, F.R.S., recognizes that "Belief in evolution is thus exactly parallel to belief in special creation—both are concepts which believers know to be true but neither, up to the present, has been capable of proof" (London: J. M. Dent & Sons, Ltd., 1971), p. x.

Evolution Operates Too Slowly for Scientific Observation

One of the nation's leading evolutionists, Theodosius Dobzhansky, has admitted:

> "The applicability of the experimental method to the study of such unique historical processes is severely restricted before all else by the time intervals involved, which far exceed the lifetime of any human experimenter. And yet, it is just such impossibility that is demanded by anti-evolutionists when they ask for 'proofs' of evolution which they would magnanimously accept as satisfactory."[2]

Note the tacit admission that "the experimental method" is an "impossibility" when applied to evolution.

Evolution Is a Dogma Incapable of Refutation

Two leading modern biologists have pointed out the fact that, since evolution cannot in any conceivable way be disproved, therefore, neither can it be proved.

> "Our theory of evolution has become . . . one which cannot be refuted by any possible observations. It is thus 'outside of empirical science,' but not necessarily false. No one can think of ways in which to test it. . . . (Evolutionary ideas) have become part of an evolutionary dogma accepted by most of us as part of our training."[3]

Similarly, Peter Medawar recognized the problem entailed by the fact that no way exists by which to test evolution.

> "There are philosophical or methodological objections to evolutionary theory. . . . It is too difficult to imagine or envisage an evolutionary episode which could not be explained by the formulae of neo-Darwinism."[4]

In other words, both the long neck of the giraffe and the short neck of the hippopotamus can presumably be explained by natural selection. A theory which incorporates everything really *explains* nothing! It is tautologous. Those who survive in the struggle for existence are the fittest because the fittest are the ones who survive.

Evolution Is an Authoritarian System to Be Believed

> "It seems at times as if many of our modern writers on evolution have had their views by some sort of revelation and they base their opinions on the evolution of life, from the simplest form to the complex, entirely on the nature of specific and intra-specific evolution. . . . It is premature, not to say arrogant, on our part if we make any dogmatic assertion as to the mode of evolution of the major branches of the animal kingdom."[5]

---

[2] Theodosius Dobzhansky, "On Methods of Evolutionary Biology and Anthropology," *American Scientist,* Vol. 45 (December, 1957), p. 388.

[3] Paul Ehrlich and L. C. Birch, "Evolutionary History and Population Biology," *Nature,* Vol. 214 (1967), p. 352.

[4] Peter Medawar, *Mathematical Challenges to the Neo-Darwinism Interpretation of Evolution* (Philadelphia: Wistar Institute Press, 1967), p. xi.

[5] G. A. Kerkut, *Implications of Evolution* (London: Pergamon, 1965), p. 155.

"But the facts of paleontology conform equally well with other interpretations. . . . e.g., divine creation, etc., and paleontology by itself can neither prove nor refute such ideas."[6]

Thomas Huxley, probably more responsible than any other one man for the acceptance of Darwinian philosophy, nevertheless recognized that:

". . . 'creation' in the ordinary sense of the word, is perfectly conceivable. I find no difficulty in conceiving that, at some former period, this universe was not in existence; and that it made its appearance in six days . . . in consequence of the volition of some pre-existing Being."[7]

The Reason for Favoring Evolution Is not because of the Scientific Evidence

An outstanding British biologist of a number of years ago made the following remarkable observation:

"If so, it will present a parallel to the theory of evolution itself, a theory universally accepted not because it can be proved by logically coherent evidence to be true but because the only alternative, special creation, is clearly incredible."[8]

The only reason for saying that special creation is incredible would be if one had certain knowledge that there was no God. Obviously, if no Creator exists, then special creation is incredible. But since a universal negative can only be proved if one has universal knowledge, such a statement requires omniscience. Thus, by denying God, Dr. Watson is claiming the attributes of God himself.

There are some scientists, at least, who find it easier to believe in the deity of an omnipotent Creator than in the deity of Professor Watson.

THE TWO MODELS OF ORIGINS

It is, as shown in the previous section, impossible to demonstrate scientifically which of the two concepts of origins is really true. Although many people teach evolution as though it were a proven fact of science, it is obvious that this is false teaching. There are literally thousands of scientists[9] and other educated intellectuals today who reject evolution, and this would certainly not be the case if evolution were as obvious as many scientists say it is.

The same is true of creation, of course. Although many believe special creation to be an absolute fact of history, they must believe this for theo-

---

[6] D. Dwight Davis, "Comparative Anatomy and the Evolution of Vertebrates," in *Genetics, Paleontology and Evolution* (ed. by Jepsen, Mayr and Simpson, Princeton University Press, 1949), p. 74.

[7] Leonard Huxley, *Life and Letters of Thomas Henry Huxley* (London: Macmillan, Vol. II, 1903), p. 429.

[8] D. M. S. Watson, "Adaptation," *Nature*, Vol. 123 (1929), p. 233.

[9] The Creation Research Society, for example, numbers over 700 M.S. and Ph.D. scientists on its rolls.

logical, rather than scientific reasons. Neither evolution nor creation can be either confirmed or falsified scientifically.[10]

Furthermore, it is clear that neither evolution nor creation is, in the proper sense, either a scientific theory or a scientific hypothesis. Though people might speak of the "theory of evolution" or of the "theory of creation," such terminology is imprecise. This is because neither can be *tested*. A valid scientific hypothesis must be capable of being formulated experimentally, such that the experimental results either confirm or reject its validity.

As noted in the statement by Ehrlich and Birch cited previously, however, there is no conceivable way to do this. Ideally, we might like to set up an experiment, the results of which would demonstrate either evolution or creation to have been true. But there is no one test, nor any series of tests, which can do this scientifically.

All of these strictures do not mean, however, that we cannot discuss this question scientifically and objectively. Indeed, it is extremely important that we do so, if we are really to understand this vital question of origins and to arrive at a satisfactory basis for the faith we must ultimately exercise in one or the other.

A more proper approach is to think in terms of two scientific models, the *evolution model* and the *creation model*. A "model" is a conceptual framework, an orderly system of thought, within which one tries to correlate observable data, and even to predict data. When alternative models exist, they can be compared as to their respective capacities for correlating such data. When, as in this case, neither can be proved, the decision between the two cannot be solely objective. Normally, in such a case, the model which correlates the greater number of data, with the smallest number of unresolved contradictory data, would be accepted as the more probably correct model.

When particular facts do show up which seem to contradict the predictions of the model, it may still be possible to assimilate the data by a slight modification of the original model. As a matter of fact, in the case of the evolution model, as Ehrlich and Birch said: "Every conceivable observation can be fitted into it."

The same generalization, of course, is true of the creation model. There is no observational fact imaginable which cannot, one way or another, be made to fit the creation model. The only way to decide objectively between them, therefore, is to note which model fits the facts and predictions with the smallest number of these secondary assumptions.

Creationists are convinced that, when this procedure is carefully followed, the creation model will always fit the facts as well as or better than will the evolution model. Evolutionists may, of course, believe otherwise. In either case, it is important that everyone have the facts at hand

---

[10] Dr. N. Heribert-Nilsson, Director of the Botanical Institute at Lund University, Sweden, said "My attempt to demonstrate evolution by an experiment carried on for more than 40 years has completely failed. . . . The idea of an evolution rests on pure belief" (*Synthetische Artbildung*, 1953).

with which to consider *both* models, rather than one only. The latter is brainwashing, not brain-using! . . .

A. THE EVOLUTION MODEL

The evolutionary system attempts to explain the origin, development, and meaning of all things in terms of natural laws and processes which operate today as they have in the past. No extraneous processes, requiring the special activity of an external agent, or Creator, are permitted. The universe, in all its aspects, evolves itself into higher levels of order (particles to people) by means of its innate properties.

To confirm that this is the essential nature of the evolution model, several recognized authorities are cited below, giving their own concepts of evolution.

> "Most enlightened persons now accept as a fact that everything in the cosmos—from heavenly bodies to human beings—has developed and continues to develop through evolutionary processes." [11]
>
> "Evolution comprises all the stages of the development of the universe: the cosmic, biological, and human or cultural developments. . . . Life is a product of the evolution of inorganic nature, and man is a product of the evolution of life." [12]
>
> "Evolution in the extended sense can be defined as a directional and essentially irreversible process occurring in time, which in its course gives rise to an increase of variety and an increasingly high level of organization in its products. Our present knowledge indeed forces us to the view that the whole of reality is evolution—a single process of self-transformation." [13]
>
> "Biological evolution can, however, be explained without recourse to a Creator or a planning agent external to the organisms themselves. There is no evidence, either, of any vital force or immanent energy directing the evolutionary process toward the production of specified kinds of organisms." [14]

Thus evolution entails a self-contained universe, in which its innate laws develop everything into higher levels of organization. Particles evolve into elements, elements into complex chemicals, complex chemicals into simple living systems, simple life forms into complex life, complex animal life into man.

Summarizing, evolution is: (1) naturalistic; (2) self-contained; (3) nonpurposive; (4) directional; (5) irreversible; (6) universal; and (7) continuing.

---

[11] Rene Dubos, "Humanistic Biology," *American Scientist*, Vol. 53 (March 1965), p. 6.

[12] Theodosius Dobzhansky, "Changing Man," *Science*, Vol. 155 (January 27, 1967), p. 409.

[13] Julian Huxley, "Evolution and Genetics," Chap. 8 in *What Is Science?* ed. J. R. Newman (New York: Simon & Schuster, 1955), p. 272.

[14] Francisco J. Ayala, "Biology as an Autonomous Science," *American Scientist*, Vol. 56 (Autumn 1968), p. 213.

B. THE CREATION MODEL

Diametrically opposed to the evolution model, the creation model involves a process of special creation which is: (1) supernaturalistic; (2) externally directed; (3) purposive; and (4) completed. Like evolution, the creation model also applies universally. It also is irreversibly directional, but its direction is downward toward lower levels of complexity rather than upward toward higher levels. The completed original creation was perfect and has since been "running down."

The creation model thus postulates a period of special creation in the beginning, during which all the basic laws and categories of nature, including the major kinds of plants and animals, as well as man, were brought into existence by special creative and integrative processes which are no longer in operation. Once the creation was finished, these processes of *creation* were replaced by processes of *conservation*, which were designed by the Creator to sustain and maintain the basic systems He had created.

In addition to the primary concept of a completed creation followed by conservation, the creation model proposes a basic principle of disintegration now at work in nature (since any significant change in a *perfect* primeval creation must be in the direction of imperfection). Also, the evidence in the earth's crust of past physical convulsions seems to warrant inclusion of post-creation global catastrophism in the model.

The two models may be easily compared by studying the table below:

Evolution Model	Creation Model
Continuing naturalistic origin	Completed supernatural origin
Net present increase in complexity	Net present decrease in complexity

The questions of the *date* of creation (old or young) and the nature of cosmic processes *since* creation (dominantly naturalistic and uniform or catastrophic) are separate issues.

It is proposed that these two models be used as systems for "predicting" data, to see which one does so more effectively. To do this, one should imagine that neither the evolutionist nor the creationist knows in advance what data will be found. They do not know what they will find but bravely make predictions, each on the basis of his own model.

The following table (p. 381) indicates the predictions that would probably be made in several important categories.

It should be noted that the tabulated predictions are predictions of the *primary models,* as defined in their most general terms as in the foregoing discussion. These primary models may be modified by secondary assumptions to fit certain conditions. For example, the basic evolution model may be extended to include harmful, as well as beneficial, mutations, but this is not a natural prediction of the basic concept of evolution. If the "predictions" of evolution, as listed in the above table, were actually observed in the natural world, they would, of course, in every case be enthusiastically acclaimed as strong confirmations of the evolution model.

Category	Evolution Model	Creation Model
Galactic Universe	Galaxies Changing	Galaxies Constant
Structure of Stars	Stars Changing into Other Types	Stars Unchanged
Other Heavenly Bodies	Building Up	Breaking Down
Types of Rock Formations	Different in Different "Ages"	Similar in All "Ages"
Appearance of Life	Life Evolving from Non-Life	Life Only from Life
Array of Organisms	Continuum of Organisms	Distinct Kinds of Organisms
Appearance of Kinds of Life	New Kinds Appearing	No New Kinds Appearing
Mutations in Organisms	Beneficial	Harmful
Natural Selection	Creative Process	Conservative Process
Age of Earth	Extremely Old	Probably Young
Fossil Record	Innumerable Transitions	Systematic Gaps
Appearance of Man	Ape-Human Intermediates	No Ape-Human Intermediates
Nature of Man	Quantitatively Superior to Animals	Qualitatively Distinct from Animals
Origin of Civilization	Slow and Gradual	Contemporaneous with Man

That fact justifies the conclusion that these are the *basic* predictions of evolution.

The above predictions are merely suggestive of the types of entities that can be used to contrast the two models. . . . Creationists maintain that the predictions of the creation model do fit the observed facts in nature better than do those of the evolution model. The data must be *explained* by the evolutionist, but they are *predicted* by the creationist.

▼ *Evolution as Fact and Theory*
STEPHEN JAY GOULD*

Kirtley Mather, who died last year at age eighty-nine, was a pillar of both science and the Christian religion in America and one of my dearest friends.

---

* Stephen Jay Gould, "Evolution as Fact and Theory," Copyright © 1981 by Stephen Jay Gould. Reprinted by permission of the author. First appeared in *Discover Magazine*.

The difference of half a century in our ages evaporated before our common interests. The most curious thing we shared was a battle we each fought at the same age. For Kirtley had gone to Tennessee with Clarence Darrow to testify for evolution at the Scopes trial of 1925. When I think that we are enmeshed again in the same struggle for one of the best documented, most compelling and exciting concepts in all of science, I don't know whether to laugh or cry.

According to idealized principles of scientific discourse, the arousal of dormant issues should reflect fresh data that give renewed life to abandoned notions. Those outside the current debate may therefore be excused for suspecting that creationists have come up with something new, or that evolutionists have generated some serious internal trouble. But nothing has changed; the creationists have not a single new fact or argument. Darrow and Bryan were at least more entertaining than we lesser antagonists today. The rise of creationism is politics, pure and simple; it represents one issue (and by no means the major concern) of the resurgent evangelical right. Arguments that seemed kooky just a decade ago have reentered the mainstream.

Creationism Is Not Science

The basic attack of the creationists falls apart on two general counts before we even reach the supposed factual details of their complaints against evolution. First, they play upon a vernacular misunderstanding of the word "theory" to convey the false impression that we evolutionists are covering up the rotten core of our edifice. Second, they misuse a popular philosophy of science to argue that they are behaving scientifically in attacking evolution. Yet the same philosophy demonstrates that their own belief is not science, and that "scientific creationism" is therefore meaningless and self-contradictory, a superb example of what Orwell called "newspeak."

In the American vernacular, "theory" often means "imperfect fact"—part of a hierarchy of confidence running downhill from fact to theory to hypothesis to guess. Thus the power of the creationist argument: Evolution is "only" a theory, and intense debate now rages about many aspects of the theory. If evolution is less than a fact, and scientists can't even make up their minds about the theory, then what confidence can we have in it? Indeed, President Reagan echoed this argument before an evangelical group in Dallas when he said (in what I devoutly hope was campaign rhetoric): "Well, it is a theory. It is a scientific theory only, and it has in recent years been challenged in the world of science—that is, not believed in the scientific community to be as infallible as it once was."

Well, evolution *is* a theory. It is also a fact. And facts and theories are different things, not rungs in a hierarchy of increasing certainty. Facts are the world's data. Theories are structures of ideas that explain and interpret facts. Facts do not go away when scientists debate rival theories to explain them. Einstein's theory of gravitation replaced Newton's, but apples did not suspend themselves in mid-air pending the outcome. And human beings evolved from apelike ancestors whether they did so by Darwin's proposed mechanism or by some other, yet to be discovered.

Moreover, "fact" does not mean "absolute certainty." The final proofs of logic and mathematics flow deductively from stated premises and achieve certainty only because they are *not* about the empirical world. Evolutionists make no claim for perpetual truth, though creationists often do (and then attack us for a style of argument that they themselves favor). In science, "fact" can only mean "confirmed to such a degree that it would be perverse to withhold provisional assent." I suppose that apples might start to rise tomorrow, but the possibility does not merit equal time in physics classrooms.

Evolutionists have been clear about this distinction between fact and theory from the very beginning, if only because we have always acknowledged how far we are from completely understanding the mechanisms (theory) by which evolution (fact) occurred. Darwin continually emphasized the difference between his two great and separate accomplishments: establishing the fact of evolution, and proposing a theory—natural selection—to explain the mechanism of evolution. He wrote in *The Descent of Man:* "I had two distinct objects in view; firstly, to show that species had not been separately created, and secondly, that natural selection had been the chief agent of change. . . . Hence if I have erred in . . . having exaggerated its [natural selection's] power. . . . I have at least, as I hope, done good service in aiding to overthrow the dogma of separate creations."

Thus Darwin acknowledged the provisional nature of natural selection while affirming the fact of evolution. The fruitful theoretical debate that Darwin initiated has never ceased. From the 1940s through the 1960s, Darwin's own theory of natural selection did achieve a temporary hegemony that it never enjoyed in his lifetime. But renewed debate characterizes our decade, and, while no biologist questions the importance of natural selection, many now doubt its ubiquity. In particular, many evolutionists argue that substantial amounts of genetic change may not be subject to natural selection and may spread through populations at random. Others are challenging Darwin's linking of natural selection with gradual, imperceptible change through all intermediary degrees; they are arguing that most evolutionary events may occur far more rapidly than Darwin envisioned.

Scientists regard debates on fundamental issues of theory as a sign of intellectual health and a source of excitement. Science is—and how else can I say it?—most fun when it plays with interesting ideas, examines their implications, and recognizes that old information may be explained in surprisingly new ways. Evolutionary theory is now enjoying this uncommon vigor. Yet amidst all this turmoil no biologist has been led to doubt the fact that evolution occurred; we are debating *how* it happened. We are all trying to explain the same thing: the tree of evolutionary descent linking all organisms by ties of genealogy. Creationists pervert and caricature this debate by conveniently neglecting the common conviction that underlies it, and by falsely suggesting that we now doubt the very phenomenon we are struggling to understand.

Using another invalid argument, creationists claim that "the dogma of separate creations," as Darwin characterized it a century ago, is a scientific theory meriting equal time with evolution in high school biology curricula. But a prevailing viewpoint among philosophers of science belies this creationist argument. Philosopher Karl Popper has argued for decades that the primary criterion of science is the falsifiability of its theories. We can never prove absolutely, but we can falsify. A set of ideas that cannot, in principle, be falsified is not science.

The entire creationist argument involves little more than a rhetorical attempt to falsify evolution by presenting supposed contradictions among its supporters. Their brand of creationism, they claim, is "scientific" because it follows the Popperian model in trying to demolish evolution. Yet Popper's argument must apply in both directions. One does not become a scientist by the simple act of trying to falsify another scientific system; one has to present an alternative system that also meets Popper's criterion—it too must be falsifiable in principle.

"Scientific creationism" is a self-contradictory, nonsense phrase precisely because it cannot be falsified. I can envision observations and experiments that would disprove any evolutionary theory I know, but I cannot imagine what potential data could lead creationists to abandon their beliefs. Unbeatable systems are dogma, not science. Lest I seem harsh or rhetorical, I quote creationism's leading intellectual, Duane Gish, Ph.D., from his recent (1978) book *Evolution? The Fossils Say No!* "By creation we mean the bringing into being by a supernatural Creator of the basic kinds of plants and animals by the process of sudden, or fiat, creation. We do not know how the Creator created, what processes He used, *for He used processes which are not now operating anywhere in the natural universe* [Gish's italics]. This is why we refer to creation as special creation. We cannot discover by scientific investigations anything about the creative processes used by the Creator." Pray tell, Dr. Gish, in the light of your last sentence, what then is "scientific" creationism?

The Fact of Evolution

Our confidence that evolution occurred centers upon three general arguments. First, we have abundant, direct, observational evidence of evolution in action, from both the field and the laboratory. It ranges from countless experiments on change in nearly everything about fruit flies subjected to artificial selection in the laboratory to the famous British moths that turned black when industrial soot darkened the trees upon which they rest. (The moths gain protection from sharp-sighted bird predators by blending into the background.) Creationists do not deny these observations; how could they? Creationists have tightened their act. They now argue that God only created "basic kinds," and allowed for limited evolutionary meandering within them. Thus toy poodles and Great Danes come from the dog kind and moths can change color, but nature cannot convert a dog to a cat or a monkey to a man.

The second and third arguments for evolution—the case for major changes—do not involve direct observation of evolution in action. They rest upon inference, but are no less secure for that reason. Major evolutionary change requires too much time for direct observation on the scale of recorded human history. All historical sciences rest upon inference, and evolution is no different from geology, cosmology, or human history in this respect. In principle, we cannot observe processes that operated in the past. We must infer them from results that still survive: living and fossil organisms for evolution, documents and artifacts of human history, strata and topography for geology.

The second argument—that the imperfection of nature reveals evolution—strikes many people as ironic, for they feel that evolution should be most elegantly displayed in the nearly perfect adaptation expressed by some organisms—the chamber of a gull's wing, or butterflies that cannot be seen in ground litter because they mimic leaves so precisely. But perfection could be imposed by a wise creator or evolved by natural selection. Perfection covers the tracks of past history. And past history—the evidence of descent—is our mark of evolution.

Evolution lies exposed in the *imperfections* that record a history of descent. Why should a rat run, a bat fly, a porpoise swim, and I type this essay with structures built of the same bones unless we all inherited them from a common ancestor? An engineer, starting from scratch, could design better limbs in each case. Why should all the large native mammals of Australia be marsupials, unless they descended from a common ancestor isolated on this island continent? Marsupials are not "better," or ideally suited for Australia; many have been wiped out by placental mammals imported by man from other continents. This principle of imperfection extends to all historical sciences. When we recognize the etymology of September, October, November, and December (seventh, eighth, ninth, and tenth, from the Latin), we know that two additional items (January and February) must have been added to an original calendar of ten months.

The third argument is more direct: Transitions are often found in the fossil record. Preserved transitions are not common—and should not be, according to our understanding of evolution (see next section)—but they are not entirely wanting, as creationists often claim. The lower jaw of reptiles contains several bones, that of mammals only one. The non-mammalian jawbones are reduced, step by step, in mammalian ancestors until they become tiny nubbins located at the back of the jaw. The "hammer" and "anvil" bones of the mammalian ear are descendants of these nubbins. How could such a transition be accomplished? the creationists ask. Surely a bone is either entirely in the jaw or in the ear. Yet paleontologists have discovered two transitional lineages or therapsids (the so-called mammal-like reptiles) with a double jaw joint—one composed of the old quadrate and articular bones (soon to become the hammer and anvil), the other of the squamosal and dentary bones (as in modern mammals). For that matter, what better transitional form could we desire than the oldest human, *Australopithecus afarensis,* with its apelike palate, its human upright stance, and a cranial capacity larger than any ape's of the same body size but a full 1,000 cubic centimeters below ours? If God made each of the half dozen human species discovered in ancient rocks, why did he create in an unbroken temporal sequence of progressively more modern features—increasing cranial capacity, reduced face and teeth, larger body size? Did he create to mimic evolution and test our faith thereby?

An Example of Creationist Argument

Faced with these facts of evolution and the philosophical bankruptcy of their own position, creationists rely upon distortion and innuendo to buttress their rhetorical claim. If I sound sharp or bitter, indeed I am— for I have become a major target of these practices.

I count myself among the evolutionists who argue for a jerky, or episodic, rather than a smoothly gradual, pace of change. In 1972 my colleague Niles Eldredge and I developed the theory of punctuated equilibrium. We argued that two outstanding facts of the fossil record— geologically "sudden" origin of new species and failure to change thereafter (stasis)—reflect the predictions of evolutionary theory, not the imperfections of the fossil record. In most theories, small isolated populations are the source of new species, and the process of speciation takes thousands or tens of thousands of years. This amount of time, so long when measured against our lives, is a geological microsecond. It represents much less than 1 per cent of the average life span for a fossil invertebrate species—more than 10 million years. Large, widespread, and well-established species, on the other hand, are not expected to change very much. We believe that the inertia of large populations explains the stasis of most fossil species over millions of years.

We proposed the theory of punctuated equilibrium largely to provide a different explanation for pervasive trends in the fossil record. Trends, we argued, cannot be attributed to gradual transformation within lineages, but must arise from the differential success of certain kinds of species. A trend, we argued, is more like climbing a flight of stairs (punctuations and stasis) than rolling up an inclined plane.

Since we proposed punctuated equilibria to explain trends, it is infuriating to be quoted again and again by creationists—whether through design or stupidity, I do not know—as admitting that the fossil record includes no transitional forms. Transitional forms are generally lacking at the species level, but are abundant between larger groups. The evolution from reptiles to mammals, as mentioned earlier, is well documented. Yet a pamphlet entitled "Harvard Scientists Agree Evolution Is a Hoax" states: "The facts of punctuated equilibrium which Gould and Eldredge . . . are forcing Darwinists to swallow fit the picture that Bryan insisted on, and which God has revealed to us in the Bible."

Continuing the distortion, several creationists have equated the theory of punctuated equilibrium with a caricature of the beliefs of Richard Goldschmidt, a great early geneticist. Goldschmidt argued, in a famous book published in 1940, that new groups can arise all at once through major mutations. He referred to these suddenly transformed creatures as "hopeful monsters." (I am attracted to some aspects of the non-caricatured version, but Goldschmidt's theory still has nothing to do with punctuated equilibrium.) Creationist Luther Sunderland talks of the "punctuated equilibrium hopeful monster theory" and tells his hopeful readers that "it amounts to tacit admission that anti-evolutionists are correct in asserting there is no fossil evidence supporting the theory that all life is connected to a common ancestor." Duane Gish writes, "According to Goldschmidt and now apparently according to Gould, a reptile laid an egg from which the first bird, feathers and all, was produced." Any evolutionist who believed such nonsense would rightly be laughed off the intellectual stage; yet the only theory that could ever envision such a scenario for the evolution of birds is creationism—God acts in the egg.

Conclusion

I am both angry at and amused by the creationists; but mostly I am deeply sad. Sad for many reasons. Sad because so many people who respond to creationist appeals are troubled for the right reason, but venting their anger at the wrong target. It is true that scientists have often been dogmatic and elitist. It is true that we have often allowed the white-coated, advertising image to represent us—"Scientists say that Brand X cures bunions ten times faster than. . . ." We have not fought it adequately because we derive benefits from appearing as a new priesthood. It is also true that faceless bureaucratic state power intrudes more and more into our lives and removes choices that should belong to individuals and communities. I can understand that requiring that evolution be taught in the schools might be seen as one more insult on all these grounds. But the culprit is not, and cannot be, evolution or any other fact of the natural world. Identify and fight your legitimate enemies by all means, but we are not among them.

I am sad because the practical result of this brouhaha will not be expanded coverage to include creationism (that would also make me sad), but the reduction or excision of evolution from high school curricula. Evolution is one of the half dozen "great ideas" developed by science. It speaks to the profound issues of genealogy that fascinate all of us—the "roots" phenomenon writ large. Where did we come from? Where did life arise? How did it develop? How are organisms related? It forces us to think, ponder, and wonder. Shall we deprive millions of this knowledge and once again teach biology as a set of dull and unconnected facts, without the thread that weaves diverse material into a supple unity?

But most of all I am saddened by a trend I am just beginning to discern among my colleagues. I sense that some now wish to mute the healthy debate about theory that has brought new life to evolutionary biology. It provides grist for creationist mills, they say, even if only by distortion. Perhaps we should lie low and rally round the flag of strict Darwinism, at least for the moment—a kind of old-time religion on our part.

But we should borrow another metaphor and recognize that we too have to tread a straight and narrow path, surrounded by roads to perdition. For if we ever begin to suppress our search to understand nature, to quench our own intellectual excitement in a misguided effort to present a united front where it does not and should not exist, then we are truly lost.

▼ DISCUSSION QUESTIONS

1. Is creation-science or evolution-science self-sealing in any of the ways described in Chapter 5? If so, does this show that these views are not really scientific? Be sure to consider how you could refute the evolutionist doctrine of the survival of the fittest or the creationist view that God created the world relatively recently.

2. The legal issues surrounding creation-science are just as controversial as the issue of whether creation-science is a science. Using the methods of legal reasoning from Chapter 11, determine whether the Arkansas act requiring balanced treatment for creation-science and evolution-science is desirable and constitutional. Do the same for laws which forbid the teaching of creation-science or evolution-science in public schools.

3. What is the point of arguing about whether evolution is a "theory" or a "fact" or a "model"? Is this debate just about words?

14

Philosophical Arguments

It is not easy to explain the character of philosophical reasoning. Indeed, the nature of philosophical reasoning is itself a philosophical problem. We can, however, acquire some sense of it by comparing philosophical reasoning with reasoning as it occurs in daily life. In the opening chapters of this book we noticed that, in everyday discussions, much is taken for granted and left unsaid. In general there is no need to state points that are already a matter of agreement. In contrast, philosophers usually try to make underlying assumptions explicit and then subject them to critical examination. But, even for the philosopher, something must trigger an interest in underlying assumptions—and this usually arises when the advance of knowledge creates fundamental conflicts within the system of hitherto accepted assumptions. Thus, much that counts as modern philosophy is an attempt to come to terms with the relationship between modern science and the traditional conception of man's place in the universe.

In recent years, a striking example of such a conflict has been generated by the rise of computer theory and computer technology. Traditionally, humans have cited the capacity to think as the feature that sets them apart from and, of course, above all other creatures. Man has been defined as a rational animal. But we now live in an age in which computers seem able to perform tasks that, had a human being performed them, would certainly count as thinking.

Not only can computers perform complex calculations very rapidly, they can also play an excellent game of chess. Do machines think? The question seems forced upon us, and it is more than a semantic quibble. In deciding it, we are also reevaluating the status of an aspect of humanity that has long been considered its unique or distinctive feature. Once we decide whether machines can think, the next question is whether human beings are not themselves merely thinking machines.

The three selections presented in this chapter address such questions. More specifically, they all consider the so-called *Turing test* for deciding whether or not a machine can think. A. M. Turing, the mathematician who first proposed this test, is one of the geniuses of this century. He not only developed much of the mathematics that underlies modern computer theory, he helped give digital computers their first remarkable application: cracking the German secret codes during the Second World War. In his essay "Computing Machinery and Intelligence,"[1] he attempted to restate the question "Can machines think?" in a way that would admit of a clear answer. He proposed that we ask whether a computer could successfully play what he called the *imitation game*. The test, and its significance, is examined in detail in the first selection: "The Turing Test: A Coffeehouse Conversation" by Douglas R. Hofstadter. The selection is followed by some brief reflections on the Turing test by Daniel C. Dennett.

The third selection is by John Searle. It comes from his review of Hofstadter and Dennett's book *The Mind's I*, and presents a systematic critique of the claims in behalf of machine intelligence.

▼ *The Turing Test: A Coffeehouse Conversation** *
DOUGLAS R. HOFSTADTER

PARTICIPANTS

Chris, a physics student; Pat, a biology student; and Sandy, a philosophy student.

CHRIS: Sandy, I want to thank you for suggesting that I read Alan Turing's article "Computing Machinery and Intelligence." It's a wonderful piece and it certainly made me think—and think about my thinking.

---

[1] A. M. Turing, "Computing Machinery and Intelligence," *Mind*, vol. LIX, no. 236 (1950).

* From Douglas R. Hofstadter and Daniel C. Dennett, *The Mind's I: Fantasies and Reflections on Self and Soul* (New York: Basic Books, 1981), pp. 69–95. This selection appeared previously as "Metamagical Themas: A coffeehouse conversation on the Turing test to determine if a machine can think," *Scientific American* (May 1981), pp. 15–36.

SANDY: Glad to hear it. Are you still as much of a skeptic about artificial intelligence as you used to be?

CHRIS: You've got me wrong. I'm not against artificial intelligence; I think it's wonderful stuff—perhaps a little crazy, but why not? I simply am convinced that you AI advocates have far underestimated the human mind, and that there are things a computer will never, ever be able to do. For instance, can you imagine a computer writing a Proust novel? The richness of imagination, the complexity of the characters . . .

SANDY: Rome wasn't built in a day!

CHRIS: In the article Turing comes through as an interesting person. Is he still alive?

SANDY: No, he died back in 1954, at just forty-one. He'd only be sixty-seven this year [1981], although he is now such a legendary figure it seems strange to imagine him still alive today.

CHRIS: How did he die?

SANDY: Almost certainly suicide. He was homosexual and had to deal with a lot of harsh treatment and stupidity from the outside world. In the end it apparently got to be too much, and he killed himself.

CHRIS: That's a sad story.

SANDY: Yes, it certainly is. What saddens me is that he never got to see the amazing progress in computing machinery and theory that has taken place.

PAT: Hey, are you going to clue me in as to what this Turing article is about?

SANDY: It is really about two things. One is the question "Can a machine think?"—or rather, "Will a machine ever think?" The way Turing answers this question—he thinks the answer is "yes," by the way—is by batting down a series of objections to the idea, one after another. The other point he tries to make is that the question is not meaningful as it stands. It's too full of emotional connotations. Many people are upset by the suggestion that people are machines, or that machines might think. Turing tries to defuse the question by casting it in less emotional terms. For instance, what do you think, Pat, of the idea of "thinking machines"?

PAT: Frankly, I find the term confusing. You know what confuses me? It's those ads in the newspapers and on TV that talk about "products that think" or "intelligent ovens" or whatever. I just don't know how seriously to take them.

SANDY: I know the kind of ads you mean, and I think they confuse a lot of people. On the one hand we're given the refrain "Computers are really dumb, you have to spell everything out for them in complete detail," and on the other hand we're bombarded with advertising hype about "smart products."

CHRIS: That's certainly true. Did you know that one computer terminal manufacturer has even taken to calling its products "dumb terminals" in order to stand out from the crowd?

SANDY: That's cute, but it just plays along with the trend toward obfuscation. The term "electronic brain" always comes to my mind when I'm thinking about this. Many people swallow it completely, while others reject it out of hand. Few have the patience to sort out the issues and decide how much of it makes sense.

PAT: Does Turing suggest some way of resolving it, some sort of IQ test for machines?

SANDY: That would be interesting, but no machine could yet come close to taking an IQ test. Instead, Turing proposes a test that theoretically could be applied to any machine to determine whether it can think or not.

PAT: Does the test give a clear-cut yes or no answer? I'd be skeptical if it claimed to.

SANDY: No, it doesn't. In a way, that's one of its advantages. It shows how the borderline is quite fuzzy and how subtle the whole question is.

PAT: So, as is usual in philosophy, it's all just a question of words.

SANDY: Maybe, but they're emotionally charged words, and so it's important, it seems to me, to explore the issues and try to map out the meanings of the crucial words. The issues are fundamental to our concept of ourselves, so we shouldn't just sweep them under the rug.

PAT: So tell me how Turing's test works.

SANDY: The idea is based on what he calls the Imitation Game. In this game a man and a woman go into separate rooms and can be interrogated by a third party, via some sort of teletype set-up. The third party can address questions to either room, but has no idea which person is in which room. For the interrogator the idea is to discern which room the woman is in. Now the woman, by her answers, tries to aid the interrogator as much as possible. The man, however, is doing his best to bamboozle the interrogator by responding as he thinks a woman might. And if he succeeds in fooling the interrogator . . .

PAT: The interrogator only gets to see written words, eh? And the sex of the author is supposed to shine through? That game sounds like a good challenge. I would very much like to participate in it someday. Would the interrogator know either the man or the woman before the test began? Would any of them know the others?

SANDY: That would probably be a bad idea. All sorts of subliminal cueing might occur if the interrogator knew one or both of them. It would be safest if all three people were totally unknown to each other.

PAT: Could you ask any question at all, with no holds barred?

SANDY: Absolutely. That's the whole idea.

PAT: Don't you think, then, that pretty quickly it would degenerate into very sex-oriented questions? I can imagine the man, overeager to act convincing, giving away the game by answering some very blunt questions that most women would find too personal to answer, even through an anonymous computer connection.

SANDY: It sounds plausible.

CHRIS: Another possibility would be to probe for knowledge of minute aspects of traditional sex-role differences, by asking about such things as dress sizes and so on. The psychology of the Imitation Game could get pretty subtle. I suppose it would make a difference if the interrogator were a woman or a man. Don't you think that a woman could spot some telltale differences more quickly than a man could?

PAT: If so, maybe *that's* how to tell a man from a woman!

SANDY: Hmm . . . that's a new twist! In any case, I don't know if this original version of the Imitation Game has ever been seriously tried out, despite the fact that it would be relatively easy to do with modern computer terminals. I have to admit, though, that I'm not sure what it would prove, whichever way it turned out.

PAT: I was wondering about that. What would it prove if the interrogator—say, a woman—couldn't tell correctly which person was the woman? It certainly wouldn't prove that the man *was* a woman!

SANDY: Exactly! What I find funny is that although I fundamentally believe in the Turing test, I'm not sure what the point is of the Imitation Game, on which it's founded!

CHRIS: I'm not any happier with the Turing test as a test for "thinking machines" than I am with the Imitation Game as a test for femininity.

PAT: From your statements I gather that the Turing test is a kind of extension of the Imitation Game, only involving a machine and a person in separate rooms.

SANDY: That's the idea, the machine tries its hardest to convince the interrogator that it is the human being, while the human tries to make it clear that he or she is not a computer.

PAT: Except for your loaded phrase "the machine tries," this sounds very interesting. But how do you know that this test will get at the essence of thinking? Maybe it's testing for the wrong things. Maybe, just to take a random illustration, someone would feel that a machine was able to think only if it could dance so well that you couldn't tell it was a machine. Or someone else could suggest some other characteristic. What's so sacred about being able to fool people by typing at them?

SANDY: I don't see how you can say such a thing. I've heard that objection before, but frankly it baffles me. So what if the machine can't tap-dance or drop a rock on your toe? If it can discourse intelligently on any subject you want, then it has shown it can think—to me, at least! As I see it, Turing has drawn, in one clean stroke, a clear division between thinking and other aspects of being human.

PAT: Now *you're* the baffling one. If one couldn't conclude anything from a man's ability to win at the Imitation Game, how could one conclude anything from a machine's ability to win at the Turing game?

CHRIS: Good question.

SANDY: It seems to me that you could conclude *something* from a man's win in the Imitation Game. You wouldn't conclude he was a woman, but you could certainly say he had good insights into the feminine mentality (if there is such a thing). Now, if a computer could fool someone into thinking it was a person, I guess you'd have to say something similar about it—that it had good insights into what it's like to be human, into "the human condition" (whatever that is).

PAT: Maybe, but that isn't necessarily equivalent to thinking, is it? It seems to me that passing the Turing test would merely prove that some machine or other could do a very good job of *simulating* thought.

CHRIS: I couldn't agree more with Pat. We all know that fancy computer programs exist today for simulating all sorts of complex phenomena. In physics, for instance, we simulate the behavior of particles, atoms, solids, liquids, gases, galaxies, and so on. But nobody confuses any of those simulations with the real thing!

SANDY: In his book *Brainstorms*, the philosopher Daniel Dennett makes a similar point about simulated hurricanes.

CHRIS: That's a nice example too. Obviously, what goes on inside a computer when it's simulating a hurricane is not a hurricane, for the machine's memory doesn't get torn to bits by 200-mile-an-hour winds, the floor of the machine room doesn't get flooded with rainwater, and so on.

SANDY: Oh, come on—that's not a fair argument! In the first place, the programmers don't claim the simulation really *is* a hurricane. It's merely a simulation of certain aspects of a hurricane. But in the second place, you're pulling a fast one when you imply that there are no downpours or 200-mile-an-hour winds in a simulated hurricane. To us there aren't any—but if the program were incredibly detailed, it could include simulated people on the ground who would experience the wind and the rain just as we do when a hurricane hits. In their minds—or, if you prefer, in their *simulated* minds—the hurricane would not be a simulation but a genuine phenomenon complete with drenching and devastation.

CHRIS: Oh, boy—what a science-fiction scenario! Now we're talking about simulating whole populations, not just a single mind!

SANDY: Well, look—I'm simply trying to show you why your argument that a simulated McCoy isn't the real McCoy is fallacious. It depends on the tacit assumption that any old observer of the simulated phenomenon is equally able to assess what's going on. But, in fact, it may take an observer with a special vantage point to recognize what is going on. In this case, it takes special "computational glasses" to see the rain and the winds and so on.

PAT: "Computational glasses"? I don't know what you're talking about!

SANDY: I mean that to see the winds and the wetness of the hurricane, you have to be able to look at it in the proper way. You—

CHRIS: No, no, no! A simulated hurricane isn't wet! No matter how much it might seem wet to simulated people, it won't ever be *genuinely* wet! And no computer will ever get torn apart in the process of simulating winds!

SANDY: Certainly not, but you're confusing levels. The laws of physics don't get torn apart by real hurricanes either. In the case of the simulated hurricane, if you go peering at the computer's memory expecting to find broken wires and so forth, you'll be disappointed. But look at the proper level. Look into the *structures* that are coded for in the memory. You'll see that some abstract links have been broken, some values of variables radically changed, and so forth. There's your flood, your devastation— real, only a little concealed, a little hard to detect.

CHRIS: I'm sorry, I just can't buy that. You're insisting that I look for a new kind of devastation, a kind never before associated with hurricanes. Using this idea, you could call *anything* a hurricane as long as its effects, seen through your special "glasses," could be called "floods and devastation."

SANDY: Right—you've got it exactly! You recognize a hurricane by its *effects*. You have no way of going in and finding some ethereal "essence of hurricane," some "human soul," located right in the middle of the eye! It's the existence of a certain kind of *pattern*—a spiral storm with an eye and so forth that makes you say it's a hurricane. Of course there are a lot of things that you'll insist on before you call something a hurricane.

PAT: Well, wouldn't you say that being an atmospheric phenomenon is one vital prerequisite? How can anything inside a computer be a storm? To me, a simulation is a simulation is a simulation!

SANDY: Then I suppose you would say that even the calculations that computers do are simulated—but they are fake calculations. Only people can do genuine calculations, right?

PAT: Well, computers get the right answers, so their calculations are not exactly fake—but they're still just *patterns*. There's no understanding going on in there. Take a cash register. Can you honestly say that you feel it is calculating something when its gears turn on each other? And a computer is just a fancy cash register, as I understand it.

SANDY: If you mean that a cash register doesn't feel like a schoolkid doing arithmetic problems, I'll agree. But is that what "calculation" means? Is that an integral part of it? If so, then contrary to what everybody has thought till now, we'll have to write a very complicated program to perform *genuine* calculations. Of course, this program will sometimes get careless and make mistakes and it will sometimes scrawl its answers illegibly, and it will occasionally doodle on its paper. . . . It won't be more reliable than the post office clerk who adds up your total by hand. Now, I happen to believe eventually such a program could be written. Then we'd know something about how post office clerks and schoolkids work.

PAT: I can't believe you could ever do that!

SANDY: Maybe, maybe not, but that's not my point. You say a cash register can't calculate. It reminds me of another favorite passage of mine from Dennett's *Brainstorms*—a rather ironic one, which is why I like it. The passage goes something like this: "Cash registers can't really calculate; they can only spin their gears. But cash registers can't really spin their gears either; they can only follow the laws of physics." Dennett said it originally about computers; I modified it to talk about cash registers. And you could use the same line of reasoning in talking about people: "People can't really calculate; all they can do is manipulate mental symbols. But they aren't really manipulating symbols; all they are doing is firing various neurons in various patterns. But they can't really make their neurons fire; they simply have to let the laws of physics make them fire for them." Et cetera. Don't you see how this Dennett-inspired *reductio ad absurdum* would lead you to conclude that calculation doesn't exist, hurricanes don't exist, nothing at a higher level than particles and the laws of physics exists? What do you gain by saying a computer only pushes symbols around and doesn't truly calculate?

PAT: The example may be extreme, but it makes my point that there is a vast difference between a real phenomenon and any simulation of it. This is so for hurricanes, and even more so for human thought.

SANDY: Look, I don't want to get tangled up in this line of argument, but let me try out one more example. If you were a radio ham listening to another ham broadcasting in Morse code and you were responding in Morse code, would it sound funny to you to refer to "the person at the other end?"

PAT: No, that would sound okay, although the existence of a person at the other end would be an assumption.

SANDY: Yes, but you wouldn't be likely to go and check it out. You're prepared to recognize personhood through those rather unusual channels. You don't have to see a human body or hear a voice—all you need is a rather abstract manifestation—a code, as it were. What I'm getting at is this. To "see" the person behind the dits and dahs, you have to be willing to do some decoding, some interpretation. It's not direct perception; it's indirect. You have to peel off a layer or two, to find the reality hidden in there. You put on your "radio-ham's glasses" to "see" the person behind the buzzes. Just the same with the simulated hurricane! You don't see it darkening the machine room—you have to decode the machine's memory. You have to put on special "memory-decoding glasses." *Then* what you see is a hurricane!

PAT: Oh, ho ho! Talk about fast ones—wait a minute! In the case of the short-wave radio, there's a real person out there, somewhere in the Fiji Islands or wherever. My decoding act as I sit by my radio simply reveals that that person exists. It's like seeing a shadow and concluding there's an object out there, casting it. One doesn't confuse the shadow with the object, however! And with the hurricane there's no *real* hurricane behind the scenes, making the computer follow its patterns. No, what you have is just a shadow hurricane without any genuine hurricane. I just refuse to confuse shadows with reality.

SANDY: All right. I don't want to drive this point into the ground. I even admit it is pretty silly to say that a simulated hurricane *is* a hurricane. But I wanted to point out that it's not as silly as you might think at first blush. And when you turn to simulated thought, you've got a very different matter on your hands from simulated hurricanes.

PAT: I don't see why. A brainstorm sounds to me like a mental hurricane. But seriously, you'll have to convince me.

SANDY: Well, to do so I'll have to make a couple of extra points about hurricanes first.

PAT: Oh, no! Well, all right, all right.

SANDY: Nobody can say just exactly what a hurricane is—that is, in totally precise terms, there's an abstract pattern that many storms share, and it's for that reason that we call those storms hurricanes. But it's not possible to make a sharp distinction between hurricanes and nonhurricanes. There are tornados, cyclones, typhoons, dust-devils. . . . Is the Great Red Spot on Jupiter a hurricane? Are sunspots hurricanes? Could there be a hurricane in a wind tunnel? In a test tube? In your imagination you can even extend the concept of "hurricane" to include a microscopic storm on the surface of a neutron star.

CHRIS: That's not so far-fetched, you know. The concept of "earthquake" has actually been extended to neutron stars. The astrophysicists say that the tiny changes in rate that once in a while are observed in the pulsing of a pulsar are caused by "glitches"—starquakes—that have just occurred on the neutron star's surface.

SANDY: Yes, I remember that now. The idea of a "glitch" strikes me as wonderfully eerie—a surrealistic kind of quivering on a surrealistic kind of surface.

CHRIS: Can you imagine—plate tectonics on a giant rotating sphere of pure nuclear matter?

SANDY: That's a wild thought. So starquakes and earthquakes can both be subsumed into a new, more abstract category. And that's how science constantly extends familiar concepts, taking them further and further from familiar experience and yet keeping some essence constant. The number system is the classic example—from positive numbers to negative numbers, then rationals, reals, complex numbers, and "on beyond zebra," as Dr. Seuss says.

PAT: I think I can see your point here, Sandy. We have many examples in biology of close relationships that are established in rather abstract ways. Often the decision about what family some species belongs to comes down to an abstract pattern shared at some level. When you base your system of classification on very abstract patterns, I suppose that a broad variety of phenomena can fall into "the same class," even if in many superficial ways the class members are utterly unlike each other. So perhaps I can glimpse, at least a little, how to you a simulated hurricane could, in some funny sense, *be* a hurricane.

CHRIS: Perhaps the word that's being extended is not "hurricane" but "be"!

PAT: How so?

CHRIS: If Turing can extend the verb "think," can't I extend the verb "be"? All I mean is that when simulated things are deliberately confused with the genuine article, somebody's doing a lot of philosophical wool-pulling. It's a lot more serious than just extending a few nouns such as "hurricane."

SANDY: I like your idea that ''be'' is being extended, but I think your slur about "wool-pulling" goes too far. Anyway, if you don't object, let me just say one more thing about simulated hurricanes and then I'll get to simulated minds. Suppose you consider a really deep simulation of a hurricane—I mean a simulation of every atom, which I admit is impossibly deep. I hope you would agree that it would then share all that abstract structure that defines the "essence of hurricane-hood." So what's to hold you back from calling it a hurricane?

PAT: I thought you were backing off from that claim of equality!

SANDY: So did I, but then these examples came up, and I was forced back to my claim. But let me back off, as I said I would do, and get back to *thought*, which is the real issue here. Thought, even more than hurricanes, is an abstract structure, a way of describing some complex events that happen in a medium called a brain. But actually thought can take place in any of several billion brains. There are all these physically very different brains, and yet they all support "the same thing"—thinking. What's important, then, is the abstract *pattern*, not the medium. The same kind of swirling can happen inside any of them, so no person can claim to think more "genuinely" than any other. Now, if we come up with some new kind of medium in which *the same style* of swirling takes place, could you deny that thinking is taking place in it?

PAT: Probably not, but you have just shifted the question. The question now is, how can you determine whether "the same style" of swirling is really happening?

SANDY: The beauty of the Turing test is that it *tells* you when!

CHRIS: I don't see that at all. How would you know that the same style of activity was occurring inside a computer as inside my mind, simply because it answered questions as I do? All you're looking at is its outside.

SANDY: But how do you know that when I speak to you, anything similar to what you call "thinking" is going on inside *me*? The Turing test is a fantastic probe, something like a particle accelerator in physics. Chris, I think you'll like this analogy. Just as in physics, when you want to understand what is going on at an atomic or subatomic level, since you can't see it directly, you scatter accelerated particles off the target in question and observe their behavior. From this you infer the internal nature of the target. The Turing text extends this idea to the mind. It treats the mind as a "target" that is not directly visible but whose structure can be deduced more abstractly. By "scattering" questions off a target mind, you learn about its internal workings, just as in physics.

CHRIS: More exactly put, you can hypothesize about what kinds of internal structures might account for the behavior observed—but they may or may not in fact exist.

SANDY: Hold on, now! Are you saying that atomic nuclei are merely hypothetical entities? After all, their existence—or should I say "hypothetical existence"?—was proven—or should I say "suggested"?—by the behavior of particles scattered off of atoms.

CHRIS: Physical systems seem to me to be much simpler than the mind, and the certainty of the inferences made is correspondingly greater.

SANDY: The experiments are also correspondingly harder to perform and to interpret. In the Turing test, you could perform many highly delicate experiments in the course of an hour. I maintain that people give other people credit for being conscious simply because of their continual external monitoring of them—which is itself something like a Turing test.

PAT: That may be roughly true, but it involves more than just conversing with people through a teletype. We see that other people have bodies, we watch their faces and expressions—we see they are fellow human beings and so we think they think.

SANDY: To me, that seems a highly anthropocentric view of what thought is. Does that mean you would sooner say a mannikin in a store thinks than a wonderfully programmed computer, simply because the mannikin looks more human?

PAT: Obviously I would need more than just vague physical resemblance to the human form to be willing to attribute the power of thought to an entity. But that organic quality, the sameness of origin, undeniably lends a degree of credibility that is very important.

SANDY: Here we disagree. I find this simply too chauvinistic. I feel that the key thing is a similarity of *internal* structure—not bodily, organic, chemical structure, but organizational structure—software. Whether an entity can think seems to me a question of whether its organization can be described in a certain way, and I'm perfectly willing to believe that the Turing test detects the presence or absence of that mode of organization. I would say that your depending on my physical body as evidence that I am a thinking being is rather shallow. The way I see it, the Turing test looks far deeper than at mere external form.

PAT: Hey now—you're not giving me much credit. It's not just the shape of a body that lends weight to the idea there's real thinking going on inside—it's also, as I said, the idea of common origin. It's the idea that you and I both sprang from DNA molecules, an idea to which I attribute much depth. Put it this way: The external form of human bodies reveals that they share a deep biological history, and it's *that* depth that lends a lot of credibility to the notion that the owner of such a body can think.

SANDY: But that is all indirect evidence. Surely you want some *direct* evidence. That is what the Turing test is for. And I think it is the *only* way to test for "thinkinghood."

CHRIS: But you could be fooled by the Turing test, just as an interrogator could think a man was a woman.

SANDY: I admit, I could be fooled if I carried out the test in too quick or too shallow a way. But I could go for the deepest things I could think of.

CHRIS: I would want to see if the program could understand jokes. That would be a real test of intelligence.

SANDY: I agree that humor probably is an acid test for a supposedly intelligent program, but equally important to me—perhaps more so—would be to test its emotional responses. So I would ask it about its reactions to certain pieces of music or works of literature—especially my favorite ones.

CHRIS: What if it said, "I don't know that piece," or even "I have no interest in music"? What if it avoided all emotional references?

SANDY: That would make me suspicious. Any consistent pattern of avoiding certain issues would raise serious doubts in me as to whether I was dealing with a thinking being.

CHRIS: Why do you say that? Why not say that you're dealing with a thinking but unemotional being?

SANDY: You've hit upon a sensitive point. I simply can't believe that emotions and thought can be divorced. Put another way, I think that emotions are an automatic by-product of the ability to think. They are implied by the very nature of thought.

CHRIS: Well, what if you're wrong? What if I produced a machine that could think but not emote? Then its intelligence might go unrecognized because it failed to pass *your* kind of test.

SANDY: I'd like you to point out to me where the boundary line between emotional questions and nonemotional ones lies. You might want to ask about the meaning of a great novel. This requires understanding of human emotions! Is that thinking or merely cool calculation? You might want to ask about a subtle choice of words. For that you need an understanding of their connotations. Turing uses examples like this in his article. You might want to ask it for advice about a complex romantic situation. It would need to know a lot about human motivations and their roots. Now if it failed at this kind of task, I would not be much inclined to say that it could think. As far as I am concerned, the ability to think, the ability to feel, and consciousness are just different facets of one phenomenon, and no one of them can be present without the others.

CHRIS: Why couldn't you build a machine that could feel nothing, but that could think and make complex decisions anyway? I don't see any contradiction there.

SANDY: Well, I do. I think that when you say that, you are visualizing a metallic, rectangular machine, probably in an air-conditioned room—a hard, angular, cold object with a million colored wires inside it, a machine that sits stock still on a tiled floor, humming or buzzing or whatever, and spinning its tapes. Such a machine can play a good game of chess, which, I freely admit, involves a lot of decision making. And yet I would never call such a machine conscious.

CHRIS: How come? To mechanists, isn't a chess-playing machine rudimentarily conscious?

SANDY: Not to this mechanist. The way I see it, consciousness has got to come from a precise pattern of organization—one that we haven't figured out how to describe in any detailed way. But I believe we will gradually come to understand it. In my view consciousness requires a certain way of mirroring the external universe internally, and the ability to respond to that external reality on the basis of the internally represented model. And then in addition, what's really crucial for a conscious machine is that it should incorporate a well-developed and flexible self-model. And it's there that all existent programs, including the best chess-playing ones, fall down.

CHRIS: Don't chess programs look ahead and say to themselves as they're figuring out their next move, "If you move here, then I'll go there, and then if you go this way, I could go that way . . ."? Isn't that a sort of self-model?

SANDY: Not really. Or, if you want, it's an extremely limited one. It's an understanding of self only in the narrowest sense. For instance, a chess-playing program has no concept of why it is playing chess, or the fact that it is a program, or is in a computer, or has a human opponent. It has no ideas about what winning and losing are, or—

PAT: How do *you* know it has no such sense? How can you presume to say what a chess program feels or knows?

SANDY: Oh, come on! We all know that certain things don't feel anything or know anything. A thrown stone doesn't know anything about parabolas, and a whirling fan doesn't know anything about air. It's true I can't *prove* those statements, but here we are verging on questions of faith.

PAT: This reminds me of a Taoist story I read. It goes something like this. Two sages were standing on a bridge over a stream. One said to the other, "I wish I were a fish. They are so happy!" The second replied, "How do you know whether fish are happy or not? You're not a fish." The first said, "But you're not me, so how do you know whether I know how fish feel?"

SANDY: Beautiful! Talking about consciousness really does call for a certain amount of restraint. Otherwise you might as well just jump on either the solipsism bandwagon—"I am the only conscious being in the universe"—or the panpsychism bandwagon—"Everything in the universe is conscious!"

PAT: Well, how do you know? Maybe everything *is* conscious.

SANDY: If you're going to join those who claim that stones and even particles like electrons have some sort of consciousness, then I guess we part company here. That's a kind of mysticism I can't fathom. As for chess programs, I happen to know how they work, and I can tell you for sure that they aren't conscious! No way!

PAT: Why not?

SANDY: They incorporate only the barest knowledge about the goals of chess. The notion of "playing" is turned into the mechanical act of comparing a lot of numbers and choosing the biggest one over and over again. A chess program has no sense of shame about losing or pride in winning. Its self-model is very crude. It gets away with doing the least it can, just enough to play a game of chess and do nothing more. Yet, interestingly enough, we still tend to talk about the "desires" of a chess-playing computer. We say, "It wants to keep its king behind a row of pawns," or "It likes to get its rooks out early," or "It thinks I don't see that hidden fork."

PAT: Well, we do the same thing with insects. We spot a lonely ant somewhere and say, "It's trying to get back home" or "It wants to drag that dead bee back to the colony." In fact, with any animal we use terms that indicate emotions, but we don't know for sure how much the animal feels. I have no trouble talking about dogs and cats being happy or sad, having desires and beliefs and so on, but of course I don't think their sadness is as deep or complex as human sadness is.

SANDY: But you wouldn't call it "simulated sadness," would you?

PAT: No, of course not. I think it's real.

SANDY: It's hard to avoid use of such teleological or mentalistic terms. I believe they're quite justified, although they shouldn't be carried too far. They simply don't have the same richness of meaning when applied to present-day chess programs as when applied to people.

CHRIS: I still can't see that intelligence has to involve emotions. Why couldn't you imagine an intelligence that simply calculates and has no feelings?

SANDY: A couple of answers here! Number one, any intelligence has to have motivations. It's simply not the case, whatever many people may think, that machines could think any more "objectively" than people do. Machines, when they look at a scene, will have to focus and filter that scene down into some preconceived categories, just as a person does. And that means seeing some things and missing others. It means giving more weight to some things than to others. This happens on every level of processing.

PAT: What do you mean?

SANDY: Take me right now, for instance. You might think that I'm just making some intellectual points, and I wouldn't need emotions to do that. But what makes me *care* about these points? Why did I stress the word "care" so heavily? Because I'm emotionally involved in this conversation! People talk to each other out of conviction, not out of hollow, mechanical reflexes. Even the most intellectual conversation is driven by underlying passions. There's an emotional undercurrent to every conversation—it's the fact that the speakers want to be listened to, understood, and respected for what they are saying.

PAT: It sounds to me as if all you're saying is that people need to be interested in what they're saying, otherwise a conversation dies.

SANDY: Right! I wouldn't bother to talk to anyone if I weren't motivated by interest. And interest is just another name for a whole constellation of subconscious biases. When I talk, all my biases work together and what you perceive on the surface level is my style, my personality. But that style arises from an immense number of tiny priorities, biases, leanings. When you add up a million of these interacting together, you get something that amounts to a lot of *desires*. It just all adds up! And that brings me to the other point, about feelingless calculation. Sure, that exists—in a cash register, a pocket calculator. I'd say it's even true of all today's computer programs. But eventually, when you put enough feelingless calculations together in a huge coordinated organization, you'll get something that has properties on another level. You can see it—in fact, you *have* to see it—not as a bunch of little calculations, but as a system of tendencies and desires and beliefs and so on. When things get complicated enough, you're forced to change your level of description. To some extent that's already happening, which is why we use words such as "want," "think," "try," and "hope," to describe chess programs and other attempts at mechanical thought. Dennett calls that kind of level switch by the observer "adopting the intentional stance." The really interesting things in AI will only begin to happen, I'd guess, when the program *itself* adopts the intentional stance toward itself!

CHRIS: That would be a very strange sort of level-crossing feedback loop.

SANDY: It certainly would. Of course, in my opinion, it's highly premature for anyone to adopt the intentional stance, in the full force of the term, toward today's programs. At least that's my opinion.

CHRIS: For me an important related question is: To what extent is it valid to adopt the intentional stance toward beings other than humans?

PAT: I would certainly adopt the intentional stance toward mammals.

SANDY: I vote for that.

CHRIS: That's interesting! How can that be, Sandy? Surely you wouldn't claim that a dog or cat can pass the Turing test? Yet don't you think that the Turing test is the only way to test for the presence of thought? How can you have these beliefs at once?

SANDY: Hmm. . . . All right. I guess I'm forced to admit that the Turing test works only above a certain level of consciousness. There can be thinking beings that could fail the test—but on the other hand, anything that passes it, in my opinion, would be a genuinely conscious, thinking being.

PAT: How can you think of a computer as a conscious being? I apologize if this sounds like a stereotype, but when I think of conscious beings, I just can't connect that thought with machines. To me consciousness is connected with soft, warm bodies, silly though that may sound.

CHRIS: That does sound odd, coming from a biologist. Don't you deal with life in terms of chemistry and physics enough for all magic to seem to vanish?

PAT: Not really. Sometimes the chemistry and physics just increase the feeling that there's something magical going on down there! Anyway, I can't always integrate my scientific knowledge with my gut-level feelings.

CHRIS: I guess I share that trait.

PAT: So how do you deal with rigid preconceptions like mine?

SANDY: I'd try to dig down under the surface of your concept of "machines" and get at the intuitive connotations that lurk there, out of sight but deeply influencing your opinions. I think that we all have a holdover image from the Industrial Revolution that sees machines as clunky iron contraptions gawkily moving under the power of some loudly chugging engine. Possibly that's even how the computer inventor Charles Babbage viewed people! After all, he called his magnificent many-geared computer the Analytical Engine.

PAT: Well, I certainly don't think people are just fancy steam shovels or even electric can openers. There's something about people, something that—that—they've got a sort of *flame* inside them, something alive, something that flickers unpredictably, wavering, uncertain—but something *creative!*

SANDY: Great! That's just the sort of thing I wanted to hear. It's very human to think that way. Your flame image makes me think of candles, of fires, of thunderstorms with lightning dancing all over the sky in crazy patterns. But do you realize that just that kind of pattern is visible on a computer's console? The flickering lights form amazing chaotic sparkling patterns. It's such a far cry from heaps of lifeless clanking metal! It *is* flamelike, by God! Why don't you let the word "machine" conjure up images of dancing patterns of light rather than of giant steam shovels?

CHRIS: That's a beautiful image, Sandy. It changes my sense of mechanism from being matter-oriented to being pattern-oriented. It makes me try to visualize the thoughts in my mind—these thoughts right now, even—as a huge spray of tiny pulses flickering in my brain.

SANDY: That's quite a poetic self-portrait for a spray of flickers to have come up with!

CHRIS: Thank you. But still, I'm not totally convinced that a machine is all that I am. I admit, my concept of machines probably does suffer from anachronistic subconscious flavors, but I'm afraid I can't change such a deeply rooted sense in a flash.

SANDY: At least you do sound open-minded. And to tell the truth, part of me does sympathize with the way you and Pat view machines. Part of me balks at calling myself a machine. It *is* a bizarre thought that a feeling being like you or me might emerge from mere circuitry. Do I surprise you?

CHRIS: You certainly surprise *me*. So tell us—do you believe in the idea of an intelligent computer, or don't you?

SANDY: It all depends on what you mean. We have all heard the question "Can computers think?" There are several possible interpretations of this (aside from the many interpretations of the word "think"). They revolve around different meanings of the words "can" and "computer."

PAT: Back to word games again. . . .

SANDY: That's right. First of all, the question might mean "Does some present-day computer think, right now?" To this I would immediately answer with a loud "no." Then it could be taken to mean, "Could some present-day computer, if suitably programmed, potentially think?" This is more like it, but I would still answer, "Probably not." The real difficulty hinges on the word "computer." The way I see it, "computer" calls up an image of just what I described earlier: an air-conditioned room with cold rectangular metallic boxes in it. But I suspect that with increasing public familiarity with computers and continued progress in computer architecture, that vision will eventually become outmoded.

PAT: Don't you think computers, as we know them, will be around for a while?

SANDY: Sure, there will have to be computers in today's image around for a long time, but advanced computers—maybe no longer called computers—will evolve and become quite different. Probably, as in the case of living organisms, there will be many branchings in the evolutionary tree. There will be computers for business, computers for schoolkids, computers for scientific calculations, computers for systems research, computers for simulation, computers for rockets going into space, and so on. Finally, there will be computers for the study of intelligence. It's really only these last that I'm thinking of—the ones with the maximum flexibility, the ones that people are deliberately attempting to make smart. I see no reason that these will stay fixed in the traditional image. Probably they will soon acquire as standard features some rudimentary sensory systems—mostly for vision and hearing, at first. They will need to be able to move around, to explore. They will have to be physically flexible. In short, they will have to become more animal-like, more self-reliant.

CHRIS: It makes me think of the robots R2D2 and C3PO in *Star Wars*.

SANDY: As a matter of fact I don't think of anything like them when I visualize intelligent machines. They're too silly, too much the product of a film designer's imagination. Not that I have a clear vision of my own. But I think it is necessary, if people are going to try realistically to imagine an artificial intelligence, to go beyond the limited, hard-edged image of computers that comes from exposure to what we have today. The only thing that all machines will always have in common is their underlying mechanicalness. That may sound cold and inflexible, but what could be more mechanical—in a wonderful way—than the operations of the DNA and proteins and organelles in our cells?

PAT: To me what goes on inside cells has a "wet," "slippery" feel to it, and what goes on inside machines is dry and rigid. It's connected with the fact that computers don't make mistakes, that computers do only what you tell them to do. Or at least that's my image of computers.

SANDY: Funny—a minute ago your image was of a flame, and now it's of something "wet and slippery." Isn't it marvelous how contradictory we can be?

PAT: I don't need your sarcasm.

SANDY: I'm not being sarcastic—I really *do* think it is marvelous.

PAT: It's just an example of the human mind's slippery nature—mine, in this case.

SANDY: True. But your image of computers is stuck in a rut. Computers certainly can make mistakes—and I don't mean on the hardware level.

Think of any present-day computer predicting the weather. It can make wrong predictions, even though its program runs flawlessly.

PAT: But that's only because you've fed it the wrong data.

SANDY: Not so. It's because weather prediction is too complex. Any such program has to make do with a limited amount of data—entirely correct data—and extrapolate from there. Sometimes it will make wrong predictions. It's no different from the farmer in the field gazing at the clouds who says, "I reckon we'll get a little snow tonight." We make models of things in our heads and use them to guess how the world will behave. We have to make do with our models, however inaccurate they may be. And if they're too inaccurate, evolution will prune us out—we'll fall over a cliff or something. And computers are the same. It's just that human designers will speed up the evolutionary process by aiming explicitly at the goal of creating intelligence, which is something nature just stumbled on.

PAT: So you think computers will make fewer mistakes as they get smarter?

SANDY: Actually, just the other way around. The smarter they get, the more they'll be in a position to tackle messy real-life domains, so they'll be more and more likely to have inaccurate models. To me, mistake making is a sign of high intelligence!

PAT: Boy—you throw me sometimes!

SANDY: I guess I'm a strange sort of advocate for machine intelligence. To some degree I straddle the fence. I think that machines won't really be intelligent in a humanlike way until they have something like that biological wetness or slipperiness to them. I don't mean literally wet—the slipperiness could be in the software. But biological-seeming or not, intelligent machines will in any case be machines. We will have designed them, built them—or grown them, but collectively we will know how they work.

PAT: It sounds like you want to have your cake and eat it too.

SANDY: You're probably right. What I'm getting at is that when artificial intelligence comes, it will be mechanical and yet at the same time organic. It will have that same astonishing flexibility that we see in life's mechanisms. And when I say "mechanisms," I *mean* "mechanisms." DNA and enzymes and so on really *are* mechanical and rigid and reliable. Wouldn't you agree, Pat?

PAT: That's true. But when they work together, a lot of unexpected things happen. There are so many complexities and rich modes of behavior that all that mechanicalness adds up to something very fluid.

SANDY: For me it's an almost unimaginable transition from the mechanical level of molecules to the living level of cells. But it's what convinces me that people are machines. That thought makes me uncomfortable in some ways, but in other ways it is an exhilarating thought.

CHRIS: If people are machines, how come it's so hard to convince them of the fact? Surely if we are machines, we ought to be able to recognize our own machinehood.

SANDY: You have to allow for emotional factors here. To be told you're a machine is, in a way, to be told that you're nothing more than your physical parts, and it brings you face to face with your own mortality. That's something nobody finds easy to face. But beyond the emotional objection, to see yourself as a machine you have to jump all the way from the bottommost mechanical level to the level where the complex lifelike activities take place. If there are many intermediate layers, they act as a shield, and the mechanical quality becomes almost invisible. I think that's how intelligent machines will seem to us—and to themselves!—when they come around.

PAT: I once heard a funny idea about what will happen when we eventually have intelligent machines. When we try to implant that intelligence into devices we'd like to control, their behavior won't be so predictable.

SANDY: They'll have a quirky little "flame" inside, maybe?

PAT: Maybe.

CHRIS: So what's so funny about that?

PAT: Well, think of military missiles. The more sophisticated their target-tracking computers get, according to this idea, the less predictably they will function. Eventually you'll have missiles that will decide they are pacifists and will turn around and go home and land quietly without blowing up. We could even have "smart bullets" that turn around in midflight because they don't want to commit suicide!

SANDY: That's a lovely thought.

CHRIS: I'm very skeptical about these ideas. Still, Sandy, I'd like to hear your predictions about when intelligent machines will come to be.

SANDY: It won't be for a long time, probably, that we'll see anything remotely resembling the level of human intelligence. It just rests on too awesomely complicated a substrate—the brain—for us to be able to duplicate it in the foreseeable future. Anyway, that's my opinion.

PAT: Do you think a program will ever pass the Turing test?

SANDY: That's a pretty hard question. I guess there are various degrees of passing such a test, when you come down to it. It's not black and white. First of all, it depends on who the interrogator is. A simpleton might be totally taken in by some programs today. But secondly, it depends on how deeply you are allowed to probe.

PAT: Then you could have a scale of Turing tests—one-minute versions, five-minute versions, hour-long versions, and so forth. Wouldn't it be interesting if some official organization sponsored a periodic competition, like the annual computer-chess championships, for programs to try to pass the Turing test?

CHRIS: The program that lasted the longest against some panel of distinguished judges would be the winner. Perhaps there could be a big prize for the first program that fools a famous judge for, say, ten minutes.

PAT: What would a program do with a prize?

CHRIS: Come now, Pat. If a program's good enough to fool the judges, don't you think it's good enough to enjoy the prize?

PAT: Sure, especially if the prize is an evening out on the town, dancing with all the interrogators!

SANDY: I'd certainly like to see something like that established. I think it could be hilarious to watch the first programs flop pathetically!

PAT: You're pretty skeptical, aren't you? Well, do you think any computer program today could pass a five-minute Turing test, given a sophisticated interrogator?

SANDY: I seriously doubt it. It's partly because no one is really working at it explicitly. However, there is one program called "Parry" which its inventors claim has already passed a rudimentary version of the Turing test. In a series of remotely conducted interviews, Parry fooled several psychiatrists who were told they were talking to either a computer or a paranoid patient. This was an improvement over an earlier version, in which psychiatrists were simply handed transcripts of short interviews and asked to determine which ones were with a genuine paranoid and which ones with a computer simulation.

PAT: You mean they didn't have the chance to ask any questions? That's a severe handicap—and it doesn't seem in the spirit of the Turing test. Imagine someone trying to tell which sex I belong to just by reading a transcript of a few remarks by me. It might be very hard! So I'm glad the procedure has been improved.

CHRIS: How do you get a computer to act like a paranoid?

SANDY: I'm not saying it *does* act like a paranoid, only that some psychiatrists, under unusual circumstances, though so. One of the things that bothered me about this pseudo-Turing test is the way Parry works. "He"—as they call him—acts like a paranoid in that he gets abruptly defensive, veers away from undesirable topics in the conversation, and, in essence, maintains control so that no one can truly probe "him." In this way, a simulation of a paranoid is a lot easier than a simulation of a normal person.

PAT: No kidding! It reminds me of the joke about the easiest kind of human for a computer program to simulate.

CHRIS: What is that?

PAT: A catatonic patient—they just sit and do nothing at all for days on end. Even I could write a computer program to do that!

SANDY: An interesting thing about Parry is that it creates no sentences on its own—it merely selects from a huge repertoire of canned sentences the one that best responds to the input sentence.

PAT: Amazing! But that would probably be impossible on a larger scale, wouldn't it?

SANDY: Yes. The number of sentences you'd need to store to be able to respond in a normal way to all possible sentences in a conversation is astronomical, really unimaginable. And they would have to be so intricately indexed for retrieval. . . . Anybody who thinks that somehow a program could be rigged up just to pull sentences out of storage like records in a jukebox, and that this program could pass the Turing test, has not thought very hard about it. The funny part about it is that it is just this kind of unrealizable program that some enemies of artificial intelligence cite when arguing against the concept of the Turing test. Instead of a truly intelligent machine, they want you to imagine a gigantic, lumbering robot that intones canned sentences in a dull monotone. It's assumed that you could see through to its mechanical level with ease, even if it were simultaneously performing tasks that we think of as fluid, intelligent processes. Then the critics say, "You see! It would still be just a machine—a mechanical device, not intelligent at all!" I see things almost the opposite way. If I were shown a machine that can do things that I can do—I mean pass the Turing test—then, instead of feeling insulted or threatened, I'd chime in with the philosopher Raymond Smullyan and say, "How wonderful machines are!"

CHRIS: If you could ask a computer just one question in the Turing test, what would it be?

SANDY: Uhmm. . . .

PAT: How about "If you could ask a computer just one question in the Turing test, what would it be?"?

▼ *Reflections*
DANIEL C. DENNETT

Many people are put off by the provision in the Turing test requiring the contestants in the Imitation Game to be in another room from the judge, so only their verbal responses can be observed. As an element in a parlor game the rule makes sense, but how could a legitimate scientific proposal include a deliberate attempt to *hide facts* from the judges? By placing the candidates for intelligence in "black boxes" and leaving nothing as evidence but a restricted range of "external behavior" (in this case, verbal output by typing), the Turing test seems to settle dogmatically on some form of behaviorism, or (worse) operationalism, or (worse still) verificationism. (These three cousins are horrible monster *isms* of the recent past, reputed to have been roundly refuted by philosophers of science and interred—but what is that sickening sound? Can they be stirring in their graves? We should have driven stakes through their hearts!) Is the Turing test just a case of what John Searle calls "operationalist sleight-of-hand"?

The Turing test certainly does make a strong claim about what matters about minds. What matters, Turing proposes, is not what kind of gray matter (if any) the candidate has between its ears, and not what it looks like or smells like, but whether it can *act*—or behave, if you like—intelligently. The particular game proposed in the Turing test, the Imitation Game, is not sacred, but just a cannily chosen test of more general intelligence. The assumption Turing was prepared to make was that nothing could possibly pass the Turing test by winning the Imitation Game without being able to perform indefinitely many other clearly intelligent actions. Had he chosen checkmating the world chess champion as his litmus test of intelligence, there would have been powerful reasons for objecting; it now seems quite probable that one could make a machine that can do that *but nothing else.* Had he chosen stealing the British Crown Jewels without using force or accomplices, or solving the Arab-Israeli conflict without bloodshed, there would be few who would make the objection that intelligence was being "reduced to" behavior or "operationally defined" in terms of behavior. (Well, no doubt *some* philosopher somewhere would set about diligently constructing an elaborate but entirely outlandish scenario in which some utter dolt stumbled into possession of the British Crown Jewels, "passing" the test and thereby "refuting" it as a good general test of intelligence. The true operationalist, of course, would then have to admit that such a lucky moron was, by operationalist lights, truly intelligent since he passed the defining test—which is no doubt why true operationalists are hard to find.)

What makes Turing's chosen test better than stealing the British Crown Jewels or solving the Arab-Israeli conflict is that the latter tests are unrepeatable (if successfully passed once!), too difficult (many manifestly intelligent people would fail them utterly) and too hard to judge objectively. Like a well-composed wager, Turing's test invites trying; it seems fair, demanding but possible, and crisply objective in the judging. The Turing test reminds one of a wager in another way, too. Its motivation is to stop an interminable, sterile debate by saying "Put up or shut up!" Turing says in effect: "Instead of arguing about the ultimate nature and essence of mind or intelligence, why don't we all agree that anything that could pass this test is *surely* intelligent, and then turn to asking how something could be designed that might pass the test fair and square?" Ironically, Turing failed to shut off the debate but simply managed to get it redirected.

Is the Turing test vulnerable to criticism because of its "black box" ideology? First, as Hofstadter notes in his dialogue, we treat *each other* as black boxes, relying on our observation of apparently intelligent behavior to ground our belief in other minds. Second, the black box ideology is in any event the ideology of all scientific investigation. We learn about the DNA molecule by probing it in various ways and seeing how it behaves in response; we learn about cancer and earthquakes and inflation in the same way. "Looking inside" the black box is often useful when macroscopic objects are our concern; we do it by bouncing "opening" probes (such as a scalpel) off the object and then scattering photons off the exposed surfaces into our eyes. Just one more black box experiment. The question must be, as Hofstadter says: Which probes will be most directly relevant to the question we want to answer? If our question is about whether some entity is intelligent, we will find no more direct, telling probes than the everyday questions we often ask each other. The extent of Turing's "behaviorism" is simply to incorporate that near truism into a handy, laboratory-style experimental test.

Another problem raised but not settled in Hofstadter's dialogue concerns representation. A computer simulation of something is typically a detailed, "automated," multi-dimensional representation of that thing, but of course there's a world of difference between representation and reality, isn't there? As John Searle says, "No one would suppose that we could produce milk and sugar by running a computer simulation of the formal sequences in lactation and photosynthesis. . . ."[1] If we devised a program that simulated a cow on a digital computer, our simulation, being a mere representation of a cow, would not, if "milked," produce milk, but at best a representation of milk. You can't drink that, no matter how good a representation it is, and no matter how thirsty you are.

But now suppose we made a computer simulation of a mathematician, and suppose it worked well. Would we complain that what we had hoped for was *proofs*, but alas, all we got instead was mere *representations* of proofs? But representations of proofs *are* proofs, aren't they? It depends on how good the proofs represented are. When cartoonists represent scientists pondering blackboards, what they typically represent as proofs or formulae on the blackboard is pure gibberish, however "realistic" these figures appear to the layman. If the simulation of the mathematician produced phony proofs like those in the cartoons, it might still simulate *something* of theoretical interest about mathematicians—their verbal mannerisms, perhaps, or their absentmindedness. On the other hand, if the simulation were designed to produce representations of the proofs a good mathematician would produce, it would be as valuable a "colleague"—in the proof-producing department—as the mathematician. That is the difference, it seems, between abstract, formal products like proofs or songs . . . and concrete, material products like milk. On which side of this divide does the mind fall? Is mentality like milk or like a song?

Before leaping into debate on this issue we might pause to ask if the principle that creates the divide is all that clear-cut at the limits to which we would have to push it, were we to conform a truly detailed, superb simulation of *any* concrete object or phenomenon. Any actual, running simulation is concretely "realized" in some hardware or other, and the vehicles of representation must themselves produce some effects in the world. If the representation of an event produces just about the same effects in the world as the event itself would, to insist that it is merely a representation begins to sound willful. . . .

▼ *The Myth of the Computer* *
JOHN R. SEARLE

[A] theory, which is fairly widely held in cognitive science, can be summarized in three propositions.

---

[1] [The quotation is from John R. Searle, "Minds, Brains, and Programs," which is reprinted in *The Mind's I* and originally appeared in *The Behavioral and Brain Sciences*, Vol. 3 (New York: Cambridge University Press, 1980). Searle makes the point again in the following selection.]

* From John R. Searle, "The Myth of the Computer," *The New York Review of Books*, April 29, 1982, p. 3. Searle is here reviewing Hofstadter and Dennett's *The Mind's I*, the source of the previous selections.

1. *Mind as Program.* What we call minds are simply very complex digital computer programs. Mental states are simply computer states and mental processes are computational processes. Any system whatever that had the right program, with the right input and output, would have to have mental states and processes in the same literal sense that you and I do, because that is all there is to mental states and processes, that is all that you and I have. The programs in question are "self-updating" or "self-designing" "systems of representations."

2. *The Irrelevance of the Neurophysiology of the Brain.* In the study of the mind actual biological facts about actual human and animal brains are irrelevant because the mind is an "abstract sort of thing" and human brains just happen to be among the indefinitely large number of kinds of computers that can have minds. Our minds happen to be embodied in our brains, but there is no essential connection between the mind and the brain. Any other computer with the right program would also have a mind.

   Theses 1 and 2 are summarized in the introduction where the authors speak of "the emerging view of the mind as software or program—as an abstract sort of thing whose identity is independent of any particular physical embodiment."

3. *The Turing Test as the Criterion of the Mental.* The conclusive proof of the presence of mental states and capacities is the ability of a system to pass the Turing test, the test devised by Alan Turing and described in his article in this book. If a system can convince a computer expert that it has mental states then it really has those mental states. If, for example, a machine could "converse" with a native Chinese speaker in such a way as to convince the speaker that it understood Chinese then it would literally understand Chinese.

The three theses are neatly lumped together when one of the editors writes, "Minds exist in brains and may come to exist in programmed machines. If and when such machines come about, their causal powers will derive not from the substances they are made of, but from their design and the programs that run in them. And the way we will know they have those causal powers is by talking to them and listening carefully to what they have to say."

We might call this collection of theses "strong artificial intelligence" (strong AI).[1] These theses are certainly not obviously true and they are seldom explicitly stated and defended.

Let us inquire first into how plausible it is to suppose that specific biochemical powers of the brain are really irrelevant to the mind. It is an amazing fact, by the way, that in twenty-seven pieces about the mind the editors have not seen fit to include any whose primary aim is to tell us how the brain actually works, and this omission obviously derives from their conviction that since "mind is an abstract sort of thing" the

---

[1] "Strong" to distinguish the position from "weak" or "cautious" AI, which holds that the computer is simply a very useful tool in the study of the mind, not that the appropriately programmed computer literally has a mind.

specific neurophysiology of the brain is incidental. This idea derives part of its appeal from the editors' keeping their discussion at a very abstract general level about "consciousness" and "mind" and "soul," but if you consider specific mental states and processes—being thirsty, wanting to go to the bathroom, worrying about your income tax, trying to solve math puzzles, feeling depressed, recalling the French word for "butter-fly"—then it seems at least a little odd to think that the brain is so irrelevant.

Take thirst, where we actually know a little about how it works. Kidney secretions of renin synthesize a substance called angiotensin. This substance goes into the hypothalamus and triggers a series of neuron firings. As far as we know these neuron firings are a very large part of the cause of thirst. Now obviously there is more to be said, for example about the relations of the hypothalamic responses to the rest of the brain, about other things going on in the hypothalamus, and about the possible distinctions between the *feeling* of thirst and the *urge* to drink. Let us suppose we have filled out the story with the rest of the biochemical causal account of thirst.

Now the theses of the mind as program and the irrelevance of the brain would tell us that what matters about this story is not the specific biochemical properties of the angiotensin or the hypothalamus but only the formal computer programs that the whole sequence instantiates. Well, let's try that out as a hypothesis and see how it works. A computer can simulate the formal properties of the sequence of chemical and electrical phenomena in the production of thirst just as much as it can simulate the formal properties of anything else—we can simulate thirst just as we can simulate hurricanes, rainstorms, five-alarm fires, internal combustion engines, photosynthesis, lactation, or the flow of currency in a depressed economy. But no one in his right mind thinks that a computer simulation of a five-alarm fire will burn down the neighborhood, or that a computer simulation of an internal combustion engine will power a car or that computer simulations of lactation and photosynthesis will produce milk and sugar. To my amazement, however, I have found that a large number of people suppose that computer simulations of mental phenomena, whether at the level of brain processes or not, literally produce mental phenomena.

Again, let's try it out. Let's program our favorite PDP-10 computer with the formal program that simulates thirst. We can even program it to point out at the end "Boy, am I thirsty!" or "Won't someone please give me a drink?" etc. Now would anyone suppose that we thereby have even the slightest reason to suppose that the computer is literally thirsty? Or that any simulation of any other mental phenomena, such as understanding stories, feeling depressed, or worrying about itemized deductions, must therefore produce the real thing? The answer, alas, is that a large number of people are committed to an ideology that requires them to believe just that. So let us carry the story a step further.

The PDP-10 is powered by electricity and perhaps its electrical properties can reproduce some of the actual causal powers of the electrochemical features of the brain in producing mental states. We certainly couldn't rule out that eventuality a priori. But remember: the thesis of strong AI is that the mind is "independent of *any* particular embodiment" because the mind is just a program and the program can be run on a computer made of anything whatever provided it is stable enough and complex enough to carry the program. The actual physical computer could be an ant colony (one of their examples), a collection of beer cans, streams of toilet paper with small stones placed on the squares, men sitting on high stools with green eye shades—anything you like.

So let us imagine our thirst-simulating program running on a computer made entirely of old beer cans, millions (or billions) of old beer cans that are rigged up to levers and powered by windmills. We can imagine that the program simulates the neuron firings at the synapses by having beer cans bang into each other, thus achieving a strict correspondence between neuron firings and beer-can bangings. And at the end of the sequence a beer can pops up on which is written "I am thirsty." Now, to repeat the question, does anyone suppose that this Rube Goldberg apparatus is literally thirsty in the sense in which you and I are?

Notice that the thesis of Hofstadter and Dennett is not that *for all we know* the collection of beer cans might be thirsty but rather that if it has the right program with the right input and output it *must be* thirsty (or understand Proust or worry about its income tax or have any other mental state) because that is all the mind is, a certain kind of computer program, and any computer made of anything at all running the right program would have to have the appropriate mental states.

I believe that everything we have learned about human and animal biology suggests that what we call "mental" phenomena are as much a part of our biological natural history as any other biological phenomena, as much a part of biology as digestion, lactation, or the secretion of bile. Much of the implausibility of the strong AI thesis derives from its resolute opposition to biology; the mind is not a concrete biological phenomenon but "an abstract sort of thing."

Still, in calling attention to the implausibility of supposing that the specific causal powers of brains are irrelevant to minds I have not yet fully exposed the preposterousness of the strong AI position, held by Hofstadter and Dennett, so let us press on and examine a bit more closely the thesis of mind as program.

Digital computer programs by definition consist of sets of purely formal operations on formally specified symbols. The ideal computer does such things as print a 0 on the tape, move one square to the left, erase a 1, move back to the right, etc. It is common to describe this as "symbol manipulation" or, to use the term favored by Hofstadter and Dennett, the whole system is a "self-updating representational system"; but these terms are at least a bit misleading since as far as the computer is concerned the symbols don't *symbolize* anything or *represent* anything. They are just formal counters.

The computer attaches no meaning, interpretation, or content to the formal symbols; and qua computer it couldn't, because if we tried to give the computer an interpretation of its symbols we could only give it more uninterpreted symbols. The interpretation of the symbols is entirely up to the programmers and users of the computer. For example, on my pocket calculator if I print "3×3=," the calculator will print "9" but it has no idea that "3" means 3 or that "9" means 9 or that anything means anything. We might put this point by saying that the computer has a syntax but no semantics. The computer manipulates formal symbols but attaches no meaning to them, and this simple observation will enable us to refuse the thesis of mind as program.

Suppose that we write a computer program to simulate the understanding of Chinese so that, for example, if the computer is asked questions in Chinese the program enables it to give answers in Chinese; if asked to summarize stories in Chinese it can give such summaries; if asked questions about the stories it has been given it will answer such questions.

Now suppose that I, who understand no Chinese at all and can't even distinguish Chinese symbols from some other kinds of symbols, am locked in a room with a number of cardboard boxes full of Chinese symbols. Suppose that I am given a book of rules in English that instruct me how to match these Chinese symbols with each other. The rules say such things as that the "squiggle-squiggle" sign is to be followed by the "squoggle-squoggle" sign. Suppose that people outside the room pass in more Chinese symbols and that following the instructions in the book I pass Chinese symbols back to them. Suppose that unknown to me the people who pass me the symbols call them "questions" and the book of instructions that I work from they call "the program"; the symbols I give back to them they call "answers to the questions" and me they call "the computer." Suppose that after a while the programmers get so good at writing the programs and I get so good at manipulating the symbols that my answers are indistinguishable from those of native Chinese speakers. I can pass the Turing test for understanding Chinese. But all the same I still don't understand a word of Chinese and neither does any other digital computer because all the computer has is what I have: a formal program that attaches no meaning, interpretation, or content to any of the symbols.

What this simple program shows is that no formal program by itself is sufficient for understanding, because it would always be possible in principle for an agent to go through the steps in the program and still not have the relevant understanding. And what works for Chinese would also work for other mental phenomena. I could, for example, go through the steps of the thirst-simulating program without feeling thirsty. The argument also, *en passant*, refutes the Turing test because it shows that a system, namely me, could pass the Turing test without having the appropriate mental states.[2] . . .

---

[2] The "Chinese room argument" is stated in detail in my article "Minds, Brains, and Programs," pages 353–373 of *The Mind's I*. It originally appeared in *The Behavioral and Brain Sciences*, Vol. 3 (Cambridge University Press, 1980), along with twenty-seven responses and a reply to the responses.

The details of how the brain works are immensely complicated and largely unknown, but some of the general principles of the relations between brain functioning and computer programs can be stated quite simply. First, we know that brain processes cause mental phenomena. Mental states are caused by and realized in the structure of the brain. From this it follows that any system that produced mental states would have to have powers equivalent to those of the brain. Such a system might use a different chemistry, but whatever its chemistry it would have to be able to cause what the brain causes. We know from the Chinese room argument that digital computer programs by themselves are never sufficient to produce mental states. Now since brains do produce minds, and since programs by themselves can't produce minds, it follows that the way the brain does it can't be by simply instantiating a computer program. (Everything, by the way, instantiates some program or other, and brains are no exception. So in that trivial sense brains, like everything else, are digital computers.) And it also follows that if you wanted to build a machine to produce mental states, a thinking machine, you couldn't do it solely in virtue of the fact that your machine ran a certain kind of computer program. The thinking machine couldn't work solely in virtue of being a digital computer but would have to duplicate the specific causal powers of the brain.

A lot of the nonsense talked about computers nowadays stems from their relative rarity and hence mystery. As computers and robots become more common, as common as telephones, washing machines, and forklift trucks, it seems likely that this aura will disappear and people will take computers for what they are, namely useful machines. In the meantime one has to try to avoid certain recurring mistakes that keep cropping up in Hofstadter and Dennett's book as well as in other current discussions.

The first is the idea that somehow computer achievements pose some sort of threat or challenge to human beings. But the fact, for example, that a calculator can outperform even the best mathematician is no more significant or threatening than the fact that a steam shovel can outperform the best human digger. (An oddity of artificial intelligence, by the way, is the slowness of the programmers in devising a program that can beat the very best chess players. From the point of view of games theory, chess is a trivial game since each side has perfect information about the other's position and possible moves, and one had to assume that computer programs will soon be able to outperform any human chess player.)

A second fallacy is the idea that there might be some special human experience beyond computer simulation because of its special humanity. We are sometimes told that computers couldn't simulate feeling depressed or falling in love or having a sense of humor. But as far as simulation is concerned you can program your computer to print out "I am depressed," "I love Sally," or "Ha, ha," as easily as you can program it to print out "$3 \times 3 = 9$." The real mistake is to suppose that simulation is duplication, and that mistake is the same regardless of what mental states we are talking about. A third mistake, basic to all the others, is the idea that if a computer can simulate having a certain mental state then we have the same grounds for supposing it really has that mental state as we have for supposing that human beings have that state. But we know from the Chinese room argument as well as from biology that this simple-minded behaviorism of the Turing test is mistaken.

Until computers and robots become as common as cars and until people are able to program and use them as easily as they now drive cars we are likely to continue to suffer from a certain mythological conception of digital computers. This book is very much a part of the present mythological era of the computer.[3]

▼ DISCUSSION QUESTIONS

1. Suppose a friend of yours for many years is seriously injured in an accident and the doctors discover that she is an extra-terrestrial made from wires, transistors, and so on. Would this be sufficient to show that your friend never really thought or felt anything?

2. Suppose that *you* are seriously injured in an accident, and the doctors discover that you are an extra-terrestrial made of wires, transistors, and so on. Would this convince you that you had never really thought or felt anything? If your answer to this question is different from your answer to the first question, explain why.

3. Some compact disc players are of such high quality that it is sometimes impossible to distinguish the sound of the disc player from the sound of a live human voice. Applied to this example, would the Turing test show that compact disc players can sing?

---

[3] For more balanced presentations of cognitive science see *Perspectives on Cognitive Science*, edited by Donald Norman (Norwood, NJ: Ablex, 1981); *Mind Design: Philosophy, Psychology and Artificial Intelligence*, edited by John Haugeland (Branford/MIT Press, 1981); Hubert Dreyfus, *What Computers Can't Do: A Critique of Artificial Intelligence* (Harper and Row, 1972).

APPENDIX
Answers to Probability Puzzles

The following are answers to the puzzles found in Chapter 10, "Taking Chances."

(1) Your first instinct may be to suppose that the chances must be 50/50 that the remaining sandwich is a ham sandwich, because that was the probability of picking the bag containing two ham sandwiches to begin with. But don't forget that drawing out a ham sandwich gives some evidence concerning which bag was selected. Because the chances are *twice* as good for drawing a ham sandwich out of the bag containing two ham sandwiches than it is for drawing it from the bag with only one ham sandwich, the chances are two in three that you are in the bag that started with two ham sandwiches. Thus, the probability that the remaining sandwich is a ham sandwich is actually 2/3.

(2) Again, the most common reaction to this puzzle is wrong. It seems obvious that the original probability of selecting the cheese sandwich (one in three) will not be affected by anything that happens after the selection is made. But don't forget that new information is provided after the initial choice, which makes a difference. In fact, the chances of getting the cheese sandwich are 2/3 if you switch.

To see this, first notice that it will be a *bad* idea to switch only if you have started by selecting the bag with the cheese sandwich in it. The probability of starting with the bag with the cheese sandwich in it is, of course, 1/3. On the other hand, 2/3 of the time you will have started with a bag with a chicken fat sandwich in it, and switching will get you the bag containing the cheese. So it is a *good* idea to switch after one of the bags containing a chicken fat sandwich is removed because two out of three times you will get the bag containing the cheese sandwich by doing so.

(3) To get a handle on the Fogelin's Palace puzzle, we can consider a simpler case where the bet only has to ride twice. Now, once more, if you win one and lose one (in whatever order), you come out behind:

	Win	Lose
Total	$150	$90

	Lose	Win
Total	$60	$90

So again, it may seem a bad idea to gamble in Fogelin's Palace.

The flaw in this reasoning is that not all possible cases have been considered. The following chart shows the results of all possible combinations of wins and losses:

W	W	$225
W	L	$ 90
L	W	$ 90
L	L	$ 36

It is easy to see that the total winnings with two wins outweigh the losses in the other three cases. More exactly, the expected value can be calculated by dividing the sum of the figures on the right (the total payoffs) by four (the total number of equally likely outcomes).

$$\text{Expected value} = \$441/4 = \$110.25$$

The same line of reasoning will show that four-bet sequences have a favorable expected value as well. You will, in fact, have more losing sequences than winning sequences, but, as in the example above, winning sequences pay off enough to outweigh the more frequent losing sequences.

COPYRIGHTS AND ACKNOWLEDGMENTS

The authors wish to thank the following publishers and copyright holders for permission to reprint material used in this book:

Basic Books, Inc., Publishers, for "The Turing Test: A Coffeehouse Conversation," by Douglas R. Hofstadter, and "Reflections," by Daniel C. Dennett. From *The Mind's I*, by Douglas R. Hofstadter and Daniel C. Dennett. Copyright © 1981 by Basic Books, Inc. Reprinted by permission of Basic Books, Inc., Publishers, New York.

Creation Life Publishers for the excerpt from *Scientific Creationism*, by Henry M. Morris, Creation Life Publishers, San Diego, California, 1974, pp. 5–13. Reprinted by permission of the publisher.

Stephen Jay Gould for "Evolution as Fact and Theory." Copyright © 1981 by Stephen Jay Gould. Reprinted by permission of the author. First appeared in *Discover Magazine*.

Edward J. Gracely for "Playing Games with Eternity: The Devil's Offer." Copyright © 1988 by Edward J. Gracely. Reprinted by permission of the author. First appeared in *Analysis*.

Harper & Row, Publishers, Inc., for pages 19–42 from *Language and Woman's Place*, by Robin Lakoff. Copyright © 1975 by Robin Lakoff. Reprinted by permission of HarperCollins Publishers, Inc.

The MIT Press for the excerpt "The Morality of Abortion," from *Abortion and the Sanctity of Human Life: A Philosophical View*, by Baruch Brody. The MIT Press, copyright 1975.

The New York Review of Books for the excerpt from "The Myth of the Computer," by John Searle, in *The New York Review of Books*, April 29, 1982. Reprinted with permission from *The New York Review of Books*. Copyright © 1982 Nyrev, Inc.

The New York Times Company for "Is Abortion Really a Moral Dilemma?" by Barbara Ehrenreich, February 7, 1985; "Fraternities, Where Men May Come to Terms with Other Men," by Rev. William Stemper, Jr., June 16, 1985; and the editorial, "Barney Frank's Right to Judgment," September 22, 1989, *The New York Times*. Copyright © 1985/89 by The New York Times Company. Reprinted by permission.

INDEX

bias
  in sampling, 229–32
  sources of, 232–6
  informal judgmental heuristics, 233–6
  prejudice, 232–3
  stereotypes, 232–3
biased sampling, fallacy of, 231
biconditionals, 170–2
Blackmun, Justice Harry, 304
Bohr, Niels, 365
borderline cases, 98–104
  vagueness and, 98–9
breaking up premises, 77–9
Brennan, Justice William, 304–5, 313–8
Brody, Baruch, "The Morality of Abortion," 333, 348–51
Bronston v. United States, 25–6, 28
Brown (Justice), 295–8
Brown v. Board of Education, 285, 299–303, 318–9
Buoyancy, Law of, 140
burden of proof, 284, 318–20
Burger, Justice Warren, 103, 304
Burt, Sir Cyril, 119–20
"but," 43

C
California v. Carney, 103
capital punishment, 90–5, 103–4, 130, 327
categorical propositions, 184–7
Catcher in the Rye, The (J. D. Salinger), 113–4
causality
  causal factors, 254–5
  causal generalizations, 241–2
  causes vs. standing conditions, 255
  finding causes, 249–54
  reasoning about, 240–1
Chinese room, the, 412, 415
choices,
  expected value of, 267–9
  relative value of, 269–71
circular arguments, 40, 121–2
civil law, 284, 319
clarity, fallacies of, 98–113
  ambiguity, 105–8
  definitions and, 110–3
  drawing the line, 102–4
  equivocation, 108–10
  "from the heap" arguments, 100–1
  slippery slope arguments, 101–2
  vagueness and, 98–99
classical logic
  existential import in, 190
  immediate inference in, 200–1
  square of opposition in, 201–6

validity of syllogisms in, 215–7
rules for testing syllogisms in, 220
close analysis
  assuring in, 57, 58, 60–61, 65–66
  discounting in, 57, 60–61, 66
  evaluative terms in, 57, 64–7
  guarding in, 57–61, 64, 66–7
  rhetorical devices in, 57–64
  warranting connectives in, 57, 58, 60, 63, 66
complementary class, 194
complex conditions, 248–9
"Computing Machinery and Intelligence" (Turing), 390
conclusion markers, 32–3
concomitant variation, 256–7
conditions
  complex, 248–9
  necessary, 174–5, 179–81, 243
  negative, 247–8
  sufficient, 173–5, 179–81, 241, 243
conditionals (*see also* "if then" sentences)
  affirming the consequent, 164
  biconditionals, 170–2
  causal, 241–2
  denying the antecedent, 163
  in everyday language, 167–9
  general, 175–8, 241–2
  hypothetical syllogism, 164
  indicative, 160–1
  imperative, 160
  material, 163
  modus ponens, 163
  modus tollens, 163
  moods of, 160–1
  propositional, 161, 175
  subjunctive, 160
  truth tables for, 161–3
Confessions (St. Augustine), 132–3
conflicts,
  in law, 291–3
  of moral principles, 323, 329–30
  of scientific interpretations, 362, 365–6
Congressional Record, 54–7
conjunction, 146–9
  propositional vs. non-propositional, 149
  rule of Relevance and, 166
  symbol for, 147
  truth conditions governing, 147
  truth-table definition for, 148
  validity for, 149–52
conjunctive necessary conditions, 249
conjunctive sufficient conditions, 248
connectives
  conjunction, 146–52
  disjunction, 152
  negation, 153

truth-functional, 153–4
warranting, *see* warranting connectives
consequent, 160
constitutionality, 99, 287
context, 323
    dependence of clarity on, 99, 106
    normal, 249–50
contextual definitions, 112n
contradictories, 202–4
contraposition, 196–7
    by limitation, 201
contraries, 202
    conversational, 207
conventions, 4–6
    semantic, 7
    syntactical, 7
conversational
    acts, 15–6, 47
    implication, 19–21, 41, 44 (*see* implication, conversational)
    rules, 17–9
        of Manner, 18
        of Quality, 18, 23, 25, 82, 319
        of Quantity, 17, 26, 168–9, 170, 180, 215
        of Relevance, 18, 82, 113, 168
        of Strength, 17, 84
    rules, violations of, 21–2
        deception, 25–6
conversion, 192–3
    by limitation, 200
Cook, Captain, 225
Cooperative Principle, 17, 25
Copernicus, 365–6
counter-examples, 131–6
    decisive, 134–5
creation-science, 373–88
criminal law, 284, 319

D
damning with faint praise, 22
Darwin, Charles, 127, 374, 383
death penalty, *see* capital punishment
deception, 25–6
decision procedure, 165
deductive vs. inductive arguments, 224–7
deep analysis, 74–96
    capital punishment, 90–5
    suppressed premises in, 81–6
"Defense of Abortion, A" (Thomson), 331–3, 334–48
definitions, 110–3
    contextual, 112n
    dictionary, 111
    disambiguating, 111
    lexical, 111
    persuasive, 48–9

precising, 111–2
role of, 112–3
stipulative, 111
systematic, 112
truth-table *see* truth tables
Dennett, Daniel C., "Reflections," 409–11
denying the antecedent, fallacy of, 163
deriving a particular conclusion from universal premises, fallacy of, 220
Dewey, 232
Dialogue Concerning the Two World Systems (Galileo), 366–73
dictionary definitions, 111
Difference, Method of, 243n
digging deeper, 89
diminishing marginal value, 270
disagreement, moral, 322–3
disambiguating definitions, 111
disappearing hedge, trick of, 43
discounting, 43–5, 290
    in close analysis, 57, 60–61, 66
    straw men, trick of, 44–5, 60
discriminatory effect vs. motive, 291
disjunction, 152
    exclusive, 152, 158–9
    inclusive, 152
disjunctive necessary conditions, 249
disjunctive sufficient conditions, 248
distinguishing precedents, 288, 293
distribution, 218–9
    fallacies of, 220
    rules for, 220
diversity, 312
domain of discourse, 187–8
double effect, 325
double entendre, 108
drawing an affirmative conclusion from a negative premise, fallacy of, 220
drawing a negative conclusion from affirmative premises, fallacy of, 220
drawing the line, clarity and, 102–4
Duggan, Timothy, 110

E
effect, discriminatory, 291
Ehrenreich, Barbara, "Is Abortion Really a 'Moral Dilemma'?" 358–60
Einstein, Albert, 118, 365
Elliott, Deni, 110
employment discrimination, 308
equal protection
    clause, 294
    interpretations of, 294–5, 298–9, 304–5, 318

equivalence
  logical, 193
  relationships among proposi-
    tions, summary, 198
  truth-functional, 159
equivocation, 108–10
ethical theory, 135–6
evaluative language, 46–9
everyday language, logical language
  and, 166–9
evidence, preponderance of, 284, 319
evolution, theory of, 127, 365, 373–
  88
exclusive disjunction, 152, 158–9
excuses, 65, 141–3, 286
existential import, 190
  in categorical syllogisms, 215–7
  in immediate inferences, 200–1
  in the square of opposition, 201–
    5
expected value, 267–9, 278
  favorable vs. unfavorable, 269
explanations, 137–41
  as arguments, 138
  causal, 240–1
  excuses as, 142
  in narrative form, 137–8
  purpose of, 137
  in science, 363–4
expressive mood, 8
evaluative language, 46–9
  in close analysis, 57, 64–7
  persuasive definitions as, 48–9
  slanting in, 47–8
"Evolution as Fact and Theory"
  (Gould), 381–7
"Extensional Versus Intuitive Reasoning" (Tversky and Kahneman), 234n

F
fact, questions of, in law, 284–5
factors, causal, 254–5
fairness, 103
fallacies
  ad hominem, 115
  of affirming the consequent, 164,
    364
  of ambiguity, 108–10
  in appeals to authority, 116–20
  of appeal to ignorance, 320
  of begging the question, 121–2
  of biased sampling, 231–2
  of circular reasoning, 121
  of clarity, 98–113
  of denying the antecedent, 163–4
  of deriving a particular conclu-
    sion from universal premises,
    220
  of distribution, 220

of drawing an affirmative conclusion from a negative premise,
  220
of drawing a negative conclusion
  from affirmative premises, 220
equivocation, 108
gambler's, 271–2
of hasty generalization, 230
of the heap, 100–1
of illicitly distributed predicate, 220
of illicitly distributed subject, 220
of quality, 220
of quantity, 220
of relevance, 113–20, 320
of self sealing, 123–6
slippery slope, 101–2
of two negative premises, 220
of undistributed middle, 220
of vacuity, 121–6
false suggestion, 25
favorable expected value, 269
Feinberg, Joel, "Abortion," 328n
Fogelin's Palace, 276, 418–9
Foot, Philippa, "The Problem of
  Abortion and the Doctrine of
  Double Effect," 325n
"for" in arguments, 33
formal analysis, 147
  of arguments, 146–222
  and everyday language, 166–72
  see also immediate inference,
    propositional logic, square of
    opposition, and syllogisms
Fourteenth Amendment, 294
"Fraternities, Where Men May Come
  to Terms with Other Men"
  (Stemper), 71–2
Freud, Sigmund, 125
fundamental principles, 89
fundamental right, 314, 318

G
Galileo Galilei Dialogue Concerning the
  two World Systems, 366–73
Gallup poll, 232
gambler's fallacy, 271–2
Geller, Uri, 117
gender classifications, 308
generalizations
  causal, 240–3
    explanation with, 240–1
    prediction with, 240
  counterexamples to, 133
  hasty, 230
  inductive, 228–36
    acceptability of premises in, 229
    fallacy of biased sampling, 231–
      2
    sample size, 229–31
    sources of bias in, 232–6
  use in explanations, 138

sufficient conditions, 173–5, 179–81,
  241, 243
  conjunctive, 248
  contextualized definition, 250
  disjunctive, 248
  minimal, 180
  sufficient condition test (SCT),
    243–45, 247, 252, 254–6, 291,
    364
suggestion, false, 25
supporting arguments, 88
suppressed premises, 87
  linguistic principles, 84
  moral, 85
  religious, 85
  shared facts, 81–3
  uses of, 85–6
suspect classifications, in law, 299,
  309, 318
Strauder v. West Virginia, 295
stigma, 305, 316–7
syllogisms
  categorical, defined, 210
  existential import in, 215–7
  hypothetical, 164
  rules for evaluating, 218–21
    distribution, 220
    quality, 219
    quantity, 220
  statistical, 237–9
  theory of, 184, 209–21
  validity of, 211–7
  Venn diagrams for, 211
syntactical conventions, 7
systematic definitions, 112

T
tangents, 75
that's just like arguing . . . , 129
Theaetetus (Plato), 133–4
"then" in arguments, 33
"thereby" test, 9
"therefore" in arguments, 33
Thomson, Judith Jarvis, "A Defense
  of Abortion," 331–3, 334–48
Treatise of Human Nature, A (Hume),
  233n, 259
trick of
  abusive assurances, 41
  disappearing hedge, 43
  discounting straw men, 44–5, 60
trigger of strict scrutiny, 299
Truman, President Harry S., 232
truth
  of premises, 37
  validity of arguments vs., 37
truth-functional connectives, 153–4
truth-functional equivalence, 159

truth tables
  conjunction, 146–52
  disjunction, 152
  conditionals, 161–3
  negation, 153
  as tests for validity, 155–8
Turing, A. M., "Computing Ma-
  chinery and Intelligence," 390
Turing test, 390, 392–3
"Turing Test: A Coffeehouse Con-
  versation, The" (Hofstadter), 390–
  409
Tversky, Amos, and Kahneman,
  Daniel
  "Belief in The Law of Small
    Numbers," 230
  "Existensional Versus Intuitive
    Reasoning," 234
Tversky, Amos, and Gilovich,
  Thomas, and Vallone, Robert,
  "The Hot Hand in Basketball: On
  Misperception of Random Se-
  quences," 277n
two negative premises, fallacy of, 220
Tyson, Mike, 101

U
undistributed middle, fallacy of, 220
unfavorable expected value, 269
United Jewish Organizations v. Carey,
  309
universal propositions, 188, 220
"Upon Julia's Clothes" (Herrick), 8
U. S. v. Cruikshank, 294
Utilitarian Principle, 135–6, 329–30

V
vacuity, fallacies of, 121–6
  begging the question, 121–2
    circular reasoning, 121–2
  self sealers, 123–6, 388
vagueness, 77, 111
  defined, 98–9
  fallacies of, 100–4
  in legal disputes, 286, 287
validity,
  of arguments, 36–7, 146, 151
  of argument forms, 151
  of arguments with categorical
    propositions, 190–1
  legal, 287
  of syllogisms, 211–7
  testing for, 155–8
Vallone, Robert, and Gilovich,
  Thomas, and Tversky, Amos,
  "The Hot Hand in Basketball: On
  Misperception of Random Sequences," 277n
value, relative, 269–71, 278

Venn diagrams, 185
  and validity, 190–1
  for syllogisms, 211

W

warranting connectives, 33–5, 79
  in close analysis, 57, 58, 60, 63, 66
  conclusion markers, 32–4

"if-then" sentences, 34–5
  reason markers, 32–4
Warren (Chief Justice), 299–302
weighing factors in morality, 333–4
White, Justice, 304

Y

Yick Wo v. Hopkins, 288–9, 295, 297
Yogi Berra, 261

A 0
B 1
C 2
D 3
E 4
F 5
G 6
H 7
I 8
J 9